I am a

~~Dreamer~~

And

~~Believer~~

Queen Bettie Jean Grose

Copyright © 2021 **Bettie Jean Grose**

All rights reserved. No part of this publication may be reproduced, distributed, or transmitted in any form or by any means, including photocopying, recording, or other electronic or mechanical methods, without the prior written permission of the publisher, except in the case of brief quotations embodied in critical reviews and certain other noncommercial uses permitted by copyright law. For permission requests, write to the publisher, addressed "Attention: Book Rights and Permission," at the address below.

Published in the United States of America

ISBN 978-1-955243-97-1 (SC)
ISBN 978-1-955243-98-8 (Ebook)

Bettie Jean Grose
7601 Lester Road Apartment 4217
Union City Georgia 30291
www.bettiejeangrose.com

Order Information and Rights Permission:

Quantity sales. Special discounts might be available on quantity purchases by corporations, associations, and others. For details, contact the publisher at the address above.

For Book Rights Adaptation and other Rights Permission. Call us at toll-free 1-888-945-8513 or send us an email at admin@stellarliterary.com.

Dedication

To my brother, Robert Lewis "Mickey" Grose who inspires me everyday of my life with his words of wisdom and encouragement. He is speaking from beyond the grave. Everyday he inspires me to say more. Everyday he tells me "you can do more". He inspires me to say this, say that, do this and to do that. He is looking at me through his eyes of love. Jesus love me, you, him, her, she, he, them and they. His memory is surrounding me with these words.

Contents

ABOUT THE AUTHOR vi
SEE A SHINING STAR A TULIP A GEMSTONE vii
INTRODUCTION xxi
I am a Dreamer and Believer #2 xxxiv
Chapter 1 1
Chapter 2 13
Chapter 3 25
Chapter 4 31
Chapter 5 48
Chapter 6 52
Chapter 7 68
Chapter 8 76
Chapter 9 87
Chapter 10 95
Chapter 11 110
Chapter 12 125
Chapter 13 137
Chapter 14 150
Chapter 15 161
Chapter 16 172
Chapter 17 179
Chapter 18 193
Chapter 19 198

Chapter 20	206
Chapter 21	214
Chapter 22	226
Chapter 23	240
Chapter 24	252
Chapter 25	258
Chapter 26	269
Chapter 27	274
Chapter 28	288
Chapter 29	304
Chapter 30	319
Chapter 31	332
Chapter 32	342
Chapter 33	349
Chapter 34	364
Chapter 35	372
Chapter 36	387
Chapter 37	399
Chapter 38	407
Chapter 39	423
Chapter 40	437
Chapter 41	453
HAVE THE TIME OF YOUR LIFE REJOICE	461

ABOUT THE AUTHOR

Bettie Jean is a 74 years old queen, mother, nana, grandmother and a believer in God The Father of Our Lord and Savior Jesus Christ. She has a Christian heart and believes that every day she opens her eyes on this solid and sacred ground, we call Earth, is a gift to her. She believes it is a present from God. She celebrates each day as her birthday. She speaks life over her life and has special adjectives that she uses to describe each day of the week. She has written manuscripts on a daily basis as she believes each day, that Our Lord gives us "our daily bread". Everyday she waits patiently to receive His Grace and Mercy. She believes that you, too, can become a dreamer believer. I can do all things through Christ who strengthen me. Christ is alive in me. He is alive in my spirit. He has given me my faith and I trusts any decision He makes concerning my life. I believe I am walking in His Divine will. I believe I have been chosen to receive His spiritual gifts and I am grateful to Him to let me be able to share with you my beliefs, opinions, dreams, hopes and experiences.

Bettie Jean Grose

I SEE A SHINING STAR
A TULIP A GEMSTONE

TESTIMONIAL 895

On Sunday afternoon our family celebrated some special events. We celebrated Bryce's 16th birthday and Auntie Ann's 67th birthday. We gathered, shared in different conversations, ate some delicious food and allowed Bryce to enjoy His sunshine that Our Lord and Savior was shining on Him. He wanted cash so he could buy what he wanted. We gave him cash. He made out like a fat bandit. He was well satisfied in how much he was given. All of these dollars had love written all over me. It was given to him from our hearts. We all gave him some advice. Advice for a 16years old when his hair make him look like a beast. I object. I want to see your eyes. That is the windowpane to your heart. Your heart glows when you have willed the reigns you had over your life so His will can be done.

You are a man, woman, boy or girl not a beast. When is the last time you saw the sparkle in your eyes? Can't find, hair is in your face, covering your eyes and covering your ears. If you can't see then certainly you can't hear. The devil has won. You have blinders on – you can't see – your ears are deaf because you have listening to diabolical, wicked, corrupt, evil thoughts. You are being entertained by diabolical spirits. Pick up your cross and run with me. Adopt a new mentality.

I want to live. I want to come alive in my senses so I can be able to think, process, perceive and ponder thought. Sing yourself a new song.

Begin to sing the words you are reading so they will digest into your spirit. May the words of my mouth that are meditating in my heart be pleasing and accepting in Thy sight. O Lord! You are My Rock and

My Redeemer. You are the Source of My Strength. You are Christ in my life. I went to the cross with you. I laid all of my burdens down at His feet. There is wisdom, knowledge and understanding emerging from the bones that we are standing on. Are you anchored? I have a direct connection and He wants to take good care of me.

I went and did laundry. I never knew how much I loved my clothes until I picked up my velvety pants and they felt so warm, comfortable and cuddly. I love my clothes, just had to tell Jesus while He was watching over me. I saw He had me in His shadow and when I reached for the doorknob Jesus was standing at the entrance of the doorway.

My daughter's house looks like an art gallery. So many interesting and intriguing pictures that provoke thought. I got lost in the Love that was being shared by all. Jesus was there. I invited Him in to our little assembly. He is always around so I honored Him, praised Him, worshipped Him, adored Him, admired Him for shining His bright lights on me, my family, my loved ones, my cousins, my friends. We all are cousins. We are kin by His Blood. His Blood is running warm throughout my bones. I was dazzled by the light in the grandchildren's eyes. They are loved. You are loved. I am loved. Moonlight becomes you. I think under His moonlight. Looks like I get a better connection. I am so involved in what is meditating in my heart until I get lost and am not conscious that I don't have any light. I enjoy His bright sunshine and His bright moonlight. He is always around, there, here and everywhere at the same time. Is He magical? Is He majestic?

Is He magnificent? Is He marvelous? Is He miraculous?

Special Message! Love Me. Please stop what you are doing and just begin to Love Me. He say's! When I say the words; "O Lord" I am honoring, saluting, admiring, adoring Him for blowing His breath of life into my lifeless soul allowing me to become a living human being all over again coming alive in my sense of hearing, smelling, tasting, seeing, thinking, feeling, touching, hoping, believing and dreaming. I am ready to praise You, honor You, salute You for allowing me the ability to be able to think, process, perceive, ponder, thought.

Let's you and I go to that land of make believe. Get ready to dream, think, hope, pray and obey a Supreme Being. His Name is Jesus and He wants to take real good care of you. He is here with me, there with you, everywhere at the same time. Isn't He amazing? Isn't it remarkable at what He can do? He can raise the dead, heal the sick, make the blind see, make the lame walk and turn water into wine. Try telling yourself - Self - Jesus is powerful, mighty, great and strong. He is trying to remold and reshape me in His image. I want to be like Him one day. I want Him to hold me so close until I am suffocated with His Presence.

I was admiring His forest of trees, weeds, bushes, flowers, insects, bugs, birds, butterflies, walruses and a school of fish. The waters that surrounded them was a calming, soothing blue. I got lost in the Sea of Blue. and I began to listen intently to the words that were meditating in my heart. I believe He wanted me alone so He could speak to me.

Did you know trees produce growth, knowledge, wisdom and understanding? Trees like you and me are living beings that depends on Him to give us life, hope, peace and introduce us too

Paradise. We are His creation. Trees gives us paper. The Earth gives us ink and when we combine the two together knowledge, wisdom and understanding circle your feet. It runs up to you like running water. You come alive. Vitamins, minerals, bones and nutrients make up your body mass. You and I are made out of bones, vitamins, minerals and nutrients. My bones are talking.

Shish! I want to hear! He says, "Gather at my feet", gather with Me at your beginning. My brain, my heart, my mind were the first to arrive then followed my body, my soul and my spirit because one day He knew I would return to Him because He had engraved me in the Palm of His Hand. He recognizes my smile. He has me in His shadow and He is taking good care of me.

Wisdom, knowledge, love, hope, peace and understanding is at His feet. Go back to where you came from. Go back to your mother's womb at your beginning and find the Giver and Sustainer of life. Find the One who knew you before you were a thought. That is where I am headed. Come and go with me, He says, find quiet time so the two of us can be together.

I will honor a Decree. I will obey an order. I will follow a command. Let me find a comfortable place to sit because I know I am going to be here right at His feet from now through Eternity. I am holding on the string that is dangling from the hem of His garment. I am a Dreamer Believer. I am in His Presence. I see Him shining His light on my shoulders, backbone, spine, hands, fingers, toes and feet. I have given Him my heart, mind, brain, body, soul and spirit so His will could be done.

He orders my steps and my tongue. There is a miracle in your mouth, He says. Speak it, receive it now achieve it. If you can dream it then you can believe it. He makes your dream and my dream come true. What are your hopes, desires, dreams and thoughts! Are your thoughts soothing, satisfying and providing joy and pleasure and satisfaction to your mind, brain, heart, body, soul and spirit?

I go through periods of fascination. I am amazed at the connection that I have made just by changing the words meditating in my heart. Proverbs 18 v:21. Your tongue has power and authority. Invite life or invite death. Your words will create. Your words will invent. Your words will convince. Your words will suggest. Your words will persuade. You can write the next chapter of your life. You can forecast your future. You can seek shelter in His swaddling Arms. This is where I am and He is heaping piles of kindness, gentleness, softness, tenderness, love, hope, peace, patience, joy, satisfaction, contentment, tranquility, harmony, serenity and love all over me. It has rolled up to my front door. It is covering my feet.

In order to get where I am going I am going to have to take some giant steps. I want to overcome the harassment that I am receiving from the devil. You can expect unrest from the devil.

Embrace a new dimension. Come under a new awareness. Dream a new reality. Listen! Think! Believe! Hope! Pray! Dream! Achieve!

Accomplish! Stop for a moment, allow these words to digest into your spirit. You want to come alive. Jesus will raise the dead. Jesus will force you to think, process, perceive and ponder thought! Jesus gives you a question mark! Tell me who you are and what do you want!

If you seek to find Jesus you will find peace, hope, joy, contentment, happiness, satisfaction, obedience, deliverance, endurance and righteousness. He combines His love and covers you from the crown of your head to the sole of your feet in His Grace and Mercy.

You allow the devil to kill you, murder you, destroy you and deceive you. The devil will paint you a picture and tell you that everything that glitters is gold. He is a liar and a thief. He will try to steal your thoughts, ideas, opinions, dreams, hopes and desires. One way to escape the devil's wrath is do Him like Jesus told me to do. "Ignore Him". This is not hard to do once you place Jesus First. I placed Jesus at the top of my list. I adopted Him as my constant companion. He told me He would take good care of me, that His yoke was easy. Pick up your cross and follow me.

I really like to read where it says "you, yes you, who are weary, worn, torn, sad, neglected, deprived and heavy laden, come and go with Me and I will give you rest. Matthew 11 v:28 - 30. Find this kind of love, acceptance, attention and affection at my feet. Are you listening to the words that are meditating in your heart? Take a moment. Compose yourself and feel Him drape a blanket of love, comfort, compassion, hope, peace and satisfaction all over you. There goes my heart. I have given Him my heart so His will could be done. He found my heart pure, clean with an upright and steadfast spirit. He wanted a place to dwell so He could have a final resting place. I gave Him all of me. I asked Him to please come into my Presence and to please allow me to enter into His Presence. Words formed together to make a concrete thought. I know what I want to happen to me from now through Eternity. My mind is made up. I am following Jesus. Jesus has the blueprint and the outline.

Jesus is the One that wrote the script.

Over yonder! Over there! At the Great Beyond! In Paradise! In the United Kingdom! In the Promised Land! Come and go with me.

Somewhere over the rainbow that I see circling my head. I see Him shining His light on me. He has His eyes fixated on me and I see a halo of colors shining all over me. This tells me that Someone is watching over me.

Can you see the different shades of green? Can you see the sparkling waters that glitters like little diamonds? There is pea green, lima bean green, aqua green, army green, money green. There are millions upon trillions of trees, weeds, bushes, flowers growing from the grass. His grass glistens in my eyesight. I see His signs and wonders. He makes the green grass shine and I have been told to wake up O sleepyhead, rise from the dead, wake up O sleepyhead, rise from your field of dreams, come and go with me, face reality and allow Your Lord to shine on you.

I heard Him call my name. Tulip, Shining Star, Rock, Diamond, Butterfly, Bird, Gemstone. I stretched out my arms, legs, body, fingers and toes. I smiled. I said "Thank You Lord"" for favoring me with a brand new occasion so I can enjoy my new mind, my new brain, my new heart, my new body, my new soul and my new spirit. I continue smiling the entire time I am in my happy space. I am so glad that I was favored to flush my kidneys and excrete my bowels. I am so grateful when His Holy Spirit nudged me so I could come alive in my senses. I began to say "Thank You

Jesus". I began to sing it. My words soon turned over into a chant. These were the words rolling off of my tongue. I was praising, honoring, worshipping, saluting all at the same time.

O Lord! You are perfect, powerful, wonderful, strong, mighty, great and divine. Stop and allow Him to drape His Everlasting Arms all around you. Let Him tell you "I have got you". Finally, I found a place where I belong. I belong in His swaddling Arms so I can be cradled into a new awareness. O Lord! Please allow me to become brand new.

O Lord! Please raise me from the dead. I want to live. I want to breathe in wisdom, knowledge and understanding. Give yourself a five minute break and eat these words. Tattoo them across your forehead, your heart. It is running over in my cup. Bones are squealing. Take off the blindfolds. Uncover your ears, your eyes and open up your heart to receive knowledge, wisdom and understanding from a 74 years old perspective.

Listen! What do you hear? Do you hear Him singing you a song! He sings my name! He calls it so gently and softly. He is talking to one of His Angels. His Bright Stars, His Shining Stars, His Rocks,

His Diamonds, His Gemstones. He is talking to me! Do you remember drinking your coffee? You were told to slow up, slurp and sip and not to be in any rush to allow Him to love you while you breathe and swallow.

I can't do it without Him being my ever present help. He is always around. He walked with me to the laundry room, allowed me to wash and dry my belongings, then fold them up and put them in their proper place. He is magical! He is majestic! He is miraculous! He performed a miracle on me when He gave me a new life, a new mind, a new heart in the Presence of a King. He has taken over. He is in-charge. He is

in-control. I allowed Him full access to every fiber of my being. I now belong to Him. He is calling the shots. I trust Him. I honor Him.

I worship Him. I obey Him. I salute Him.

He is my constant companion. He is my commander-in-chief. He is My Authoritative Ruler. He is My Supreme Being. He is My God. His

Name is Jesus. God told Jesus to not to ever forget about me because I was engraved in the Palm of His Hand. Jesus keeps reminding Him that I was given an assignment to complete and He is pleased with my performance. I have achieved one of the goals He had sat for me.

I began to listen! I began to listen so I could hear Him when He called my name. I had to adjust to what I was telling myself. I had to accept facts as truths.

Remember yesterday! You were a butterfly! Coasting, floating, gliding and waltzing from one happy space to another happy space because I was delighted in what He had prepared for me. He gave me food to eat and water to drink. I am elated, satisfied and captivated by His Presence. He says "Thy art with me" and He is going to take real good care of me if I allow Him too.

You are wanted, needed, appreciated, accepted, adored, admired, worshipped, treasured, idolized, cherished and honored by a King

if you allow Him to love you. O Lord! Please love me. O Lord!

Shower me with Your hugs and kisses. O Lord! I want You to be proud of me. I love you so, He says. I will always love you today, everyday, now, 24/7, around the clock, every hour, every minute, every second and right at this present nanosecond and millisecond of time. There is a fire burning in my bones. I can't sit still, I have to sway and swerve my body. I am so happy and grateful that I am alive and in His Presence.

He orchestrates my ideas, thoughts, opinions, beliefs, hopes, dreams, behavior, attitudes, ambitions and aspirations. He can handle it!

He wants to know your thoughts, ideas, beliefs, dreams, opinions and desires. He wants to know what you are made out of! Got any wisdom, truth, knowledge, understanding, honesty, justice, equality, sacrifices, obedience, endurance, love, hope, peace, faithfulness, salvation, redemption, manifestation and righteousness locked up in those bones? Open up the door and let Mercy and Grace rush in.

He is showering me with His Unfailing Love, His Unconditional Love, His Grace and Mercy and His Divine Devotion. He is allowing it run rapidly throughout my bones. I am covered by His Blood.

I asked. It was early in the morning hours when I first began my conversation with Him. I greeted, honored and saluted Him early. When I first opened my eyes, He was standing near my bedside with His Righteous Right Hand extended out to me and I grabbed it. I was not going to allow Him to get away from me. I honored Him because He had watched over me while I slumbered and slept and gave me a new version of myself. The old me has long ago passed away. Jesus raised me from the dead. He gave me a new life, a new mind, a new start, a new birth, a new identity, a new beginning and a new opportunity to be born again.

O Lord please come into my presence and O Lord please allow me to enter into Your Presence. O Lord please shadow us, O Lord please shelter us, O Lord please favor us, O Lord please cover us with Your Blood, O Lord please grant us Your Grace and Mercy, O Lord please strengthen us physically, mentally, emotionally, psychologically,

morally and spiritually, O Lord please forgive us of our sins because we don't always do things perfectly and correctly, O Lord please forgive our enemies because they know not what they do, O Lord please protect us from all plagues, pandemics, disasters and turmoil, O Lord please prosper us materialistically, financially and spiritually, O Lord please do not cast us away from Your Presence and O Lord please allow Your Holy Spirit to dwell in us again on this day. In Jesus' Name I Pray - Amen.

Did you pray along with me? Did you ask for you, me, him, her, she, he, them and they? We are all sheep in His Pasture and He wants to take good care of us if we allow Him too. Now is the perfect time to celebrate our new arrival. We are alive. Jesus raised me and you from the dead. We are no longer blind! We can see that Our Lord loves His creation. He loves me and you, him, her, she, he, them and they. He loves the tall ones, short ones, big ones, little ones, skinny ones, fat ones, gay or straight. We are all sheep in His Pasture. Psalm 100.

I am a child of a King. I am one of God's children. I am one of His sheep in His Pasture. I am one of His Favorites. My name has been changed. I have a new identity. Call me Holy Roller, pastor, preacher, teacher, speaker, dreamer, believer. I will answer to all of these titles.

I have news to share. I am testifying everyday that He blows His breath of life into my lifeless soul so I can become a living human being all over again in His Presence. I am living my life in the Presence of a King.

He is ordering my steps. I am in love with Jesus because He is the First One that ever loved me.

I see Him peering through the window at me, guiding me every step of the way. Sometimes when I am writing, after I pen a particular thought, His sun begins to shine brighter. I know to linger because this is where He wants me to devote more time. He is speaking to me. I am listening to every word. I am recording the words I need to live by.

Psalm 23 says "Thy art with me". Joshua 1 v:9 says "I will go with you wherever you go". These words are tattooed across my chest and my forehead. Listen! What are you telling yourself? Tell self - Self

He is with me. Self - He loves me. Come away with me and let's go to the lighthouse. There is wisdom, knowledge and understanding waiting at the rooftop. He raises me higher than my present situation, circumstance and condition. He renews my strength and uplift my spirits. He is the Source of My Strength, Salvation, Redemption and Manifestation. He has positioned my head in front of this computer and made me place my hand on the keyboard while He talks with me.

Take a time out! Find silence and solitude! This is what you must have in order to enter into His Presence. Just the two of you! Just He and I!

Just me and Him! We are cut from the same cloth! We both want the same thing! He wants me to become free just like His birds and butterflies. They float, coast, glide and waltz through His atmosphere. They know they have A Supreme Being watching over them. They are confident in knowing that He took care of them on yesterday and He has returned today to satisfy them with His morning grace and mercy. He told them to let it last them all throughout their day. Psalm 90 v:14.

He is talking to me. When Jesus walked in the door, He was bearing gifts. He draped a blanket of love, compassion and affection, hope and peace all over me. It was interwoven in a blanket made just for me.

He is reaching out to greet me. I will always love you. If you didn't hear Me the first time listen closely, "I will love you always". If you have been deprived and neglected from hearing these words, listen to Him whisper words of comfort, inspiration and encouragement into your hearts and ears.

In His Presence

In The Name of Jesus – Amen

Bettie jean Grose

INTRODUCTION

"God converses". He chooses who to use as a teacher, motivational speaker, Holy Roller, pastor, evangelist, preacher or lecturer. He makes His selection based on the progress we have made. Am I worthy to call on His Holy Name? He leads me besides the still waters. He restores my soul. Psalm 23. The First One I think about is Him. His Name is Jesus. The baby that had no where to lay His Head. Let's adore Him. Let's admire Him. He is the same baby that we worship today. I worship Him.

Jesus placed a safeguard around my brain, my heart, my mind, my body, my soul and my spirit. He gave me His Grace and Mercy and it has been following me from one happy space to another one. While I was walking I was talking. O Lord! You are mighty, powerful, strong and great. O Lord! You are magnificent, marvelous, fantastic, fabulous, magical, majestic, miraculous, splendid, superb, superior, spectacular, outstanding, wonderful and divine. I know how to praise Him. Sing it along with me. Just take one attribute and get to the bottom of it. Go in-depth with your thinking, dreaming and believing. He is listening. He hears the words meditating in my heart and your heart.

After I finished with my morning routine, His Holy Spirit urged me to recline in my happy space and place my head upon His chest so I could breathe His sweet breath forevermore and I went to thinking, dreaming, hoping, praying and trusting in Him. He wanted to give me His Fruit of His Spirits. Galatians 5 v:22. They are His kindness, gentleness, tenderness, softness, faithfulness, love, hope, peace, graciousness, deliverance, obedience and righteousness. His Faithfulness will endure if you believe, hope, pray, love, trust and embrace what is in the Great Beyond. Don't you want to go to Paradise, to the Promised Land?

It is right over there, over here, over yonder in the great unknown. He makes me lie down in green pastures. He leads me besides the still waters. He will never ever let me forget who is number one. He restores my soul by telling me over and over, again and again, "I will always love you". He says it twice. "I will love you always". This is what I heard when I opened my eyes. I worship You. I idolize You. I honor You. I treasure You. You are the One that I am trying to please. I want to make You proud of me.

The words of my mouth availeth much. My vocabulary is what matters. Speak it, receive it now achieve it. Say what you mean and mean what you say. Our God is awesome. By now you know I call Him Jesus. He is My God! He is The One that saved me. II give Him all of the honor and the praise. I salute Him. He is so good to me.

He allowed me to begin my morning routine all over again under the guidance of His Holy Spirit. I can't do nothing without His Holy Spirit being my guide. It is like a second self. I listen. I look. I learn. I hope. I pray. I think. I dream. I believe. I have faith, hope and trust in Jesus. He is right by myside. He is just that close to me. He is underneath my breath and regulating the air that I breathe. He is underneath my skin and can feel each time my heart beats. I am covered by His blood. His blood is the same blood that is running through my veins, your veins, his veins, her veins and their veins. The young ones, the old ones, the tall ones, the short ones, the little ones, the big ones, the fat ones, the skinny ones - gay or straight. We are all sheep in His Pasture. Psalm 100.

I reside in you since you have given me your heart, He says. My heart is pure with a steadfast and an upright spirit. Psalm 51. I will never stop believing that I have Someone watching over me. I can tell by what I see. I can tell by what I hear. He is all over me. He has me surrounded and I am captivated and mesmerized with what He is showing me. When I looked out of the window I saw His grass glistening. Little diamonds, little sparkles were sprinkled throughout the lawn. He is watching me. Don't you want Him to be watching you? Don't you want His eyes fixated on you? Ask Him. Ask Him over and over, again and again. O Lord! Please come into my presence and O Lord please allow me into Your Presence. O Lord! Please bestow Your Grace and Mercy all over me. Please cover me from the crown of my head to the sole of my feet in Your Love, Compassion, Acceptance, Attention, Affection and Divine Devotion till the end of time.

All during my life I have been uttering His Name. I first learned at my mama's knees to say "O Lord". These two words carry a multitude of blessings. When you say O Lord! You complete the sentence. I can only tell you what I say. I can only share with you my morning confession, my morning affirmations, my morning prayer and my morning mantra. O Lord! Please shelter us, please shadow us, please favor us, please cover us with Your Blood, please grant us Your Grace and Mercy, O Lord please strengthen us physically, mentally, emotionally, psychologically, morally and spiritually, O Lord please forgive us of our sins because we don't always do things perfectly and correctly, O Lord please forgive our enemies because they know not what they do, O Lord please protect us from all plagues, pandemics, disasters and turmoil, O Lord please prosper us materialistically, financially and spiritually, O Lord please do not cast us away from Your Presence and O Lord please allow Your Holy Spirit to dwell in us again on today. In Jesus' Name I Pray - Amen.

He waits patiently on me while I release the words and thoughts that are meditating in my heart. He listens. He responds. I hear complete silence so I drift off into winter white wonderland. I dreamed I had a baby pig and he was white all over. I began to love my pig, adore him and provide for him. This is what Christ is doing for me. He loves me. He restores my soul. This is what I keep hearing. He admires me and He will protect me from all hurt, harm and danger. He will provide all of my needs. He will allow His Holy Spirit to become my guide.

I asked. O Lord! You are mighty, powerful, strong and great and You will never ever leave my side. I depend on Thee. I tell Him often how much I admire Him for making me successful in writing my testimonies on a daily basis. Sometimes I get carried away. There is so much to say.

By now you know I talk all of the time. I talk while I am asleep. I am forever calling on His Holy Name because I don't want Him to get away from me. He is the Last One I think about when I close my eyes for sleep. He is always present in my memory bank. I know who watched over me during the morning, at noonday, in the evening and at night. I know who was standing beside my bed with His Righteous Right Hand extended out to me. I grabbed it. I was glad that He had returned to take good care of me. He came early to satisfy His Tulip with His Grace and Mercy and told me to let it last me all during my day. Psalm 90 v:14. I know how to obey a command. I know how to follow an order. I know how to honor a Decree. I will never stop believing that He has His eyes fixated on me. I asked. O Lord! Please shadow us. O Lord! Please keep a constant watch over me, you, him, her, she, he, them and they. I pray for all of us. We are all sheep in His Pasture and we all need to be taught the basics in life and the first basic there is - is to "Listen". Then you look, learn, dream and think. Keep your eye in the sky waiting upon His return. Can't you see the blue skies, the yellow sun, the golden air, the blue water? These are messages from nature and creation. Look out of the window and let Him blind you with His eyes of love. He sees me and you, him, her, she, he, them and they as jewels. We are stars, rocks and gemstones. I will let my little light shine. I will praise His Name even though you may not want to. Allow me to be me. This is what I want to do. Listen to me as I worship Him.

He is looking for a few stars who He can trust to tell the truth. He wants honesty, justice, truth, honor and valor to prevail. You must have self-respect, self-control, self-discipline along with dignity and integrity if you want to eat a piece of this pie. You ready? Where is your faith, your hope, your trust, your belief in the Unseen? It is Wednesday morning, October 13, 2021. I have never ever seen this wonderful and miraculous Wednesday morning before. I say it is miraculous because Jesus performed a miracle on me when He raised me from the dead.

He heard me when I was moving from one happy space to another happy space. He heard my cry. He heard me say "Thank

You Jesus" for allowing me to do what I needed to do. He kept me safe in His Everlasting Arms. I returned to reclaim my spot. His Arms were waiting. They are soft, cuddly and delicate. It was like laying my head on a bed of cotton, silk, satin and velvet. Similar to the petals on His tulip in His Flower Garden. What do I do? I begin speaking. I begin talking to the One who blew His breath of life into my lifeless soul and allowed me to be closed in my right mind with a reasonable portion of my health and strength so I could praise and worship You for allowing me to come alive in my sense of hearing, seeing, tasting, smelling, touching, feeling, believing, hoping, dreaming and be able to "think, process, perceive and ponder thought".

Who woke you up this morning? Who is the Giver and Sustainer of Life? Who rules the Universe? Who has all power in the hem of His garment? Who placed your name on the "wake-up" list? Who favored you with a new beginning, a new start, a new mind, a new heart, a new brain, a new body, a new soul and a new spirit? Deep down in my soul He lives. He has come alive in my heart. This is what He wants. He wants your heart so He can have a place to dwell so He can have a final resting place. This is so easy to do. Will the reigns you have on your life over to Him and allow His will to be done in your life. I commit, I submit, I surrender my total self over to Him so His will can be done. I give myself away so He can use me.

You beautiful doll! You beautiful star! You beautiful rock! You beautiful gemstone! This is what He thinks of me. You are one of a kind. You stepped out of a dream. Aren't you happy? Aren't you gleaming with pride and joy? I am. Look what He thinks of me, you, him, her, she, he, them and they. Someone pinch me. Is He watching over me? Is He talking to me? I didn't know He cared that much. "Cast all of your cares on me because I care for you". 1st Peter 5 v:7. I want to see you smile. When I look at you I want to see love, peace, hope, joy and happiness. This is what He expects to see. This is what He wants you to feel. Examine each one. I see Him. He has His eyes fixated on me. He is looking at me through the window. I feel His fresh breeze of air cascading across my shoulders letting me know that He is near.

I can begin by celebrating the arrival of my brand new day. It is a gift and I am to enjoy it, glorify it, magnify it, celebrate it and be thankful for everything in it while I rejoice in it. I am grateful that He gave me everything I would need to cleanse and clothe my body. I am grateful for the coffee and coffee pot. I am grateful for the remote control that I use to select the channel and the volume that is pleasant for my ears to hear. I am grateful for His sunshine. I see Him. I see Him peering at me through His eyes of love. I saw the sparkle in my eyes when I looked into the mirror. He is watching over me. I ask Him on several occasions to make Satan, Lucifer, the devil, the enemy to leave my body alone. He tells me to "ignore Satan". The next time you feel pain or some sort of discomfort call on Him, tell Him about it and listen intently for Him to speak. I hear Him. My ears are tuned toward Heaven's door. I hear Him when He is ready to crack the door open to release His wisdom, knowledge and understanding.

He can have "all of me". I am a willing participant. I will do as I am told to do. I was pulled to this computer and shown a village of people living in harmony, peace, patience, contentment, tranquility and serenity. The people in the village knew that they had a Supreme Being watching over them. They were content and complacent with what they had. Is mankind complacent and content with what Our King has given them? Do we have the patience to wait on Him to return to give us our daily Grace and Mercy? You get this on a daily basis after you have saturated His atmosphere with words of praise and worship.

Yesterday! Golden moments of reflection. Anytime is the right time to be in the Presence of Our Lord. It was love at the beginning, midday, evening and at night. He wants your mind, your brain, your heart, your body, your soul and your spirit. He wants "all of you". He wants to be the One holding your hand. This is just how much He loves you. He doesn't ever want you to feel like you are alone. He will tell you, I am always nearby. Just call on my Name and I will be there faster than a bolt of lightening. This is just how fast He appeared in my life. It is instantaneous. He was there within a flash. Find Him. You want to develop your very own personal, private and intimate relationship with Him. Let Him call the shots. Allow Him full access to every fiber of your being. O Lord! You can have all of me.

"Only you". Only you are important. You recognize the One who has power and authority over your life. Only you know what words to use to shatter the ceiling in Heaven. You begin early honoring and praising Him and watch Him release the blessings He has in reserve for you in your life. I see you. I see you uncovering your brain and opening your mind up to new thoughts, ideas and aspirations. I can "think". This is my right given to me by God. I have the right to choose what is the best life for me. No one can take your right to decide away from you. You make the choice. Break through all of the barriers and let your voice be heard. I will accept the fact that I allow someone else to do my thinking. Not anymore, I can "think" for myself. I make the choice.

I chose Jesus to be First. I chose Jesus to be the Head of My Life. He told me at Psalm 23, "The Lord is My Shepherd" I shall lack nothing. I accepted Jesus as My Lord and Savior and I asked Him to please come to see about me. O Lord! You know the steps you desire for me to take. I am just a willing participant. As long as He speaks then I am willing to listen. I want to hear what He has to say. Every word that He says is important. I want to hear more.

Did you know that you are wanted, needed, accepted, appreciated, admired, adored, idolized, worshipped, cherished and honored by a King? Settle back. Speak it. Receive it. Achieve it. The spotlight is on you. You are a chosen star, rock and a gemstone. He sees you with a glow in your eyes. He is looking through His sheep and He spotted you.

There is my child. Hoping, wishing and praying, dreaming and thinking about the possibility of living her life in the Presence of a King.

Anybody for dancing? I escaped. I put on the full armor of God. I have on His breastplate of righteousness. I will never stop believing that He is making a way for me to continue to complete my assignment.

It is a beautiful sunshiny day. He has His trees, weeds, bushes, flowers, birds, insects, bugs, butterflies, green lizards and every living creature that He created in His shadow. If I remain in

Him then He will remain in me. Yep! Another love story. He loves me. Yes! Jesus loves me.

He sat me down to this computer and allowed me to open it up so I could reach you with a new message of love, hope, peace and understanding. All praise to Thee. I shout glory and mercy to Him for being so good to me.

Pull up a chair and listen closely. There is news floating in His atmosphere that He will come to see about you. I am in His Hands.

He is ordering my steps. He is orchestrating my thoughts, ideas,

opinions, beliefs, behaviors, attitudes, traditions, dreams, desires and aspirations. He is allowing me to form an opinion as we speak. He is allowing me to spill the contents of my heart. My heart is open wide to share with you the love that He is sharing with me. "I love you".

This is what He is saying to me, you, him, her, she, he, them and they.

I love all of the Ones in the North, East, South and West. I want my love to circle the globe. You can help by sharing a love song. "Yes! Jesus loves me. Yes! Jesus loves me. For the Bible tells me so and if I love Him and obey, He will make me glad someday. Look forward for a brighter day.

As I was waltzing, floating, coasting and gliding from one happy space to another one, I was asked "do you have courage and confidence in that mind, brain, heart, body, soul and spirit. Is it in your backbone, shoulders, legs, feet and toes? I began to stand up straighter. I believe that Jesus loves me and will get into my bones. I told you on yesterday that bones were talking. My bones are saying "yes! You can. My bones are telling me to worship Him, salute Him, honor Him with every step I take. Let Him loosen up the knots that you have in your spine. Stand in place before you move and compose yourself.

My message to you today is to "compose yourself" and tell self – self this is what we are going to believe, hope and pray for. We pray that He will come to see about us. We pray that He gives us the ability to "think" and "choose". Mellow out. Make your choice and be confident that you have made the right choice. This is what I have decided. I have decided to give Him my hand because I am engraved in the Palm of His Hand.

He will never ever forget about me. Isaiah 49 v:15-16.

I am among the stars. I was able to squeeze in before the door closed.

He allowed me into His Kingdom and made sure I was comfortable and had everything I needed. Do you want peace, patience, contentment, tranquility, health, hope, happiness, harmony and serenity? Jesus is the Source that you need to consult. He has the answers to what, who, why, where, when and how. You were born free. Return to the cradle and claim your inheritance. He wants to cradle you in His Everlasting Arms. This is what He can do if you allow Him too. He must get your permission. You have to ask. It is important that you ask the right questions and have the right answers. You want Everlasting Life?

Do you believe? Do you hope, pray, dream, think and desire to have a new life? You must believe, trust and have faith in what you see with your own two eyes. Read Psalm 23. "The Lord is My Shepherd",

I shall lack nothing. I can't get pass the first sentence. O Lord!

Please give me Your love, compassion, acceptance, attention, affection, deliverance, obedience, graciousness, love, hope and righteousness.

Blue eyes! Green eyes! Brown eyes! Black eyes! Hazel eyes!

What now My love? Do you want kindness, gentleness, tenderness, softness to be showered all over you? O Lord! Give it to me and I promise I will share the love that you are giving me with my brothers and sisters all around the globe. Spread the message. Jesus loves me, you, him, her, she, he, them and they. He wants you to have a drink of water. He wants you to get your daily bread. He is here with me, there with you and everywhere at the same time. He is the Same God that watched over your ancestors, descendants, foreparents and slaves and has returned to watch over me and you on this glorious and wonderful Wednesday morning. A new era in time. It is the sacred hour of

12:20 p.m. Golden moments of reflection. I get to enjoy His Presence all by myself. It is just us "two". It is just me and Him. It is just He and I. I get a chance to balance myself on a bed of rocks. Trying to keep from falling in. This is the photograph that I have flashing across my computer screen. I am dancing, laughing all of the way. What a grand occasion for Him to hold my hand.

Yesterday when I was doing laundry I had to walk back and forth.

When I reached for the door latch, Jesus told me "I will hold your hand". He allowed Grace and Mercy to settle on each shoulder and I continued on to complete the assignment that I had been given. I knew He was in control. I allowed Him to encircle me.

He walks with me. He talks with me. He converses with me. He hears me and is making a mental note of the words that are meditating in my heart on this Wednesday morning. I must disappear into a Sea of

Bronze. A Sea of Brown. Brown skies. Brown waters. Brown mountains. Brown rocks. Brown trees. Brown bushes. Brown weeds.

Brown caves. It is just He and I preparing for the next phase.

In His Presence

In The Name of Jesus - Amen

Bettie jean Grose

I am a Dreamer and Believer #2

In His Presence

In The Name of Jesus – Amen

Bettie Jean Grose

Chapter 1

Yes! It is that time again. It is time for church. Let me take you there. So, pull up a chair, sit up straight, find your happy space, put your feet up and get comfortable and get prepared for me to tell what Jesus has done for me. My job is to save somebody's soul for Christ. I have a new mind, new beliefs, new thoughts, new ideas, and nothing compares to the love and devotion, and attention that I am getting on this "Good Friday" morning, March 26th, 2021, here at Gene Miller Manor in Christian City in Union City, Georgia, South of Atlanta's Airport. He is great, mighty, powerful, wonderful, magical, majestic, outstanding, spectacular, and wonderful to me. I am so important to Him that He decided to spend time in my presence and assure me that He is watching over me and is listening to every word that I say.

Cannot find anyone who I would want to spend time with this morning, but You. You are my King, My Savior, My Healer, My Deliverer, My Burden-Barrier, My Lily in the Valley, My Bright and Morning Star, My Strong Tower, My Rock, My Redeemer, My Way-maker, My Heart Regulator, My Mind Regulator, My Strength, and My Joy and I praise and honor and salute You for being so good to me. You are present in my life to protect me from all hurt, harm, and danger. You are present in my life to provide for all my needs. You are present in my life to allow Your Holy Spirit to be my guide as I get ready to embrace the adventure that You have planned for me on a day that I have never seen before.

He is "wonderful". He came early in the morning hours to satisfy me with His morning mercy and love and told me to let it last me all during my day. Psalm 90 v:14. I can follow orders. I can follow His Decree. Hallelujah! Praise His Name. He touched me with His finger of Love and whispered in my ear "wake up O sleepyhead", rise from the dead, and let the Lord shine on you. The next thing I did was to turn over, sit up straight and place my two feet on His floor and go into my happy space and do what I needed to do. I had been given my marching orders and I obeyed. Once again, he bestowed His kindness, gentleness, softness on me and I am grateful that he chose to favor me with a brand-new day and a brand-new beginning. I have a brand-new mind. A brand-new birth, a brand-new identity. I know who I am, and I know whose I am. I am so glad to be in His Presence.

After I finished up in my happy space, I returned to my spot where my head was resting. I had it buried in His Everlasting Arms. Here I am safe and secure from all hurt, harm, and danger. This is where I seek refuge from the enemy. I was being cradled in His Everlasting arms and this is where I wanted to return to. I pulled the covers up close to my neck and ask O Lord please come into my presence and O Lord please allow me to come into Your Presence. These words have saved my soul. These words have given me Salvation and Redemption. These are words I say every morning I open my eyes. "Thank You, Jesus" is what I sing when I am moving about. I honor Him. I praise Him. I worship Him. I salute Him. I am so confident that He heard my prayer that I continue talking. I ask O Lord please shelter us, O Lord please shadow us, O Lord please favor us, O Lord please cover us with Your Blood, O Lord please grant us Your Grace and Mercy, O Lord please strengthen us physically, mentally, psychologically, morally and spiritually, O Lord please protect us from all plagues, pandemics, disasters, and turmoil, O Lord please prosper us physically, materialistically, financially and spiritually, O Lord please do not cast us away from Your Presence and please O Lord allow Your Holy Spirit to dwell in us again on this day. In Jesus' Name, I Pray - Amen.

I did not drift back to La La Land. Since I could not, I chose just to celebrate that I have a new day because I know who woke me up this morning and this created smiles, joy, and pleasure in my heart. I had been favored and I honored Him for being so good to me. Later during the morning hours, I waltzed out to my happy space and made myself a pot of coffee. You know how I enjoy my coffee in His Presence. I bowed my head in praise and worship and began reciting His twenty-third Psalm. Surely goodness and mercy shall follow me all the days of my life if I dwell in His secret place, His shelter, and in His Presence because I know "Thy art with me."

His Holy Spirit led me to turn on some music and the lyrics in this song resonated in my heart this morning. It says, "I give myself to You." My life is not my own. I belong to You. Use me. O, Lord! Take me and hide me underneath Your Loving Arms. I gave myself away to Him many moons ago. I am convinced that I belong to Him, and this is what I have accepted to be true. This has given me peace, joy, and satisfaction. What a beautiful morning. His sun is shining. After the rain, winds, tornadoes, the weather is settling down. God is upset. God is not pleased with His sheep in His Pasture, and He is doing all He can to get our attention. Listen to me I am talking. This is what He is saying. This morning He is telling me to be strong and courageous and talk to Me. You can tell me anything. Share your thoughts, hopes, dreams, wants, and desires with Me. He says, "He will guard them as my secrets." I can tell Him anything and I can ask Him for anything. He understands me. He listens to me, and He tells me that I am His own. I have a confidant. I have a constant companion. When I pull up a chair to this computer, He takes a seat right beside me.

Good news. Joy is on its way. Peace is on its way. Help is on the way. People are crying out "help" to the top of their lungs. This is what I have been waiting for, His Love, His Grace, and Mercy, His Divine Devotion. Here it comes! Let me share "hope" with you this morning. Earlier during the morning hours when I opened my eyes, I saw daylight and I began to smile because I was alive and He blew His breath of life into my lifeless body, allowing me to become a living soul all over again, ready to praise, honor and worship Him for being so good to me. He is wonderful! He is magnificent! He is marvelous. He is miraculous because He performed a miracle on me and raised me from the dead and gave me a life to live. I am glad that I am alive. I enjoy waking up in His Presence because I know He has come to take real good care of me. At this sacred moment in time, He allowed me to be closed in my right mind with a reasonable portion of my health and strength and I knew how to honor and praise Him. Who chose to wake me up this morning? Who do I salute, praise and worship? Who woke you up this morning? Have you honored Him and showed Him your gratitude? You are wasting time. Do it now while you have a chance and ask Him for His love, admiration, and affection to be bestowed on you, me, your loved ones, your family, and your friends. You must pray for all of us, your brothers and sisters in the North, East, South, and West. Jesus said "we must love everybody" if we want to see the Kingdom of God. Me, myself, and I want it. I want to walk Hand in Hand with Jesus. What must I do to make this happen?

Believe. Trust and have faith in yourself that it can be done.

The sheep in His Pasture are out of control. They are denying that God exists. They refuse to believe the truth. His Grace and Mercy, His Divine Devotion, His Unfailing Love, and His Unconditional Love were given to my mother, father, sisters, brother, cousins, and friends. He has the same Grace and Mercy ready for me to receive. I had to ask. I had to develop a personal, private, and intimate relationship with Our Lord and Savior Jesus Christ and talk to Him.

His sheep, my brothers, and my sisters are doing this and that and disregarding the One who makes it possible for them to wake up every day and inhale and exhale His air in and out of their lungs. He is the reason we are alive. It was His choice, His decision to allow us to come alive in our senses and begin to "think and process thought." The evil spirit of "Hate" is trying to raise its ugly head. Satan, Lucifer, the devil, the enemy is saying to God's sheep, His children, that they do not need God, that they can make it on their own. What a disappointment.

Do they realize that we are walking away from righteousness? Do they realize what they are filling their hearts with? No! They do not. It is "hate". They have abandoned their faith. They have decided that they do not need God and a sense of direction. Satan has convinced them that they can do what they want to do. Sorry! A lie. Deception. They have given up "hope". They have abandoned their dreams. Do not accept your life as it is. Say to yourself "I want more". I want an "everlasting life" so I can live in perfect harmony and perfect peace while I am here on Earth. This is what you are searching for - right?

Come in out of the rain and let me talk to you for a little while. His sheep are intoxicated with disbelief. Their minds and hearts have been convinced to accept anything. They say, "this is the way of the world, that is how it is done nowadays". We are on a collision course with death and destruction. We have no morals. God and his written word have been shelved to the corner. Nobody is consulting God to find out what is His plan for your life and my life. Jeremiah 29 v:11, says "there is a plan designed - just for you and me." A plan to prosper you and not to harm you, a plan to give you hope and a future. Find it in your Bible. Read it, digest it, commit it to memory. You were created for a purpose. His sheep have lost their sense of direction and they are looking around and there must be some sign of hope and peace available to them.

Man, woman, boys and girls, princes and princesses are drunk with stupidity because they have been fed the lie that it is permissible to hate the ones that do not look like you. Look around you. There is a new day on the horizon. Come to grips and face reality. We are all sheep in His Pasture, and He sees that our hearts are filled with hate. He is demanding that our hearts be filled with love and compassion and empathy. My God! My Lord! My Jesus! He wants you to join with Him hand and hand and when you do, He will strengthen you physically, mentally, emotionally, psychologically, morally, and spiritually. He will heal our hearts. He is the One with the power to change our hearts. He wants to dwell in our hearts. You must yearn for a change in your heart. Hate is all you have known. No one has ever told you three simple words and they are "I love you." Some people have never heard these words. This is the truth. Think about it. Love is absent from the minds of people today. They put up barriers. They have adopted a philosophy. I hate you and you hate me. How confusing? People justify this statement. People have these words tattooed across their hearts. Their hearts are filled with hate. You must face reality and realize we are in pandemics, having plagues, facing disasters and turmoil.

The pandemic of Hate. Can you see it? Can you feel it? It is surrounding you and me. Come in a little closer and let Him speak to you. He has a message for you. It is for your ears only. I love You. These are the words we all need to hear. How many times have you heard it? You are to be commended for having someone to love you. Do you know the greatest love? Do you know where you can find it? I do. You find it when you realize who watched over you while you slumbered and slept and favored you with a brand-new day and a brand-new mind. This is what He did for me. Oh! Jesus "I love You" and "thank you" for being so good to me on this glorious, gorgeous semi-cloudy, gray day. His love lives in my heart every day, all day, 24/7, around the clock - every hour - every minute - every second and right at this precise and present moment in time.

You and I do not know where death is. There so many mass shootings. People carrying bombs and explosives. We do not know when it will our last day. I recommend that you get your ducks in a row, in other words, make a declaration that you will make Jesus Christ your Lord and Savior and you surrender the reigns you have on your life over to Him so His will can be done. We need protection. We need guidance. Somebody needs to tell the story. Do you want hope?

Do not fall asleep. It is time to wake up and face reality. Do you know who loves you now, today, tomorrow, and will love you through Eternity? It is Jesus. The baby in a manger. The baby that had nowhere to lay His head. It is Jesus who is watching over you as you go here and there. Have you praised Him for the Love and Affection that He has given you? Watch me! O, Lord! You are great! Oh, Lord! You are mighty! Please guide my thoughts, actions, deeds, opinions, beliefs, traditions, and desires on this day on your solid and sacred ground we call Earth, on Your Planet, and in Your Universe.

This is your world. Take it back from Satan, Lucifer, the devil, the enemy. How do you do that? First, gather the facts. What you will need has already been supplied to you. You will need faith. You must be able to believe. You must be able to trust. There is a pillar that you can lean on. You will need your Bible, His written word, and His Holy Spirit. This is what I did, and it worked for me. You have been a slave to Satan too long. You are his prisoner, and it is time to ask God the Father of Our Lord and Savior Jesus Christ to make Satan release the chains and shackles he has skillfully placed around your neck, mind, brain, heart, body, soul, and spirit. He is holding you so tight that you are unable to breathe, think and process thought. You are chained and bound. He keeps telling you to do this or do that, everybody else is doing it. We cannot follow the world. We must come to a complete stop and say "no" I am not going to live with hate, lies, and deceit in my heart. Living this kind of life will fail. Hate creates savages and barbarians and heathens and misfits. Rage and anger and hate are spewing from their ears. This is what is dwelling in their hearts. Tell yourself "I want a clean heart". I want a golden heart. You have made a big declaration. You have committed to a change. A word of encouragement, this is what you must yearn to have. Plan your escape. Open your Bible and read.

St. Mark, Chapter 7 and listen to Jesus tell you how to get a clean heart and a steadfast spirit.

What comes out of a person is what makes him have an unclean heart. Out of the heart of man comes evil thoughts, sexual immorality, theft, murder, adultery, coveting, wickedness, deceit, sensuality, envy, slander, pride, and foolishness. All these evil things come from within, and they defile a person.

People are hurting, crying out, and dying. Look what is dwelling in their hearts. They are hungry for a change. They need to know that there is a safe place you can go where you will be safe and secure. What is your desire? Are you living to try to please God or yourself? Serious question. Take some time to answer. Do not let the world govern you. You have a choice. You have self-control and free will. It is a basic guaranteed human right. You can make a choice. What do you want? What are you trying to achieve? You can receive a clean heart and a steadfast spirit. I am trying to please God this morning. I must convince you to have the desire to change your heart, beliefs, opinions, traditions, ideas, thoughts, and desires. The Grace of God has appeared to me, and He has given me salvation. He has this available to all the people. They need to be taught to turn away from ungodliness and worldly passions and to live self-controlled, upright, and godly lives in this present age. Read Titus 2 v:11-12.

God is trying to bust the door down with His word and you are rejecting Him because you will not open your Bible and allow Him to talk to you. Decide for the rest of your life that this is what I want. I want His Unfailing Love, His Unconditional Love, His Grace and Mercy, and His Divine Devotion. It is available if you ask. You have work to do. Submit yourself to Him. Commit yourself to Him.

Surrender yourself to Him. I decided to make Jesus Christ the head of my life and this is the best decision I could have ever made. This gave me peace and confidence and the courage to keep waking up and doing His will.

I am resting in His word. My heart is filled with love, wisdom, knowledge, understanding, justice, honesty, truth, self-respect, self-discipline, self-control, free-will, dignity, integrity, honor, valor, redemption, salvation, and righteousness. Is this what is residing in your heart? A long time ago I learned that I belong to Him. He gave me an assignment and I am moving forward every day to meet my destiny.

You cannot live an immoral life and expect God to give you His Grace and Mercy, Love, and Divine Devotion. People are lost. Are you dead? I believe you are. I believe you have died and been buried alive. Your heart is dead. You cannot feel. There is no compassion, love, and tolerance for each other. You have decided to live a life that you have created for yourself. Have you thought about consulting God and asking Him to lead you out of that wilderness that you find yourself in? I am headed over yonder, over there, to paradise, to the promised land, the Great Beyond. This is the direction I am pursuing, and I want to give you a glimpse of what I see.

It is time to begin questioning your character and morals. Ask yourself is this right? Have I given up on finding peace, happiness, joy, salvation, redemption, truth, honesty, justice, love, and righteousness? Do not hang your head in disbelief. Ask yourself "what have I done".

Have I accepted my life as it is and never considered changing my beliefs, opinions, ideas, thoughts, traditions, and desires?

Satan has made you accept the fact that you have no reason to live. He has made you settle in your present condition and situation and wait to die. You are merely eating, sleeping, and breathing, just existing and not living an abundant and joyful life filled with purpose, dedication and satisfaction.

Wait a minute! Hold up! There is "good news". Matthew 11 v:28 says, "you, who are weary, worn and heavy laden, come unto me and I will give you rest. Does this sound like you? Want Perfect Peace? Want tranquility, contentment, harmony, serenity, health, love, joy, happiness, and love? Jesus got it. Jesus, has it waiting for you. Want me to tell you how good He is to me. I just must take you to church. Decompress! Let all the air out of that engine. Breathe, take a sigh of relief. You can rest now because you have saved, redeemed, and been given a new life to live in the Presence of a King. Stop searching. Go to the source.

The moment that you cry out "Lord! Save me", He will appear quicker than a bolt of lightning. Accept Christ as your Savior and ask Him to talk to God on your behalf. Jesus Christ saved me one day. Jesus keeps me in perfect peace. The moment I accepted Christ He made me a promise that "He would never leave me nor forsake me". Hebrews 13 v:5. I trust Him. I believe Him. I have faith in Him. I have placed all my hope, faith and trust, and belief in Him. Jesus saves. Jesus can save your soul. You must be willing to do the work. You must decide. You do have a choice. You have free will and self-control. Okay! Let us see! Do I choose life or death? I want to live. Do I want a counselor and a comforter to help me live my life? Say - Yes! Admit it - you cannot do it on your own. Accept the fact that you need help because you are not satisfied with your achievements, accomplishments and the conditions that you find yourself in.

You must do one thing that He commands and that is "believe". I can go to Christ and give Him my entire all. I give myself away. He saved me and I will worship Him, honor Him, praise Him, and share with the world just how good He is to me.

Are you all in like I am? Have you committed, submitted, and surrendered your life over to Him so His will can be done? If not, then let us get started. Ask Him. This is what I did. Oh, Lord! Please come to see about me. Oh, Lord! Please reshape me, remold me and make me into the person You had designed me to be before I was in my mother's womb. Jeremiah 1.

If we believe in Him, if we abide in Him, if we remain in Him, if we draw nearer to Him, then we can shatter the ceiling in Heaven and ask Him to release the blessings that He has in reserve for you and me.

Chapter 2

It is a foggy-rainy glorious and gorgeous day. I am in His Presence, and He is taking good care of me. I enjoy all my days because I know who decided for me to come alive in my senses so I could think, and process thought. It was King Jesus and I owe Him a debt of gratitude. Thank You, Lord, for smiling on me and favoring me with a new day and a new mind. Let us begin all over again is what He said to me. I hurried up and said "yes". Will today be a repeat? He said, "if I want it to be". So, I danced off into my happy space to cleanse and clothe my body after I became awake on this Saturday morning, March 27th, 2021, here at Gene Miller Manor in Christian City, in Union City, Georgia, south of the airport.

At the age of 74, it finds me magnificent, marvelous, splendid, superb, fabulous, fantastic, outstanding, spectacular, and wonderful. How can that be - you asked? When you know that you have been saved from that fire that rages in your mind, brain, heart, soul, body, and spirit, you have the right to become alive again. I am alive. I am inhaling and exhaling His air out of my lungs. He is regulating my heartbeat. He is the One that decided for me to open my eyes this Saturday morning to embrace the adventure that He has planned for me.

The grass is about to start glowing this morning. I am getting ready to teach you a lesson on love and devotion. I will be fertilizing it with His written word. I have verses in scripture that I must research. I will be getting myself some fuel because I know what it takes to keep this little light shining. I know what it takes to keep the engine running. Love, more love, more love. Affection and Admiration from the One who first loved me. He is awake this morning and has directed me to pull out a chair, get comfortable and listen as He speaks to me. Oh! I want Him. I need Him and I love Him. I need for Him to pull me into His shelter and keep me in His shadow. I am a little child playing in the wide-open field and I need to tell you just how good He is to me. He allows me to float, glide, coast through His air just like a bird. He allows me to do what I want to do, and I want to please Him. I cannot let an hour pass by without my saluting, praising, honoring, and saluting Him for what He is doing for me right at this specific moment in time at the sacred hour of noon.

I am over the rainbow. I have disappeared into His sunrise and in His sunset. We are getting close to meeting Him face to face. In the meantime, He wants you and I to get our house in order. He wants us to spread the word that "Jesus saves". What do you mean? I can only tell you what He did for me. Jesus heard my cry. I said, "Oh Lord, please save me". He appeared and saved me from me. I was destroying my beliefs, my faith, and my life. I was responsible for my failure. It was only because I did not believe and put my hope, faith, and trust in Thee. I will not remember all the trials and tribulations, disappointments that I faced because He is playing my favorite song. I recollect the time He told me "I will always love you" and I did not hear Him, and He said it again, this time in a different manner, "I will love you always". I had never heard these words before. Naturally, I could not contain all the joy, satisfaction, and jubilation that I felt. It took me some time to readjust myself.

The first time in my life that I had heard these words. I wanted to hear more. So, I began hanging out with Him. I began to enjoy the time we shared. First, I had to change my vocabulary. I had to change the words that I was releasing into His atmosphere. I was sabotaging myself. I was the one destroying my hopes, dreams, wants, beliefs, opinions, thoughts, ideas, traditions, and desires with the words in my mouth. I was so guilty of not thinking and processing thought. One day His Holy Spirit led me to the right vessel I needed to hear so I could get back on course. I learned that I was headed into self-destruction. I learned I had been given a life to live and it was my choice if I wanted life or death. Proverbs 18 v:21 - The tongue. I was already dead and buried. This is the conclusion I came to. I was taught that I am great. I am a masterpiece. I am a fine specimen of workmanship. Come up out of that grave. I was taught that Jesus can raise the dead. If I put my hope, faith, trust, and belief in Jesus, I could receive a life to live in the Presence of a King.

This is a glorious and gorgeous foggy rainy day that I see. I see Jesus. I feel Jesus. I know He is close by. I know He is here because He lives within the four chambers of my heart. After all, I swept all the evil spirits away and allowed Him full access to replenish them with His love, kindness, gentleness, and righteousness. Oh! I love You, Lord. You are my source of strength, joy, and happiness because it is You who lives within me. You opened the doors and windows to show me where my blessings come from.

You bestow on me your love, kindness, goodness in the morning, at noon, in the evening, and at night. It has been a long time since I have felt this way. You fill me with pride, satisfaction, joy, and glee all day, every day, around the clock, 24/7, every hour - every moment - every second, and at this present and the precise moment in time.

My mind, my brain, my heart, my soul, my body, and my spirit is awake this morning. I am not dead in my senses so that makes me able to think. I can process thought. I have been given that right. It was given to me by Jesus from Our Heavenly Father. I know who touched me with His finger of love and blew His breath of life into my lifeless soul so I could be raised from the dead, ready to praise, honor, worship, salute, and cherish Him. Our God the Father of Our Lord and Savior Jesus Christ is so good to me. He gave me a Savior. He gave you a Savior. He is the One that I have placed my hope, trust, and faith in for the remainder of my day, today, tomorrow and forevermore.

I can only do it one day at a time. I rejoice when I receive a new day. I celebrate it. I magnify it, I enjoy it and I am thankful for everything in it. Psalm 118 v:24 tells me this is what I am supposed to do when I receive a gift of a brand-new day. I feel so good. I am ready to embrace my morning because I know who is leading the way and holding my hand. It is Jesus. He is my protector, my provider, my healer. He is My Savior, and He loves to hear my voice when I call on His Holy Name.

Want a dose of reality? Want to face facts? Do you know he is a "Beautiful Savior?" Well! Tell Him. Give Him your praise and honor. Wish you were here so we could praise Him together but since you are not, I will continue the pathway that He has chosen for me on this brand-new Saturday morning that I have never seen before. I will continue to talk about Him. Good morning! Wake up! I am about to share with you some amazing news. I am going to give you a glimpse of the kind of love that I am getting. It is Extraordinary Love. It is not ordinary love that you have for your brothers and sisters. This is a special love that you can only receive from a King.

He is so far away. He pulls me in closer to Him. I have seen the light. This is how I can explain to you the relationship that I have developed with Him. He is a "way maker". Jesus is my way maker, my strong tower, my strength, and my joy. I want His Love. Yes! I do. I need His Love. This is where I seek refuge. I need Him to shelter me and to shadow me. He allows me to be cradled in His Everlasting Arms. I belong to Thee. I am a child of a King. I am one of God's children. I am one of His sheep in His Pasture and He is taking good care of me.

He sees my smile when I look into the mirror, and He sees the sparkle I have in my eye. Look into the mirror and see if you have that sparkle. Stay long enough to see it. When you see the sparkle, that is Him, speaking to you calling you His "Shining Star". Go back a second time and listen for Him to say, "You are my only love".

Go with me as I take you back to the beginning of my morning. When I opened my eyes, I began praising and worshipping, and honoring Him for waking me up this morning. When I went to La La Land, I did not know what would happen. I confided in Him before I drifted off into La La Land. O, Lord! Please keep us safe. Please keep us locked in tight in Your Presence. Then I found my favorite spot. My head was buried in His chest so I could breathe His sweet breath forevermore and I began to dream.

When I opened my eyes on this Saturday morning, He was present with His Hand stretched out to me, I grabbed it and He allowed me to go into my happy space and do what I needed to do.

And of course, I returned and went into dreamland, my wonderland, you know La La Land. His Arms are so snuggly, warm, and comfortable. I love being cradled. You should try it, I recommend it. He allows you to dream sweet, pleasant dreams because He allows you to float into His Presence. Lay your head on your pillow, fluff it, a smile because you know you are in His Presence. I am always in His Presence.

While I was getting nestled back in His Arms, I began to whisper these words, and they gently, softly were O Lord please come into my presence and O Lord please allow me into Your Presence. In other words, I just said "O Lord please come to see about me". This is what I heard my mamma say. If mama said it and it worked for her, then it should work for me, and guess what I found out, "it did".

I remained just where I was, in His Presence and I began talking. I ask O Lord please shelter us, O Lord please shadow us, O Lord please favor us, O Lord please cover us with Your Blood, O Lord please grant us Your Grace and Mercy, O Lord please strengthen us physically, mentally, emotionally, psychologically, morally and spiritually, O Lord please forgive us of our sins because we don't always do things correctly and perfectly, O Lord please prosperous us physically, materialistically, financially and spiritually, O Lord pleases forgive our enemies because they know not what they do, O Lord please protect us from all plagues, pandemics, disasters, and turmoil, O Lord please do not cast us away from Your Presence and please O Lord do not take Your Holy Spirit away from us on this day. In Jesus' Name, I Pray - Amen.

What does your affirmation, morning prayer, morning confession or morning mantra say? Do you greet Him with "hello" or "good morning"? I smiled and said, "what a wonderful Savior". I greet my Savior in the humblest and meekness way I know how because He is My King, and He deserves my best.

His Peace, Love, Hope, Joy, Wisdom, Knowledge, Understanding, Equality, Justice, Honesty, Truth, Salvation, Redemption, and Righteousness will consume you. You must allow Him to enter your hearts and replace hate with His Love and Devotion. This is what He did for me. It will make you feel brand new. You will come into such awareness. You will be placed on a higher dimension than you are already on. All of a sudden everything will become brighter. Pull your heart out - lay it on the table and examine it. What do you see? You know your heart. No one else does. That is why each of us has a heart. First, it must be filled with Love for yourself. Hello! You must love yourself from the crown of your head to the sole of your feet because you are covered in His blood. You do not belong to self; you belong to Jesus. He died for you. He gave up His life for you so you could be saved. What kind of heart did Jesus have? A heart made from pure gold.

Your heart should be filled with Love for, self-first, then your brothers and sisters in the North, East, South, and West. It should be filled with love for those who are young, old, tall, short, big, thin, black, brown, yellow, white, straight, or gay. All of us are His sheep in His Pasture. Psalm 100.

Why do I write? To release the love, hope, peace, trust, and happiness that He has given to me. I want to share with the world that there is another life for you to live. Come in out of the rain. Open your mind and imagination and ask the question "what if"? You are responsible for finding His love, hope, peace, trust, and happiness and I am willing to help you. What He has given to me should be shared. It might be you who He is calling on this Saturday morning to preach to someone about how good He is to you. Just testify about His goodness. What else is there to talk about? Give honor and recognition to the One who watched over you while you slumbered and slept. Give honor and recognition to the One who woke you up this morning. It is up to me to bring this to your attention. That is part of my assignment. I am just keeping it real with you. He whispers joy, hope, and peace into my heart. This is what is spewing out of my ears. I depend on Him for all my needs. I go with the flow. I lounge, I eat, I sit, I read, I meditate. I find comfort, joy, peace, satisfaction being in His Presence. I hear horns and drums. A soft melody. The window is cracked, and I am feeling a breeze of fresh air rush in through His window.

Just had to have my say! You knew when you pulled up a chair that I was going to take you to my favorite spot. Yes! Church or Sunday School. We must go back to the cradle and start our lives all over again. Remember how you were pampered? Yes! You do. You were given everything you needed and wanted. You and I had loving parents who provided great care for us. Imagine who wants to take great care of you now that you are a man or woman? Can you grasp a vision of His love on this bright sunshiny morning? The weather changed. When I began it was gray and cloudy and after spending some time with you, I see rays of sunshine. That tells me that He is watching over me, and you and He gave us in His shadow. You were an infant presented to the world. He was holding your hand. He wants to hold it now at this present and precise moment in time.

What are you saying to yourself? Is she serious? Get serious and drink some water. He is my silent Love, I can talk about Him, all day, at the crack of dawn or nightfall. I know He is with me. Psalm 23 says it. I know He will go with me everywhere I go. I know He went me into my happy space, and I made myself a pot of coffee, ate my banana, took my meds, and prepared to begin my morning routine. Here I am, at this computer, celebrating the life of the Wonderful One. How can I "Thank Him"? Do you ask? By saying three precious words that He likes to hear and that is "Thank You, Jesus". Every time He hears it makes His heart pumps faster. He is so satisfied that you realized where your health and strength come from. He has given you and me everything we needed to cleanse and clothe our bodies so we could prepare to perform the tasks at hand.

I know Jesus is real. I can tell by the way I feel. He lets me know that I "belong" to Him. He plays my favorite song. He talks to me meekly and humbly. His voice is so soft and gentle. He loves it when I play instrumental music. I hear His pianos, violins, horns, tubas, harmonicas, trombones, guitars, and drums. My thoughts began to flow, and I can share with you what is meditating in my heart.

His Holy Spirit said to me "you know who loves you, don't you?" I replied "Yes" I do. At that time, I was drinking a bottle of His chilled spring water that He allowed to escape from His mountains, His rocks, His brooks, His rivers, His streams, His dams, His creeks, and His rivers. Sparkles started coming from the bottle. He is shining a light on me. His eye is on the sparrow then it certainly is on me and you. We both are blessed and highly favored.

Is He great or what? Isn't this amazing? Look what He did for me.

Let me talk about the water that my sister, Vivian Ann, and my family use to drink that came from a well. It was cold coming out from the faucet. It tasted oh so good. Look what Jesus did. He gave us pure well water to drink, cook with and do laundry.

Teach me how to love you O Lord! Teach me what pleases you because this is my aim and purpose. I just want to do God's will. I want to follow His Plan. Satan tries to interrupt my flow of thoughts. Jesus asked me if I knew I was under demonic attack coming from demonic sources? I said "yes" I do. Adjust yourself because you know what is expected of you. There is a story for you to tell. Then he showed me a white rabbit.

I see a white rabbit hopping around on the white ground. He is jumping and ducking in and out of the snow. This reminds me of when I lived in Maine. We played in the snow, we got cold, but we loved it just like His rabbit is doing. I have different pictures of nature cascading across the computer screen when it is idling.

His rabbit is so free. It can hop, here and there because He has someone who loves Him. Jesus loves me and I know why? He treats me as a newborn. He supplies all my needs, He will protect me from all hurt, harm, or danger and He will allow His Holy Spirit to become my guide. He is "beautiful". Did you grasp that?

He neither sleeps nor slumbers. He watches over me all day, every day, around the clock, 24/7, every hour, every minute, every second, and right at this present moment in time.

How do you convince a 15-year-old, who has schoolwork, ROTC, a job and who is learning how to drive that these words are true? I know Jesus will give him everything he needs if he believes, trust, obey and have faith? He is trying out dating and spending time with the fellows. Wish for me special blessings. Pray for me. I have work to do.

I had to learn to adopt a new behavior. I had to exercise self-control and restraint. I can enjoy a magnificent and marvelous, fulfilling and rewarding life if I choose to. I had a choice. I could live with my old self, but this was not what I wanted to do. I got a chance to live on the other side of the mountain and I loved it. I made up in my mind that I would make Jesus first and make Him the Head of My Life. You see I knew that He looked at me through the eyes of Love and Devotion. He had His eye on me. I see His rainbow colors when I look at His sun at a certain angle. I see a light. I am confident that He is watching over His trees, grass, flowers, weeds, bushes, insects, bugs, animals, and everything that He created. He created me and He created you.

Back to my rabbit. My white rabbit is loving the cold weather and I want to join the rabbit and play outside in the snow. He is white and his feet are brown because he lives under the ground. God takes care of me. I live above ground. I have food, shelter and common sense. He loves His rabbit, and He provides everything His rabbit will need. Ah! Shucks. He is taking good care of me because I am the cream of the crop. I am one of His finest and He said He would "take good care of me".

Want me to tell you what time it is? It will be brief? It is time for your heart to receive an "overhaul". Your heart needs to be made brand new. It is a joy and a pleasure to tell you just how good He is to me. It is time to shut up, sit down and listen. Return to the basics. Return to what you know will work. How did my mamma, daddy, aunties, uncles, cousins, and friends make it out of the wilderness? They had hope, faith, trust, and peace. I got it.

The preachers have been holding back on you. Do you want to live in Heaven or hell? Right now, not when you die. It is what is in that heart of yours that will matter. This is what is keeping you alive. What are you filling it with? Fill it with godliness and righteousness so we can sing in the Sunshine a song that He wants to hear.

I have come to realize that He is keeping me alive for a reason. I must tell it. There was a plan devised for me. I have got to say it. It is so important that today you make a better day than yesterday. Yell! Stop sending in the clowns. We cannot pretend anymore that we are content, happy, and satisfied when we are not. The truth will set you free.

You can turn over a new leaf. Start brand new and let Jesus hold your hand. He will force you to take a mental note and say this is not what God had intended for me. I missed my turn-off. I should have taken the detour when I ran upon it. Now it is time for you to get back on the right road, one filled with hope for your future so you can complete your destiny. You are alive for a purpose. Use your imagination. You have knowledge, wisdom, and understanding, don't you?

He is hovering over me like a helicopter. He is stuck to me. I cannot go anyplace without Him. He is my constant companion. My Sargent in Arms. My Commander-in-Chief. I love it. Look in the Big Book - His Bible. Surely His Goodness and Mercy shall follow me all the days of my life as long as I dwell in His Shelter, His Secret Place, or His Presence. Psalm 91.

Chapter 3

What is new? How do you keep the music playing in your head? You embed His Spirit into your mind, brain, heart, soul, body, and spirit. You keep your mind on Jesus and what He is doing for you. He is saving your soul every hour, every minute, every second, all day, every day, 24/7. He sure is good to me, and I keep this at my forefront. It is your Lord and Savior who allowed me to go outside and breathe some of His fresh air and hear His birds sing and chirp. I went outside, sat with one of my Bible Study Scholars and we celebrated that we knew the Lord. We enjoyed each other. We commented on how we love the peace, love, and joy that He was showing us. Some people do not know, do they? I asked! He replied, "They sure don't". I told him it is up to us, you, and I to spread the word. We continued to swing and enjoy the moment.

I captured precious moments when I sat in the swing, rocked back and forth, and delighted in the treasures that He had prepared for me. Franco is his name. He saw a blue-green-yellow lizard and he immediately tried to show it to me. I saw it. It got away so fast. I did not take him too fast. His Holy Spirit gave me the words to say. He was listening to opera, and we commented on how gentle, soft, and kind this type of music sounds to our ears and how satisfying it is to your brain, mind, and heart.

I walked to the mailbox and subsequently went outside so I could spend some alone time in His Presence outdoors. When I returned to my mansion I decided to talk on the phone to my daughter and son. My daughter, Tamara, and her husband were enjoying outside. We had a lot to share. My son, Nate was watching a movie and of course, I had to take them to church.

That is what mammas and daddies do.

You must be born again and learn to love the entire world. Chances are you never thought about loving your brothers and sisters in the North, South, East, and West. It is a new day. America must learn to love, share, give before our time is up. We do not have forever to get it together. We only have a short window to act.

Want to go to Paradise, over yonder, over there in the Great Beyond? Say yes and I will have you convinced that it is a great day to be alive in His Presence. You are alive so you can explore the world that is wrapped around you. If you want to go to Paradise, then we must learn to love those brown people in South America who is harvesting and shipping coffee to America on a twenty-four-seven basis. They work Monday through Sunday to get it on our breakfast table. Nowadays, there is a coffee rush in the morning, noonday, in the evening, and at night. Is not God wonderful to give us what we need? Can you imagine waking up to no coffee? Suppose their villages were hit with unforeseen weather tragedies. Suppose their crops were destroyed and them along with it. What would we do? Jesus said, "We must love everybody". Before you can enjoy the horn of plenty, you must have a clean heart and an upright spirit. The only source I can tell you about is Jesus. He is our advocate to the Father. Your Heavenly Father is listening to Jesus, and I am sure I am going to do what He tells me to do because I want to please Him. I want The Lord to continue waking me up and shinning His bright light on me. Psalm 36 v:10, "continue Your Love on those that know you and who are upright in heart. That is what it says. Want Him to continue to love you then learn to love Him back?

The One I belong to belongs to nobody else but me. He saved my soul and I promised I would serve Him the rest of my life. Now I have the chance to prove myself and my love for Him. If I keep telling you how He showers me with His Unfailing Love, His Unconditional Love, His Grace and Mercy, and His Divine Devotion, you might question your beliefs, opinions, thoughts, ideas, traditions, and desires. What do you want? Do you want Him to watch over you 24/7, then ask Him? He is right close by you. He can hear you. There is no need to get loud or boisterous. He can hear you. He hears your thoughts. He crafted you in His image and made you a fine specimen of His workmanship.

Want me to point you to the Stairways to Heaven? I do it for this reason only. Jesus saved my soul. He gave me a brand-new beginning, a brand-new birth, a brand-new mind, a brand-new identity because I was born again. Oh! My Child! You must return to the cradle and become alive in your senses so you can think, and process thought? Who woke you up this morning and gave you a sound mind with a reasonable portion of my health and strength? God did it. He told Jesus to watch over me. He told me I was in "good hands". He knew me as a suckling baby and said He would never forget about me because I was carved in the Palms of His Hands. Isaiah 49 v:15-16.

So, I settled back and just went with the flow. I stayed outside for about two hours, breathing His fresh air, and listening to His birds worship Him. They were worshipping Him so I joined in with the birds and told the birds, "I will salute Him too" because He is so good to me on a Saturday afternoon at the 5 o'clock hour. Do you see that I am seeing a new world this afternoon? I saw Lofoten Islands in Norway. The world is passing us by. We are missing what He has prepared for us because we will not slow down to a snail's space and just breathe and realize that you are blessed and highly favored as you take a breath.

I am making plans for a family get-together. Easter Sunday, I have made plans to visit with my daughter, my son-in-law, and my grandson. I have not seen him since he got his job. Almost six figures. Isn't God good? He knows what time it is. Grandma takes him to church every chance she gets. His favorite comment to me is "Yes mam". Music to my ears. He understands. He listens. This is what America must do - begin to listen. If we begin to listen and produce thought, then we will be saved.

Newsflash! We are the walking dead! Why do you say that? Look around you, what do you see. People, more people, sheep that lives in His Pasture. What direction are His sheep headed in? Where are they trying to get to? What are they trying to achieve? Perfect peace, happiness, joy, salvation, redemption, faith, justice, honesty, love, and righteousness. Want it? They come in out of the rain! Claim your seat because you want to hear more. Want me to share more with you. I am the author of "You Can Be My Tulip". It is faith-based on actual conversations and interactions that I have had with Our Lord and Savior Jesus Christ. He is with me. When I pulled out the computer chair, He was there, and He pulled up a seat right beside me. Isn't He wonderful? Isn't He amazing? I tell Him often that "You light up My Life". I adore You; I admire You; I worship You; I honor You; I salute You; I cherish You and I idolize You because You gave me the gift of life. I became alive. I separated my old self from my new self. I changed my thinking, my behavior, my attitude and began to dream again. I dreamed of myself into a new reality. I dreamed myself into His Presence with the words that I release from my vocabulary throughout my day.

O Lord please come into my presence and O Lord please allow me into Your Presence and when You come to see about me, please take good care of me. This is the way you must go home. You must pass by Jesus before you can get a seat in His Kingdom. You want to be a member of God's Household - right? You want your inheritance, right? You want what belongs to you - right? You want Salvation - right? It is free.

You must commit, submit, and surrender yourself to Thee so His will can be done. If I do not tell another breathing soul but you, know that there is another life that you can live. It is up to you what you choose. Choose life. Do not choose death! Tell Jesus you want to become alive in His Spirit. You are a child of a King. You are one of God's children, you are one of His sheep in His Pasture and you should stop and allow Him to take good care of you.

Find your love letter in the Bible. He is sending love through every verse in scripture that you read. There is so much love being shown to you when you read your Bible, it appears to jump off the page. Let His words of wisdom come alive in your mind, heart, brain, body, soul, and spirit. If He has His eye on the sparrow or the skylark, then He has His eye on me. Remember the oldies yet goodies. The same Grace and Mercy, Love and Devotion that He is giving to me is the same Love, Grace, and Mercy He wants to give to you. He wants to put a song in your heart, and He expects you to have praise on your tongue all day, every day, 24/7, around the clock, every hour, every minute, every second, and right at this present moment in time. In His Presence, can't you tell? I am going to disappear and enjoy my pizza, my bowl of chilled grapes, and my soda and water. This is what He provided for me.

Isn't He awesome? Isn't He wonderful? He has prepared a table before me. My cup is running over. My cup is filled with Love, and I want to share it with you.

Chapter 4

I sing a long song. There are a lot of words to my song. Got time to go to church. I am coming up out of that valley and with your help you and I can make it. It is written right before you that "I am the truth, the way and the light!! It is in the Bible! Have you read it, if not, find it? Then settle back, and just think - think - dream - think some more - where are you? What is controlling your thoughts? What is controlling your ideas? Who is supplying you with words of knowledge, wisdom and understanding? Is it God, Jesus Christ, My Lord and Savior, Jesus Christ or is it Satan?

Satan said "I will get them through their senses. I will make your sheep unable to think. I will capture their mind, their wants, and desires. God said "I will only distribute my ability to think to the noblemen, women, and humble boys and girls. There will only be a few who will stand up and be a man or woman. There will only be a few who will listen. Satan said! God said! For those are my chosen few, the ones I brought up out of the valley. For them, I have peace, patience, joy, happiness, salvation, redemption, love, and righteousness. Listen to me. Satan wants your soul, and He has pulled you over to His side of the fence. I got them through their eyes, I will shine gold in front of their eyes. Satan said. God said my children have a heart of gold and they will always love each other. My children have been set aside and taught to have faith that one day I will come to see about them. Those of us who believe must not allow Satan to enter our eardrums. His evil spirit of hate will destroy you. Listen to Satan. He says.

I will tear them apart with lusts. More of this, more of that, keep it coming I can never get enough of what I am seeing, eating, hearing, and tasting is what they say. I say this. Life on the other side is better. You will be happy, satisfied, joyous, appreciative if you come to spend just a little time with me on the other side. It is by invitation only. I asked to be invited to the party, they were praising God, glorifying His Name, and being thankful for everything in sight and I wanted to join them.

Thank You, Lord, for my eyes. It is dusk dawn, and I am allowed to dream. Dream off into one of His sunsets. Dream off into one of His sunrises. Dance under the moonlight. It is peaceful, serene, soft, and gentle to your mind, your brain, your heart, your body, your soul, and your spirit. Want true love from a King? It is available to you. It is right under your nose. You have not found Him because you refuse to think. Here is a sample of my conversation with my baby girl.

My daughter was having a "rainy day". No joy! No hope! Her name is Aishah. Oh! She is a smart little cookie. Done forgot her upbringing. Done forgot what her mama taught her at her knees. To believe in yourself. God will watch over us. You are a Princess, and you should be acting just like one. You are a doll, sitting on the shelf, ready to take home to nurture and grow into what you were designed to be. Let her grow! She is still a bulb in the ground. This is what Our Lord told me. She needs to sit down, lie down, stand up and begin to "think" and "process thought". This is your guaranteed right from Jesus from God. Want your inheritance? Then go to the source of your strength. Find out what does He want you to do.

Come to paradise with me. Let me take you to church. Nope, Sunday School will do. We are happy together, He and I. Me and Him. Just us two. We are happy. We love each other. I am kind, gentle, soft, beautiful, courageous, delightful because He is with me. I must impress. He is the "Wind Beneath My Wings." I am mounted upon an eagle, and he is about to take off. He will go with me down this golden road that He has paved just for me.

God, Our Heavenly Father of Our Lord and Savior Jesus Christ, we begin our mornings together. He tells me "I will never find anyone like me. I listen. I ask at the crack of dawn for Him to please come into my presence and I ask Him to allow me into His Presence. He hears me. He listens to me. That is the most important thing you have is someone who will listen to your thoughts and ideas. No one has the time. You can talk to Jesus. You can confide in Him. You can tell Him anything. He wants to know your desires, wants, needs, opinions, beliefs, ideas. In other words, He wants to know just how you think.

Are you worshipping the One who gave His sheep a sunrise and a sunset? It is His Will that today be the day when you throw in the towel and say I have had enough of this nonsense. When I was a child, I acted like a child. I was free and happy, content and satisfied with whatever I had because I knew tomorrow would be a better day. Yesterday was beautiful, magnificent, and marvelous. I received a portion of my daily bread. There is more. I can get a little nugget of wisdom, knowledge, and understanding for just believing, trusting, and having faith that One Day He is coming back, and I want to be ready.

It is here. I have a story to tell. Let Him find me joyous, praising Him, saluting Him, glorifying Him, and rejoicing in Him.

When I get His attention in the morning time, I dare to keep talking. I have a built-in desire to communicate with My Heavenly Father, but I must tell Jesus first what I want and need and ask Him to talk to the Father on my behalf. O, Lord! I want to learn. I want to know more. Teach me, Master. Where should I lay my head? I want Peace. I want Love and Affection and Admiration.

I can tell you where to get it! You get it from the Prince of Peace, Jesus Christ, Our Lord and Savior, the Son of God. I have a smile on my face with joy and contentment radiating in my heart. I cannot smile and have this much confidence to write unless He allows me to. I am so convinced that I am doing the right thing. I am following His will. I am so confident that He heard my prayer and will answer my prayer, I drift back off into His Wonderland, Over Yonder, Over There, in the Great Beyond, in Paradise.

He reassures me that I am loved, appreciated, needed, wanted, admired, accepted, and adored by a King. He allows me each morning I open my eyes to wake up in His Presence with a sound mind and a reasonable portion of my health and strength. I can "think and process thought". God has smiled at you and told you what time it is. Put on your thinking cap. Let foolishness go. Let the world go. Let it travel on without you. You will not be a part of this foolishness. You will not feed off their food. You will develop your thoughts and ideas and remember when. That time He saved you.

You made a promise. Are you keeping your promise? I promised to love Him until I die. So, I will dwell over in this patch of cotton, while you dribble over there. I am not following the world; I have crossed over to embrace a new pathway. So now I will talk to My Savior most sincerely and humbly I know.

Thank You Jesus for watching over me while I slumbered and slept. Please continue to love me all day, every day, 24/7, around the clock, every hour, every minute, every second, and right at this present and precise moment. He is able!

I am making dinner. Beef Briskets, mashed potatoes, and steamed broccoli. Sounds yummy right? I know it will be good. Love in that pot. Love while they are cooking and when you finish. Know who made it possible. Pay some respect. Oh, Lord!

I "thank Thee" for guiding my footsteps, my tongue and my heart, my brain, my body, my soul, and my spirit. I will seal it with My Holy Spirit.

You, you are precious and there are only a few of you that believe and trust and hope in their future as you do. He has placed me on a pedestal. I admit it. I am on a higher dimension. I saw Him yesterday. I felt Him yesterday. He has reappeared and wants me to clap my hands, pat my feet, sway, and swerve my body to the music that I hear on His music channels. He is so remarkable. I am left in "awe" and disbelief. Oh! How He loves me, and He tells me that I am His own because I know how to keep quiet and open my mouth and pour out the words that are meditating in my heart.

Pastors say we gotta hit the streets with this message of hope, peace, and love. You have a job to do. I have a job to do. That is what Jesus did. He walked among the masses. He was with the poor and rich. He was with all His children. He was watching over all His sheep in His Pasture, but they went outside the gate, and they got lost. Somebody prayed for me. Somebody had a long talk with Jesus about me and they asked Him to please take care of me and He did just that. He answered their prayer. He allowed me to come in out of the rain and so I began to "think and ponder thought". They prayed that one day I would wake up. This is just what I did! I woke up. I stopped sleeping so much and came into a new awareness. Life is what you make it. If you want joy, then He will give you joy. If you want to bathe in sorrow and sadness, He will allow you to do that too.

Good News! Come to where there is rest for the weary soul. Every day is different for me. I get excited about the adventure He has planned for me so I carefully plan my morning routine so I will be ready to listen to His voice when He wants to speak to me.

It is me and Jesus, together on this Palm Sunday. Spend a portion of your Sunday afternoon in His Presence. Spend time in His Presence and allow His spirit to come alive in your mind, brain, heart, body, soul, and spirit. I am a new creature in Christ. I am a spiritual being having a human experience. All of this will soon pass away, and I will have missed the opportunity of a lifetime. To live my life hanging on to that vine and not die on the vine.

My Special Angel! Do you ever tire of thinking, reading, and writing?

"No" was my reply. I have so much to say. It is my season. 74 years of knowledge, memories, and events that are stored in my memory bank and I am so glad that You are allowing my blessings that You have in reserve for me to be released.

It is Palm Sunday! Christians, Believers, celebrate the entry of Jesus into Jerusalem by carrying palm fronds. This marked the high point of His earthly ministry. Palm Sunday is the beginning of Holy Week. On Palm Sunday the people threw clothes, palms of small branches in front of Him as a sign of homage. They had heard about Him being a healer, a miracle worker sent by God and the people did not want to hear it. Palm branches are a sign of peace and victory. Palm Sunday warns how our lives can be torn upside down in a matter of minutes. Life can be fine one day and the next day it could be turmoil. Bad times come to all of us. Bad times came to Jesus in about a week, but what did Jesus do. He confided in His Father and asked Him for direction and guidance. Who do we confide in? Who do you and I confide in?

We find ourselves having to adjust and adapt. Just like Jesus did. Christ's life changed in a week. One He was hailed as a hero, adored by thousands then put to death in the most horrible manner devised by man, "Crucifixion". Agree with me that our lives can be happy and sound one day and the next day it will change. It could become a catastrophic failure.

If we control our emotions, we can allow God to be in control of our lives. God is in control, and we must accept and adjust to His Plan. The lesson of Palm Sunday is that anyone can have their destiny, their lives changed overnight. God remembers that and He will always keep His Promise and that is "He will never leave us nor forsake us". You can depend on God to get you through to the other side.

So now I know! I am on a pathway designed by God. He knows the way He wants me to go, and I am obedient to His word because I know who I am trying to please. It was His decision, His decision to give me love, hope, peace, and develop a plan for my future. He tells me "I am His own" and He will take good care of me if I trust, believe, and have faith in Him. I am confident that He knows the direction He wants this little light to shine.

He made the decision that I could be raised from the dead and become a living soul ready to honor worship and praise Him for once again giving me a life to live in the Presence of a King. He is almighty! He is great! His truth surpasses all my understanding. If I remain in Him, then He will remain in me. If I abide in Him, then He will abide by me. If I draw nearer to Him, then He will draw nearer to me.

Know what I am going to do? I am going to hold on to His Unchanging Hand with all my strength because I can do all things through Christ who strengthens me. Again, and again, over, and over I find myself in His Presence. This is what I cherish, being alone with Him in solitude so He can whisper to me His words of wisdom, knowledge, and understanding that are designed just for me. He will speak to you if you talk to Him. Tell Him what is on your mind. I write my testimony and it is designed for you to read and come away with your meaning and understanding. You want to learn something. You want to come away with renewed strength that will uplift your spirits. Consult God through Jesus and ask Him what is His Plan?

Oh, Sweet Sunshine! You are my favorite. There is no one else like you. Oh, Lord! I am truly devoted to You, and I want You to continue waking me up in Your Presence. You have watched over me while I slumbered and slept and reached out Your Hand to me when I opened my eyes. When I wake up, He is there at my bedside waiting for me to honor, praise, worship, and salute Him for favoring me with another brand-new Sunday. Palm Sunday, March 28th, 2021, finds me in Perfect Peace, Harmony, Tranquility, Serenity knowing that I am in Your Presence all day, every day,

24/7, around the clock – every hour – every minute – every second and right at this present and the precise moment in time.

Take a chance! Knock and the door shall be opened. Seek and you shall find. Want to change your life? Want to become alive in your senses so you can think, and process thought? Then spend some time alone with Him. You find the spot and He will be right there waiting for you. Find out what He wants to tell you. Sit down, turn off the noise and think.

You are in the presence of a King. Now is the time for you to express to Him your thoughts, ideas, wants, needs, and desires. 1st Peter 5 v:7. Cast all your cares on me because I care for you. Wow! Did you hear that? Game changer. I have someone to talk to. I have someone who cares about me. I have someone who will care, share, and give to me what I need to complete the adventure that He has planned for me. Ask Him.

Have you praised Him for what He has already done and what He is going to do in your life? Dream. Know what! You have made Him so happy by coming to Him first. Before anyone else, let me consult Jesus on this and get His opinion is what you must tell yourself. Already you have shown your gratification when you first opened your eyes and saw a foggy, cloudy, rainy warm Palm Sunday.

His Holy Spirit glided me into my happy space in the wee hours of dawn, early to do what I needed to do. "Thank You Jesus" – You have given me a sound mind and a reasonable portion of my health and strength. I say "Thank You Jesus" once again You favored me. I humbly and meekly salute A King. You are the greatest!

After I finished in my happy space, as you can see and hear, I went to talk. I want Him to know that I know who my source of strength and joy is. I saturate His atmosphere with words of praise because He is worthy to be praised. He died a horrible death for our sins so that I could one day be saved. He made me. Yes, Jesus made me take back my life from Satan through His Presence and His Holy Spirit. He demanded that I make a change. My head had been headed in the wrong direction for too long. Sit down and listen, that is what I was told! I obeyed an order. I listened. The more I listened the more I wanted to hear. His story was impelling. He showed me how I could obtain a new life to live in the Presence of a King. I like it. Come away with me and dance the old-fashioned way. Slow, gently, kindly, softly, meekly. That is the way, now let me hold your hand on this foggy wet day. The only way I can repay Him for giving me a new life, a new mind, a new beginning, a new birth, a new identity is to tell someone else what He has done for me.

Any listeners? Comprehend what you are reading. Someone is talking who has firsthand knowledge of Jesus, God, and His Ministry. She was taught from the cradle up but one day she followed the ways of the world. She came back. He has me surrounded in Love, Peace, Patience, joy, happiness, satisfaction, and glee. Can your God do all of that? Then pull back the covers and see what you have. I cannot be wrong about this for the Bible tells me that "God is Love" 1st John 4 v:8. I feel His gentleness, softness being generated to me through the music I am listening to. Instrumental music, violins, tubas, accordions, horns are easy to listen to as it calms my mind, heart, brain, body, soul, and spirit.

Jesus is my source of inspiration and encouragement. If I remain in Him, then He will remain in me. Surely His Goodness and Mercy shall follow me if I dwell in His shelter, His secret place, or His Presence. There is no one like Jesus. Nothing can compare to His goodness. Nothing can compare to the type of love and affection that He is sprinkling all over me. I hear His birds singing and chirping, they are having fun, praising Him for His rainwater. They have moisture. The leaves caught His rain and are holding it for them to drink. He provides for all His creation, and He is providing me a piece of that bread.

News Flash! I have a friend. I am glad that I have a friend. This is the best friend a man or woman, boy or girl or child could have. My friend's name is Jesus. Want to know more? Nature Boy! Nature Girl! This is where you were born under a star-lit sky. A full moon and all of creation have gathered to see what I had crafted. I crafted you in my image and I am proud of the fine art of workmanship that I put together.

Since the birds are praising Him, I will join in with the birds and allow Him to set my thoughts free on this windy spring-like day. His birds are singing praises to the Son of God. They know it is about that time when it will go into total darkness for about three hours. I can do it like the birds. I can do the same. We have a choice. We have been given free will believe what we want to believe. We have self-control. You make the choice. Come on in out of that rain?

I adore Him and how I idolize Him. Want to know why? He is the King of Kings and The Lord of Lords. He is the Son of God, and He is the connection that we must get to God. He is our mediator; He is our go-between. Before you can talk to our Heavenly Father, you must pass by the King. You must have His permission to enter His Presence. We must establish a relationship with Jesus, and He will speak to God on our behalf. So! Have you had a personal, private, and intimate conversation with The King?

We gotta get the news out. Anyway, we can. Put Jesus First. Before you begin your morning, just about the crack of day, begin talking to Him. He is allowing you to come alive. You are waking up in His Presence and He expects you to acknowledge His Presence. We do not. He is taking a mental note. She did not, he did not, they did not honor me for favoring them with a new beginning, nor a brand-new day but you did. Let me acknowledge the One that saved my soul. This is what He did for me. The more I began to find out, the more I wanted to know. Let us just say I got curious. It sparked my interest. I positioned myself so I could get a clearer picture of where I was trying to go. Then it hit me "there is another life". I can have it if I want to. It is my choice. I wanted to hear the preacher's words. He said "this is not it, this is not all, there is another life for you to live in the Presence of a King.

When the preacher said, "he can do this and He can do that", I put on my running shoes, meaning that I was going to find out the truth for myself. I just had to learn more. I yearned for a change in my life, and I was told I had the opportunity to make Jesus My Lord and Savior. This is what I did. I wanted it so badly.

I remember waking up at odd hours of the night because Jesus wanted to speak to me. I was at a learning session. He was pulling me up out of my grave. Yes! "My Grave". I dug it for myself. No peace, no joy, no happiness, no satisfaction, no mercy, no justice, no truth, no honesty, no salvation, no redemption, no love, and no righteousness until I met Jesus. My life changed. Today I lift His Name on High. This Palm Sunday. He is my healer, physically and spiritually, my Lily in the Valley, my Bright and Morning Star, my way maker, my burden barrier, my joy, and my strength. I keep Him close by my side by asking Him not to ever leave me to the fowler's snare.

What a beautiful Savior. He is allowing me to write, drink His spring water and smell the aroma of pot roast. One of my favorite things is to write and share with you the highlights of our conversations. He is right here beside me. I pulled out the chair and there is room for the two of us. This is what He is doing for me. He is giving me a new mind, a new beginning, a new birth, a new identity, and He is allowing me to be born again in the presence of a King.

It is the sacred hour of 4 pm on this Palm Sunday and I am in His Presence. Do you want to know what Satan has done to you? Satan, Lucifer, the devil, the enemy has stopped you from thinking. Are you happy? Really, happy? Do you see flowers in your world? Do you see the beauty of a flower bed? There are so many varieties of flowers designed for your eyes only. Don't you "thank Him" for your eyes? I do! I can stop right now and thank Him for my eyesight. I can see. I can look around and see the trees, the flowers, the weeds, the bushes, the insects, the bugs, and all His animals in His creation.

Think about the time you were happy! Happy! Experiencing joy, satisfaction, peace, and harmony. Do you see me? Do you hear what I am saying? Am I preaching to the masses or just you? You can grow like a flower from the bulb up to be a full-grown plant, tree, or flower? You grew from the bottom up. He got me at the bottom of the grave, at the bulb stage. He is the One that allowed me to be blossomed outgrow, be alive like His trees, roses, tulips, bugs, insects, the bees, the butterflies. They are God's creation, and they light up your life. His bees light up the night sky. They come around during sunset. Aren't they breathtaking? Especially the lightning bug. He glows as He floats through His air. He floats. He glides. That is what His butterfly does. It is so content, peaceful, happy, and satisfied because they are honoring, praising, and saluting the One that made them. Does a man do that?

Slow up! Let your mind, brain, heart, body, soul, and spirit, free themselves. Let it go! Stroll on His white sandy beaches. See the glow of His beautiful, spacious, blue sky. The ocean is nearby with its waves that crash into His rocks and mountains located out there. You have got to have peace in your life. You must be willing to smell a rose. Stop! Look! Listen! What is going through your head right now? Don't you see the sign of hate coming around the mountain?

There are demonic forces ready to take over our minds, hearts, brains, bodies, souls, and spirits. I see that but I also see hope. Imagine one day waking up and it is all over! One thing I need to know is who possesses your soul? He has Risen! He has come alive in me, and I believe He has come alive in you. There is that spark. You know who you belong to. You know who you are and whose you are. Willing to lay down your life? He will be with you! Not to worry, you are in good hands. He told Jesus what He had to do, and Jesus accepted His fate. Jesus trusted. Jesus believed. Jesus had faith.

Let me blow my own horn! I am a child of a King. I am one of God's children. I am one of His sheep in His Pasture. Satan tried to snare me. He tried to swish me away from believing in the One who set me free, the One that loved me first. Jesus came first.

Listen up! Somebody is calling your name. Who is calling your name? Jesus is! He is beckoning for you. He wants your full attention. I am going to hang with Jesus because He knows the way to the Father. After all, that is who is holding His Hand. Jesus is holding my hand and taught me how to say the word "Hallelujah". He has risen! He came up out of that grave and said, "let my people go". Satan said "no" I will put their eyes out. I will shine gold in front of their faces, and they will listen to me. I will make it impossible for them to see, listen, taste, or smell any signs of You. Satan said!

Satan, Lucifer, the devil, the enemy cannot take away your ability to think, achieve, process thought. This causes you not to dream. Read any great books lately? Read the Bible lately? Nope! I pick it up every chance I get but that is not often. Just do not have the time, man. Take time. Be at ease! You are new at this! I do not have much to say. Tell me what to say! Begin with "Hello". I am here to talk to You for a little while. What are your wants, desires, opinions, beliefs, traditions, and desires? You have His full attention. Want a suggestion, talk to Him, tell Him just what is going on. Admit to Him that you are not happy. Something is missing. After you begin talking to Him, He will give you so much peace you will find yourself spending hours and hours in His Presence.

It is not your ordinary love – it is Extraordinary Love coming from a King. Has Satan silenced you? Has he taken that drive, that desire, that determination away? Did you let him kill your dreams? You allowed him to stop you from dreaming, didn't you? Jesus will come to you like a stranger in the night to save you from this wicked and corrupt world that you see, hear, taste, and feel.

There is another alternative. You have chosen the wrong road. Your road is at a dead end. My road has wide open spaces for me to float, glide, coast into my Palm Sunday afternoon. You know who has all power- don't you? On my road there is caring, sharing, giving, and loving being given to all His sheep in His Pasture. Want to cross the road? Give Him your Hand. Accept what you have and ask Him for more. More of His Love, His Affection, His Admiration. While you are asking me to ask for you, me, your family, my family, my loved ones, your loved ones, your friends, and my friends. There we are all covered. We are all sheep in His Pasture. Psalm 100.

I ask for so much. I bow my head. I close my eyes and I began reciting the words that are meditating in my heart. He heard me yesterday and I am sure He is listening to every word I say on my brand-new Palm Sunday afternoon. I want to go where Jesus is. First, you must find Him here on His solid and sacred ground we call Earth on His Planet and in His Universe before you can find Him out there. Where are you looking for Jesus? Good News! He lives within the four walls of your heart. That is what He told me. He told me I have been with you for 74 years, want 74 more? Yes! Yes! I do. Send me back as a butterfly so I can tell the masses in the South, North, East, and West that they must slow down to a snail's pace, listen, and pay attention before they can hear the words of my mouth.

Become a little child. You have been to Sunday school. You have been taught the basics of what I was singing on this Palm Sunday. I went to dreaming. He says, "I will shed my light on Thee". He wants you to know before it is too late. He is getting ready to close the gate. Only the righteousness and pure in heart shall be saved. What condition is your heart in? Who are you trying to please?

Chapter 5

Tell you what! We talk. Just the two of us. I will talk to you, and you will talk with me. Like a conversation. I will play me and you at the same time. It is Palm Sunday at nighttime. What are you doing? I am eating dinner. What are you doing? I am writing.

I am enjoying being in His Presence and wanted you to join me. I am expecting you to say.

"I feel like praising Him also". Then we both join in and share just how good He as been to me throughout my day. I believe He is going to be good when I get ready to go to La La Land because I am spending every awakening moment in His Presence.

I am planting a seed in the ground, and I expect to reap a big harvest. I have 17 seeds planted in the ground. They are scattered all over the United States. They live in different parts of the country. To see some of my seeds I must take a road trip or a plane ride. How will I accomplish this? I have no idea, but I have got to get to one of my great-grandchildren because she does not know how to sit down, be still, sit at attention and think. Children do not listen. They have not been taught to listen, sit at attention, and follow the leader. Just basics, our kids are lacking. We must go into these schools, orphanages, camps, and prisons.

The prisoner will tell you firsthand what he did not do. And that was listening. Man! I did not listen. I was told about a man who could raise you from the dead. I was told that there was a man that I need to pray to because He would take care of me. I was told that on Friday nights, they should be spent in prayer. When I got to be an adult, I forgot about all of that because I wanted to see what I could do on my own. It is a party? The biggest party in town. We are going to have some fun.

In the meantime, mama and grandma, grandpa and granddaddy were going to church on Friday Night. Sometimes it would last three nights. Friday night, Saturday night, Sunday night. That is too much church for me. I want to find the girls, women, dope, booze, cigarettes. Do not forget the music. Wide-open funk. Let us get downright nasty and dirty with it. It is free for all. Everything is free.

Jesus said, "look at my sheep". They have lost their way. They stopped listening to their mama, papa, grandma and them, those cousins, those mothers in the church, those deacons on the deacon board. They stopped listening to the preacher because it was too much theatrics. Now his sheep are wondering. Satan showed up and told God's sheep, look at me I am all shiny. I am glittering in gold. Off they went searching for anything that shines. This put them to sleep. Satan had you then. I will shine more glitter and gold since they like that. Then I will attack their ears. I have their eyes. They are blinded. Satan said "I will determine what kind of music you listen to? I will get them by their ears. What are you listening to? Who is making noise up in your head? Are you reading your Bible? Are you letting God talk to you through Jesus Christ, Our Lord, and Savior? Who are you talking to? You are talking to somebody. Satan has cursed your tongue. The words that come out of your mouth are destroying your future. What do you want? It is willing to listen. His Name is Jesus. He is a Beautiful Savior that died an excruciating death possible known to man.

He was a man sent by God to die for all our sins. He hung on an old, rugged cross where He bled and died. He died for me so I could come alive in my senses and glorify Him for making a sacrifice so that I could be saved. Beautiful Savior. Don't you adore Him? Don't you admire Him? He has come to pull you up out of that grave. You dug your own grave with the words that you release from your mouth. You say what is in your heart. What kind of food have you been feeding your heart? You know a man is fed in more than one way, don't you? He is fed wisdom, knowledge, and understanding. He is fed physically, emotionally, mentally, psychologically, and spiritually. What are you eating? How big is your appetite? Do you want to enjoy a marvelous, magnificent, splendid, superb, spectacular, and wonderful night? Then spend it in His Presence doing what you do best. Relax, Enjoy the moment. Spend some time with me. I have got "good news". I know someone who will protect you from all hurt, harm, and danger. I know someone who will provide for all your needs. I know of someone who will allow His Holy Spirit to be your guide.

He will not let me forget that I can depend on Him. He says "I will be here for you" all day, every day, 24/7, around the clock, every hour every minute every second, and right at this present moment in time.

Getting ready to escape into a world filled with Love. Getting ready for His music to penetrate my mind, my brain, my heart, my body, my soul, and my spirit. I hear a ping sound after each musical instrument. It sounds like a sweet good night kiss. Getting ready to place my head in His chest so I can breathe His sweet breath from now through Eternity forevermore. Goodnight!

Pleasant Dreams. May He surround you with His Peace, Love, Protection, and Guidance.

Come in out of that rain!

Chapter 6

A roller-coaster ride. Get prepared. It is church time. It is a time for the meeting of two minds. I share. You listen. Your comment. Fair deal? Then come fly with me! Wonderful! This is His Name! Oh! He is magnificent, marvelous, splendid, superb, fabulous, fantastic, outstanding, and spectacular on this Monday morning, March 29th, 2021, that we have never seen before. It is a new era in time. A new day and He is present in our lives. Hallelujah! We are alive. We have been raised from the dead. He has given me a new self.

Good morning Sunshine! I wish upon a star. Jesus is a Star, and He has pulled up a chair right next to me because He is interested in what I am about to say. It is going to be good I can tell. New morning, new mind, new ideas, new thoughts, new treasures to find. Tell Satan, Lucifer, the devil, the enemy to take off the masquerade. He has cast a veil of darkness over your eyes. Yes! you have blinders on. Take them off now. Pull back the layers of lies, deceit, and hate that He is trying to overshadow your thoughts and your true ideals with.

Go with me on the other side of the world. Go with me as I pass through the shadows of death. Psalm 23. I will never be defeated. I will always exalt His Name in praise. Let me tell you about that mean old sneaky, sly devil. His name is Satan, the devil, the enemy, Lucifer. He already said, "she will never give God the Father of Our Lord and Savior Jesus Christ a praise all day, every day, 24/7, around the clock, every hour, every minute, every second and right at this present and the precise moment in time."

The devil is a liar! I proved it to him because I see God, My Lord, My Jesus through the eyes of Love. He loves me and cherishes and idolizes me and now that I know this, I must turn my attention on Him, the One that gave me a life to live in the Presence of a King. He is "almighty". Powerful words are what I am told.

Satan is scared. Somebody is sounding a horn! Is it you? You got a job to do it and just do it. That is what Nike says, "just do it." Our Nation needs to be warned that the devil is planning an attack. He is declaring all-out war. We as Christians, Believers, gotta stay the course. We must be committed to doing His will. Not sometimes but all the time. He has a message for you, and it is for your ears only. It is time to stop the foolishness. Take off that suit and let us go to war. There is a war between good and evil. Bad versus Good!

Admit it - I want to change. I want a new me! I want a new beginning each morning I open my eyes. I want to begin admitting that He is the greatest early in the wee hours of dawn. Teach me how! Listen up boys and girls, men and women, princes, princesses, Kings and Queens, and children. A King is coming to town! Don't you want to go to see Him? He comes with wisdom, knowledge, understanding, fun, and games. His Name is Jesus.

Jesus stopped by my mansion, my pad, my home, my castle. This is where we live. We have some of our best conversations within these four walls. I love it. It is my peace of Heaven while I am down here on Earth. It is home! Peace and happiness live at home because all of us in this house honor Our Creator, Our God, Our Jesus, Our Lord and Savior Jesus Christ, and whatever He says goes.

I see His Love. I see His blossoms on His trees and His flowers. I witness a lot through my eyes. It is about to start raining in words of knowledge and wisdom. He gave me my eyes and I am looking past my current circumstance or situation and seeing God come to my rescue. I will never leave you nor forsake you. Hebrews 13 v:5. This is His promise to you and me. I see your effort now let us talk.

Make an effort to crossover. Make an effort to get to the other side of the road so you can dodge Satan. Get under His wings as quick as you can. Read it in your Bibles. Psalm 91. I am here to protect you. I will go with you everywhere you go. If you want to go into the kitchen, I will go, if you want to go into the bathroom, I will help you, if you want to go into the bedroom, I will help you, if you want to want to go in the den, I will help you, if you want to go into the living room, I will be there too.

I am everywhere. You asked. You got the courage to stand up to Satan and open the door of knowledge that you have had invested into your head for 74 years. You must have a lot of stories to tell. Only the good ones, I am leaving those doors shut. I will enjoy my new life. I am not taking any of the old with me. It is a new me and I am proud that I was chosen, selected to be one of the carriers of some good news.

I am not finished with telling you about Satan. He is a thief. He is a murderer. He is a destroyer. Satan said, "she will never put Jesus first". Another lie. I developed a habit of waking up calling on His Holy Name. I wake with a smile on my face, with joy and pleasure radiating from my heart because I know who favored me with a brand-new beginning. If you do something for thirty days - you can call this a habit - that you will naturally gravitate toward it. Develop this habit. This is the best habit you could develop. Talk to Our Savior when you first open your eyes. Told you to come in out of that rain.

Oh, Lord! Thank You! Again I "Thank You". I began to salute, honor, and praise Him the second I wake up. I owe Him Grace and Honor for being so good to me. This is what you must do. This is a recipe for success! Honor the Giver of Life with praises of worship and admiration and you will realize it is an honor and a privilege to be awakened in the Presence of a King and being called a child of the Living God.

CeCe Winans sings this song "Never be defeated". Sing it along with her at your earliest convenience. (On YouTube) Let me give you what the words mean to me. Each time the devil raises his head, start giving God praise and learn to say, "Hallelujah Anyhow". Good days, bad days, days of sheer disbelief. Call on Him, He hears you. He wants you to hear Him. He has something powerful to tell you.

When Jesus was on His way to the cross, He began talking to His Heavenly Father and He said, not my will but Your will must be done.

His will is being done in my life. I have been called to spread a message of love, hope, and peace to you, him, her, she, them, and they. All of God's sheep must gather around and hear some good news.

Heard any good news lately? What are your preachers telling you? Are they opening avenues so you can think? Did they tell you that we got to hit the streets with a message of love, hope, and peace if you want to be saved? Now that you know who you are and whose you are, you must share it with the world. Find a way. That is your job. Tell yourself "I must tell somebody". I want to make a difference in somebody's life. If I can lead them to Christ, I will have done my job.

Once you begin the adventure that has been placed before you, you will be rewarded in Love and Kindness and Gentleness and Softness from A Savior who is seated at the Right Hand of the Father who is talking on our behalf. What can I do? I can open my Bible and get myself some daily bread to sustain me throughout my day.

He came early in the morning hours to give me His morning grace and grace and He told me to let it last me throughout my day.

Psalm 90 v:14. When I opened my eyes, I sat up straight with my feet dangling off the bed and said, "Thank You Jesus" and began to sing my song. I went into my happy space to do what I needed to do, and I was so happy that I had received the "go ahead" signal. I had to honor Him. I had to praise Him. I had to worship Him. As I was doing so, I was getting snuggled back into my spot. I had my head lying in His chest so I could breathe His sweet breath and I did not want to depart.

I was eager to return and when I did, I began talking. I ask O Lord please come into my presence and O Lord please allow me into Your Presence.

As I was doing this, I was tugging at the covers trying to get them close to my neck so I could feel the warmth and gentle touch that they provided. I was happy that He chose to love on me this morning. I was happy that He chose to raise me from the dead.

Before I got to my grave, He pulled me up. Young lady! The Sergeant in Arms! Listen to Him speak. He is serious. He wants to know why, when, what, and how.

I know you are not finished. He proceeded to say; You have not lived the life that was intended for you. This is what He said. I stopped, took note, and began to listen. I began to inquire. I wanted to find out more, so I listened to what He had to say. His words changed my life. His actions saved my soul. I am a new creature in Christ because of what He did. In a matter of seconds my beliefs, opinions, ideas, and thoughts changed.

I came under His Authoritative Power. He made me so aware of what I had been missing. I have been missing out on communing with Thee. I had missed out on being in His Presence. I had every opportunity in the world to come back inside the gate, but I strayed into green pastures, the unknown. That is when I found Jesus. He was so meek and mild. I inquired why are you so quiet He said, Shish!

Little girl, "I am communing with the father. I am talking to Him."

So, I took a seat and just waited, and He began speaking and I began to listen. I had to take a big sigh of relief! I was so amazed when He told me He had been watching over me for 74 years.

I immediately wanted to show my gratitude. He said "the only way to Thank Me is if you tell someone else. I have got to get the word out.

A Man is coming to town who can raise the dead. He gives away new life, new hope, new dreams, new ambitions, new beliefs, new opinions, new ideas, and new thoughts every time He raises you from the dead. He can make your brand new. I must celebrate my new day and my new beginning. You will become a new creature in Christ. Like a human being having a spiritual experience.

Listen up! You have a friend who is glued to your heart. He has found a dwelling place and He wants a place to rest on this sunshiny, warm, spring day on His solid and sacred ground we call Earth on His Planet and in His Universe. Breathe some of the air that I am breathing. Drink some of the water I am drinking while the blood is still running warm in your veins, and you can still choose right over wrong.

After I was tucked into those Everlasting Arms, I went to talk.

Yes! I went to confess what was meditating in my heart. This is my affirmation. This is what I say each time I open my eyes. O Lord please come into my presence and O Lord please allow me into Your Presence. O Lord please shelter us, O Lord please shadow us, O Lord please favor us, O Lord please cover us with Your Blood, O Lord please strengthen us physically, mentally, emotionally, psychologically, morally and spiritually, O Lord please forgive us of our sins because we don't always do things perfectly or correctly, O Lord please forgive our enemies because they know not what they do, O Lord please prosper us physically, materialistically, financially and spiritually, O Lord please protect us from all plagues, pandemics, disasters, and turmoil, O Lord please do not cast us away from Your Presence and O Lord please allow Your Holy Spirit to dwell in us again on this day. In Jesus' Name, I Pray – Amen.

I must get my affirmation out. I tell Him what is meditating in my heart. I know who my source of strength and joy is. I know who made the decision I could live one more day and I am going to celebrate it. Who can I share my happiness with? It must be you! You have been selected to hear the fresh and new words that are meditating in my heart.

So how do you like your coffee! He will make it just the way you like it! Drink it under the moonlight! Then find you some Final Love. Aren't you tired of trying to get the world to love you? Cannot find it there! You got to go further. The ultimate sacrifice was given by Jesus when He gave up His life for me so I could be saved. How do I pay my respects, show honor, glory, and gratitude? Worship Him. Praise Him. Hallelujah Anyhow! He is the greatest. There is no greater than Him. He paid the price so now I can live. I can live up to my full potential. I will be the man-woman, boy, or girl that He had designed me to before I was in my mother's womb. Find this when you read Jeremiah 1. He knew you and He knew me when we were only a thought.

It is pouring down rain! You have so many wasted nights and wasted days. Idle time – just doing nothing! If you are doing something – you are not enjoying it – you are just following the world. The world is full of sinful lusts. A want for this, want for that – never satisfied with what has been already provided for you. Deep dark shadows. Uncover the truth. Do you stop for a moment and consider the source? Who provided all of this? Who is the One that provided all my needs? Who is the One that said He would allow His Holy Spirit to become my guide?

Use your memory bank! It is stored up in your head in your brains. Think. That is what Socrates and Aristotle did. Great thinkers! They were men of honor and character that had integrity. You have been in your coffin too long. The world is a great big circle, and it is traveling fast, and you must slow yourself down long enough to enjoy the gift of life that God has given you. Tell yourself "I must find my space". I must find out where do I fit in this big puzzle. Just do it. Go for it. Do like everybody else is doing. They are praying, studying, meditating, and reading His written word. They are happy. They are at peace. This is what I am so desperately trying to find. Did you say? You can find it at Jesus' Feet. He is hanging on that cross. The pain that He felt. Those awful pains in His hands, His feet, His toes, His ankles, His side, His head. Yet He endured it all because He was determined to do His Master's Will. That is why He was created. To do His Father's Will.

Okay! It is decision time. Ask yourself "why did I allow this to happen to me"? Here I am, unhappy, dissatisfied, weary, worried. I am not living a joyous life. It is not bright and merry. What must I do?

Pick up a new leaf. Change lanes. The highway is too crowded. Find your peace and happiness. You can find it in Jesus. A regular household words! Remember! Your mamma, daddy, grandmas, grandpas, cousins, friends, brothers, and sisters called on that Name.

If He saved them then most certainly, He could save you if you allow Him in. Use Him as an umbrella. Cover yourself with Him. Let it rain!

Do you see His sunshine? Do you see His green trees swaying and swerving while He is blowing His breath on them? They are so happy being able to perform their duties. The trees cleanse the air and provide fresh oxygen for us to inhale and exhale out of our lungs. The trees bump into each other's branches as they want to please Him so much. You and I are on a Divine Path, one ordered by Our Lord and Savior Jesus Christ. Rock with me. Are you willing to go the distance it takes to get to that Promised Land, Over yonder, Over there in the Great Beyond?

Teach me O Lord how to act and what to say. Examine my heart and sweep away any negative influence. Sweep away all those evil spirits that want to live in my heart. I give myself to Thee so You can use me as a vessel in Your Kingdom to spread Your Holy Word. One soul at a time, that is what I am after. I must convince you to look around the mountain. Look over the hills. Look at what is right before your eyes and witness a miracle. It was a miracle that He performed for you on this morning that you have never seen before. You are alive in your senses, and you know right from wrong. You know good and bad, and you know which one you desire to tuck under your arms. Rock with me.

Oh, Lord! Keep me close. Do not ever let me get from under Your wings. I read in Psalms 91 that You will cover me with Your feathers and under Your wings, I can seek refuge. Under Your wings, I will be safe and secure if I believe, trust, and have faith that if your eye is on the sparrow then it most certainly is on me. It is "Hallelujah" time. Don't you agree? We have something to be proud of. We no longer live in the land of the wicked and corrupt, we have been saved by the Grace of God and given new ideas, new thoughts, new beliefs, new opinions, new traditions, and new desires. We have pulled off the old clothes and put on new clothes. 2 Corinthians 5 v:17 says, "Therefore if any man is in Christ, then he is a new creature because all things are passed away and behold, all things have become new. Agree? He is My Rock and My Redeemer. Psalm 19 v:14 says "may the words of my mouth and the meditation in my heart be acceptable in Thy sight. He is watching over our tongues and our feet. He is guiding our pathways. He is so "happy" that you are coming in out of that rain? He wants to shower you with His Unfailing Love, His Unconditional Love, His Grace and Mercy, and His Divine Devotion around the clock, all day, every day, 24/7, every hour - every minute - every second and right at this present and the precise moment in time. Let Him.

Knock and the door shall open. Pick up your Bibles. Explore it. Find comfort and joy in reading His words of wisdom. Seek and you shall find. Turn the pages and begin to write the next chapter of your life. Okay! You have tried it on your own, now turn it over to God and let Him choose the path for you. It has already been decided what you should do and become. It is recorded in the Lamb's Book of Life, your name and what duty you are to perform. I do not know the plan that He has for you. I only know what I have been told. I only know why I was created. I am only a vessel trying to put you on the right path. You have taken a detour and now it is time to get on the right road so you can fulfill your destiny.

You are someone special. He has His eyes on you. He is waiting for you to become alive in your senses so you can "think and process thought". He wants to get you alone so He can tell you what He thinks of you. He wants you to one day lay your head upon His chest and rest in His Everlasting Arms so He can take real good care of you. I am there! I am on board! I earned my spot. I asked for it. Contour your lips and begin to speak into His atmosphere the words that are meditating in your heart. Tell Him your thoughts. He already knows them but wants to hear you admit it to yourself. So! Talk to yourself. Sing to yourself. What are you telling yourself? Are you happy with the words you have chosen? It is a brand-new day, a day to enjoy, rejoice, magnify, glorify, and celebrate your new beginning. Psalm 118 v:24, tells you what to do when you get a gift of a brand-new day.

Jesus is the Star. What happens when you wish upon a star? Your prayers are answered. I savored the aroma and taste of my coffee this morning. His Holy Spirit said, "this is what He does", He satisfies your every need, and He will allow you to have more mornings like this one if you glorify Him for making it possible for you to be able to drink a cup of your delicious brew that you yearn for each morning you open your eyes. He allowed my taste buds to come alive so I could taste and smell what I was drinking. It was oh so good! Isn't He wonderful? Isn't He great? Isn't He powerful? Isn't He mighty? He is miraculous because He raised me from the dead. He is the One who decided for me to come alive in my senses so I can "think and process thought."

You on board! We will be climbing to a higher dimension. Do not worry! I know the captain. I have my hand in His Hand and He is leading the way. He captured my mind and thoughts when I first opened my eyes and realized that I had been given a sound mind with a reasonable portion of my health and strength.

Who watched over me, and you while we slumbered and slept? Who blew His breath of life into our lifeless souls and bodies and allowed us to witness the miracle of a new day? These are thoughts to ponder! Who did you praise for your being able to open your eyes so that you can embrace the adventure that He has planned for you today? I know who tapped me with His finger of Love and said "O sleepyhead" wake up, rise from the dead, and let The Lord shine on you. Thank You Jesus is what I said. Then these words developed into a sweet, sweet song. Love and admiration were flowing through the arteries in my heart, and I felt special.

Let me tell you how He makes me feel! I am so well protected, important, needed, wanted, accepted, appreciated, adored, admired, and idolized when He is near me. I want to be in His Presence. He goes with me everywhere I go, Joshua 1 v:9. He is with me "Thy Art with me."

Psalms 23. Surely His Goodness and mercy shall follow me all the days of my life if I dwell in that Secret Place, that Shelter, in His Presence.

He is so close to me. He hears my thoughts, ideas, opinions, beliefs, traditions, and He knows my desires. If I remain in Him, then He will remain in me. I choose to remain where I am. This is a choice that I make every time I take a breath and each time my heartbeats. I love Him so much! Every opportunity I get I will praise Him for being so good to me. He is alive. He lives with my heart and my spirit. I am One with God, My Lord, My Jesus, My Beautiful Savior.

Save a dance for me! I cannot keep quiet! Yes! I will say it! Yes! I will tell it! I among the living. I am not dead. I am proud to be called a child of a King, one of God's children, and a sheep in His Pasture who is grazing on fresh green grass this Monday morning. The Jewish people celebrate "Passover". You and I can join in with them on their celebration because you know, and I know He is passing through saving souls. He has His vessels located throughout His Kingdom here on Earth trying to spread the word. I can only tell you what He has done for me. I can only tell you what He can do for you now that you have decided to continue reading. By now, you know, two things, I will take you to church and you may have to stay awhile until I have concluded my message. So, take your time. Read, relax, and think about what you just read and what your ears heard. I do. It has worked for me. I am your witness. Once you change the words in your vocabulary your life will suddenly change.

I am never too old to dream. A dream is what it is. Imagine you live your life in the Presence of a King. This can be done. It takes patience resting in those bones. Take the time. Turn it off. All the noise. Place His Written Word before your eyes and let the words jump off the page straight into your heart. Do you see how bright His sun is shining? He has you and He has me in His shadow. I know who is watching over me and listening to every word I say. It is Him. Jesus. That is who is responsible for my writing. That is the One who plans how my adventure will unfold. I am glad about it. I am glad that I gave myself away to Him so He could use me.

Jesus is the only One we should try to please. He is watching over you just like He is watching over His trees, flowers, weeds, bushes, insects, bugs, and all His creation especially man and woman, boys, and girls.

Ask someone who knows about His Love, Kindness, Gentleness, Softness, and His Goodness.

It was His will that I pick up pen and paper and begin to write. He allowed me the opportunity to be at peace long enough to be able to think and process thought. When I first began, His Holy Spirit told me "I'll help you". I am fulfilling a divine destiny and serving a purpose. It has been ordered and ordained by A Holy One. I am on a mission to complete the assignment that I have been given and that is to tell you, my brothers, and sisters, in the North, East South, and West how He saved my soul.

Get wisdom. Get knowledge. Get an understanding. Read Proverbs. The book is known as the Book of Wisdom. Tattoo these verses in scripture across your heart. If you open your heart, He will begin to speak to you.

Oh, Lord! You can depend on me to share with the world the words meditating in my heart. I will be the one who will spend my time in Your Presence all day, every day, around the clock, 24/7, every hour - every minute - every second and right at this present and the precise moment in time.

Oh, Lord! I am looking for a brighter day. I am looking for more knowledge, wisdom, and understanding. The Bible says, "praise Him". The preacher says, "praise Him". They told the truth. This is your secret weapon. This is body armor. This is what will save your soul. Use your words of wisdom that you have glued to the walls of your heart.

Want to see your life make a turn-a-round? Find you a place so the two of you can have some alone time. Man and woman, boys, and girls I am talking to you. Sit up straight and listen and pay attention to the words of my mouth. I am trying to lead you out of that wilderness. I moved to the other side of the road. I changed lanes. I came from behind the fence. Then I saw it. I can have this and that if I open the windows in Heaven and shatter His ceiling with words of Admiration and Praise.

Spend a little time with Jesus. This is what you must-do if you want your life to change. Do you want to enjoy the smell of cherry blossoms? Do you want Him to touch you with the same finger of

Love that He touched me with? Then exalt His Name in Praise and watch Him turn your life around. Keep that song in your heart and keep that praise on your tongue. Your life will never be the same because you put Jesus first. When I made Jesus the head of my life, it was the best decision I could have ever made. I went fighting for my freedom. I went to call on His Holy Name, asking Oh Lord please save my soul, and this is what He did.

Chapter 7

I see a white sandy beach with pure blue water, making waves. A swishing sound. Overhead I see His big blue spacious skies with just one or two mini white clouds. White is beautiful? Deceit? Lies. Hate. Look at God at work, showing off what He has provided for us. He wants us to care, share and give to each other out of the kindness, gentleness, and softness that is residing in our hearts. It is His Precious Love that He wants to give you. Look beyond those skies, there is more. Only the pure in heart shall see God.

Don't you see His handiwork? Do not you see His oceans, His rocks, His volcanos - they too are dissatisfied in man's behavior. Luna Skye is her name. It is a cartoon. Luna lives on the moon, and she cannot understand why man is not happy and is reaping in self-destruction. Luna wants to know why, and I can tell her why. My answer begins, Luna, let me tell you a story. You were created for a purpose! You were created by God and Jesus and given a name. Your mission was to live on this solid and sacred ground while you are alive in your senses to think, multiply the believers in knowing that there is life beyond what they see on Earth. You were made to worship God. My Lord! My Jesus. You were to be a vessel to carry the good news.

Man and woman were created to live in peace and harmony with each other and enjoy the fruits of the land. Their aim and purpose changed. They were being controlled through their senses and stopped "thinking".

Do you know what I did? I got my foot wedged just inside Come up out of that grave!! Want me to repeat myself? You have dug your own grave. Stop this now! Come on! You were given a brain, a mind, a heart, a body, a soul, and a spirit. Who controls all of these? Who is your go-between? Do not know? Well! His Name is Jesus. You got to go through Him before you can reach the Kingdom of God that He has prepared for His precious few. Only a few will make it in. If I, were you, I would abandon the ship you are own and come over to my side and get in the boat with me and Peter, Tom, Dick, Harry, Jane, and the rest of the crew? These are the ones that are going to make it. The ones who believe, trust, have faith, and realize that there is only one true Living God, and His Name is Jesus. Our King of Kings, Our Lord of Lords, that is Him. That is His original Name. It was shortened down through the years. I heard my grandmamma and my mamma, and my daddy says, "O Lord", it was good enough for them - then I will begin to say it now. Oh, Lord! Please save me! Do not close the door before I get my foot in the door. The door. I was looking, I was knocking. I was yelling. "Let me in". I want to be protected, safe, and secure from all hurt, harm, or danger. I want to trust in the One who will supply all my needs. I want His Holy Spirit to become my guide. Okay! Then you must come over to the other side. There is a special place for those who believe. They are called the children of God. They live in the Great Beyond. Beyond this solar system. Over yonder. Over there.

We must become as a little child. Saying: Teach me, O Master. Teach me Thy ways. Teach me Thy wants and Thy needs. Teach me again. I heard you say that "Jesus loves me" but I sang it so much until these words became the only words I knew. It is not too late for me to say it – is it? No! You are my precious love, and I could never say "no" to you.

It is a gorgeous afternoon at the sacred hour of 5 p.m. Capture those sacred hours – you are spending it in His Presence because He is with me and you all day, every day, 24/7, around the clock, every hour – every minute – every second of the day. Every hour, every minute – every second and right at this present moment in time. Just had to say it unless you had forgotten it. I told you where I was when I first began to open and tell you what is meditating in my heart on such a glorious, sunshiny, windy, spring-like day. It is a day the Lord has made and expects you and I to rejoice, enjoy it, glorify it, celebrate it and be thankful for everything in it.

I admit it "I will always be in Love with You". You are my secret weapon and I rely on you to cover me with Your Blood and grant me Your Grace and Mercy and give me Your Divine Devotion. Precious Love. Can we ever get enough? Never! That is why I am going to continue to count my blessings, one by one so I do not miss any. I want Him to know just how good He has been to me, and I must show Him my gratitude and I can do it with the words of my mouth. Is He alive in your spirit like He is in mine? Are you nuts? It is springtime. It is a joyous occasion. New flowers, new trees, new identities being shown. New encouragement. New inspiration. Are you serious? You did not know? Each new day that I open my eyes, Jesus wakes me up to a new beginning. New aspirations. New dreams. New hopes. New future. This power takes control of me, and it makes me want to praise Him, call on His Holy Name. I yield. There is not a fight left in me. This is what I want to do also. Join in. The Angels are already praising Him, and He expects man and woman, boy and girl to honor, salute, glorify and give Him the Highest Praise. Hallelujah! P.S. You got a new day.

    I went outside and spent a great part of my afternoon outside. I went for a walk, and I took His Twenty-Third Psalm with me. This is what I was reciting while I was walking. His birds were singing words of praise and worship. They were chirping and whistling. They were happy swinging from tree to tree. His birds are happy. They float, they glide, they coast through His air. They fly so gracefully. It is almost like a trance the way they flutter their wings. They appear to just stop and rest and spend their time enjoying what they are doing. Man, woman, boy, child, girl, infants spend some time alone in His Presence. Just the two of you. Put on your favorite music and just jam. Float if you can, waltz, skip, hop and jump if this is all you can do. You have a life to live. Stop wasting time. You need to decide to join in with me and the birds and rejoice and celebrate each day that He allows you to open your eyes. Have yourself a merry little birthday. You have the best company.

    Oh! I am glad. I am so glad that I am alive today. I got up out of that grave that I had dug for myself. In that grave. In there went my old thoughts, ideas, beliefs, opinions, traditions, and desires. Look at the opportunity you have. You have the opportunity to come alive in your senses and begin to "think" and "process thought". This is something you have not done in a long time. When is the last time you spent some alone time in His Presence? Just the two of you.

    Let us face the music. You have forgotten how it felt to be alone with Him, haven't you? Take your time, slowly, you can do this. It takes practice. You must develop a habit. You must yearn to be in His Presence. Say it as I say it; I want this. This will be good for me. This is what I need. I can change my life with the words in my mouth. Yes! There is a miracle in your mouth. It is locked up in there, you must position your tongue and heart to come together as one. You have a mind. You have a brain. You can control your emotions. He will strengthen you physically, mentally, emotionally, psychologically, morally, and spiritually – only if you ask. I know where my health and strength come from. I am standing on His shoulders. He is the One propping me up. I must stand up high and straight because I weigh my shoulders. I must set a good example for the children. I must teach the children. I must show the children how to enjoy the life that God has given them. Caring, giving, sharing. These habits are going to have to be taught at an incredibly early age. What kind of seed are you planting? What are you giving your seed for it to grow? You are giving your seed the only thing it needs which is Love. Some of the children are not getting it. Our hearts must be saddened to know that some children and adults have never heard the words "I love you". These poor souls are lost. They have no hope. It is our job to bring to them hope, peace, love, and affection. We must be considerate and tolerant of the condition we find ourselves in and be thankful for the opportunity to do what we are doing right at this specific moment in time.

    We got it so good. We do not have to want anything. Everything is laid out for us to partake in and enjoy. Some of us cannot get enough. Some of us do not know when it is time to quit. They want to continue and on like a locomotive. When you find those people, who want to go non-stop – shut them out – you do not have time for that foolishness. Everyone should be able to govern themselves and not let someone else control them. Who is controlling your appetite? Who is telling you what to eat and when to eat? Do you know what hunger pains feel like? Try fasting? Try omitting certain meals and food and wait until you get hungry before eating again. If you wait until you get hungry then you will learn to be "thankful" for every morsel of food that you are getting.

Do we stop and take the time and savor the taste of what we are eating? We are too busy doing two things at one time. We never know when enough is enough. Have you lost your mind? Look around you, examine what is going on in the atmosphere. Pandemics, plagues, disasters, and turmoil. Will it ever end. No! That is why you must put on new clothes and shoes and get out of town while you still can cross that river. You want to go to the other side of the world. You want to go where Jesus is. Take my advice. There is a place of peace, and the sign is all over the place saying, "You can rest now".

I will "Hallow" His Name because He has kept me at peace. Tranquility, Harmony, Serenity, Happiness, Joy, and Righteousness is found when you say His Name. He is the author and finisher of my fate. He is my beginning and my end.

Okay! I tried His kindness, gentleness, and softness. It is like being on a cloud suspended in the air. It is gentle. His love is kind. There is no other love like it. You can lean back or recline in your favorite chair and listen to the sound of His instruments, all in harmony and providing a melody that soothes the mind, brain, heart, body, soul, and spirit. We gotta love each other! Yep! Must do if you want your soul to be saved. Want to live in Paradise? Do not let this opportunity pass you by. Have a candlelight dinner.

Just the two of you. Or do like I am getting ready to do. I will be dining in the Presence of a King. It is almost dinner time. I will take my time and enjoy every delicious bite I take. I will savor the taste. I will give Him the praise for making it possible. Nourishment for my body so I can continue my evening routine.

Spending time in His Presence is what I enjoy doing. Can't you tell? Jesus is my silent partner, personal and private companion, my enabler, my empower, my strength, my joy, and my love. He is the source of my inspiration. In Him, I have found justice, truth, honor, honesty, salvation, redemption, faithfulness, self-control, love, and righteousness. I found Perfect Peace. I know who is watching over me and is listening to every word I say. Jeremiah 29 v:12. He is a mighty good God! He is an "awesome God". Great Balls of Fire! He is bursting out of that tightly fitted jar that you had put Him in. Open the jar and let Him come out. Demand your freedom from Satan. Take back your life from Him. Ask God the Father of Our Lord and Savior Jesus Christ to help you. Go ahead and say "you can do this if you accept Jesus Christ as your Lord and Savior. If you do, He will allow His Holy Spirit to become your guide.

Say! You will do it. Say! Yes, I will. Say! Yes, I can. Yes, I have the courage I need to fight the enemy. I have praise on my tongue and a song in my heart. It has three words, "Thank You, Jesus". Examine your heart and accept the Love that He is trying to give you. You are His secret love. It will just be between the two of you. You love Him and He loves you. A match only made in Heaven.

Ask Him to make you into the person He had designed you to be when you were a thought. He knew you and me before we were the sparkle in our mom's and dad's eyes. He crafted us in His image and made a snapshot of you and promised He would never leave you nor forsake you. He has not forgotten about you. He remembers you. You are carved in the Palms of His Hand. Isaiah 49 v:15-16. Isn't He wonderful? Isn't He spectacular? Isn't He magical? Isn't He majestic? Isn't He miraculous?

I believe in You! This is what He is saying to me. I am a big girl. You can do all things through Christ who strengthens you. I can do this. I can continue to write my testimony if I can. Surely goodness and mercy shall follow those who dwell in His shelter, His secret place, and His Presence.

Chapter 8

Do not read unless you want to. This is what is new to me. I was so thankful that I completed the assessment interview that I wanted to praise Him for allowing me to plan my morning routine so I would not be late in keeping this appointment. I am proud to report that I was able to walk to the office and mailbox and walk back to my apartment. I walked yesterday. His sun was shining oh so bright. It was calling me. I had to follow the leader. His Holy Spirit is the One that encouraged me to go. I walked halfway around the building.

The church is now in session. Let Peace be among you. Let sure joy, bliss, pleasure surround you when you open the window on a spring day. Here at Gene Miller Manor in Christian City, Union City, Georgia, south of the airport, this is what happened to me. I wanted to write.

I am listening to a banjo. It is taking me on a country mile. On a long walk. I am taking a scenic route. Less building and more trees. More homes, more people on the patios waving as the cars pass by. We let that tradition of asking each other how are you pass by? Really, we stopped caring. We stopped listening to each other. What I had to say was more important. Yep! But listen to me and hear me out. Do not be so quick to interrupt. There is a message here.

How is your day? I am talking about a peaceful sheer bliss kind of day. This is what I was given. In His Presence where I can walk under a tree and admire the new leaves that are hanging on to that source of life they know. Your immediate reply is - Whatever! I am so tired I cannot think! What is rattling around in that brain? God gave it to you. What are you doing? I see what you are going to do! What you will do is disappoint God. He is Our Commander-in-Chief. You gotta go through Jesus before you get to Him. You were chosen at birth to be a boy or a girl. It was decided on a long time ago. There was a plan with your name written on it. It was already written what you would become. But do I get a chance to change that? Yes! Yes! You can. I am glad you asked. First, you need to have a little talk with Jesus. He comes highly recommended. You were the sparkle in His eye. You were the chosen one. You were singled out to be a winner from all the rest.

Say it! Sure, I am the best! I stopped dreaming. I became a mom, pop, you name it. I wore a lot of hats. I came from below the ground. I came from the dirt. Then I went to blossoming again. I grew up with a lot of responsibility. I had to think fast. I used my brain. Not just used to rest my head but to cradle me in His Everlasting Arms.

Okay! You heard a snapshot of my life now lets you and I go and become a leaf on a tree. His leaves are hanging on for dear life. They are saying they were here first, and you are trying to destroy me, soon, all you will have is dust to breathe, the air will be so contaminated. Man cannot breathe. Another epidemic. Man gasping for air. No more ventilators. Stop killing each other by chopping down every tree that you see. The trees gotta live too. They were here before we were, and they will be here when we are gone. Let us save a tree for the children. Somebody got to tell them how a man wanted to build buildings that would reach the moon. Chopped down the vegetation. Chop down the tree to build a house. Stop it! America has enough houses. You are destroying Earth. You are destroying a planet. You are wasting away. Pretty soon you will be a million miles away and never hear the bird's tweet and chirp while listening to an accordion again. It is soft music and soft lighting. This is when you can do some of your important thinking. I am not ready to die. I must convince you to tell yourself that there is another life other than this one so you can convince someone else. There is that word "responsibility". You are responsible for your fate. What do I want to become? What do I want to become? Let me dream about it. To be recognized as one of His sheep in His Pasture because I know once inside that gate that He will take good care of me.

Once you get inside the gate you will hold your spot for dear life. You never want to let go of His Unchanging Hand. He is the same today, tomorrow and in the future to come. He just stopped by to pay you and me a visit. A fireside chat on a gray spring-like day. Will March come in like a lamb and go out like a lion?

His sheep are taking their final breath with this Coronavirus. He is sweeping the nation so more souls can take their place. Find a way to honor your loved ones. Set aside today as their day and celebrate today as if it is your last. We do not know. We must be always prepared because our name could be called at any day, any hour, anytime.

Got your house in order. You ready? No! You do not need more time. The time is now! Your choice. Use your self-control. Use your willpower. Use your ability to think. I believe I will stick with the One that I know I can trust in. I believe I will stick with the One that is propping me up. I believe I am going to stick with Jesus. He knows the way. He has a plan with my name written on it and He promises to never leave me nor forsake me. I am going to depend on Him. He has never failed me yet. I have been hanging on for 74 years. He is the Same God that met me at the cradle. He was there. He remembers me as a suckling babe. How can a mother forget its suckling baby, there is a special bond that you develop when you hold me? You talk so gently, sweetly, and kindly to me. Just like a whisper. The same way that Jesus deposits pieces of silver and gold into your ears. Softly, gently.

Are you dear to His heart? Will He do anything for you? He will give you what you need if you depend on Him as the supplier! He will love me today, right at this present and the precise moment in time just like He will love me tomorrow. He wants me to celebrate this day first. Before tomorrow gets here. I must capture this sacred hour of 6 p.m. We are living too fast. We are putting too much into our schedule. When you gain the freedom, you desire you will find that you only want to do one thing at a time. If I am going to write I write. If I am going to eat, then I eat. If I am going to recline and relax then I must set the mood. Nothing happens automatically. You gotta work for it. You must make an effort to locate your peace and happiness. If you need alone time, then take it. You owe it to yourself to live your life the way God intended for you to live it.

Join me. I am in The Presence of a King. This is what makes me happy. I can smile, shout, sway and swerve my body, clap my hands, pat my feet, wiggle my toes, whatever I can do, I am doing it. I will not wither away into an old bulb. I still have life in me. I have a light that I want to shine. I will listen. I will open up my ears to hear any sound that He might make. He is angry with the nation. They refuse to think. They refuse to see the handwriting on the wall. Man! This thing is about to end. What will we do? Find a safety net. Find someone who can save you. Go to the other side.

Let us you and I play a game. You pretend and I pretend. I am going to drink wine, beer, and alcohol all night and all day. Man! Where are you trying to get to? You do not need that. I have a better idea. Let us talk to the man and ask Him if He is satisfied with you abusing your body like that? He said No! Your body is a temple. A human sacrifice. Your body is a landmark in History. You are a man and woman of noble character. You have goals, beliefs, opinions, traditions, desires built off into those shoulders. You were destined for greatness. I was disappointed that you did not stand up to the masses when it was your time to shine and tell the world what The Lord did for you.

We gotta teach the children. Save them. Mothers, Fathers, men, or women, boy or girl. Do you want to survive? Then find a young soul that is lost and put them on the right track. Somebody showed you the right way – right? Somebody told you these words "I love You". These sheep that are in the pasture at this present era in time have never heard these words. It is my job and your job to tell them.

Kindness, gentleness, softness – this they have never felt. The ones that are lost. They do not know because no one taught them that there was a King who watched over them all day, every day, 24/7, around the clock – every hour – every moment of their lives. They do not know about

Jesus but you do. Joy and satisfaction should light up your heart and face when you hear His Name because you can recall what He has done for you and what He is doing at this moment in time. You know who is watching over you - right? We know who has given us the strength to bear. How Great Thy Art? It is just Me and Him. He and I.

Just "us two".

A man, woman, boy, or girl is whistling. It is a calm melody. Bells are ringing. He is walking through the woods on a spring-like sunny afternoon. The birds are pecking in the grass. They are feeding. He provides for them just like He provides for me and you. Isn't He wonderful? Isn't He spectacular? Isn't He outstanding? I guess you will never know if you aborted your flight. If you did not stick with me then you have lost a great opportunity to hear my next thought. I am happy. I am satisfied. I am where I want to be. In His Presence. Tucked away in our Hide-A-Way. Join me! There is plenty of room in His big, spacious, blue Arms located in His sky. Big Arms - right? Drifting! I was lost in a sea of green leaves hanging on to a limb and the limb was holding on to the tree. It is such a peaceful view. All shapes different colors coming together in one to make a big bouquet. Those are My Angels. He brags! One of His Angels was holding a sheet of green joy, love, and admiration over me. I am in a Heavenly, divinely place made just for me and you. Green is the most dominant color. I sat and stared at it for about half an hour and just dreamed this and dreamed that. The leaves on the trees are trying to tell us something. They belong here too. Just like you.

Somebody prayed for me. Somebody prayed for you. Do you know what that means? Somebody pleaded your case over you to God and He heard you when said Oh Lord! Have Mercy! Just the mumbling of these words is all He heard. My daddy could not say it properly, He just hollowed out "Ah Lord"! We knew what that meant. He was counting on the Master to show up. I heard my mamma say, "Ah Lord". She was calling on Him to make a way and He answered her prayer. If it was mamma, papa, aunt, uncle, cousin, or friend. He heard their prayer. So, when you look at your family, stop and "Thank Him" for watching over you and your loved ones all these many years and the ones who prayed for you.

I woke up. I had no hope and happiness and peace and understanding until I met Jesus and He said to me "come and go with me, my yoke is easy. Matthew 11th chapter. I went. He nodded in my direction, and I knew what that meant. I had to face the fact of did I want to be there in His company? I did not hesitate for a moment I immediately and spontaneously answered "This is where I want to be" In Your Presence, Your Honor, Your Majesty, Your Superior One, Your Marvelous, Your magnificent, Your fabulous, Your fantastic, Your outstanding, Your wonderful and spectacular Savior.

He welcomed me with open arms. He laid out the red carpet because one of His angels had come home. She has come back to where she belongs. I found myself wrapped up in His Everlasting Arms earlier during the morning hours. I have written one testimonial for the day but felt very compelled to pick up where I left off.

Today I had a personal assessment interview with the service coordinator. It was scheduled to be a one-hour session, but we finished in less time than that. She asked the questions, and I gave her the answers. I had the memory test. My four objects to remember were Walmart, cup, letter. Cannot remember the last one. I passed the memory test with flying colors. I made an A. I was so proud to know there is nothing wrong with my memory. I know who to honor, cherish, worship, admire and adore for this miracle. It is a miracle that we are closed in our right mind. I am 74. Pulling for 74 more. Just asking? What will I do? Write! More writing! So since 74 more is not guaranteed. I might as well proceed to complete the mission I have assigned during my allotted time.

Hallelujah! He is making a way for you to connect with me and a way for me to connect to you. It is all in His Plan. You were destined to be where you are and doing what you are doing right at this present and the precise moment in time. If you have been reading my books, then you know what time it is and what kind of attire you will need for the occasion of spending time with me while I tell you what I am being told. He speaks to you in so many ways. Only if you are open. Only if you have not given up the idea that there is more out there for me.

You have a lifetime to live. This is what you think. No, the only day you must live is today. Tuesday. A brand new day. Take time out and smell the roses. Stroll with me.

Each time the leaf on the tree moved, it was speaking to man, saying "I belong here, I was here first." Just keep me O Lord. Please hold my hand. You created a doll, and I was sitting on a shelf, and someone decided to take me home. They dressed me in so many outfits. I changed clothes so I often. I stopped dreaming. I became obsessed with clothes. I began to realize I worship clothes. I am so glad God stepped in and took the blinders off my eyes. All the time I should have been worshiping the One who gave me the clothes, I was worshipping and showing gratitude to Satan. Told you He would steal your ideas, kill your hopes and dreams, and destroy your belief in Our Divine Creator.

Man feels vibrations. What feels good is what I want to have. Satan got you by your senses. Satan knows what you like, and Satan will continue to supply your demand. You got to get up and put on your wartime clothes. You got to fight that enemy. Hate is raising its ugly head. The Hispanic Population is sheep in His Pasture just like America's men and women, boys, and girls. They are suffering from disillusion. They were just released from one world of hate into a new world of hate. America says, "she loves". That is why they are trying to get here. In America you are free - they have been told.

Free from what? There is hate and prejudices deeply rooted in the hearts of men who live there. There is separatism. They play favorites and it is based on the color of your skin. There is hate, anger, convulsions, rage, and wrath written on their faces. It is coming out the side of their head. It is being released through the ears. What are you listening too? Who are you following? Who orders you around? Who tells you what to do and what to think? Satan. The devil the enemy. Lucifer. That is who responsible for the pandemics, plagues, disasters, and turmoil that you see ravaging the city. We are a city located upon a hill. The sheep are restless. There are good sheep and then there are bad sheep. How can you tell? It is how they bark. It is how they talk to each other. Once you learn their language you can control them. Once they hear Your Voice, Oh Master, they will stand up and take notice.

What language are you speaking? Are you sharing, caring, and giving? Are you grabbing everything you get your hands on? What about settling down and doing one thing at a time. If you are going to cook then cook, embrace it, do not dread it. You must put love in those pots, and you get His tenderness, gentleness, and softness each time you stir the pot. Who gave you your strength for you to be able to move a muscle? How important are your fingers to you? Man, I cannot live without these fingers. These fingers make things happen. These fingers just might save a soul for Christ. Somebody will read about it. That wonderful life that comes to those who believe, trust, and have faith that there is another life beyond what we have now at this present time. We are just passing through. Where do you want to go? Hang with me and I will take you there.

Talking about dependency. I depend on Thee. He is my way-maker. He surrounds me with everything I need so I can write, share, and give away what is being given to me at this present and the precise moment in time. When I need Him, He is there? He is here, there, everywhere at the same time. Isn't He magical? Majestic. He is my Rock and my Redeemer. It is in Him who I trust. I have faith in Thee. I know of all the bridges came across just to make it to the other side. There were roadblocks, boulders in the road, but I dodged them and readjusted myself, and got back on the right road that is leading me up the King's Highway.

You and I are Heaven bound! Brace yourself! This is 74 years of knowledge, growth, and wisdom that you are getting. I have paved the way for so many of you to begin to question why do you exist? Who am I? Man, woman, boy or girl, there is only one. No choice. That decision was made when you were only a thought. It is explained when you read Jeremiah. Pay close attention to Jeremiah 1. Spend some time there – do not rush through – allow the words that were spoken to Jeremiah to penetrate the walls of your heart, your brain, your mind, your body, your soul, and your spirit. It is important. You are not alone! There is help available to you. Ask Him to save your soul? Ask Him to lead you out of the valley. You are ready to return home. A place of comfort and joy, peace, and relaxation, with wisdom, justice, honesty, equality oozing from the walls. I am drenched in His Grace and Mercy, His Unfailing Love, His Unconditional Love, His Grace and Mercy, and His Divine Devotion.

Psalm 23 says "Surely His goodness and mercy shall follow me all the days of my life as long as I dwell in His shelter, His Secret Place of His Presence. If I remain in Him, then He will remain in me. If I abide in Him, then He will abide in me. If I draw nearer to Him, then He will draw nearer to me.

I admit it. I stay in the church. Anytime you call me I am in church. I devote so much time to reading, writing, meditating, pondering, believing, trusting, and loving everything I do. I love writing. I know it will always be a good conversation. I know who needs me. I have a purpose. You are not doomed! There is life on the other side. You must jump ship. You must climb aboard. Where this ship sails, nobody will know but she is on her way to the Great beyond. Come on and get aboard. Claim your seat while you have a chance.

Chapter 9

Cannot end my day yet! There is more to tell you. I watched the news and listened to one of His tv vessels. And the question was asked " am I trying to please God or am I trying to please man? This made me question my morals, my character, my ideas, my thoughts, my opinions, my beliefs, my dreams and my desires. Who I want to please is the One that created me? Who I want to please is the One who is watching over me and listening to every word that is meditating in my heart. I want to return to Him and be in His Presence all day, everyday, 24/7, around the clock, and right at this present moment in time. I must practice being in His Presence here on His solid and sacred ground we call Earth on His Planet and in His Universe. I have got to get it right down here before I can go over there, over yonder, in the Great beyond.

Let me pick up my song. Thank You Jesus for giving me ears to hear. Thank you for giving me a brain so I can think. Thank you for giving me a heart so I can feel. Thank you for giving me a mind so I can remember. I know about the Love that I am receiving from a King. This is my only source of knowledge. I know He loved me yesterday. I know He loved me this morning because He sat with me the entire time I was writing. He allowed His Holy Spirit to pull me away from my morning routine and mop the kitchen and bathroom. Change the rugs. Tidy up and make everything shine. I felt so good I was able to bend, stoop and move about to complete this job. After I finished, I felt so good that I came in here, sat down, with a bottle of His delicious, chilled spring water, and began to write.

I am doing what God has intended for me to do. Tell you about the incredible relationship that He and I have formed. It is the gentle hour of 8 pm. You know how I say to capture the moments that you are in His Presence. Like right now. I talked on the phone to two of my family members. It was a joy and pleasure to talk to them, we had interesting things to say to each other. My son, Gregory is having to teach his grandchildren how to share, care and give. I told him to start at the knee level. They share. Just him and the boy and then share with the girl. Teach them to love each other so that they will want to share. This is what is missing in this day in age. Love is not being shown. We are not giving, sharing, and caring. This is what Jesus did.

He raised me from the dead and allowed His Holy Spirit to become my guide. I wanted to please Him. After I finished my morning routine, I set aside a quiet time just for the two of us and I said, "Thank You, Master". Once again You showed me just how much you cared. You wanted to see me at my best. I did not disappoint Him. He has created someone great, a masterpiece, and a fine specimen of His workmanship. I knew if I put Jesus first, that He would walk with me, talk with me, and guide me in the direction that He plans for me to go.

I let Him have His way. I play follow the leader. He has a plan, and He is the best of planners. Want to know how I know? Because I gave myself away to Him totally so His will could be done. He led me to the right preacher. This preacher said it is impossible to fulfill the Ten Commandments unless you are in His Presence all day, everyday, 24/7, around the clock – every hour – every minute – every second and right at this present moment in time unless you are under the influence of His Holy Spirit. Know what? He is right.

Let me tell you about His Holy Spirit. It holds you accountable for your thoughts and actions. It tells you what you need to do and accomplish. His Holy Spirit creates a desire in you to please God. His Holy Spirit coaxes, urges, suggests, influence and persuade you to do the right thing. Evil, Satan, the devil, the enemy, take a back seat. Get away from me. I am a child of a King, and I will not give up where He has placed me without a fight. I belong here and this is where I have been placed and this is where I will stay. Be firm in your denial of the Satanic influences. Know this, I am safe and secure under His Arms because He has me covered under His feathers. Psalm 91.

Nope! Not giving an inch. I shall not be moved. I remember when I was loose and fancy-free. I lived that life but today is different. I know whose I am, and I know who I am. You are going to wake up one morning and realize what you have missed. There is another life. You can wake up tomorrow morning and you will be set free of all that baggage that Satan had piled on your shoulders. Shake it off. It is too much a burden to carry around the wounds facing the world. Be free. Watch His birds. Watch the leaves on His trees. Watch how they cluster together in a bunch. They made room for each other. Every leaf wants to be connected to a vine. Are you connected to that vine? How deep are your roots? Are you willing to hold on to your belief that You know He is going to take good care of you? I am. Psalm 90 v:14, it says "I will satisfy you early in the wee hours of dawn with your morning grace and mercy, just trust me. I will come everyday to touch you with my finger of love, you gotta remember who it is that is touching you. Can you remember that?

Every morning I open my eyes, He is there present at my bedside with His Hand extended out to me. My child! come this way – there is an adventure planned just for you. How can I refuse an invitation like this? He is going to provide for all my needs, protect me from all hurt, harm, and danger and allow His Holy Spirit to become my guide. Name me one person who would pass up this opportunity. He is with me. I am writing, it is nighttime. Just cannot turn Him loose. He keeps giving signals to me making me want to sit down and listen to the words that are meditating in my heart.

There are tears in Heaven. God, Jesus, My Lord, and Savior are unhappy. Their sheep are going farther and farther away from reality. First, they are blind. They cannot see the handwriting on the wall. Earth is about to be destroyed. Only a few will be saved. The others will be swept away like dust. They will return to what they came from if they do not come alive in their senses and begin to think, and process thought. Time is being wasted. Resources are being wasted. You are not showing your gratitude for what God has given you.

These sheep use too much water, they are not going to save any for the children. This Land was made for you and yours so we gotta protect it. We must save the trees, oceans, wildlife. We must save the planet. What are you doing to save our planet? Stop wasting water. Do not let the faucet of water run while you are brushing your teeth. Turn it off while you are washing dishes. Save some for the children. If we do not save some for the next generation, they will die of thirst. No one told them to conserve and to prepare for a rainy day. A day when there is no water. Ask the hurricane survivors just how that feels. We are blessed and highly favored but we do not think like that, do we?

If it had not been for God on our side, what would we have done? Our fore parents taught us to be thankful for everything that we have. Treat it as if it is a gift from God. Be grateful. Be thankful. Surely you have set an example for your generation to follow. What are you teaching these kids? That they can make it on their own. This is the wrong example to set. Teach them who they are, they are a child of a King, and when they are old, they will not forget about it. Teach them morals, build character, be on guard for what they are putting in their heart. Your heart should be made from pure gold. I know this is risky to say. But listen up. You are responsible for the evil spirits that want to reside in the four chambers of your heart. It is filled with love or hate. Good or bad. You decide. You are the decision maker. What kind of heart do you want to offer to God and ask Him to bless each night you close your eyes for sleep.

I want to offer Him a clean heart so He can dwell and have a final resting place. This should be your answer, if it is not, then you will have to start all over again in first grade. God made you and He made you in perfect form. He gave you what you needed to multiply, grow, and return to Him in Perfect Peace. He did not give you a life to live and allow you to live it without giving you basic commands. He wanted you to always remember Him. He is God! The Creator and Ruler of The Universe. He gave us a Savior. We must first get the Savior's approval to get our inheritance. You became a member of God's household the moment you accepted Jesus Christ as Your Lord and Savior. This was the best decision you could have ever made. Put Jesus first. Let Him go before you because He knows the way. He has a plan. Who do you trust with your life? Where have you placed your confidence? In whom have you placed your confidence? Take your time, this can be unsettling questions. Make sure you answer honestly. Make sure your answer agrees with your heart. You must have principles to lean on. You must take your time in answering because you want to cross over, and you need to be sure that this is what you want to do. Who are you trying to please man or God? Or are you trying to please yourself?

I want peace, patience, harmony, tranquility, serenity, fairness, equality, truth, honesty, justice, integrity, salvation, redemption, love, and righteousness. Where can I get it? I can give you the source that I use. I found it in Jesus. I found joy, happiness, peace, and contentment in His Presence and I believe you can find it too. Go exploring with me. Come let us pretend. Pretend you wake up tomorrow and it was the end of your life. What would you regret or what would you rejoice over? How did you spend your last day here on His Earth? Were you in His Presence asking Him to let His will be done? Did you have some alone time with Him? I did. This was the time that I was most happy and content. He was holding my hand and I was saying to Him, "My heart belongs to You", I want to please You. You are the one in charge. You call the shots. Whatever you tell me to say, I will say it. You have ordered my steps and I trust you to take real good care of me.

It is because of you that I am the way I am. It is because of Your Unfailing Love, Your Unconditional Love, Your Grace and Mercy, and Your Divine Devotion that I can sit here and compose a thought. It is His Divine Intervention that is empowering me to write sentence after sentence. It brings me divine joy and pleasure to know that I have a Savior who is watching over me and is listening to every word that I say.

There are millions of blessings that I can thank Him for! Too many to count on fingers and toes. He allows me to shatter the ceiling in Heaven with my praise and He allows my blessings that He has in reserve for me to be released to me. They come fluttering in like the wings of a bird. They come rushing by like the breeze that shakes the trees. I am so happy. I am overcome with joy and emotion. I know I am different. I know I am one of a kind. I know there is no one else like me. I was chosen to be His Tulip because I believed in His promise - that He would return to take good care of me.

He keeps waking me up in His Presence. He keeps giving me a sound mind with a reasonable portion of my health and strength. I am alive and I am glad that I am alive today to witness another miracle. It is Him who gave me a life to live in the Presence of a King. He is my influence. He is my inspiration and encouragement. I wait patiently to take my turn. He is keeping me alive for a reason. My destiny and purpose are about to meet. That is why I must tell you everything I can while it is my season.

This is my song. "I love Jesus, I love Jesus, yes I do, because He is the first one that ever loved me. Sing it with me. Do not be coy or shy. You can do it. Take control of the words that are meditating in your heart. Replace the words of your mouth with words of praise, worship, and admiration for Our King who is seated at the Right Hand of The Father. Ask Him to strengthen you physically, mentally, emotionally, morally, and spiritually. You have a Pillar of Faith. This is who you can lean on. My Rock and My Redeemer.

We have an advocate. We have a mediator. He is our go between.

He is on our side. It is Jesus who will plead our case. Jesus - I am hopelessly devoted to You. It is You I am trying to please. It is You who I want to be satisfied with my accomplishments. All my honor, all my worship, all my praise, all my Love, and all my glory is given to You. Listen as this tulip honor and salute Our King.

Chapter 10

Oh! I am under Grace. This is the most important thing to be under, it is nice. I hear birds, I see birds, I see raindrops, I see joy, I see love. I saw His birds just floating, gliding, coasting along, and enjoying it. They flap their wings. Give me my wings now? That is the message here listen up, the more time you invest in His Presence the more knowledgeable you become. Flap my wings! I am free. I am a bird. I am the red bird you saw when I gave you sight far enough for you to see the bird. Who gave you those eyes? I know who did, it. I came from a safe place to deal with this. What is wrong? There is no peace. One side verse the other side. Hate comes in. An evil spirit and His Name are Satan, Lucifer, the enemy, the devil - the one that looks like He has horns coming out of His ears. Cannot you see that smoke? It is hatred.

Take a hike through the Woods at Gene Miller Manor and you will find someone there who knows what she needs before she can get the next sentence out and He is right there with the answer. He is alright! He glows.

He shines because I have been released from the devil's horns. One morning I was shaken because I knew this was it, gave up, about to give it, and guess who walked in the door. It was Jesus! Right on Time. I know who I can depend on. Do you know who you depend on to make everything alright? He turned on a light. He turned on a glow. He turned and looked at me and saw the sparkle in my eye.

I must stop here and say "Ain't He Grand? I have got to give up the Name, He knows how to handle some things. He brought me into a garden of red roses because I had been buried in the ground. You know you and I come from the root. We are deeply connected through the ground that we stand on. What is in that heart? Man! Got any morals you care to share!

The Earthman, Our United States of America, Our Nation at this day in time must go to war with words. At this time, I command all other states to come under one authority. Let Our Creator decide who should live here on Earth. Not the Heathens. Yep, them too, you see God is a Universal God, not just my God, your God, His God, Her God, Their God, them who do not believe, yes, you are too. Wake up! People. Stop sleeping! He is blowing His horn and He is not happy with His sheep in His Pasture.

Witness with me. I give honor and praise and worship to the One that saved me. I know who woke me up this morning, it was Our Lord and Savior, Jesus Christ, yes that is His Name. My Lord and Savior. I call Him my Savior brother man and brother woman, my sister, my brother, women, and men, child, boy or girl. He makes all things possible! He does! He is the One that sits high and makes the rules. He has given us liberty, justice, and grace, what more can we ask for other than His Divine Love and Affection. He is showering me with His love and Affection, His Unfailing Love, His Unconditional Love, His Grace and Mercy, and His Divine Devotion. The last time I checked He was giving me His Grace and mercy on my left, Grace and Mercy on my right, Grace, and Mercy in front of me, Grace, and Mercy in the back of me, Grace, and mercy on top of me and Grace and Mercy underneath me. You see! I am covered in His Grace and Mercy from the crown of my head to the sole of my feet. He is mighty? Who can snap a forest down in a couple of seconds? Nobody but God and He is so dissatisfied. He is downright appalled at the ideas that you allow to float around in your head. Has the word happy ever surfaced in your head? Happiness - that is a foreign word. What is the meaning of this so-called Happiness? You asked. It is about Peace. He gives it to His birds. He gives it to His sheep in His Pasture. It has been distributed all over the land. Jesus - This joy that you have the first time you meet Him. Want me to tell you how to meet Him? Curious yet? I will tell you what worked for me. It was concentration, I kept listening, there is another world just for you and if you trust in me, I will take you there. Wear ballerinas, you will be doing a lot of gliding here and there, I am going to be with you every step of the way. This is what He said to Joshua. He said I will be with you every step of the way. Yep! Right beside you - being your cheerleader. Look who is backing you, look who is holding you up? Isn't He great? Is not He marvelous, fantastic, spectacular, superb, and wonderful on this Wednesday morning, March 31st, 2021, the end of March, and it is going out like a raining lion? He is whispering in my ear. Everything is so still when it rains. These are moments that you should choose to meditate. Be in His Presence. On a rainy, foggy day, sweatpants, loose-fitting clothes, you will be happier, you will be able to move more freer when trying to relax. In between times, I honored Him for allowing me to be in His Presence one more time, every chance I got, I was walking, moving, breathing, and counting my blessings by being able to recite His Twenty-Third Psalm. Standing on His word. He said He would take care of me. He said "toss all of those dirty rags over to me, I will wash them and make them as white as snow. Toss all your worries on me. Stand firm in your beliefs.

Black Lives Matter Movement. Learn their language. Listen to how they talk to one another. One authority over another authority. White and Black. A Fight, Conflict, Rage, Anger, Hate, Deceit, Lies, surface. Righteousness shows up and asks the question who is responsible for this nonsense? My people should live in peace. I have provided harmony, tranquility, serenity to those who chose to spend every awakening second in My Presence. People! I sent you a King. He is Your Savior. Are you treating Him as such?

Oh, Father God of Our Lord and Savior Jesus Christ gets all my honor, my worship, my glory, my love, my admiration, my idolization. Yep! That is Him. The One that sits high and looks low. He is looking for the salt that He has here on Earth. Not too happy with how things are looking. He is a little disappointed – He had faith and hope and trust for you, but you abandoned it. You stop listening to Grandma and Grandpa. They were trying to aim your mind, your brain, your heart, your soul, and your spirit in the right direction. Could you become meek and humble? Can you do two things at one time? Do you believe He is watching over you then start talking to Him? He is not far off. He is right there. He keeps the blood running warm in your veins. Thank You, Lord, for my heart. I will protect my heart and give it all back to you because I know you gave me a golden heart and I want to return it to you the same way you gave it to me. Pure in heart. Precious Love. Goldilocks, Cinderella, boys and girls, women, and men. My angel, my bird, my tulip, "Now run along and be blessed." They disappeared into pure joy, pleasure, contentment, only plain old peace.

A man dropped his guard and experienced torment. Hate showed up in disguise. A man went through hell. Suffering from plagues, pandemics, disasters, and turmoil. Just like today - but only the strong survived. Those who ate bread and water will survive, all your need is bread and water, then you could make it. Man, we are killing ourselves. Food and more food. Gotta have it. Slow up from that overeating. Who eats 2 chickens, 6 burgers, tons of sodas, ice cream all in one sitting? Now you know that is too much food. Yep! You know do not you. But I want it. Your eyes are playing tricks on you. Your eyes have been gorged out. Your eye socket is blank. There is no life in those eyes because those eyes have been looking at the wrong thing. Overload of food. Then there comes glitter and Gold - Satan - do I need to go into detail? If I must. Gold and glitter make them happy; I will shine more of it in their direction each time I return. Food makes them happy. Keep giving it to them. Satan kept showing up until God began speaking through His leaves on His trees. Man stops. Do not cut down our trees. Save some for the children. What will cleanse their air? The trees. That is their purpose " to cleanse the air" and provide pure air for our nostrils. I love each leaf on my tree just like I love you. You are nothing but a leaf hanging on to a tree limb. Okay, little leaf - what are you doing here - there are so many of you - yes, we want to hold on and drink from the vine just like you do.

What is wrong with the man? He does not want to drink from this fountain of truth. He wants to do his own thing. Man cannot do that. There are limitations on man. He must do what pleases

God so he can develop into his full potential. Only God will make him into the man that he was designed to be. Has man stopped and consulted with God? Has he asked God, "O Lord what is your plan for me?"

Tell the world these words "I love You". Show the world the true meaning of the word love. Love is powerful. There is a miracle in your mouth. Your mouth can move mountains if you speak to it, have faith, and believe and trust in the One who knows the plan. Proverbs 18 v:21. The power you have in that tongue. Life or death! Choose life. Dwell in the pathway that has been chosen for you. This is fulfilling and rewarding. Find your place of peace. He has changed me from the inside out. I cleaned out my heart so He could dwell and have a final resting place.

Satan tricked you into believing that you should wear and have things that glitter that is made from gold. Satan grabbed your attention fast. You started listening to Him whisper in your ear. This is what He did to me. He would whisper around the clock and made me want to give up and accept my fate. But God showed up, Jesus, His Holy Spirit was on the scene and made some sweeping changes. Everything in my heart that did not belong there had to go. He assured me that He would provide me with what I needed. Strength, joy, peace, happiness, faithfulness, love, and righteousness. This is the type of fruit that He was bringing. All I had to do was to believe and trust and have faith in myself. I wanted a change. He sees me as the sparkle in His eye. This morning He called me Shining Star, you have a full day planned.

The man was saved because an angel told him, it is time to clean his heart out.

A man heard the call, give it up man, come on board. There is room for one more. You believers got a job to do. You gotta warn the others of the pending dangers ahead if they choose to get off the main road. The main road leads to peace, rest, and relaxation - you can pick up peace on this road. In this place, you can get just comfortable and enjoy the flow as you coast along on His sacred and solid ground. Do you know where you came from don't you? That is what you will return as, nothing but dirt, so now that you have received a new life then stand on some principles. Have some morals. Have some things that you just will not do. Have affirmations so you can do the things God intended for you to do.

I am glad to be alive. Once again, He did it again. What did He do? He touched me with His finger of Love and told me to "wake up" O sleepyhead, rise from the dead, and let the Lord shine on you. Without hesitation, I placed my two feet on His floor and hallowed His Holy Name because He allowed me to do what I needed to do. I will praise Him. I will honor Him. I will salute Him. I will worship Him. I will glorify Him. I will rejoice in Him. This is what I am supposed to do now that I realize that He has favored me with a brand new day and a brand new beginning.

He is looking for a Star this morning. He is looking for someone to bestow His Grace and Mercy upon, is it you? Look around, listen up boys and girls, a King is coming to town, and He is the barrier of good deeds and mercy. Where is He? He is here, there, and everywhere. His written word is buried in the Bible, and you must open it up and read it so you can help solve the mystery of why man does not listen to God and do what He tells you to do. Man is dead! Man has died and been buried! Why do you say that? Man has buried his thoughts, his ideas, his hopes, his ambitions, his beliefs, his opinions, his traditions, his dreams, and his future in the grave. How do you know? Look around at the people. Where are they going? They do not have a clue of what direction to go in. They are lost, wandering sheep in His Pasture. How can we gather the sheep into the gate? By speaking their language. Tell them what they want to hear, and you

can corral them at any time. That is what is controlling man. He is listening to everybody speak except God. He abandoned the idea that God knew you when you were a thought. He abandoned the idea that we have a Superior Power watching over us right now at this present moment in time. He abandoned the idea that there is another life other than the one you are living. He gave up hope for his future. He stopped dreaming!

I can see clearly now. It is not raining; I see His Sunshine and His white clouds located throughout His skies. I see that He has not forgotten about me. I see He knew me as a suckling babe. I see that I am engraved in the Palms of His Hands. Help yourself to praise Him. Did you see how I opened the door to show you how to praise Him? This is what He enjoys most, His sheep giving honor and recognition to the One that woke them up this morning. Honoring Him Adoring Him Admiring Him Saluting Him is what I am supposed to do. This is my job. Kneel at the feet of The King. If I keep my promises to Him, then He will keep His promises to me. Since I have honored and adored Him, He is going to open the windows of Heaven now that I have shattered the ceiling and release to me the blessings that He has in reserve "just for me".

Today is laundry day. I am busy washing and folding clothes. I praise God that He gave me the mindset I needed to get the job done. I walked to the laundry room with the laundry basket in tow.

I put the clothes in the washing machine, waited, then returned to put them in the dryer. Now that I have some in-between time, I found a good way to spend my downtime. Write. Tell Him "I Love You", that is what I am saying. You smiled at me once again. You convinced me that I was blessed and highly favored when You blew Your breath of life into my lifeless body and allowed me to become a living soul all over again - ready - yes ready- to honor you and praise you for being so good to me. When I opened my eyes to a great and brand new day, I quickly turned over, placed my two feet on His floor, and began to count my blessings by singing an old familiar hymn, "Thank You, Jesus". You should try it sometimes and see if it works for you. I take my time when I am flushing my kidneys. The entire time I am "Thanking Him" that my kidneys are working properly. After I finish, I hurry back to reclaim my spot. I was tucked in so comfortably and securely in His Everlasting Arms. He was cradling me. Do you know how it feels to be cradled? It is Love. It is a gentle, kind, compassionate, delicate, tender kind of love' like His Fruits of His Spirit.

Can you cradle yourself? Yes! Show yourself some kindness, tenderness, softness, gentleness, and moments of soft joy and total happiness. Waltz with Him. Prance, glide, float in His Presence. You know who is protecting you from all hurt, harm, and danger. You know who it is that will supply all your needs, and you know who will allow His Holy Spirit to be your guide.

Hey there! I am talking to you. Just trying to get you in closer to His Kingdom. He has for us here on Earth. It is a new day that you have been given. It is not like yesterday. Today is different. It has come with its events and adventures. The best way to describe it is to say; Look at me I am alive, and I know who is responsible for me being closed in my right mind with a reasonable portion of my health and strength. It is My God, My Lord, My Jesus, My Savior. This is who I worship, and this is the authority that I live by. He is the Leader and whatever He says goes. My happiness depends on how I worship Him, honor Him, and glorify Him. Want the ground to be level that you are standing on? Then lean on your Rock and your Redeemer and do not depend on your limited understanding. Wake Up! The Commander-in-Chief is here, and He is setting the rules for us to follow. He showered you with His Unfailing Love, His Unconditional Love, His Grace and Mercy, and His Divine Devotion in hopes that you would raise your head above the water and begin to drink of what you see.

Try some that are old fashion like thinking. First of all, you decided I can do this on my own. I can take control of my life! Is this what you said? No! You cannot stop fooling yourself that you are in control of your destiny, only God is. He has the plan. He has the outline. Sorry! Some of you are drowning. Drowning in your limitations. Thinking your life is your own and you can do with it what pleases you. Wrong! Wrong again! You need the leadership of a Supreme Being. You need God to show you the way. Your path has already been carved. Now is the time for you to set aside quiet time and ask the question that has been gnawing at you for sometime now. Why was I born? How do I fit into this big puzzle of life? Why am I here? Who made me and why? What is going to happen to me? Be born, grow up, work on a job for forty years, grow old and die? Hold up! Wait! That is not it. This is not the life God intended for you to live. Wake up! Listen to the birds sing their song of joy and praise, they want you to join in with them to salute the One that created them. Thank You, Lord, for my ears. I can hear good. I hear Your whispers. Listen up! Do not let the rocks cry out. His rocks are alive you know - trees and flowers and plants are living in those rocks. In Colorado, trees are growing that are rooted to the side of the mountains. Where is your soul, mind, brain, heart, body, and spirit anchored?

I am holding on to the vine. That tree of knowledge, that tree that gives me life. This tree is bearing good fruit. This tree is here with a message of love, hope, and peace. I finished the laundry and went to the grocery store on this rainy, serene, glorious, and gorgeous day. I drew near to Him early in the morning hours and He, in turn, drew near to me after I saturated His atmosphere with words of praise and admiration. That is what I have been doing all day. Just to be near Him is satisfaction for me. He watched over me as I embraced the adventure that He had planned for me today and enabled me to complete each task. Isn't He wonderful? Isn't He fantastic?

Isn't He almighty? Yes! A thousand more "yes's". I am confident that He is watching over me all day, everyday, 24/7, around the clock, every hour - every minute - every second and right at this present moment in time.

Gather around and listen to the teacher! Psalm 23 says "The Lord is My Shepherd; I shall not want". I am one of His sheep in His pasture and He is taking care of you just like He is taking good care of me. I recognize where my health and strength come from. I know who is holding the key to my happiness and future. Only God can give you what you need. He gave us a Savior. Someone to call our counselor and comforter. He knew man would need to be consoled in his beliefs. That is why Jesus assured us, that we who are weary, worn, and heavy laden can enter His Presence and rest.

Do you stop and show yourself any love? Do you pile it on a mountain high?

Like a sundae. Softness, gentleness, kindness, and tenderness - more and more - repeat to yourself "I love you". Who are you talking to? You are telling yourself these words. Nobody has ever told you these words and there is something you need to know. I know the One who loved you before you were a thought. I know who will share, care, and give these words to you each time your heartbeats. These are delicate moments that you should share with yourself before you share them with the world. The world will destroy your beliefs, opinions, ideas, thoughts, traditions, ambitions, and desires if you are not solely anchored in Jesus. Who is propping you up? What are you leaning on? Me, myself, and I are leaning on His word. Read Philippians 2 v:13. "For it is God who works in you, both to will and to work for His good pleasure." He has begun a great work in you and me and He knows the work we do will glorify His Name. Sound the alarm! Somebody needs to be told that "Jesus loves you". He loves you and me and his whole wide world. Look at what He gave us. Do you see the birds? Do you hear them singing and chirping? They go nonstop, just like me, do not know when to stop. It gets so good to me, and I only want more of His Divine Devotion, Grace and Mercy, His Unfailing Love, His Unconditional Love. When He walked in, He brought with Him my portion of my daily bread. Just a little bit at a time. He cannot share all the knowledge and wisdom and understanding that He has in reserve for me all at one time.

It must be spread out over a period. I want and I need the Love on tomorrow that He is giving me today. You see why I write. It is a daily occurrence. I wake up in His Presence - ready to go. Boy! Am I pumped!

He is sprinkling all this Love over me, and I want to share it with you. He will give it to you, but you must ask. Oh, Lord! Please love me all day, everyday, around the clock, 24/7, every hour - every minute - every second, and at this present moment in time. In Jesus' Name, I Pray. Amen.

Find yourself a Bible and turn to Isaiah 49 v:15-16 and read where it says.

"I remember you", " I will never forget about you". Read

Jeremiah 29 v:11 where it says "I developed a plan for you, one that will prosper you, not harm you, but a plan that will give you hope and a future. Let us see! Take a deep sigh of relief. You are in school, and we have a full session planned for you today. He remembers you and He remember me. We were each given an assignment to complete while we are here on His solid and sacred ground, we call Earth on His Planet and in His Universe. I found my calling. He anointed my head with oil. He gave me the wisdom, knowledge, and understanding I would need to get the job done.

He will give the same to you. You were created by God to be a barrier to good news. You must tell everyone, someone, that you have discovered the keys to peace, happiness, joy, honesty, truth, justice, salvation, redemption, love, and righteousness. It is through knowing Jesus Christ and reading His Holy Word. He made it so plain. Trust, believe, and have faith. This is what He commanded.

One day you and I will float, coast, glide through these green pastures, the unknown to see what it is out there. There is another world. I have discovered the Passage to Paradise. You must know Jesus. You must be hand in hand. He is holding your hand and you are holding His Hand.

Got it? Once you trust Him with your life, once you give your total self to Thee and let Him remold and reshape you into the person, He had designed you to be before you were the sparkle in mom's and dad's eye, there was a plan made for you. Don't you want to know what it was? Ask Him! He is the One with the secret.

Gotta spend some time with Him and find out what He has for you. Did you know that already - right? If not - you do - this is a requirement. You devote so many hours to your job how many hours do you devote to God? This is who you need to talk to and ask Him for a clean heart and a steadfast spirit.

It is impossible for you to escape what He has planned for you. If you want peace, patience, faith, hope, truth, honesty, justice, salvation, redemption, love, and righteousness, then you are at the right place. You have reached your destination, now you will be crowned based on the contents of your heart not the color of your skin.

Won't that be a great day? Oh, Lord! Look at my heart, examine it closely and see that no evil spirits are residing in it. God wants you to do some housecleaning. Get rid of hate. Get rid of lies. Get rid of deception. Man must decide to come over to the other side of the road. Right now, man is all over the roadway running around like lost sheep. Do you want peace, joy, love, and happiness? Then come to Jesus, just as you are. Men, women, boy or girl, old ones, young ones, tall ones, short ones, big ones, little ones, thin ones, thick ones, gay or straight. This is your chance to get a new beginning. A new life. A new identity. A new birth. You want to change. You must yearn and desire for a change.

Now come and go with me! You are there and I am here, and He is with you and me at the same time. He is listening to every word we say. He is watching over us as we go here, go there, and allow us to safely return to our homes. He has made plans for us for tomorrow because I enjoyed spending time in His Presence today. I am looking forward to tomorrow so that I can enjoy it just like I enjoyed this Wednesday at 5 pm.

Now when I see you the next time, I want to see life in those bones, a heart radiating with glee and cheer. I expect to see a ray of sunshine, a sign of hope, contentment. Be joyous and happy because you know who is smiling at you and watching every step you make and every mumbling word that you utter. He hears it, He is listening. Jeremiah 29 v:12.

Chapter 11

I see sunshine. I see trees swaying and swerving, they appear to frolic and dance, they are so happy. The branches appear to bump into each other. On yesterday, they received their food, and today they are getting more food. The trees are saluting, rejoicing in that He is taking good care of them. He gave them what they needed and now they got to trust Him that He will come back to see about us. Man, woman, boy, child, girl, step up to the plate. It is your time at bat. You got to go all in and give it everything you got. You are fighting for your life? The battle has just begun between you and Satan. Tell God to make Satan leave you alone. You gotta trust Him. Call on the One that watched over your mama and daddy, sisters, and brother. He will supply everything you need. Got any faith, trust, hope, justice, peace, love, and happiness?

Here is a clue! God has got it. Somebody has been holding out on you they are not telling you the truth, I have a Savior, I have a way-maker, I got a stronghold on myself because I committed, submitted, and surrendered my total self over to Him and said O Lord, please reshape me, remold me and make me into the person you had designed for me to be when I was only a thought! You can at least clap your hands and give up your praise, your worship, your salute. I do. I do this every morning when I open my eyes, my spirit wakes up and tells me everything is okay, you can open your eyes now, I know someone who will take good care of you. It is Jesus. God Himself that has come to see about me and you.

It had to be God that woke us up this morning closed in our right mind with a reasonable portion of my health and strength. God's Grace!

He has got plenty and He wants to lavish it all over you but each time He begins, He must stop, because you will not sit still long enough to find out what surprises He will give you today.

Can man worship and rejoice like His trees? He came yesterday to give you your morning mercy and He allowed it to last you all day long. Did you stop and thank Him? I did and He remembered that I remembered to thank The One who made my yesterday possible. He has returned to give me what I need to continue to grow, flourish and produce good fruit. It is in the words that you speak, this is how you can gain your freedom from Satan. Lucifer, the devil, the enemy. Satan is listening and He is whispering in your ear. Can you slow down long enough to hear what God has to say to you on this brand new Thursday morning, April 1st, 2021.

I did and he is telling me to "get ready". You are being prepared to go to the finish line. If I am writing my future everyday then I will continue to say, I know He is watching over me and He is listening to every word I say. I will be careful; I do not want my words to offend Him, so I am careful about the words I release into His atmosphere. I am doubly cautious about what I am putting in my heart.

I see a light. I see the light that He is shining all over His world. The spotlight is on you. He is looking at you carefully and asking himself – what can I do to persuade her to invest all her faith, her belief, and her trust in me. He is always thinking about you and rejoices when you give Him the credit that He is due for raising you from the dead and allowing you to come alive in your senses and choose words that will give your life. It is only God's Grace that I am here today, alive, in person, a real human being telling you she is speaking to a higher power. I made it to the other side. Only through His Grace and Mercy and when I found Him, He had His Unfailing Love, His Unconditional Love, His Grace and Mercy, His Divine Devotion waiting for me.

In other words, listen up! This is going to be good I just know it is. There is life, there is strength, there is joy, there is happiness, there is love, there is righteousness, there is hope and there is a future reserved just for the "two of you". And how do you know? I have been there, I been to the Promised Land, I go there every night I close my eyes and get ready to embrace a brand new day. I am there at this sacred hour - in His Presence. I get excited just like His trees. I admit it quick "The Lord sure is good to me." It is a brand new day, let me get prepared because my adventure will be exciting because Jesus is leading the way, He is your cheerleader. He is right there beside you; He is your double. Do you see Him in your shadow? Pull your head to the ground and look and see if you see Him in your shadow. He is watching over you right at this present, precise moment in time just like He is watching over me.

Hey! Hey! Take your seat, you might be here for a while. You know by now I surprise you. I start writing nonstop. Right? I got so much to tell you, so take a break if you need to, then come back and refresh yourself and follow me on this flow of energy that I am experiencing. Hey! Listen up here - take Home Economics - the basics in cooking - it will come in handy when you are trying to remember this or that in any situation you find yourself in. What is going off in your head? Any light being shined on you?

He is shining His light this morning and it is very bright. What is in your head? What is in that noggin? What have you got up there? Any knowledge? Let us you and I do this comfortably! Are you ready to travel? Say Yes! Knowledge is based on the noise that is up in your head.

Your head is not a hat rack. Something just to hold a hat over. What is under that hat is what matters? Got any morals? Developed any character yet? You know those things that you gather so you can become a man or woman. Whatever you send out from that heart and mouth will come back to the rest of your shoulders. You are preaching your life everyday you open your mouth. Spend a little time in His Presence, allow Him to give you the food, nourishment you will need to continue to grow. He has an assignment for you. Stop! Ask Him? Are you trying to talk to me? Yes! He replies. Take your time because I always have time for you. I will listen, what is it? I cannot believe you want to talk to me. Oh! Yes, I have wanted to talk to you a long time ago, but you were too busy and said one day she will come to her senses and begin to think and ponder thought as to why did you give me a mother named Bettie Jean Grose? Teacher, Lecturer, Queen, Mother, Nana, Sister, Auntie, Cousin, and Friend. I answer to all those names. I wear my hats proudly.

Look at Mom! See what Mom does in her spare time. She spends it with her Personal, Private and Intimate Lord and Savior Jesus Christ.

He is always available, and she loves talking to Him and He loves listening to the words that are meditating in her heart.

Honor Him, Salute Him, Worship Him, Praise Him. Rock with me?

You are right there with me being a cheerleader, right? Urging me on - right? I know I could count on you because we are counting on a Savior, right? Right On Sista, tell me more. You must start early in the morning, the first time He wakes you. Praising His Name. Calling on Him. Worshipping Him. Before the

sun rises while you have some quiet time. Say these mumbling words "Thank You Jesus" and watch the songbird begin to fly.

Keep those words sealed to your lips and tattooed across your heart and tell them every chance you get. I expect you will have a chance to say them once you realize who is responsible for all these gifts.

Oh, Lord! Thank You for a great morning. It is sunshiny and cold, and I am getting ready to go to the barbershop. When I opened my eyes, guess what I did? I saturated His atmosphere with words of praise and worship. Then His Holy Spirit allowed me to glide into my happy space and do what I needed to do. Jesus was still watching over me. He is here, there, everywhere right at this present and precise nanosecond.

Nonstop. Morning, noon, evening, night, 24/7, around the clock - every hour - every minute - every second and right at this present moment in time. Oh! He is here with me, no doubt about it. Is He with you also? Then let us rock and roll.

Let me tell you about my morning, it is interesting, you will learn a lot. You see the Same God, Same Jesus, Same Holy Spirit that is watching over me at this present time is the Same God,

Same Jesus, Same Holy Spirit that is watching over you. Light bulb? Told you He was here, there, and everywhere. Right now, He is watching over those sons and daughters, and He has tears in His eyes. You are such a disappointment. How have my sheep been so mistaken and mislead? They are blinded. They cannot see the light. It is in His Holy word. Read the Book of John.

Wake up! Come alive in your senses and begin to think. Who and What made it possible for you to see another day? Who breathed His breath of life into your corpse and made you come alive again on this Thursday, April 1st? Did he favor you to return in human form and start your day all over again? Did you think to say a word to the One who watched over you while you slumbered and slept? Did you say a mumbling word to the One who was standing at your bedside ready to catch your hand and lead you on the adventure that He had planned for you on today, "April Fool's Day"? Words are so important. I will explain later.

Stop sleeping in your grave. You have been given a marvelous, glorious, outstanding, and perfect day. Don't you have everything you need?

I do! I am so happy! I am downright elated that He surprised me with another day. I could have come back as a bird or a flower. You chose to touch me with your finger of Love and tell me "Wake up O sleepyhead, rise from the dead and let the Lord shine on you!! He is shining a light in my direction. I see its glow.

I can back it up. I saw it in the Bible. When I read His Psalm 23, a light bulb went off in my head. It says "Yea though you may walk through the valley of the shadow of death, fear no evil, for Thy Art with me. Okay! Now that means He sees me here at this computer pecking away at this keyboard and sharing with you the highlights of the text that we have covered. He is giving me my daily share of His daily bread. He wants you to begin to eat also.

Bump The Funk! Its time has come and gone. My sheep will not look like beasts, sheep, and monsters. My sheep know what they are – they are either a man or woman who stands firm on His belief that God is on The Throne and Jesus is His Right Hand Man. Cannot get to the Father unless you go through Jesus. Jesus must recommend that you become a member of God's Household. I have my papers. I have all the credentials I will need. I have a clean heart and a steadfast spirit, and He keeps opening highways, byways for me to travel. Look like I have a long road ahead of me, but I know who will be there cheering me on.

I am one of the sheep in His Pasture who is trying to do His will.

I am listening so I can learn how to come in closer inside the gate. If I remain in Him, then He will remain in me. If I abide in Him, then He will abide in me. If I draw nearer to Him, then He will draw nearer to me.

Shish! The class is in session. Did you see me tell you that this will be a continuous cycle for me? I will praise Him everyday of my life because He is worthy to be praised. He lifted the veil from my eyes. I can see now. My life changed because I demanded it from myself with God's help. I had a conversation with Him. I am in His Presence, and He wants me to tell you how I was rewarded for getting all my tasks done yesterday and today.

His Holy Spirit had me reclining and I was thanking Him for everything He allowed me to do. Just dreaming. It felt so good to be cradled in His Everlasting Arms. In them, I know I am safe and secure. As one of His horns was blowing, His Holy Spirit reminded me I would be hungry in about an hour. So, I began to ponder, what will I eat? His Holy Spirit glided me into the kitchen, my happy space, and I began to cook a full breakfast. Beef Sausage that came from one of His farm animals. Thank You, Lord, for your cow. It gave me meat, butter, cream, and cheese. You knew I would need these ingredients to prepare my breakfast foods.

Scrambled eggs and cheese. Again, from His farm animal, His chicken.

His chicken gave me the eggs and the chicken gave me meat. Steamy hot buttered grits that came from your wheat farm. Isn't He amazing?

He knew my needs before I did. He went ahead of me and prepared me to have on hand everything I would need to make a rewarding and satisfying breakfast. Oh! It was oh so good! Wish I could have shared it. Maybe you will reward yourself and your loved ones with a surprise like I received.

I cannot hide the fact that I love Him. He is so good to me. I have placed Jesus First. Put God in front of you. Ask Him to bestow His Grace and Mercy on you from the crown of your head to the sole of your feet. When I made Jesus the Head of My Life, everything changed, and I know this was the best decision I could have ever made. I will rejoice.

In the beginning, was the Word and the Word was with God. Let us treat Word as a person. The word was with God, and He supplied God with words. Word kept talking to God. Just Word is speaking to me and you right at this present and the precise moment in time. Your fate and knowledge are determined by what words you are putting in your head and allowing them to manifest into reality in your heart. What is that noise in your head? Do you know it is His Grace and Mercy that is keeping you alive? He is keeping me alive for a reason and I am excited. I am thrilled to know that I have a purpose. Confidence, yeah!

Do you know how to talk to Him? He is empowering me with His Amazing Grace. He can do the same for you. Oh! I am going after the ones that I can reach and tell them "Man, woman, boy or girl, there is

another life you can live. You can change the outcome of the race. Each day you start at the beginning, you can come out as a winner. You have not been taught about this thing called "life". No one has ever told you these words and they are "I Love You". These sheep have no one to care for, give or share their lives with. They do not know what the meaning of love is. Never seen it, never had it, never read it, never said it, and never experienced it. Any empathy?

Cannot we find a way to reach the masses and tell them, I love you, but I know who loves you the most? It is Jesus, Our Lord, and Savior. You see in the beginning we were created with Words. Words came to live inside of us. You stopped listening to yourself. You stopped listening to what Grandma and Grandpa had to say. It was their belief and faith that allowed them to wake up each day to chop a patch of cotton. A better day is coming. It will not be like this always. One day this thing is going to turn around.

The time has come for you to take notes. I cannot do this on my own. I need help. Once you realize you need help and ask for help, He will tell you, I have been right here near you all the days of your life and I will continue to watch over you all day, everyday,

24/7, around the clock - every hour - every minute - every second and at this precise and present moment in time if you give Me praise.

Let me remind you that I am your constant companion, your shadow, sidekick, cheerleader, your best buddy, God said. Someone needs to give you the definition of a way maker, a burden barrier, a healer, a promise keeper, a strong tower, strength, and joy. His Name is Jesus, and you can cast all your cares upon Him because He cares for you.

1st Peter 5 v:7.

My granddaughter, Tisse, sent me the words to the morning mantra that she is teaching her son. She is telling Him that He is "amazing" and having him get louder and louder each time he says it. He repeats this three times. Is this the making of a genius, exceptional intellectual, just plain smart? You have seen those kids! You want to meet your parents.

Tisse sees a light. It is shining bright in her direction. If she continues to fertilize her mind, her knowledge, wisdom, and understanding will increase.

Everyday is a learning day. It is always exciting and that is the reason I honor, cherish, worship, and praise Him when I open my eyes. I had finished up in the bathroom, I rushed back to claim my spot. I was resting comfortably, all nestled in, into a bed of warmth and softness. When I got settled in, I pulled the covers up close and tight and asked O Lord please come into my presence and O Lord please allow me into Your Presence and He did just that. I was so happy that I had no aches and pains, Thank You Lord, and He opened a space just for me to hide. He was waiting on my return. This is where I wanted to be. Safe from all hurt harm or danger and wait on Him to supply all my needs. I began talking! I had a smile on my face, and I got busy saying my affirmations. O Lord please shelter us, O Lord please shadow us, O Lord please favor us, O Lord please cover us with Your Blood, O Lord please grant us Your Grace and Mercy, O Lord please strengthen us physically, mentally, emotionally, psychologically, morally, and spiritually, O Lord please forgive us of our sins because we don't always do things perfectly and correctly, O Lord please forgive our enemies because they know not what they do, O Lord please protect us from all plagues, pandemics, disasters, and turmoil, O Lord please prosper us physically, materialistically, financially and spiritually, O Lord please do not cast us away from Your Presence and O Lord please allow Your Holy Spirit to dwell in us again on this day. In Jesus' Name, I Pray - Amen.

I had a smile on my face as I confessing what was meditating in my heart. It meditates there day and night. These words have saved my life. These words saved me. These words gave my life a new meaning. What about that! I saw myself under God's eyes. I was looking at myself through the eyes of God and He saw me as a Shining Star, A Sparkle in His Eyes, a Tulip, a Tree, or a Red Bird. He was excited to see me under His light.

When He saw me, He saw a ray of sunshine. I was happy, joyous, content, peaceful, and happy with where He has placed me. Boy! Am I grateful that He granted me His Grace and Mercy. I could not continue in the role that I am playing unless He holds my hand and guides my tongue and my footsteps. I know where my health and strength come from. Amen!

Done deal. It is sealed. We all recognize who we must humble ourselves before. We know who we must bow our heads unto. We know who woke us up this morning. We know who gave us sight to see, ears to hear, mouth to talk, a mind to think, a brain to coordinate thought, and allowed us to embrace right over wrong.

I am from the old school. I was yelled at for not listening. I was taught well how to listen. Put everything aside. The phone, the tv, the noise and concentrate on what you are getting ready to do and that is to "think and process thought". Stop the wiggling! Control yourself. Clear your mind and brain of any fog and travel with me.

There is a better way of living. You are merely existing. Eating, breathing, and sleeping. Don't you want to come alive in your senses and begin to live the life that you would adore and enjoy in the Presence of a King? He is all around me this morning, pumping me up because I have seen the light and I want to share it with you. There is that word again.

L. O. V. E. Love. Yes! It is a subject that comes up each time I begin to write. We must love each other, brothers and sisters in the North, East, South, and West. We must rid our hearts of evil spirits and the number one spirit to remove is Hate. It is the devil!

Next time you are strolling, got some idle time, sit back, relax, and recline and ask yourself do I have hate in my heart? Then sit back and begin to ponder this question over and over and the first person you will decide that you hate is yourself. I hate myself - is that what you are telling me? Yes! Afraid so! Do you love yourself? Are you what God intended for you to become? Is He pleased with the words that are meditating in your heart? Is He pleased with the words that He is allowed to hear that is being released from your mouth?

Are you amazed at what you just read? It is true. We do not show compassion, empathy, kindness, tenderness, gentleness, softness to ourselves then how can we show it to others? Cannot be done. Before you love someone else you must first love yourself. Facts or Fiction. I must set an example because I want Him to watch over me, my family, my loved ones, and my friends. What a beautiful sunshiny Spring-like day!

I am magnificent, marvelous, fabulous, fantastic, splendid, superb, outstanding, spectacular, and wonderful because He did it again. He favored me with a new beginning, a new mind, a new birth, a new identity, and I have been born again. I love me. I love everything about me. I love my hair, my face, my

nose, my eyes, my mouth, my teeth, my chin, my neck, my body, my soul, and my spirit. I love everything about me. He does. Courage. He tells me "It is a slam dunk - you know what I think about you."

Take a sip of water, sit back, relax, and let what you just read saturate in those bones, brains, mind, heart, body, soul, and spirit. Whatever you tell yourself - this is what you can become. Words made the world and words can make a man. I need some hope and happiness. I need to know that He is with me as I sip my chilled spring water that He allowed to escape from His mountains, rocks, rivers, brooks, valleys, and streams into a bottle just the right size for my hands to hold. He is dynamite!

You cannot beat Him. You cannot top that. Let me hear how you pay honor to Him for showering you with everything you need materialistically to complete your new day. All these gifts, where did they come from?

Bottled water, cranberry juice, chilled pineapple, who provided the funds I would need to purchase these items from the store and position them on the shelves in the pantry so I would have access to them at my convenience?

The Word that was, in the beginning, became flesh and it decided to live within us. His word should live in your heart. Nothing else. The words that live in your heart, mind, brain, body, soul, and spirit must come alive. Digest the word that you are saying. Define it so you will understand what you are trying to comprehend. Whatever you tell yourself this is what you will become. The sheep in His Pasture stopped dreaming, they stopped showing appreciation for what He is giving to them. He has given them life and it is up to them to define what life means to them. I, myself, and I wanted to become alive in my new self. I yearned for a change. It was granted to me once I began using His words correctly. I began to use words that would change my whole lifestyle and upbringing. I know I am not alone because He told.

Joshua 1 v:9, "I will go with you everywhere you go" so that means.

He is right beside me. How awesome is that?

Just who do I think is giving me my daily bread! I know it is Jesus, sitting and whispering words into my vocabulary for me to use now and today and tomorrow.

Jesus taught us to "love". We must give it up. Hate. You must divorce yourself from hate. You had to come to face reality. Hate has been holding you back from reaching your full potential because you have not stopped and realized that Jesus Our God Himself is nothing but love and He wants to dwell in our hearts so He can have a dwelling place.

He wants your heart to return to Him as He gave it to you.

A heart made from gold.

Chapter 12

I could not do it without Him. I could not make a sentence without His help. He adores me. He admires me. It is church time. Never say never! You can do all things through Christ who strengthens me. This is tattooed across my heart. If you Love My God! My Lord! My Jesus! My Lord and Savior! Like I do, you can identify with me saying never say never. Say never will I let the devil, Satan, the enemy, Lucifer take my mind, heart, brain, body, soul, and spirit. My spirit is alive because Jesus decided to raise me from the dead early in the wee hours of the morning. I saw the moon. Early, right? He knew I needed to wake up early so His Holy Spirit tugged at me and after Jesus whispered in my ear "wake up O sleepyhead" rise from the dead and let the Lord shine on you, I turned over and went into my happy space to do what I needed to do. This is the way I salute a King. "Thank You Jesus" are the words to my song. I sing it in and on the way out. Isn't He wonderful? He allowed me to flush my kidneys. "Thank You, Lord, they are working fine. He did it. He is the One that led me to the right doctors and resources to listen to so I would not have renal failure.

I need Jesus all day, everyday, 247, around the clock - every hour - every minute - every second and right at this present moment in time. I just finished my hour-long waterfall. It was nice. You know how I describe my waterfalls. If not then get ready to hear one of His sheep honor Him for allowing her to stand on her own two legs, long enough to scrub each nook and cranny. When I lather up, I tell myself, "You are lathering up in His Grace and Mercy" and the soapy cloth glides all over my body. After I dry my body off, I put on lotion. I call my lotion "Divine Devotion". It goes on so smoothly and it feels so good being applied to my clean body. Isn't He wonderful? Isn't He awesome? He is the One who is guiding this sheep on this Good Friday. Friday before the Resurrection.

On this Friday, Jesus was drugged to an old, rugged cross, he hung there, bled, and died for we could be set free on our sins. He died for my sins and your sins. He rose again on the third day, and He is saying to you this morning, "Come alive – let me raise you from the dead". You are alive but dead. Your mind has not been renewed. You are dreaming through the eyes of Satan. He has blinded you. Jesus says, "I am the way, the truth, and the light". I will use my Resurrection Power to raise you from the dead, but you must want me to. Jesus cannot do anything unless we permit Him. You must put forth the effort to knock, seek so you shall find. Unless we ask Jesus for His Love and Blessings we are doomed. God said, "I have given you a Savior". Yes! He went to the cross, but I saved Him before any nail was driven into His body. I had yanked His Spirit out of His body so He could be with Me. God says "I want to save you – you must be willing to change – you must yearn to come alive in your senses so you can be loved while you think, and process thought. You can have a new beginning. It is written.

You can trust in God. You can depend on Jesus. I do. He has never failed me, and I know I am loved, wanted, needed, accepted, appreciated, adored, admired, and idolized by a Savior. I want you to receive the same kind of attention that I am getting on this Good Friday, April 2nd, 2021, here at Gene Miller Manor in Christian City,

Union City, Georgia, south of the airport. I see planes going east and I pray and ask "O Lord please watch over those people and the plane and let them get safely to their destination. Yes! I pray for all of us, and it is time for you to change up the words that you release from that mouth. You are only reciting the words that are in your heart. A man will speak his mind. What is in that brain and mind and heart of yours?

This morning finds me excited to embrace the adventure My Lord has planned for me. If you love Jesus now is the time for you to tell someone just how good, He is to you. I am not ashamed to open the jar and let words of praise and admiration come out and saturate His atmosphere with words of praise and worship. This satisfies Him. Oh! He is alive. Know how I know? Because He watches over me, and He listens to every word I say. I cannot stop praising Him every chance I get. He opens doors for me to walk through. I had to pack my suitcase, shower, and prepare to spend the week with my daughter. Jesus had told me that "I will be with you". Psalm 23 "For Thy art with me".

I will go with you wherever you go. He told Joshua the same words at Joshua 1 v:9.

I know that He loves me, He just finished admiring my smile and my joy and peace as I was able to waltz from one happy space to another happy space completing each task. I know that He cares for me. He cares if I am happy, contented, tranquil, and satisfied. He wants me to have Perfect Peace and joy. I can only do that if I accept the fact that He has His trees, weeds, bushes, flowers, insects, bugs, and everything He created in His Shadow. He cares for me, and He cares for you. It is written that His Love Endures Forever. Do not you hear the birds singing and chirping.

They are doing what you should be doing - praising Him for one more day of sunshine on this glorious and gorgeous day in April. Easter weekend. It is beautiful, isn't it? Everything is so calm, not much wind blowing, just soaking in His rays of sunshine.

Thank You, Lord, for giving Your creation what they need. Peace and patience are what I am getting. I am listening to His angel's praise and worship His Name through song. His Love is Everlasting, and His Love is all you need. When I opened my eyes, I said, "Thank You Jesus" and then He took full control. Good morning sunshine. I placed a smile on my face as my heart was filled with joy knowing that He had returned to see about me and plans to take good care of me just like He did on Thursday, yesterday.

Again, I got a chance to wake up in His Presence. He touched me with His finger of Love and blew His breath of life into my lifeless body allowing me to wake up in His Presence. He was there at my bedside with His hand stretched out to me. I grabbed it. I was content and thankful that He had come to see about me. He favored me with a brand new day and a brand new mind. I went to praising, honoring, saluting, and glorifying Him for being so good to me by saying "Thank You, Jesus". He made the decision that I could come alive in my senses so I could think, and process thought. Quickly, I realized that it is Jesus who watched over me while I slumbered and slept and my first words were "O Lord, I Love Thee", Thank You! Thank You! For everything.

When He heard me give Him praise, He immediately paid attention to what I had to say. O Lord please come into my presence and O Lord please allow me into Your Presence. He never failed me. I was so confident that He heard my prayer and was going to answer my prayer, I continued to lift His Name. I was sincere and honest when I was speaking to Him. O Lord please shelter us, O Lord please shadow us, O Lord please favor us, O Lord please cover us with Your Blood, O Lord please grant us Your Grace and Mercy, O Lord please strengthen us physically, mentally, emotionally, psychologically, and spiritually, O Lord please forgive us of our sins because we don't always do things perfectly or correctly, O Lord please forgive our enemies because they know not what they do, O Lord please prosper us physically, materialistically, financially and spiritually, O Lord please protect us from all plagues, pandemics, disasters, and turmoil, O Lord please do not cast us away from Your Presence and O Lord please allow Your Holy Spirit to dwell in us again on today. In Jesus' Name, I Pray - Amen.

What He is doing for me should be spread among the living sheep that are in His Pasture. There is another life for you to live in the Presence of a King. How do you know? Jesus gave me a new mind, new beginning, new birth, new identity, and He allowed me to be born again. He rose from the grave so that I may have

life and have an abundant life. I am rejoicing on this morning because I know He loves me. He continues to shower me with the blessings that He has in reserve for me.

Sit down, relax, take a sigh of relief, you have work to do. Help me praise Him, honor Him, salute Him, glorify Him, and magnify Him. Isn't He wonderful? Isn't He amazing? Isn't He great? Isn't He mighty? He is to me. He turned my head and pointed it straight in front of me and told me I will show you the path that you need to be on. Follow me and I will give you peace. Follow me and I will give you rest. Jesus rescued me from the enemy. Jesus reinvented me. I am a new creature in Christ. I am a spiritual being having a human experience.

I gave my life to Jesus. How did I do that? I committed, I submitted, I surrendered my life over to Him so His will could be done. I ask O Lord please reshape me, remold me and make me into the person You had designed me to be before I was in my mother's womb. This was my prayer and instantaneously He appeared asking me "you want me to walk with you", I said "Yes! I do and He took me by the hand and said, "come and go with me". How was I to know that this was a new beginning for me? I quickly learned that I had been saved from the corrupt and wicked world ruled by Satan.

Satan has you blinded. Jesus opened my eyes, and I could see the light that He was shining in my direction. I was so amazed when I learned that if I believe, trust, and have faith that He will protect me from all hurt, harm, or danger, will provide all my needs, and let His Holy Spirit become my guide. You are looking at the world through Satan's eyes. He is guiding your eyes away from the reality that God wants you to see. Let us try with the basics, something as simple as a bird chirping. Do you listen and enjoy the chirping and singing? I do because I look at the birds praising God, Our Creator, for giving them life. This is the same praise I have for Him. I say, "Thank You Jesus" at a moment's notice. I then go into praise. O Lord "Thank You" for my ears - my hearing - I can hear Your birds singing praises to Your name. They are delighted that You came to see about them by letting the leaves on the trees collect droplets of water for them to drink. He looks out for His birds, and I believe He will look out for me. He is supplying them with what they need and every day I open my eyes,

He gives me my daily bread. If His eye is on the sparrow then I know He has His eye on me.

I know who is my beginning. I know who is my end. Hallelujah anyhow! He is worthy to be praised and honored by one of His sheep that He rose from the dead. My life changed. My viewpoint changed. My ideas, thoughts, beliefs, opinions, traditions, and desires changed. I welcomed the change. I was tired, weary worn, and worried but guess what He did. He snatched me out of the condition and circumstance I was in and placed my feet on solid ground and told me I am Your Rock, and I am Your Redeemer. My heart was pounding as I was in disbelief. I did not know anyone loved me. I had not heard these words before. He made a complete sentence, so I knew it was a fact. I knew it was true when He said to me "I will always love you". At first, I did not hear Him, so He said it again. this time He rephrased it and said, "I will love you always". My heart was sealed. The deal had been made. I knew I had become a member of God's household and I had been given the assignment to complete. Tell someone about your fortune.

You cannot shut me up! I have something to say. The words that you allow to be released from your mouth are words being sent up like an umbrella. These words will come back to rest on your shoulders. Make yourself a pool of love, happiness, and joy and dive into it and let it cover you from the crown of your head to the sole of your feet. This is where I am. I am indebted to Him. He saved my life. I am saved, redeemed, and filled with His Holy Spirit and I will tell the world, my brothers and sisters in the North, East, South, and West that no one has ever loved me the way Jesus has.

As I was getting ready to go into my happy space, He draped a curtain of His Unfailing Love, His Unconditional Love, His Grace and Mercy, and His Divine Devotion all over me. I am free this morning to enjoy a wonderful, magnificent, marvelous, spectacular day. He loves me and I accept that I am one of His sheep in His Pasture who will carry the torch. I will carry the flame. I will yell it "Jesus saves". What do I mean? He gave me the opportunity to be born again. Take off those old clothes and put on your new clothes. I shed them in a flash because I wanted what He had to offer me. He offered me a new beginning. He offered me the opportunity to come alive in my senses so I could think, and process thought. There is no one like Him. He is Holy and we should worship Him at His feet. He is a beautiful Savior. When I pulled out my chair to sit and record the words that were meditating in my heart, He pulled a chair right beside me and assured me that He would help me say what I was trying to say.

He is alive. I am in His Presence. There is nobody like Jesus. He comes every morning to satisfy you with His morning mercy and love and tells you to let it last you throughout your day. Psalm 90 v:14. Are you listening? I am giving you a detailed account of the relationship that I have developed with My Savior, Our Lord, and Savior, Jesus Christ. You know Him, He is the Lord of Lords and the King of Kings. I know why He loves me so! I do not take my thoughts or eyes off Him. I am always searching for new thoughts because I made Jesus The Head of My Life. I put Jesus first. He is the One that I am trying to please and I know I cannot please Him with an unclean heart. That is why I cleaned my heart out and asked Him to fill it with His Love and His steadfast spirit. I ask Him to allow His Presence to remain in me because I sure will remain in Him. He supplies all my needs. It is something grand? To know that you are loved – is priceless. Once you begin receiving His Extraordinary Love, you will come back for more. You will keep returning to that place where you found comfort, joy, and peace. In His Presence is where you can find it and it is available all day, everyday, 24/7, around the clock – every hour – every minute – every second and right at this present moment in time. Ask Him.

It worked for me. He is propping me up this morning. I am pumped. I know who gave me the green light. I know who told me to press on. I know who told me to keep coming. Keep writing. Keep shouting it. Keep telling your story. Keep telling the world how good He is to me. This is what I was told, and I will continue to share with you what is meditating in my heart.

I am getting it from the source. This is firsthand knowledge. Talk to me and I will tell you that you are writing your life story everyday that you live. You are writing the next chapter in your life. You are responsible for how it unfolds. Control your emotions, ideas, thoughts, beliefs, opinions, traditions, hopes, and dreams. Wow! There is another life that you can live. It has been well hidden from you but now is your chance to experience it for yourself. Carve out some alone time and spend it in His Presence. This is the best feeling. Allow Him to cradle you in His Everlasting Arms so you will be safe and secure. He wants to. He is circling above you just waiting for you to ask for His help.

Speak! O, Lord! Show me the way that you want me to go. I will say what you tell me to say. I will do what you tell me to do. I will open up my Bible and read Your Holy Word and I will tattoo Your Word across my chest. Once you open your heart, mind, brain, body, soul, and spirit to Him, He will take you on a vacation.

Your mind will be free of all worries. You will be made over again. You will become brand new because you have opened your heart, brain, mind, body, soul, and spirit to new possibilities. New thoughts! New ideas! Amaze yourself? Just do it! Believe, trust, and have faith that you have made the right decision and ask Him to take you by your hand and lead you to that Promised Land. Oh! I am there. I am comfortably seated in His Presence, and I will continue to listen. This is the only way He can talk to you. Lay everything aside and come to Him just as you are. He is so accepting. You will never be rejected. He has tons and tons of Love that He wants to give you. Ask Him if this is true? Wait for His answer! You will not be disappointed you will have a heart, mind, brain, body, soul, and spirit in Perfect Peace and Harmony.

On my computer screen, I have scenes of nature flashing across it. I just finished being at one of His lakes and I saw mountains of ice formed in the water. The ice was melting, and the water had made a pathway for it to flow. Isn't God amazing? He is so amazing. He has so much He wants us to see. He made this world. He made it for me and you. Can you see the beauty in His snow-covered mountain peaks? I see serenity.

I see peace, harmony, tranquility, contentment, joy, and happiness.

I am off to enjoy dining on rotisserie chicken and chilled watermelon bites. Thank You for allowing me to enter your space. If you were the only person in the world, who would you want to hold your hand?

I know who I would want to hold my hand. It would be Our Lord and Savior Jesus Christ. This is who is guiding my thoughts and my pathway. I lift His Name on High. Earlier during the morning when I had the cup of my delicious brew, my coffee, I said while I was ladling it back and forth to cool to my desired temperature, "O Lord" if I remain in You then You will remain in me, then I continued and said.

"O Lord if you abide in me then I will abide in You, I finished up with,

O Lord if I draw nearer to Thee then You will draw nearer to me.

Brown eyes, hazel eyes, black eyes, blue eyes, and green eyes. What is your color? You know these eyes were given to us by God. He positioned them where they need to be so you could look forward and never lose sight of what you see. Do you see unanswered prayers and dreams? Well! Today is the day to shed those overcoats of doubt, fear, and disbelief. Your thoughts torment you. Enter His Presence with Praise and Thanksgiving and ask Him to supply you with the thoughts you will need. Turn it over to Him. Give yourself away freely to Him.

Let go of the reigns you have over your life and surrender your total self to Him so His will can be done.

Let us celebrate the arrival of Our King. Let us celebrate that He used His Resurrection Power to raise us from the dead. This is what He did for me. I am truly blessed and highly favored on a Friday morning that I have never seen before. Join me as I honor the One who woke me up this morning. God raised Jesus from the dead and told Him, now save the world. He is standing at your door knocking, open it up wide and let Him in and let Him have His way. He is coming bringing you His Love and Devotion.

I will keep my dream alive. I am being cradled in His Everlasting Arms where I am safe and secure. He has risen. In my life, I know He is the King.

Chapter 13

It is church time. Are you ready? Are you relaxed? Are you excited about what you are about to hear? Close the door - shut out the noise. Zone out. Turn the tv off, the phone off, and enjoy some easy listening music as you absorb the words that are meditating in my heart. Are you glad to be alive? Yes! You are! Think about it. Do not just zoom past these words. Ponder your thoughts! This is what you will need to do to come alive in your thought pattern. We are going to use your sixth sense. To think! It is not impossible to think. You choose the time and place that you want to travel with me. It may be early in the morning, midday or late in the afternoon, or maybe at night. You have a choice of when to read and meditate. Isn't that wonderful to know that you choose to be in His Presence? Slow up and allow Him to overtake you.

Feel His Presence. Feel Him as He touches your mind, your brain, your heart, your body, your soul, and your spirit. You deserve a "get-a-way". Come and go with me. Let me tell you how He has changed my life. Let me tell you just what He is doing for me.

Let me begin by telling you the words that I said while I was ladling my coffee back and forth to cool. If I remain in Him, then He will remain in me. If I abide in Him, then He will abide in me. If I draw nearer to Him, then He will draw nearer to me. These are important words to remember. When you repeat these words know what you are saying. Listen! When I say "If I remain in Him" then He will remain in me. I must remember that every day, all day, 24/7, around the clock - every hour - every minute - every second and right at this present and the precise moment in time that I am in His Presence, and I am asking for His Unconditional Love, His Unchanging Love, His Faithfulness. His Grace and Mercy and His Divine Devotion to be given to me. Memory. Memories. I remember yesterday! I remember the Love and tender devotion that I received.

Ask Him to give you the same! Do not rush! Take your time. That is all you have is time. You have time to do this and time to do that. Right now, open up the door and let His sunshine in.

Join me as I change lanes depending on the circumstances that are following me. I am at a windmill. His breezes are flowing in through the windows and His birds are singing away. My mind, brain, body, soul, and spirit all come under His authority. I do not belong to myself any longer. I belong to Our God, Our Lord, Our Savior Jesus Christ. This is who is ruling my mind, thoughts, ideas, opinions, beliefs, traditions, dreams and desires. I surrendered. I committed. I submitted my total self over to Him so His will could be done. He has captured my soul and has given me His Spirit. I am a new creature in Christ. I am a spiritual being housed in a human body. I do not belong here. I cannot live in a world of deceit, lies, and hate. I had to gravitate to a higher level of consciousness and ask myself "how are we going to save the children"? Will, we let them self-destruct and become extinct?

It is not impossible for us to teach our kids that they must have self-control. These kids need to know that they have free will and they are the ones who decide what to do. Our kids need to be taught to listen. Our kids are choosing the wrong path. What will they become? Liars, murderers, thieves, and misfits. Is this what we see in the next generation. Satan, Lucifer, the enemy, the devil has taken over the hearts and minds of these young children and some adults. They have no idea of how to show gratitude because they have not been taught to appreciate what they see, feel, hear, smell, touch and taste. You have five senses and they have been dulled until you feel numb. Throw up your hands and ask Him what must I do? How can I repay you for the Love that you are showering all over me, my loved ones, my family, and my friends?

Moms and dads. Take notes. We must sit these children down and tell them about the God that we serve. Make them take a "time out". That Same God that guided your mother and father, your grandmother and grandfather, your aunts and uncles, cousins and friends is the same God that is watching over you at this present moment in time. Our God, Our Lord, Our Jesus, is kind, compassionate, considerate, and tolerant of us because we are a child of a King, we are one of God's children and we are sheep in His Pasture. Psalm 100. We must begin to act like it.

Long ago I was bouncing off the air. I was listening to Satan's whispers. This came to a complete halt. I had to stop listening because He was leading me in the direction I did not want to go in, and I cried out "O Lord please save me". He heard my cry. He answered my call for "help." He made me change lanes. I was on the wrong highway, so He redirected my path, hopes, dreams, and my future. He gave me new hope. He gave me a new mind. He gave me a new beginning. I was yanked up out of that coffin and told to "come alive and live". Do you want to live in hell or Heaven? I chose Peace. He had extended His Right Hand of Righteousness to me, and I grabbed it.

So now I am the dancing, prancing, and floating Queen. I floated right out of bed early in the wee hours of dawn and went into my happy space and did what I needed to do. Hallelujah! Praise His Name. He allowed me to flush my kidneys numerous times. Each time I began singing my song "Thank You Jesus" on the way in and on the way out. I nestled back under the covers, pulling them close to my neck and saying O Lord please come into my presence and O Lord please allow me into Your Presence. Before I drift back to La La Land I continue talking because I know He is listening to the words that are meditating in my heart.

I begin my conversation with Him by asking O Lord please shelter us, O Lord please shadow us, O Lord please favor us, O Lord please cover us with Your Blood, O Lord please grant us Your Grace and Mercy and, O Lord please strengthen us physically, mentally, emotionally, morally and spiritually, O Lord please forgive our sins because we may not always do things perfectly and correctly, O Lord please forgive our enemies because they know not what they do, O Lord please protect us from all plagues, pandemics, disasters, and turmoil, O Lord please prosper us physically,, materialistically, financially and spiritually, O Lord please do not cast us away from Your Presence and O Lord pleases allow Your Holy Spirit to dwell in us again on this day. In Jesus' Name, I Pray - Amen.

Dignity, love, trust, kindness, happiness, joy, and self-respect must be taught to the ones that surround us. We must love each other. We cannot escape it. If we want Jesus' Love, His Admiration we must open our hearts so they can be cleansed of the evil spirits of hate, lies, and deceit. Do not deceive yourself into believing that you love all your brothers and sisters in the North, East, South, and West when you have not begun to love yourself.

What a lovely day. It is great to be alive in my senses and know I can choose to celebrate it just the way it fits me. I choose what kind of day I am having. I ask early that He come to see about me, and I ask early that when He comes to please take really good care of me. It is the Springtime of the year. Monday, April 12th, 2021, at this sacred hour of 1 o'clock and I am being loved, admired, appreciated, wanted, accepted, adored, idolized, and loved by a King. Who does this you may ask? Jesus does! Jesus loves everything about me because He crafted me in His image. He knows what He created. He has equipped me with the tools I need to get a job done. I have had a lot of assignments in my lifetime but none as important as the one I have been given by my Lord and Savior Jesus Christ. Be attentive and become a good listener. He "says" I am home. I am all alone in His Presence. I am relaxed because I know He is cradling me in His Everlasting Arms that are as wide as His big blue spacious skies. I am wedged in. There is room for you to come on in. I will save a spot just for you. There is no other love like it. This love will save your soul. He is My Rock and My Redeemer, and it is so good to be in His Presence because I know He is taking good care of me.

Do you have a "Happy Heart? Is it filled with joy, love and admiration and happiness for everything? Mine is! I am joyful because when He touched me with His finger of Love and whispered in my ear "wake up O sleepyhead" rise from the dead and let the Lord shine on you, I did just what He said. I welcomed Him to blow His breath of life into my lifeless body allowing me to become a living soul all over again just like yesterday. Oh! My Yesterday!

It is a joy and privilege to be alive on this magnificent and marvelous Monday morning in His Presence. He decided for me to come alive in my senses so I could look around and begin to "think and "process thought". He is the One making all this possible. He favored me and He favored you with one more day. A day that we have never seen before and now that we have a brand new day – what are we going to do about it? I know, let us build a "wonderland".

It is a day that I can come alive, come out of that coffin, and begin to live my life to the fullness in the Presence of a King. It is wonderful, where I am, I am leaning back in my chair, and I see stalks of cane mounted on the side of a rock bed. Must be nice to lounge in the place where His rocks are stored and enjoying His rays of sunshine penetrating my heart, my mind, my brain, my body, my soul, and my spirit. I know who loves me. I know who adores me. I know who admires me. I know who cherishes me. I know who idolizes me. The One who gave His life to save me from a world of corruption, wickedness, confusion, and sorrow.

In His Name! In His Name! Ask anything you want In Jesus' Name! What do you want? Do you want peace, harmony, contentment, serenity, justice, equality, patience, salvation, redemption, love, and righteousness? I can give you a great source and He will supply all your needs. His Name is Jesu Christ, Our Lord, and Savior. It is all in His Hands! He is highly recommended. This is where my source of strength and health comes from. He lifted me. He lifted me higher than my current circumstances, conditions and situations and allowed me to escape into a world of love, peace, harmony. Oh! Yeah! I am satisfied. We are alone and we can share. He tells me and I write.

There is another world that you can live in. It is filled with corridor after corridor of beautiful flowers, plants, animals, and trees. You are surrounded by love and gentle devotion at this present and the precise moment in time. Know that you are special. Know that you are important. Know that you are a child of a King. Know that you are one of God's children. Know that you are just one of His sheep in His Pasture and He wants to take good care of you. Psalm 23 says.

"The Lord is My Shepherd, and I shall not want.

Don't you want to leave this world knowing that you did something to aid mankind? In other words, make this world a better place for the ones that will come behind you. We cannot be silent. Then you must spread the word to the children that are being blinded by what they see. Satan has dulled all your senses. Will you ever know how to feel?

Do you know what it is to feel someone else's pain? Can you empathize with mankind? These children have not been told that they are loved. This is where you come in, somehow, someway. We must "tell others "About the peace, love, affection, grace and mercy, and tender devotion that we receive from Our Lord and Savior Jesus Christ. Jesus can save your soul. Jesus will allow you to come inside the gate and

close the door on your old self. He will give you a "do over". He will give you another chance. He will allow you to come alive in your senses so you can "think". Call Him and ask Him to recreate you and reinvent you.

Can you sing a song" There are three precious simple words "Thank You Jesus" are the only lyrics. They tell a story. The more

I say "these words" the more I can shatter the ceiling in Heaven and ask Him to release to me the blessings that He has in reserve for me. I sing it often, as I find so much joy and comfort in knowing these three words. These three words saved my life. I began just repeating it as I pranced from one happy space to another one. He is giving me His undivided attention. What can I tell you about it? His Love is so tender, soft, meek, and mild.

    I did not know how much I appreciated my hands and fingers until I was washing and rinsing them in His hot and cold water. They were sudsy and I washed them back and forth and said "Thank You Jesus" for my fingers and hands. They mean so much to me. Without them, I could not express the words that are meditating in my heart. Do you see the sunshine draping through the windows? It feels so nice outside. Have you ever looked at a tree long enough to see it glisten. Each leaf catches His sun rays, and they glow like a diamond in the dark. I see glittering trees. They sparkle. His trees are so complacent because they are doing what trees do. They cleanse the air and resupply the air with pure and fresh oxygen for us to breathe. Isn't He wonderful? Isn't He worthy to be praised? He is always thinking of you. Can't you tell? Who makes everything possible for you to enjoy the peace, love, and devotion that you are experiencing at this moment in time. Place this in your memory bank. "I am loved". Say it more than one time to yourself. Let your ears hear it. Let your heart feel it. How does it feel to be wanted, needed, appreciated, accepted, adored, admired, idolized, and loved by a King? Read it again! Stop and examine each one. When you break away, you will feel as if you are skating on ice. You will feel so good. So special. So important.

I belong here. In His Presence. Don't you?

I witnessed so much this past Easter week. It was a weeklong celebration, and it has continued to this day. Love is all around us. Love follows us around like a bad cold. His Love is surrounding me as I hit key after key. I know I can accomplish nothing without His Guidance. He wants to love you just like I am being loved. He wants to cradle you in His Everlasting Arms, and you should allow Him too, so you can feel His Love. This is the same type of love that He gives to His tulips in His Flower Garden. He comes early in the morning to satisfy us with His morning grace and mercy and tells us to let it last throughout the day because He is coming back to see about us.

Give Him your heart. Let Him transform it. Let Him fill it with joy, laughter, happiness, love, and righteousness. This is what He wants to do. You must give up the reigns you have over your life to Him so His will can be done. Ask Him as I did, say "O Lord please reshape me, remold me and make me into the person You had designed for me to be before I was the sparkle in my mom's and dad's eye.

Enter a Land of Dreams where your hopes, wishes, and desires come true. I want to know more, don't you? I want to see more, don't you?

I want to experience more, don't you? I want to go out there, over yonder in the Great Beyond. They tell me that there is happiness, joy, and peace in that Land. It is, only if you remain in His Presence and allow His Presence to reside in you. I am free. I obtained my freedom a long time ago. Years ago, I crossed over. Years ago, I changed lanes. Now I am on the right road.

I have come from a mighty long way. Just to know that I am traveling in the right direction gives me so much peace, joy, and jubilation. I cannot stop singing my song. I cannot stop preaching. You know me by now, that I might get long winded and try to say it all at one time.

I am living this day as if it is my last day. We do not know where death is, but we can live this day because it is a gift given to us by a King. King Jesus! That who it is. Yes! I want to be in His Presence. There is no other place I would rather be. He is watching over me. He has me and my fingers, my mind, my brain, my heart, my body, my soul, and my spirit in His shadow. What a joy and a privilege to know that we are loved. Isn't that remarkable? Isn't this reassuring to know that you have someone who is hovering over you like a helicopter.

He wants to know your thoughts. He wants to know if you have come alive in your senses and begun to think. The Same Grace that you are experiencing is the Same Grace that He gave to your mom and dad before you were conceived. You were chosen. You were selected. You have received a word and you must go past and beyond what you see. It is not time for you to go. There is work to do. Tell the children about the One who watches over you while you slumber and sleep. Tell the children He is there to catch their hand and lead them through the wilderness that is about to face.

I came back from the edge. I have a story to tell the young ones, old ones, big ones, thin ones, tall ones, short ones, gay or straight. Change the words that you allow to escape from your mouth.

It is all about the words that you tell yourself! Proverbs 18 v:21, the tongue. There is a miracle in your mouth. Your brain, your mind, your body, your heart, your soul, and your spirit absorb revelation each day that you are allowed to open your eyes. What can I learn today? Is there solace in hearing His birds chirp and sing praises to His Name.

Is there peace when I feel the petals of His tulips, azalea bushes, and roses? Yes! A thousand times! Yes!

What have you been missing? You have been missing His magic, His majestic and The miraculous things that He has been doing for me.

Do we reap what we sow? Do we hear what He is saying? God has chosen the best for those who surrender to His will. You and I need more love and joy in our hearts. We must open our hearts to receive the Love and Devotion that He wants to put in them. I cannot make it without Him being in control. Can you?

Oh, Lord! Do not ever leave me to fend for myself! I cannot make it without Your Grace and Mercy and that is why I ask for it everyday you allow me to open my eyes. He has allowed me to be closed in my right mind with a reasonable portion of my health and strength and I am truly and sincerely "grateful". He allowed me to come into His Presence. He wants me to explore the world of beauty that surrounds me. Have you ever watched His Clouds in His sky? His clouds just hang there. They are suspended in the air and will not move until He directs them to. Can we become like His clouds?

Do you have the peace, harmony, and contentment that His clouds have? It is time for you to disconnect from this world of danger, turmoil, and confusion. Look at it from another angle. When Jesus said "you, who are weary, worn, and heavy laden, give it up, come unto me and rest, he meant every word He said. Give it up. There are too many Gods hanging around your house. There are too many Gods lodging in your head. What is the noise that is rattling around in your head? The nose in your head will come back to rest on your shoulders. I should know I am the one preaching to you about love, hope, and peace. I am the one seeking Divine Intervention. I ask everyday, all day, 24/7, around the clock - every hour - every minute - every second and right at this present and the precise moment in time to come and see about me.

Everyday is a challenge and that is how I know I cannot make it without Him leading the way, directing my footsteps, and directing my tongue. Yesterday I was young, gifted, and black. Yesterday I received His Unconditional Love, His Unfailing Love, His Unchanging Love, His faithfulness, His Grace, and Mercy, and His Genuine and Devine Devotion and He has returned to give me the same kind of love that He gave me yesterday. Am I glad to be alive and among the living? Yes! I am. I have much to say and I have such a short window frame.

I receive a little Kiss each morning and I know I can place my two feet on His floor because I know who is watching over me and listening to every word I say. Come and go with me! Just a tiny taste of Heaven is what I am getting? Because I have self-control. Because I have free will. I am allowed to come alive in my senses so I can think and behold The Lamb of God. He is worthy. He is the One who we should idolize and try to walk on the land that He walked on. I chose to walk with Him holding my hand.

The only way to make it is to give up your heart and allow Him to fill it with His love and His Devotion. Then you can say "I made it". I made it to that Promised Land. I embrace each day because I know my adventure will lead me to His Glory! I glorify, magnify, salute, worship, honor, and cherish Him for being so good to me. Right about now I am going to enjoy being in His Presence and receive the Love He has for me.

Did I take you to church? Now and then it happens. I get so much peace and contentment, joy, and happiness when I am "hallowing" His Holy Name. Yep! I got the joy! Yep! I got peace!

Yep! I got happy! The rocks will not have to cry out for me. I will cry out and tell the world "Just how good He is to me". He holds the key to my happiness and my future. He is the One with the Plan.

Jeremiah 29 v:11.

Chapter 14

There is good news surrounding us. Dreams! Wonders of the mind! Let me try and recapture the moments I spent in His Presence in this warm sunny 84-degree weather on His brand-new Tuesday morning that I have never seen before. It is Tuesday, April 13th, 2021, here at Gene Miller Manor in Christian City in Union City, Georgia in the year of Our Lord and Savior Jesus Christ. I am glad that I am alive! I must tell you about it. Come and travel with me on the adventure that He has allowed me to embrace. Smile! You know it is going to be good nourishment for your brain, mind, heart, body, soul, and spirit. Ready!

Prepare to be placed on a higher dimension. Plan to allow your heart and mind to embrace new thoughts, new ideas, and new opinions. Prepare to dream. Prepare to float, coast and glide. Quiet time.

In His Presence.

I was so involved in writing letters earlier during the morning hours. I had to sound off on Senator Reverend Warnock and tell him to tell the Evangelicals and the Christian Community that it is time for them to get a new heart, a do - over, a heart transplant. Those evil spirits that are lodged in that heart must come out. Jesus said it at St. Mark, Chapter 7, what makes a man's heart unclean. If you are a follower of Christ, then you too must clear away all those evil spirits that is holding you back from the comfort and joy and peace that you receive when you receive the Love of Christ.

Hate, deceit, lies, confusion come from Satan, Lucifer, the devil, the enemy. Satan comes to kill, maim, steal, and destroy your beliefs, thoughts, ideas, opinions, traditions, dreams and desires. Satan tells you to hate anything and everything that do not look like you. Go ahead and develop an uncomfortable feeling about them. They do not look like you. This is what white supremacy teaches. You are not my color therefore I feel superior to you, and you are inferior to me. Man must change his heart! Man must come to grips with the reality! Man must decide of what or who he is going to follow! Man must take a big sigh of relief and tackle the challenges that his heart holds. Do I hate? No! As of today's date, in history and time, I am honestly and sincerely saying "I don't hate anyone". Jesus gave us an order. Jesus gave us a command and that is we must love each other. That is the only way you will see God manifest in your life.

Want Our God, Our Lord, Our Savior to come alive in our lives, then ask Him. Tell him you will clean out your heart so He can dwell and have a final resting place. He knows your name and He is listening to every word you say. I am glad that He is smiling at me amid the problems going on in the outside world. You see I live each day as if it is my last day. We do not know where death is. I want to be in that number when He calls the roll up yonder. You know in the Great Beyond. That secret place where you and He dwell. So, I will celebrate my new day as my birthday. I have a new beginning and I want to share it with you. It is just us "two". It is just Him and me. I have become complacent in knowing that He has me in His shadow. I pray for you and me. I use the word "us" in all my affirmations. The only way He will continue to shine His light on me is if I shine my light on others.

Church time. Let us gather and give Him praise for being so good to you and me. I went outside and enjoyed a walk with His rays of sunshine cascading across my body. I heard His birds, chirping, and singing. I saw His trees glisten as I stared at them. See if you can look at a tree long enough until it gleams like an uncut diamond. This is what His birds see. They see the light that He has shining from His trees, and they gravitate toward it because they know they are safe and secure from all hurt, harm, or danger.

His Holy Spirit led me off into a house cleaning mode. I cleaned the bathroom, kitchen and dusted the furniture. I gave myself a facial. It was pure joy to me to be able to do this housecleaning. I am alive, not dead. I know how to make everything sparkle as if it is brand new. I have a heart and I remember how it looked when I first saw it and I wanted to capture that same moment all over again. It was sheer joy and pleasure to see it gleam and glow. As you can tell I enjoyed my cleaning routine on this glorious and beautiful day.

So, what is new! We must fight hate every time we see him raise his ugly head. I want to see another day and I am sure the young African American men who were recently murdered did not know about Jesus Christ and what He could do for their soul. One thing we must teach our offspring that they must realize and is to obey the "police". They are already scared and trigger happy, and they will use any excuse in the book to wipe us out. Right? We must teach our children to be smarter than the police. Say "Yes sir" officer, this is what they want to hear. Now you know what you are up against. Your back is against the wall. One strike is your color and origin! This is what matters most. They have already assumed that they are approaching a thief, or a murderer and they respond according to what is meditating in their heart. They hate you! They hate me!

Truth be told! There is a new man in town whose job is to call them out. Call out the heathens, barbarians, hoodlums, thieves, and murderers. Those who have their heart filled with "hate". Certainly, you have experienced it firsthand. They call us "nigger" under their breath. Now you know what they think about you, you can follow orders. Rise! Raise yourself above your present circumstances and conditions. Your mom and dad taught you to obey law enforcement officers. Auntie or Uncle told you. We must obey Authority.

If you want to see tomorrow, then there are things we need to do today.

Gather under one accord! Tell the Christians and Believers to take a stand and demand that the Black Lives Matter Movement be heard. Hate! Anger! Rage! Lies. This is what they are eating for breakfast, lunch, and dinner. Our appetites have changed. We want truth, honesty, justice, love, faith, sincerity, salvation, redemption, and righteousness to be equal for all. This is what I want. I am just one of His vessels that He is using to tell the world that they must give up the dreadful feelings of "hate". Today! Decide to divorce yourself from the evil spirit of "hate". You oversee your emotions. You decide. You have self-control and free will. Exercise the judgment that Jesus has placed inside of your heart.

To each its own. Everyone has their own opinion. I can only tell you on what side of the mountain I am on. If He ever left me alone, I do not know what I would do. I depend on Him for everything. He supplies all my needs, and I am glad to know that I am a child of a King, one of God's children, and one of His sheep in his pasture.

When I was pulled from my coffin by the Holy Spirit, I was told to "wake up O sleepyhead, rise from the dead and let the Lord shine on you". I did just that after He whispered in my ear these three words. "I Love You". He had favored me with a brand new day that I have never seen before. I woke up in His Presence and He was there at my bedside ready to take me by my hand. I want to be one of His angels. Their job is to bow, praise, worship, honor, and salute Our King. This is what I do all day, everyday, 24/7, around the clock – every hour – every minute – every second, and at this present moment in time.

I just finished looking at the architectural structures that our forefathers gave to America. They were ancient cathedrals. All were built by slaves with their bare hands. Hate has been around a long time but "Thank You Jesus" now we can read, write, and do arithmetic. Are you reading the handwriting on the wall? The white race wants us brown, black, yellow sheep to become extinct. If they could wipe us off the map.

Let you and I talk about some good things. Like it is an honor and privilege the He touched you with His finger of love on this morning and allowed you to become a living soul closed in your right mind with a reasonable portion of your health and strength. Isn't He wonderful? Isn't He amazing? If I am close to Him, He will guide my pathway. If I remain in Him, then He will remain in me. If I abide in Him, then He will abide in me. If I drawer nearer to Him, then He will draw nearer to me and give me my daily bread.

One more time I get to "hallow" His Name. One more time I get the chance to tell you just how good He is to me. It was early in the morning hours when I woke to go into my happy space. I was so glad for my happy space I sang three precious words on the way in and on the way out. "Thank You, Jesus". He allowed me to do what I needed to do. Thank You, Lord. You did it again! You have given me a new day to come alive in my senses so I can think, and process thought. Thank You, Lord, for deciding to favor me with a brand new gift of a new day. What must I do with it?

Breathe some of His fresh air. Float around in His sun. Feel His gentle breeze across your face, neck, and arms. Feel Him as he encompasses you totally in His Presence. I am captivated. I am mesmerized today because He did not forget about me. He knows I will sing a song everyday about how good He is to me. I must share it with someone, and you have been chosen to hear the words that are meditating in my heart at this 4 o'clock sacred hour in His afternoon.

Are you floating along with me? Are you happy? You have got some peace, joy, and happiness wrapped up into those bones - right? If you do not, then you must get busy. Find something that you enjoy doing and place your energy on that one thing and let it satisfy your fleshly and earthly desires. Mine is writing. Can't you tell? No matter what the subject is "I have got something to say".

We must teach our children how to love one another and not to hate. Tall order you think? I do not - children imitate their mothers and fathers, sisters and brothers and friends. Show your child some love and when He gets older it will not depart from his heart. We are grooming young men, women, boys, and girls how to carry the torch and live in the land of the free and home of the brave.

Racism - we must attack it head on. Is anyone too scared to call out the race card? I am not! I have seventy-four years of memories. I knew how to move to the back of the bus and let them sit upfront. I often wondered why we did this, and it became evident that they felt superior over us in the back of the bus. It is a new day. I want the absolute best that life has to offer and that is Peace in the valley. There is peace in the valley for you and me. We must move a few stones out of the way so we can see the path that has been chosen for you and me.

I went into my happy space, and I had everything I needed to cleanse and clothe my body. A big deal for me. I took my time. One sock and one shoe on, Thank You, Lord. Little miracles keep happening. Before I knew anything, I was finished. I lingered in my happy space as I embraced the adventure that was planned for me today.

My heart was healthy, happy, and contented, so I was able to make myself a pot of coffee and thank Him for being so kind and generous to me on my brand new magnificent, marvelous, splendid, and supreme Tuesday morning. While ladling my coffee back and forth to cool I recited His Twenty-Third Psalm. Surely goodness and mercy shall follow me, if I dwell in His secret place, in His shelter, and His Presence.

For Thy Art with me. Psalm 23. All day. Everyday. 24/7. Around the clock - every hour - every minute - every second and at this present and the precise moment in time.

Join in with me. Pat your feet, sway, and serve your body because Jesus has lifted the curtain from your eyes that had you blind. It was a disguise. A masquerade. You are important. You are special. You are needed to carry a message. You are wanted. You are appreciated. You were given an assignment before you were in your mother's womb. Newsflash! He knew you before you were a thought. Jeremiah 1. Ask Him?

He knows what kind of heart He placed in you. He placed in you His golden heart. You were given a heart that glows in the darkness and the light. My heart is glowing with words of love, hope, and peace. We must find that peace that only He can give us. We must search high and low and find that spot where He wants us to be. Me! I find myself being swaddled in His Everlasting Arms breathing His sweet breath forevermore. Come aboard! There is plenty of room. His Arms are as wide as His big blue spacious skies. You see He has plenty of room for His clouds to remain fixated on their appointed station.

Why does He love me so? I do not have an answer for you, but you can bet it is because I ask Him every morning when my two feet hit His floor to love me by saying "Thank You, Jesus." I would be lost without His love and mercy. He comes early in the morning hours and showers me with His grace and mercy and tells me to let it last me throughout my day. I follow His orders. I obey His decree.

So, after I finish in my happy space, I hurry back to reclaim my spot. I had my head buried in His chest breathing His sweet breath. It was so tender, mild, and soft so I snuggled in real tight and said "O Lord please come into my presence and O Lord please allow me into Your Presence.

He made sure I was nestled in, and I began talking by asking O Lord please shelter us, O Lord please shadow us, O Lord please favor us, O Lord please cover us with Your Blood, O Lord please grant us Your Grace and Mercy, O Lord please strengthen us physically, mentally, emotionally, psychologically, morally, and spiritually, O Lord please forgive us of our sins because we may not always do things correctly or perfectly, O Lord please forgive our enemies because they know not what they do, O Lord please prosper us physically, materialistically, financially and spiritually, O Lord please protect us from all plagues, pandemics, disasters, and turmoil, O Lord please do not cast us away from Your Presence and O Lord please allow Your Holy Spirit to dwell in us again on this day. In Jesus' Name, I Pray - Amen.

Think He heard me? I believe He did! I believe that since He has His trees, His weeds, His bushes, His flowers, His grass, His birds, and His butterflies in His shadow that He has me and you in His shadow. The Lord is my Shepherd, and I shall not want. I am asking for something special to happen to me this Tuesday. If I remain in Him, then He will remain in me. If I abide in Him, then He will abide in me. If I draw nearer to Him, then He will draw nearer to me. This is what I said while I was sipping on my delicious cup of morning brew. I did not know coffee could taste so good. It is especially delicious when you are drinking it in the Presence of a King.

It is no secret! He watches over me. He listens to my thoughts and opinions and decides what is best for me. I ordered a back brace so I could stand up straight. When I first tried it on, it seemed to work. I thought I had found a secret. Not much support. Though I will keep wearing it. I must give it time for its healing properties to work - right? I will hang in here with it. It does not constrict my movement. My fingers and hands are free, and I get busy and start typing away.

I talked with Jerome Williams, my aide, earlier today. He is doing great. He is getting his place through Hud. He is excited and I was excited for him. He is the one that said, "God is good" Ain't He? I replied, "you can't beat Him, and we laughed." He received some important personal mail and I made him aware of it. He was happy this morning and I am glad that He is achieving some of his lifelong goals.

He is doing quite well. He is doing good. I am glad about it. I pray for him when I say my prayers. I pray for you, me, him, her, she, them, and they. My prayers cover all His sheep in His Pasture. This is what He told me to do. He told me to "love you as much as I love myself" and I can do just what He said.

Can you get too much Heaven? I do not think so. I am enjoying a springtime breeze as I listen to some easy listening music and allow my thoughts to flow. With Jesus, He will give you that Perfect Peace. That Perfect Peace will make you clean up an entire house. It will be a joy and delight to restore everything in its proper place. I cannot get good "cellphone" coverage. Cannot go to my favorite spot "Google". There I can find out anything and everything. I need your prayers. You pray for me, and I will pray for you. Deal! I need all the prayers I can get. Keep them coming, moving, and going. Everyday you should have morning prayer, a morning affirmation, a morning mantra, a morning confession. This is your protection against the enemy. Declare who you are and who you are when you open your eyes!

You are invited to join in with me as I saturate His atmosphere with words of praise and admiration when I first open my eyes. You want God's peace, don't you? Then go to Him with a clear conscience because you have not done anything wrong and ask Him to come to see about you and when He does ask Him to please take good care of you. This is what I am asking for when I say "O Lord please come into my presence and O Lord please allow me into Your Presence.

Just keeping it real. This is the best way I can describe to you so you can receive His Unfailing Love, His Unchanging Love, His Unconditional Love, His Grace, and Mercy, and His Genuine and Divine Devotion. It is like living on an island or in the backwoods of the country. Stroll with me. Go back on memory lane and remember the love your grandma and grandpa and your daddy and momma had for you. They knew way back then that He would save your soul and give you everything you need only if you would believe, have faith, and trust that there is a better life for you to live. Want to live? Then come alive in His Spirit. Ask Him? Tell Him what you want. You want a beautiful and memorable afternoon than spend some time in His Presence. Oh, Lord! Here I am. How great Thy Art!

Let Him change your name! You too can become a shining star. A masterpiece. His favorite. His Tulip planted in His Flower Garden, and He will return to give you what you need so you can continue to flourish and grow.

Chapter 15

It is time for Him to renew your strength, comfort your soul and uplift your spirits. Be still! Want joy and peace for your soul? Relax and accept the fact that you are loved. What a beautiful Savior that we have. Worship with me. There is no one like Him. There is no one like Jesus. Agreed! Who can enter your heart, brain, mind, body, soul, and spirit and make you come alive in your senses so you can "think and process thought"? No one but Jesus, our beautiful and wonderful Savior. He is watching over His Sheep in His Pasture and will touch you with His finger of love and make you rise from the dead. Our God, Our King, Our Rock, Our Redeemer, Jesus Christ, My Lord, and Savior. I cling to Him. I hold on to His precious Name. It is springtime and I have been approved to enter His Household. I am confident that I am. Cannot do it without Him holding my hand. Confidence – do you have enough to have a talk with Him and ask Him to talk with you?

I do! You can do this. Practice until you get it perfect. Practice until you shatter the ceiling in Heaven with your praise and worship. This is what I did.

I honor Him because "today" is a great day for me because I am alive. I can breathe His air. I can see His trees, flowers, sunshine, bugs, insects, His weeds, and His bushes. I can smell His Honeysuckle vine. It grows wild and it is such a beautiful smell. Those who suffer from allergies are missing out. Aishah, my youngest daughter has allergies "bad". I ask for your prayers for her.

With this Honeysuckle vine - I will share with you how it makes you feel. A sense of calm and jubilation overtakes you as you inhale and exhale His air that He allows you to breathe in your lungs. Thank You, Lord! For my lungs! Thank You Lord for every breath I take because You are holding me. You are cradling me in Your Everlasting Arms because you said at Isaiah 49 v:15-16 - that you would never forget about me.

I know Him and He knows me. Know how I know? He told me. It is amazing what you will learn about yourself when you set aside private time to be in His Presence. Just the two of you - alone. Let Him comfort you. Allow Him to enter Your heart so He can dwell and have a final resting place. Let Him massage every bone in your body with His Divine Devotion. The more time you invest in Him will become so exhilarating, thrilling, and powerful because He dictates it. I hear His birds singing and chirping, they are so glad they are alive that they will sing about it, and I can sing praises to His Name. If they sing, then so will I.

I think I will sit back, drink my water, breathe in and out, and allow Him to put His Loving Arms around me. He sure is good to me! Hallelujah! Birds cry out so joyfully- why can't I. Listen to the birds they are sending you a message that they too will soon disappear if we do not change our lives. We are to live in peace with each other.

We are getting dangerously close to the edge. Our life as we know it, will all come to an end. At that time, we will all be "extinct" because of man's ignorance. He has designed a blueprint for us to follow. It is His Bible. His guidance is in there. It is laced with big dreams and wishes but you must slow it up a bit.

The evil spirit of hate will destroy us as a people, as a nation, and as a Kingdom unless we allow God, Jesus, The Holy Spirit to enter our hearts and lives and allow Him to take over. Oh, Lord! I surrender myself to

Thee. I give myself a way to You so Your will can be done. The reigns I had over my life - I gladly handed them over so His will could be done.

Take it easy, slow down, a snails' pace. Begin to relish in His sunshine. Get His sunshine therapy. It is rays of love, hope, and pleasure being generated to you through the rays of His sun. Let your mind, brain, heart, body, soul, and spirit relax, meditate, and thank Him for the wonderful air that you breathe. It is His breath.

This morning, I cry "Holy", and He is worthy to be praised. He came early to satisfy me with His morning grace and mercy and told me to let it last me all day long. I can do this. If I remain in Him, then He will remain in me. John 15 v:5. If I abide in Him then He will abide in me. If I draw nearer to Him, then He will draw nearer to me. James 4 v:8. He is the Only One I know who a Savior is, healer, way-maker, provider, protector, pillar of strength, and who fills your heart with peace, love, joy, wisdom, knowledge, honesty, justice, salvation, redemption happiness, pleasure, and righteousness. He is present in your life to give you The Fruits of His Spirits. Galatians 5 v:22. There is so much kindness, gentleness, softness, faithfulness, salvation, and redemption provided to you because you have self-control. You make the choice. Life or death comes by way of the tongue. Proverbs 18 v:21. You speak it. You say it. It goes up and comes back to rest on your shoulders. You dictate what your thoughts will be. You dictate what your future will be with the words that come out of your mouth.

Today is the day He chose to blow His breath of life into my lifeless body and save my soul. He saved me. He changed my way of acting and thinking. He told me "There is another life for you to live if you come and go with me. My yoke is easy and I will give you rest."

Read Matthew 11 v:28 and continue so you can hear Him tell you as He told me "My yoke is easy". You must believe, trust, and have faith in His Holy Word. Our God, Our Jesus, is speaking.

I am glad that I am alive on this day. This day is brand new to me. I have never seen this Tuesday, April 14th, 2021, before. I come ready this morning to lift His Name in prayer here at Gene Miller Manor in Christian City in Union City, Georgia. May He continue to hold us in the Palms of His Hands. I come to exalt His Holy Name for being so good to me. Help me out! Whatever you need this morning, you can find it in His Everlasting Arms which are in His big blue spacious skies.

He raised me from the dead. He whispered in my ear these words; "wake up O sleepyhead, rise from the dead and let the Lord shine on you". These words brought joy and comfort to my soul because I realized then that He had watched over me all night long while I slumbered and slept. When I awoke, I was closed in my right mind with a reasonable portion of my health and strength. I wanted to come alive and live the life that I had been given in the Presence of a King. I rolled over from my happy space, sat up straight and placed my feet on His floor, and began to sing my song of "Thank You Jesus" because I realized at that point that He is so good to me. He allowed me to go into my happy space and do what

I needed to do. For this, I am "grateful". I owe Him a debt of gratitude for showering me with His Unfailing Love, His Unconditional Love, His Grace and Mercy, and His Divine Devotion.

It is the sacred hour of 10 a.m. and I know He is in control of my thoughts, ideas, actions, opinions, beliefs, traditions, and desires. I cannot make it without Him. He is my source of strength, wisdom, knowledge, and joy. I am one of His sheep in His Pasture just like you seeking to climb to new heights, arrive at a new dimension. My life and your life will never be the same if you drink some of this water. We have tapped in on an energy that is available to all His sheep in His Pasture. Shake your head and say if they only new that there was another life that they could live". You and I know there is joy, peace, happiness in that Land. In His Presence. Psalm 23 says, "Surely His goodness and mercy shall follow me all of the days of my life as long as I dwell in His shelter, His secret place and in His Presence.

He will make you feel brand new. He will give you a new mind and a new beginning each morning you open your eyes because you and I realize that He performed a miracle on us by allowing us to see another day as we realize who made it all possible. I will serve, honor, cherish and obey My God, My Lord, My Savior Jesus Christ all the days of my life while I am on His Earth, on His Planet, and in His Universe. Wherever I go, Whatever I do, I know, "He is with me". That is what it says in Psalm 23. "Yea though I walk through the shadows of death, fear no evil, for Thy art with me." Confidence. Let me shed the layers of darkness that have covered my eyes, my heart, my mind, my brain, my body, my soul, and my spirit. Now! I can see. I see what lies ahead. I see that we must fight the evil spirit of hate before it overcomes the world that God created for you and me. Get ready! Our work has just begun. We cannot sit quietly and hold our hands. You and I must get busy and tell the world what Our God, Our Lord, Our Jesus has done for you and me.

To get to where I am I had to jump over boulders and wade through the raging seas. I depend on Jesus this morning. I am leaning on His Everlasting Arms. He is the One that saved my soul. He is the One that stretched out His Righteous Right Hand to me and guess what I did, I "grabbed" it. He guaranteed me that I would find peace, happiness, joy, truth, justice, honesty, salvation, redemption, love, and righteousness if I cast all my cares on Him because He cares for me. 1st Peter 5 v:7.

It is a guarantee that if I lean on Him, He will prop me up on His Pillar of Faith. I only need to believe, trust, and have faith that He will keep His Promises to me. In Hebrew 5 v:13, He said "I will never leave you nor forsake you". He has kept His Promise every day now that He has raised me from the dead. I will tell it. If it had not been for the Lord shining His Grace and Mercy on me, I don't know, where would I be. Oh! For His grace and mercy, I will continue to let this little light of my shine. Oh, Lord! Please give me more. More of your wisdom, knowledge so I can get an understanding of what I am to do to glorify Your Name.

I know who woke me up early this morning and brought joy and pleasure, peace and happiness, and joy to my day. It was Jesus. He was stirring around quite early in the wee hours of the morning. Touching His sheep, telling them "You have been given a new day now what are you going to do with it?" Psalm 118 v:24 tells you what to do when you open your eyes. Rejoice! In your spirit and your soul – be "grateful". Magnify it. Glorify it, celebrate it and be thankful for everything in it. This is the decree that was given to me and you. I can do this easily. I know who favored me with a new beginning and I am glad that I was chosen to be among the living and not the dead. Every day that you see is a privilege and honor given to you by Almighty God, My Lord, My Savior Jesus Christ. Rejoice! He loves you and He loves me. Let Him shine His light on you. Saturate His atmosphere and your heart with words of praise and admiration. He magnifies in your heart. He will come alive in your spirit because you are building your hopes, dreams, and future on Him. Have faith. Believe, Trust. Lean not to your understanding. Live your life by faith and not by sight.

Peace! Is this what you want? Then listen closely to the next set of words. It is a descriptive form of words aimed to stir you on the inside. That is what Jesus does He restores you from the inside out not from the outside in. If you allow Him to, He will push "evil spirits" away from your heart.

Once upon a time, I overheard a conversation. Somebody is talking this morning and telling me that there is another life to live. Someone is talking to me this morning telling me that I need to slow up and set aside a private time so I can develop a relationship with Our Lord and Savior Jesus Christ. Someone is telling me that I need to establish a personal, private, and intimate conversation with Him. Just do it! You will feel His Spirit all over you. You will become content and complacent as you come to realize that there is Someone who wants to hear your thoughts, hopes, ideas, dreams, and aspirations. Use your sixth sense. Listen to what you are telling yourself! Oh, Lord! Please hear my prayer. Please hear my supplication. Please hear my confession. Please hear my affirmations.

You are I are needed, accepted, wanted, admired, adored, cherished, and idolized by Our King. This is the joy that you can shout about. You are loved, appreciated, and adored by Our Savior. He is listening to every word you say. Read Jeremiah 29 v:12. Jeremiah 29 v:11 says, "there was a plan developed just for me and you". You and I are new creatures in Christ and old things have passed away. 2nd Corinthians 5 v:17. We have a new way of talking and thinking. This morning is all about giving Him our praise and worship because He is so good to us. He favored us with a new beginning, a new soul, a new spirit, a new brain, a new mind, a new heart, and a new body. I cannot give up now. A pathway has been carved for me to follow. I believe. I trust and I have faith that He is the One orchestrating my ideas, thoughts, and beliefs. I know what He has done for me, and I know you know what He has done for you.

It is time to worship Him. Isn't He grand? Isn't He marvelous? Isn't He magnificent? Isn't He mighty? Isn't He wonderful? Yes, He is, and He is keeping me alive for a reason. Everyday, all day, 24/7, around the clock, every hour - every minute - every second, and at this present and the precise moment in time I will testify as to His goodness. He is using me for a season to tell you how He saved a wretch like me. Bow and worship Him. Talk to Him, He is waiting. He is listening and wants to know what is meditating in your heart. Realize that He wishes to cradle you in His Everlasting Arms if you allow Him to. He is mighty? He is greater than great. This is what I was told. He keeps me in perfect peace. Come before the Lord with Thanksgiving and Praise. Glorify Him and let Him know that He is the King over your life, and you will exalt His Name.

He has placed me on a "pedestal". He is telling me that "I will love you always". And in case I didn't hear Him the first time, He will rephrase it and say, "I will always love you". Can you see the Love and Admiration that He has readily available to me? Now I can sit back, relax, and allow Him to captivate me, surround me, and mesmerize me with His Unfailing Love, His Unconditional Love, His Grace and Mercy, and His Divine Devotion.

He is so good to me that I am walking on air. I am prancing and bouncing around from one happy space to another one. Earlier during the morning hours, I said my affirmations. I ask O Lord please come into my presence and O Lord please allow me into Your Presence. While I had His attention and while He was listening to me, I continued to say the words that were meditating in my heart.

O Lord please shadow us, O Lord please shelter us, O Lord please favor us, O Lord please cover us with Your Blood, O Lord please grant us Your Grace and Mercy, O Lord please strengthen us physically, mentally, emotionally, psychologically, morally and spiritually, O Lord please forgive us of our sins because we don't always do things correctly or perfectly, O Lord please forgive my enemies because they know not what they do, O Lord please prosper us physically, materialistically, financially and spiritually, O Lord please protect us from all plagues, pandemics, disasters, and turmoil, O Lord please do not cast us away from Your Presence and please O Lord allow Your Holy Spirit to dwell in us again on this day. In Jesus' Name, I Pray - Amen.

I just asked Him to take care of us. You can do the same. The more prayers and praises go up, the more His blessings will shower down upon us. After I finish saying my morning prayer, I began to give Him Glory. I began to praise His Holy Name because He did it again. He came to see about me and showered His Love and Affection all over me. I am "grateful". I owe Him my life. He changed my life. I wanted Him too. I yearned for a better life. I begged. I ask "O Lord! Please save my soul." He calmly, softly, gently, and kindly said to me "You, who are worn, weary, and heavy-laden, come and go with me and I will give you rest. Read Matthew 11 v:28 again. His yoke is easy. He is on one side, and I am on the other side, and I will allow Him to be my guide. I tried because I thought I had to do it on my own. Oh No! You are not to walk the pathway that He has carved out for you - all alone. He is there to guide you, protect you and provide for your every need. He is there to steer you in the right direction. You want to follow the Leader.

I decided that I wanted a new beginning. A new identity. A new birth.

This is what I asked for and He answered my prayer. He empowers my day today to say "Hallelujah". He is giving me what I need to move these fingers all over this keyboard. He is filling my heart with pride and joy because He is encouraging me to write sentence after sentence.

There is more. Psalm 121 reads "I will lift my eyes unto the hills, from whence cometh my help." I will open His Holy Word and read it and allow His words to comfort my soul. He is alive in my spirit. I am a spiritual being having a human experience. And you are too. You are no longer a part of this wicked, corrupt, and a wicked world ruled by Satan and His Army. You have been raised higher. You are on a new dimension. You have received divine revelation and you know that you don't belong here. You belong in

God's Kingdom that He has right here on Earth. You are now officially a member of God's Household. Tell someone that there is another world that they can live in and that they should join you. You and I both know the way. I will tell it. Will you?

I can do all things through Christ who strengthens me.

Chapter 16

Wait a minute! Slow up! You are moving too fast to realize that you are loved, needed, and protected. By whom - do you ask? Shut it down - Our Lord and Savior want to spend some quality time with you. You want to renew your strength; you want to uplift your spirits and you want to come alive in your senses so you can think, and process thought? Right?

Listen! You still have time to listen! That is all you have is time. Spend this sacred hour of 7 o'clock with me as I take you on a journey that is designed for those who live in the Great Beyond. There is peace, satisfaction, love, righteousness, justice, honesty, salvation, and redemption in that Land that you are about to embrace.

You need to start your morning, noon, and night off by asking to be in His Presence. Oh, Lord! Thank You for cradling me in Your Everlasting Arms all this day long. It is Tuesday night. 7:30 p.m. I tried to listen to some of His tv vessels, but I got tired and just had to sit down and tell you that there is another life you can live. Bump the turmoil, bump the confusion, bump the stress, bump the depression, bump the temptations, bump the trials and tribulations and the storms.

We belong to God, Jesus, Our Lord, and Savior. When I open my eyes each day that He raises me from the dead, I know who to salute. I know what to celebrate. I know whom to glorify. I know whom to magnify. It was my God who was standing beside my bed waiting for me so He could catch me by my hand and lead me on today's adventure that He had planned for me. I cannot listen to too many tv vessels, His preachers are too emotional. I need a level head. I need someone who is going to have a private chat just with me. Preachers! Tell me something that will soothe my aching mind, brain, heart, body, soul, and spirit. Tell me that "Jesus loves me". Reassure me that He is on my side. Read Psalm 23 and He tells you that He is Your Shepherd - He will watch over you and you shall not want for anything. Aren't you hunting for some peace, joy, happiness, and satisfaction?

Who wants to pray? Wrong time of the day - yes, or no? I cannot help it. I - all day, everyday, 24/7, around the clock, every hour - every minute - every second - at this present moment in time - I am asking to be in His Presence. I know you loved me Lord early in the morning and You told me to let it last me throughout my day. Right now, He is showering me with His Unfailing Love, His Unconditional Love, His Grace and Mercy, and His Divine Devotion.

Who said we would get to know each other on such a personal and intimate basis? I know Him and He knows me. He knows my thoughts, ideas, opinions, beliefs, traditions, and desires and He is guiding me every step of the way. He reassures me that He will go with me everywhere I go. Joshua 1 v:9. I have been sheltering in place all day in His Presence. It has just been the "two of us" all day and it will be just the "two of us" the entire evening and throughout the night.

You see when I lay down to close my eyes to drift off into La La Land, I am dancing on one of His clouds because His Arms that are cradling me are so soft and comfortable. He invites me to rejoice in how I spent my day. Okay! I get comfortable when I lay my head in His chest to breathe His sweet breath forevermore. I know one day that I will float away and if it is this night then I am satisfied that I honored and saluted A King for being so good to me.

Please O, Lord! Do not leave me! I am depending on you now just like I depended on You yesterday. Guess what? He did it again. He came early in the wee hours of the morning. He satisfied me with His morning Love, Grace and Mercy, and His Divine Devotion. I felt so good. Oooh! Wee! He loves me. So, when I looked into the mirror at His Shining star, I said "Hi". Speak! You think you are important – right? Yes! So, you think you are special – right? My answer was yes, and I pranced away – feeling His Love all over me. I am loved. You are loved but you gotta put the work in so you can reap the results. You reap what you sow.

What are the words rattling around in your head? Am I in control and do I make wise decisions? You do not if you do not place God out front. You must make Jesus first. You must give Him all the authority because He is the One that will make the best decision for you. Trust in Him. Believe Him. Jeremiah 29 v:11 says, "He has a plan for my life".

Want advice about His plans? Get in the boat! Take refuge. Seek safety. Seek security. Find a way to get to know Him. This is the best decision I ever made. Making Jesus the Head of My Life changed my life. He deserves all the Praise. Lift His Name on High. I will because I know what He is doing for me. He is opening highways and byways, avenues, expressways for me and that means I have a lot to say. I cannot be quiet. There is something that you must know. Jesus is real. His Love is real. His affection is pure and divine. He calmly rests beside you and guides your thoughts, ideas, ambitions, traditions, beliefs, and opinions. He whispers so you must be tuned in to hear His words that are designed for your ears only.

There is too much noise sounding off into your head. Stop! Drop! Tune everything out. You need quiet time for you to realize that He is there watching over you, listening to everything you say and making mental notes of your aspirations, dreams, and hopes. Oh, Lord! Help me to become what you intend for me to be! It is a new day, and you should get busy and recapture the moments you spent today in His Presence because tomorrow is another day. Did you stop and thank Him for giving you one more day? Now that it is about to come to end, ask Him just like I will - to order your pathway.

My mom used to yell at me and say to me "child - you gotta change your heart". I had no earthly idea of what she meant. I thought she was just sounding off at the mouth. So, what she said went into one ear and came out on the other ear. Boy! Did I learn? The words you speak out of your mouth will develop your mind, brain, heart, body, soul, and spirit. No preacher told me that there was another life to live other than the one I saw with my own two eyes. No preacher told me that there would be a great day - when I gave up the reigns, I had over my life to Him so His will could be done. I was left to fend for myself, and I did just that. Injustice - inequality. No truth, honesty, salvation, redemption, love, and righteousness were preached to me. If it, was it went right out of the window? I experienced it. I took it. That is before I began to learn how to read, write and process thought. The words in my mouth are what determines my future. Hallelujah! Did you know that? I didn't until I read Isaiah 41 v:10. It says, "I am your God", I will stretch my Righteous Right Hand out to you. When I read this verse, it sealed the deal, immediately I was linked into a domain ruled by A King.

The mountains moved. I came close to the shore. I got out of the boat and started telling the world how much He loves me and that He is available to hold your hand just like He is holding my hand. He is the One that I want to be by my side. He is my constant companion. He calls the shots. He directs my footsteps. He has shown me the way. He has told me what to do and I am going to follow the outline that He has designed just for me. I am glad about it. I can spread the word. I can tell somebody just how He is shining a light on me. As He was shining His light I began to bud out like a flower and bear some good fruit.

I can think. I can write. I can glorify Him for being so good to me.

Where is He right now? He has His spotlight on me and He has His spotlight on you. Isn't that unbelievable? Isn't that terrific? He can keep an eye on you, me, him, he, them, and they at the same time.

Is He alive? Yes! He is. He watches over me and you all day, everyday, 24/7, around the clock, every hour, every minute, every second, and right at this present and the precise moment in time. I welcome His attention. I want His Love and Admiration.

Recently, about an hour ago, I looked into the mirror as I was washing my hands and I was asked, did you accomplish the goals you set out to do this morning? Nope! I had made business plans, but they can be put on hold and right now I am going to eat some dinner, relax and tell Him all about my day and ask Him to open the gates to Heaven so I can shatter the ceiling with my words of praise and worship because He sure is good to me. Two testimonies in one day. God has been at work all during the day in my life and His Holy Spirit, said: "do you want to write?" I stopped reclining, put on some music, and pulled out the chair and you know what happened next. I was on a mission. I wanted to share what was meditating in my heart. I wanted to talk, and I have the best audience and the best gear to get the job done.

I can sit here; admire the various shades of green I see on His trees that open with new leaves. I see His Pine Trees, they never change colors, they stand firm and tall, they are the money colored green. His pine trees are strong and mighty. I am strong because He enables me with what I need to get the job done. I am mighty because I will never give up writing, talking about what My Lord and Savior Jesus Christ is doing for me right at this precise moment in time. Okay! I am in His Presence. It is calm, soothing, peaceful, and content within my soul. He has never disappointed me. I stay close to Him. If I remain in Him, then He will remain in me. John15 v:5. I want to bear good fruit. I want to make Him proud of me. I want to please Him. I want to satisfy Him. If I draw nearer to Him, then He will draw nearer to me.

What am I telling myself? I am telling myself that I can do all things if I continue to trust, believe, and have faith that He is watching over me with His eyes and He is listening to every word I say with His ears. He sees me and He sees you. He hears me and He hears you. He recognizes my voice because I call on Him so often. He recognizes me because each morning I open my eyes I "hallow" His Name. He is expecting me to keep our channel for constant conversation open. I talk to Him, and He talks to me. I listen. I listen so hard; I can hear the train's whistle. My mind is tuned in to hear the words that He allows to meditate in my heart. I am not turning back. I have come too far. I made it. I am there. I am here. I am among the believers. I am among the ones who have allowed Him to move into our hearts so He can dwell and have a final resting place.

I can do this for the rest of my life. Being in His Presence. He will cover me with His feathers and under His wings, I will seek refuge from the fowler's snare. Psalm 91. I am not moving. I am not going anywhere. This is forever. I will not give up what I have been able to accomplish. Love, Peace, and Happiness - where can you find it? I know! You find it at His feet - seated at His Throne of Grace and Mercy. I belong here. This is where I was headed before I started listing to Satan and allowed him to be my guide. I learned. I learned fast. I had to. I was given a choice and I chose to live a life in the presence of a King.

His yoke is easy. He is on one side, and I am on the other one and I will allow His will to be done. He is the leader. I will follow. I will do what I am told to do, and I will say what I am told to say. Everyday, I am

meditating, talking to Him, reading His religious magazines and books. Everyday He makes sure I receive my daily bread. I am receiving the blessings that He has in reserve just for me. Trust me, He has got this.

Trust me, He is in control. Trust me, He wants to be your guiding light.

Chapter 17

Sometimes I must get real! There is so much to say. Want to go to church? You have an open invitation to come in, relax, put on your favorite pair of pj's, turn on some easy listening music and go with the flow of words that are being generated from the lips, mind, heart, brain, head, soul, body, and spirit of a 74-year-old queen, mother, nana, grandmother, auntie, sister, father, cousin, and friend. Surely somewhere you fall into that category. You are your individual, and you have self-control and free will. Right?

You can turn me off, but curiosity will get the best of you. Tell yourself you want to hear more. If you, do I have some stories to tell about my capture. I was released from the shackles that Satan, Lucifer, the devil the enemy had placed on my back. I began to shed the overcoats. The biggest overcoat I had to shed was when I realized that Jesus Christ loved me. He had been kept telling me this so one day I set aside some quiet time and said "okay! Here I am "love on me". I began to say my prayers softly and gently and kindly, humbly, and meekly. Oh, Lord! I know you have all power. I know it was You who touched me with Your finger of love and whispered in my ear, "wake up" O sleepyhead, rise from the dead and let the Lord shine on you. I pushed the covers away and raised my hands in Praise for Thee. You did it again! You showed up on this brand new Thursday morning that I have never seen before to satisfy me with Your morning mercy and love and told me to let it last me all during my day. I am awake this morning. I have been raised from the dead and I have got something to say. Want to know a secret? You are dead! You are in your coffin! Want to know how? Then stick around.

The time has come to remove the layers of darkness that are covering your eyes. Now that your eyes have been opened you are obligated to tell your children, your mama and daddy, your sisters and brothers, your nieces, nephews, cousins, and friends, one by one, what the Lord can do for them right now at this present and the present moment in time. He will shower you with His Unfailing Love, His Unconditional Love, His Unchanging Love, His Grace and Mercy, and His Divine Devotion. You know how to relate to your loved ones, if you do not then ask Him to put the right words in your mouth so you will be able to reach them regardless of what level of understanding they are on.

Do you know what He is doing for you? I will tell you what He is doing for me. He pulled me out of the coffin and told me to "get ready" to embrace the adventure that He has outlined for me to follow. He did it. Again, He allowed me to be closed in my right mind with a reasonable portion of my health and strength so I could get to this computer and release the words that are meditating in my heart.

There must be order in your life. A Divine Revelation from My God, My Lord, and My Jesus! A manifestation. Listen! He wants to talk to you. He wants to hear your thoughts and ideas this Thursday morning, April 15th, 2021. I am at Gene Miller Manor in Christian City in Union City; Georgia and He has all of us residents in His shadow. I asked for it. He has me in His shadow. He has you in His shadow. This I know because He raised me from the dead and allowed me to go into my happy space, my bathroom, and do what I needed to do. He is mighty and powerful! He decided to favor me with a new day. He allowed me to flush my kidneys and excrete my bowels. Isn't He wonderful? Do not He deserve praise. One "shout out". Keep talking, it will get good to you, if you don't be filled with pride, love, and devotion from the inside out then you require some deep meditation. Now that I realize He allowed His will to be done, I am forever "grateful" to Him for showering me with His Love, Grace, and Mercy.

What do you want to hear this morning? Do you want to hear just how good He is to me? In the wee hours of the morning, He stretched out His Righteous Right Hand to me and I grabbed it. I had the perfect experience when I went into my happy space. I had been given everything I needed to cleanse and clothe my body. After I finished up, I waltzed into another one of the happy spaces and made myself a pot of coffee.

Earlier during the morning hours, I knew who to honor, worship, and cherish for me being allowed to open my eyes to a semi-cloudy, gray looking day. I love foggy days, just like I love sunny days. God is at work! He is getting ready to feed His creation. He will supply His trees, weeds, bushes, flowers, grass, insects, bugs, and all the animals that He created with His rain so they will be nourished and allowed to continue to grow, be fruitful and multiply. He has equipped me with a brain, heart, mind, body, soul, and spirit and I can process thought. Isn't that wonderful? Isn't that magnificent? Isn't that marvelous? I think so.

Blessings keep coming, over and over, again and again as long as I keep my Hand in His Unchanging Hand. His Hand will always be the same. He has me engraved in the Palms of His Hands. He will never forget about me. Bragging rights! He will hold my hand and I will have my hand locked in real tight. I don't want Him to ever leave me nor forsake me. I am one of His children. I am a child of a King. I am one of His sheep in His Pasture just like you and He is taking real good care of me. Thought you would like to know! I am alive. I am not dead. There is life in my body, and I have much fruit to bear. I am a living witness to what He is doing for me right at this present moment in time. I am in the mood for His Divine Devotion, and I will recline back and allow Him to drape buckets of love from the crown of my head to the sole of my feet again and again, over, and over, forevermore.

One blessing I must praise Him for is, my being able to sit and compose a thought. I can "think". Okay! His Psalm 23 tells me that "Thy art with me"! What can I do with this type of ammunition? I can go there, go here, say this, and say that because I know who is orchestrating my thoughts. He is alive. He lives within my heart. Hallelujah! Glory to God in the Highest, He is worthy to be praised. He watched over me while I slumbered and slept and when I returned to my happy space to reclaim my spot, I began talking. I had already saturated His atmosphere with words of praise and admiration by singing my song; "Thank You, Jesus". As I began to get nestled in tight, I said my morning prayer, my morning confession, my morning mantra, my morning affirmation, and that is "O Lord please come into my presence and O Lord please allow me into Your Presence." He heard me. He was listening. He knew I was one of His children and I would salute Him and glorify Him for being so good to me for giving me another brand new opportunity to get it right.

I was being cradled in His Everlasting Arms and I knew this, so I began talking. I ask O Lord please shelter us, O Lord please shadow us,

O Lord please favor us, O Lord please cover us with Your Blood,

O Lord please grant us Your Grace and Mercy, O Lord please strengthen us physically, mentally, emotionally, psychologically, morally, and spiritually, O Lord please forgive us of our sins because we don't always do things correctly and perfectly, O Lord please forgive our enemies because they know what they do, O Lord please protect us from all plagues, pandemics, disasters, and turmoil, O Lord please prosper us physically, materialistically, financially and physically, O Lord please do not cast us away from Your Presence and O Lord please allow Your Holy Spirit to dwell in us again on this day.

In Jesus' Name, I Pray - Amen.

What is your morning mantra? Affirmation? Prayer? Confession?

Now is a good time to repeat it. This can be done at any time, all day, everyday, 24/7, around the clock - every hour - every minute - every nanosecond, right at this present and the precise moment in time. Silently or loudly give Him your praise and worship. He deserves it! You were raised from your grave. You were given another opportunity to live. Whether you are glued to that computer screen or if you are strolling in His sunshine, He is with you. I like to reassure myself and I say, "Thy art with me". Psalm 23.

I got to know Him, and I got to know what He can do. He saved me. I was going under for the last time. Satan, Lucifer, the devil, the enemy had dragged me so low. I was about to give up when I heard about a man named "Jesus". I had hope! Jessie Jackson is the one that said, "Keep hope alive". My interpretation is "yes! you can dream. So, I went to work. I read Matthew 11 v:28 and it says, "you, yes you, the one who is worn, weary, tired and heavy laden – come unto me and I will give you rest". I closed the book gently and began to pray my silent, personal, private, and intimate conversation with the One who died on Calvary so my sins would be forgiven, and I would be saved.

He is here with me this morning. He is preaching to me this morning and telling me to just be still and let His will be done. I am praying. I am meditating. If I remain in Him, then He will remain in me. I am in a cocoon. He has me wrapped in a bubble. It is me and Him only. He charts my course and directs my tongue and my pathway. The search is over. I found the prize. I found His Treasure of knowledge when I opened my Bible and allowed Him to begin talking to me. Listen! Be quiet! Our God, Our Lord, Our Jesus is speaking. He is talking to me, and He is talking to you.

Let you and I consider the facts. Don't you know who woke you up this morning? Don't you know who favored you with a new beginning? Don't you know who pulled you out of that coffin, placed your feet on solid ground so you could salute, honor, worship, and salute the "Giver of Life"? My nephew, TJ Grose, told me, "Auntie" when I opened my eyes, that was enough for me. Jesus delights in us when we delight in Him. Help me lift His Name in jubilation. He sits high and looks low, and He has found me, and you this morning and He is anxious to know just how we will celebrate the new gift of a new day that He has given us.

Let Him reign forever in your life. I will let His will be done. It is with great pleasure, pride, and joy that I can devote so much time and energy to talking about my favorite subject. "Jesus

Christ". I will write early in the morning hours, on noonday, in the evening, and at night if I am directed to. I am never too busy to hear a word coming from Our Lord and Savior Jesus Christ. He is the One we should worship, honor, cherish and obey. He is Alpha and Omega. He is our beginning, and He is our end. He knew me and you before we were in our mother's womb. Jeremiah 1. He planned for me and you. Jeremiah 29 v:12.

I promise to glorify Him, magnify Him, and rejoice in His Presence. While I was ladling my coffee back and forth to cool to its desired temperature, I recited His Twenty-Third Psalm. These words made a way for me to come alive in His Presence. Surely, He says, "grace and mercy" shall follow me all the days of my life if I dwell in His secret place, in His shelter, and His Presence. What kind of relationship have I developed? Psalm 91. Because He loves me, I can call on Him.

I wanted a change. I wanted this. I wanted to divorce my old self from my new self. I changed from old clothes and put on new clothes. I began to read His Bible. I began to speak the word over myself, my family, my loved ones, and my friends. When I say my prayers, I am praying for you, me, he, him, her, she, them, and they. Try this and see how free it makes you feel. You will change from the inside out. You will become a new creature in Christ from within. He - Jesus- gave up His life for me and you so we can be saved. They pierced Him in His Hands, Feet, and Side. He bled and died just for me and you. He arose from the grave with all power, and He came to tell me to stop sleeping - open your mind, brain, heart, body, soul, and spirit and read His Holy Word. Read where it says, "I am Your God" and you don't need anything or anyone else", I will be your guiding light.

What can I say? He is the One that is empowering me. He is walking with me - every step I take - He keeps the line of communication open. The only thing I must do is hold to the peace, patience, joy, happiness, contentment, and love that He is giving to me. He has shown me the way and I must take this opportunity to tell you that I am going to stay on the battlefield. It is a battle everyday to maintain your mind on Him. You must push away all those other thoughts that want to occupy your brain and mind and call on His Holy Name. Just ask Him. "O Lord please come to see about me." Smile. Go visit the mirror and see what you see. If I, were you, I would keep talking. Shatter the ceiling in Heaven and develop your line of communication.

Some mornings I ask, "where are you" and He assures me that "I am right here", I never left you alone. I am always thinking of you. In Isaiah 49 v:15-16, it says "I will never forget about you - you are engraved in the Palms of my Hands. You are responsible for building your fire. You raise yourself from the dead. You are in control of your emotions. Remember in my affirmations, I ask Him to strengthen us physically, mentally, emotionally, psychologically, morally, and spiritually. I ask Him to push back all my emotions and let me concentrate on His goodness. Build your fire throughout your day. I will take you to church. It is a pleasure and a privilege for me to be able to shine my little light on a Thursday morning, a glorious and precious day.

If you have made Jesus the Head of Your Life, you can make it. You can cross over. You can stroll beside the lake of blue water with His waves flowing in and out and observe His snow covered mountain peaks and find peace, solace, and understanding. This is what is waiting on you on the other side. Love, joy, peace, happiness, righteousness, salvation, redemption, justice, equality, honesty, and truth shall prevail. It is written. His work is not finished because He will not let up until all the world glorifies His Name. He has provided all of this for me and you. What a delight to know that He will place peace right before my eyes for me to see. This is a glimpse of the kind of Love that I am receiving on this glorious and gorgeous day.

I see a light shining! I want to continue to be able to grow and to keep dreaming. I want all the blessings that He has in reserve for me. Eyes have not seen; ears have not heard what He has for me. For those who love Him, there is a special prize. He will uplift your spirits and renew your strength if you woke up to Him overseeing your life. Let His will be done. Allow Him to love you. He is the Only One that matters. If He is holding your hand then you do not need anything or anybody else. You and I come under His Authority; He rules the pack. He runs the show.

So how did you greet your new Thursday? Did you open with words of praise and admiration for a King who favored you with a brand new day in this era of time, on His solid and sacred Earth, on His Planet, and as a member of His Universe. I am safe. I am just the turtle that is covered by its hard shell. Have you ever touched the shell of a turtle? I have. At the fishing creek. It is hard as a rock. No predators can harm it. That is just how I am this morning, laying back, reclining, and letting Him whisper thoughts into my ears.

It is a new day - are you celebrating it? I am! I had everything I needed to cleanse and clothe my body. Isn't He wonderful? Isn't He magnificent to know what I would need? He provided for me and yes, I am "grateful". It is just the two of us, of course, He is looking out. He is the One that said I will be with you always. He is the same One that said I will always love you. In case you didn't hear Him the first time, He will say it again "I will love you always". Notice the difference between the two. Cement this into your brain! Lock it in tight! You need to put on the full armor of God because there will be battles for you to fight. Satan, Lucifer, the devil, the enemy will not let you go until you demand it. Stand up to Him and put your foot down.

Tell Our Lord, I Want You, I need You and I love You, please accept me into Your Kingdom that You have prepared for me down here on Earth. Just how bad do you want it. Read 2nd Timothy Chapter 3. It begins in the Message Bible to read as follows; Don't be naive! Don't be silly! There are difficult days ahead. As the end approaches, people are going to be self-absorbed, lover of themselves, money-hungry, self-promoting, stuck up - profane, contemptuous of parents, willing to disobey and neglect their parents, crude, coarse, dog-eat-dog world, unbending, slanderers, impulsively wild, savage, cynical, treacherous, ruthless, bloated windbags, addicted to lust and allergic to God They put on a show about religion, but behind the scenes they are animals. Stay clear of these people.

How can we keep a message of love, hope, and peace alive? Are you a member of the categories named above? Take time out. Examine yourself. Who is talking about God, Jesus, Our Lord, and Savior?

In three seconds or less, you can tell if they were sent by God or by the devil. Our Lord speaks to us just that fast. Like a bolt of lightning, He is there. Waiting, listening, and giving you a plan of action all the while you are listening. Plainly and simply - it is a new day.

He is with me, and I can't stop honoring, glorifying, magnifying Him for being so good to me. For the rest of my life, I will honor, cherish, obey, and salute the One that loved me first before I was a thought. He is right there. Open that heart, mind, soul, spirit, body, and brain and let Him in. He is right beside you. He is on my right, on my left, in front of me, in the back of me, on top of me, and underneath me. Seems like I am covered in His Grace and Mercy from the crown of my forehead to the sole of my feet. I am covered by His blood, and He will never leave me or forsake me. He promised at Hebrews 13 v:5.

Think back! It was not too long ago that you realized that He loved you. Right? He loved you enough to ride with you on your trip as you went back and forth. He equipped you with everything you would need. Right? Did he keep you safe from all hurt, harm, and danger - right?

He watched over you as you went back and forth yesterday and has returned to do it all over again. Aren't you special? Aren't you important? Aren't you loved, wanted, needed, accepted, appreciated, adored, admired, cherished, idolized, and worshipped by a King?

He smiles on you just like He smiled on me, and I love Him. He is my everything. He is the reason that I write so I can tell you and the world around me that He loves us. He loves every nook and cranny. We are His and He wants His sheep to come back inside the Pasture where they will be showered with His Unfailing Love, His Unchanging Love, His Unconditional Love, His Grace and Mercy, and His Divine Devotion.

Are you glad to be alive? Tell someone. Show someone just how glad you are. In your speech, in your mannerisms, tell Him how much you love Him. Tell your loved ones that you love them. They need to hear it. You say it now and then, but you must develop a habit of telling them that you love them today because today might be your last day.

Let us you and I ask Him to allow us to borrow more time. I have a lot to say. Don't you? He gave me a new identity, a new beginning, a new birth, a new mind, and another opportunity to praise, honor, worship, and cherish Him for being so good to me. I must tell it. Do you know it is an honor and a privilege to be able to breathe His air in and out of your lungs? Do you know it is a privilege and honor for Him to allow your heart to beat at its normal rhythm on a day that you have never seen before?

Go ahead! Take a break, drink some of the chilled water that He allowed to escape from His mountains, rivers, brooks, streams, and canals into a bottle just the right size for your hands to hold. How do these words fit into your daily worship? Stop! Examine what you think when you reach for a bottle of water with the hands and fingers and arms that He gave you. You have a reasonable portion of your health and strength. Who provided this for you? Just think! Just ponder some thoughts!

I am dreaming of a brighter day. I am dreaming of being more fruitful in the days to come. I can't stop now. He is keeping me alive for a reason. I have no idea what dimension I will be on. He keeps allowing me to travel to new heights.

Either you are a child of a King, one of God's children, or one of His sheep in His Pasture. Where do you fit in His puzzle? Your choice?

You are in control? You control your desires and wants? Right?

Do you want the best that life has to offer? Right? The release the reigns you have over your life to Him and allow His will to be done. I give myself a way to Thee so He can use me. This is my affirmation. I am following the pathway that has been designed just for me.

Are you listening? Are you cheering me on? Well! I am the most beautiful creature that He has created because I am showing Him in every way I can that I am grateful to be alive and breathing His air in and out of my lungs. I want to testify. I am not ashamed. I want to go forth and lead His sheep to the troth so they can drink some of the water that I am drinking.

It was after I looked out of the window that I realized that He had His spotlight on me during this foggy - partly cloudy day. His light shines brightest when I am reclining with my head buried in His chest so I can breathe His sweet breath. His Arms are open so wide. There is room for the two of us. You and I. You choose your spot. I have claimed mine.

I am a member of God's household.

Go ahead try to shake the tree and I will not fall because the ground I am standing on is solid and the foundation will not crumble. I am a branch on the vine. I am anchored to the root of the tree. You can't pull me up by hand. There is no turning back! You don't get a do-over. Make up your mind once and for all. For life, I am committed to my beliefs, opinions, thoughts, ideas, traditions because I know who saved my soul.

I just want to be near Him. If I draw nearer to Him, then He will draw nearer to me. Oh, Lord! I call on Your Holy Name because You saved me. I will honor You. I will worship You. I will cherish You. I will obey You. I will salute You.

My daughter-in-law, Lavetta Denson, says "Grammy! I am living the dream". Kudos to Lavetta. I can identify with her because I am in Christian City, watching His trees sway back and forth, honoring Him for making them a tree. I am sanctified with His Grace and Mercy.

The rocks will not have to cry out for me. I can do it on my own. This I know I can do. I can raise my hands, pat my feet, sway, and swerve my body because I know I am in His Presence. I have a lot to be proud of.

Chapter 18

Got a couple of minutes to spare? Go ahead! Get comfortable, relax your mind, brain, heart, body, soul, and spirit, and take a ride with me on this Thursday night here in my mansion provided to me by a King. It is our domain; it is our hide-a-way. Chances are you have never read a testimony quite like mine. I keep it real with you. There is a source of energy that draws and pulls me to this computer. It has a Name. It is His Holy Spirit. I began to canvas the mail and I find myself winding up in this writing position. Regardless of the time, it happens often as you already know. It is the sacred hour of 10 p.m. and I have got something to say. Ready for me?

What or who is my favorite subject? You guessed it - it is Jesus Christ and I have a lot to say. I never tire. I do not get exhausted easily. I can go from sun up to sundown. Our dad taught us not to ever go to bed in the daytime. There is too much to see and too much to do. He worked from sun up to sundown and instilled the same off into His children and grandchildren. So, after sleeping all night long, I am ready to go when I open my eyes and give Him worship for being so good to me.

Let me share with you how my day has unfolded. I watched some tv and learned a couple of things. People are reaching out to the masses of people with a message of love, hope, and peace, just like I am. The only problem is that it is coming from so many directions. So, I listen to the tv vessels, enjoy some easy listening music while drinking a bottle of His chilled water. My takeaway after hearing their messages is that I can't forget how He saved me. I cannot forget how He watched over my mama and daddy, sisters and brothers, cousins, and friends, and me. Only through His Divine Intervention was anything made possible.

We had a 2-bedroom home with 1 bath and about 15 stayed in that house. Everyone always had a bed to lie on or a pallet, everyone one of them was fed breakfast, lunch, and dinner. How did we do it? God knows! My mom would come through the kitchen look at me and go outside and sit under the tree and left me in the kitchen to cook and serve. I watched her - I saw how she did it. I have some of her cooking recipes and techniques tattooed across my brain, mind and heart, body, soul, and spirit. I watched her and learned how to cook quickly. She was a school dietician. It was watching her several times through the day was how I learned how to cook food in large quantities. I learned quickly and I enjoyed it. Our foods would taste so good, and we had plenty of it. We fed everyone in the house and the neighbor's three kids. Hallelujah! Isn't He great? Isn't He grand? Isn't He spectacular?

I think so. I am working under a shadow of light. I don't need that much electricity going off into my body. I enjoy His dusk dawn hours. Just before nightfall, I am writing, looking at a body of blue water, full of waves, with trees that have no leaves. It is wintertime and the mountains are covered in snow. I didn't know how much He loved me until He allowed me to escape to see some artwork that would calm me down and allow my thoughts to flow.

Do you remember when your first met the Lord? Do you remember when He stepped in, and everything worked out fine because you left all of your cares at His feet? After all, He says "I care for you"! You called out His Name aloud, over and over again.

This is the Same Name that I am worshipping, saluting, honoring, cherishing, idolizing, and obeying. Jesus came to my rescue.

I am building a stairway to the planets and the stars. I sure want to visit Pluto, Venus, Neptune, Saturn, Mars, and Jupiter. Reckon I will see them in my dreams. There is another life you can live. It is the opportunity of a lifetime. No more troubles of this world, you will be free just like His butterflies that you see float and coast through His Air. The only way for this to occur is you must remove the evil spirit of hate out of your heart so Jesus can dwell and have a final resting place. I said this earlier. It is worth repeating because someone didn't hear me. We listen but we are listening to the wrong thing. We are not listening to God, Jesus, My Lord, and Savior when He speaks to us.

What is clogging your eardrum? What are you telling yourself? You are writing your future by the words that are meditating in your head. What kind of noise is rattling in your mind, brain, heart, body, soul, and spirit? Our Lord says, "He wants all parts of you". Let me sing you a song. It is getting about my time to go to La La Land. I will undress, change into nightwear, place my head on my soft pillows, snuggle under the covers and place my head in His chest so I can breathe His sweet breath forevermore.

Be ready for the next phase. Peace and love and admiration to you, your family, your loved ones, and your friends.

Read the New Testament, King James Version, or Message Bible and witness how the Apostle Paul suffered through crisis and hardships. He never turned loose of The One that was holding his hand. Even though he was beaten, battered, and bruised, He never gave up hope. He knew God would take care of Him if He believed and worshiped His Son, Jesus Christ. The Apostle Paul was anchored to that vine that was connected to the root. He is My Rock and My Redeemer. I depend on His for everything! I am anchored. I have unshakeable faith! I believe.

I trust. I know what He is doing for me, and I wanted you to hear how He is the winds beneath my wings.

I mount up on the backs of Eagles because I have a story to tell. His Eagle is so special. They are allowed to mate while in flight. If He has His eye on His Eagles, then He sure has His eye on me and you. Want to know how I know? Because He wants me to recall yesterday. Yesterday was grand and spectacular and wonderful. I spent most of the day cleaning and writing. They were interchangeable. Yesterday He remained in my presence because I remained in His Presence. I set the tone of the day when I ladle my coffee back and forth, I recite His Twenty-Third Psalm, and this follows me around like a magnet. These words are glued to my mind, brain, heart, body, soul, and spirit. "Surely goodness and mercy shall follow me all the days of my life if I dwell in His secret place, dwell in His shelter, and dwell in His Presence.

Looks like I am covered. I know what He did for me way back when and certainly on yesterday. My today was like my yesterday. It has been exhilarating, eventful, and fruitful. I wrote a testimonial earlier during the day. After I finished listening to the tv ministers, I began to think, and process thought. TD Jakes talked about using your memory. He told His audience to think back to when you first had an encounter with the Lord. Of course, this was a praise moment. If you close your eyes and think how you made it over, you must respond with praise. Me, myself, and I just silently confirm what I already knew – that He is taking care of me right at this precise and present nanosecond. Like right now. He tells me He is keeping me in His shadow. Psalm 91.

Chapter 19

Want your day interrupted with some "good news"? I just finished enjoying an oasis of blue colors. A blue sky, a blue body of water, blue houses, blue lights, blue snow. It was cool, calm, and relaxing because I have no fire raging in my soul. I am satisfied with where my tongue has made me accomplish and learn. I use my tongue the way Our Lord and Savior has ordered me to. He gave us Divine Wisdom and Revelation when He told you "I love you"' and in case you didn't hear Him the first time is because you were not listening for a word that you would receive from Heaven. You didn't have time to sit and listen! But now you are trusting, right? You are faithful – right? You believe right? I do. There is another life for you to live. It is like a new awakening. You come alive and begin to think and process thought. There is a higher dimension that you can go to. You can go higher, the world is yours, it was built and constructed with you in mind. Try to find you a little fresh air, now and then, it renews your strength and uplifts your spirits. This is the revelation that is being released through the meditations of my heart.

Proverbs 18 v:21, that tongue. It brings life or death. I asked! Yes, I asked! That is all you have to do is ask! He will come to see about you and me at the same time. It is a new day and He loved me, and you yesterday well guess what? He has reappeared again to take good care of us. Don't you know who you are? You are a child of a King, you are one of God's children, you are one of His sheep in His Pasture. Surely you fit in either one of these people that I just described. Who are you? Whose are you?

Psalm 100! It reads "child, you and me, we are His shining Star, His favorite, and I am sure you have the time to set aside just to praise His Holy Name. Enter into His Presence with Praise and Thanksgiving! I want His Grace and Mercy. It has been following me all morning long. We are His sheep. Just you and me. Ask Him to grant us His Grace and Mercy. Have church right where you are! Whoever you are! Honor Him, Obey Him, Listen to Him. He is casting a wide net and only the pure in heart shall see God. Only the ones that got you in their heart, will get in?

I feel like a "Tumble Weed", I flow with the wind, and I am breathing dust. Because you are drying up all the forest. My sheep need the forest to breathe. So do like I do, catch you a breath of His fresh air that He is breathing on you! O, Lord! Where am I? I know it is Springtime and I have been made brand new, all over again. It is my season to grow, climb mountains, go over there, over yonder, in the Great Beyond while I have a chance. I am at Peace.

You need to just stop what you are doing and begin talking to Him? Ask Him! Go ahead and ask Him to show Himself within you. This is what He does for me. I come alive. I am glad to be alive. He has raised me from the dead and given me His spacious, big blue Everlasting Arms for me to rest my head in! Wow! Want to go with me. We are going to have to go to church. I cannot keep it in. I have got 74 years of wisdom and knowledge to share with you. I must tell you about what I have embraced, learned, and adapted to. I am only asking for 74 more. 74 after that and on through Eternity so one day I will be able to lay my head upon His chest and breathe His sweet breath forevermore.

A tribute and an honor to the Family of Deacon Essau Studymine at Mt. Gilgal Baptist Church, in Dry Branch, Georgia - our church that mom and daddy helped to build. Their beliefs were good then and I am a living witness they are still good on today. Their beliefs built a firm foundation in all of us. Everyday they were grateful because they tended to the Lord's business of providing for His sheep and taking us to church. The Lord just kept blessing them, their children, their childen's children, and it has manifested in my soul, and I must cry out. No rock will need to cry out for me. There is no raging fire within my soul, my brain, my mind, my heart, my body, my soul, and my spirit. I gave myself away totally to Thee.

Where is the fire burning? In your mind? In your heart? In your brain? In your body? In your soul? In your spirit? Oops! Times up? You may want to linger a while and ask yourself some questions? Am I where I want to be? Am I satisfied with what I see? Am I willing to look the other way? What have you become? Self-assessment. Take inventory and come to where you need to be. Come into the Pillar of Faith that I am leaning On. A pillar of rocks, they go high so that means if I am going to get higher into His Kingdom, you and I must let go of those rocks that are holding you back from receiving all that God, Jesus, My Lord, and Savior have for you.

You and I are under His care - right? I need you to agree with me! Right now. What He has created in me is because I began to listen to my sixth sense. My ability to "think and process thought? Only Jesus can free your mind so you will think only the thoughts that He wants to deposit in it? It is a new day? Someone must open the door and stare "hate" in the face and say that is enough.

It is time for a change. It is time for a believer in Grace and Mercy to occupy the Throne that I laid down for us. It is all in your tongue! That is where the secret lies! Whatever you speak you can conceive. Satan, Lucifer, the devil, the enemy has stopped you from thinking and dreaming. What if? Ask yourself? Is she for real? Just as real as a leaf on a tree.

I saw a crying tree. At one moment their leaves were firm, green, and had strength. Then later they began to wither and fade away because their source of strength was cut off.

I have nature and art exhibits flashing on my computer screen and every so often it takes me there where I just stroll in His sand in between my toes. It feels funny. I am enjoying a breeze of His fresh air because I have work to do. Come and dance with me! I must take you there! My Good Friday! April 16th, 2021, at the Gene Miller Manor Apartments.

When you say your prayers and sincerely honestly mean what you say, Our Lord and Savior will answer your prayer. Oh, I wish you could embrace the adventure that He has planned for me today. I have been walking back and forth from one happy space to another one. I checked the mail and went outside to catch a breath of fresh air because His Holy Spirit suggested it to me and told me I could. I received assurance that He was going to be with me, so I continued to do what I had planned to do.

This morning when I said my affirmations, His Holy Spirit told me to switch up my words. Stop asking and start saying "Thank You". So here goes. I will try it out on you at this 3 o'clock sacred hour.

I have to tell you about my morning. After listening to Him tell me "Wake up O sleepyhead" rise from the dead and let the Lord shine on you, I pulled my head from under the covers and welcomed in my new gray - semi foggy - glorious and wonderful day. We belong together. That is what I am told. I belong to Him, and He belongs to me. If I remain in Him, then He will remain in me.

Want to go around a mountain? Stick with me. Brace yourself because it is good news that I must share with you on this enchanted, glorious, and wonderful brand-new day. I have a brand-new mind! Let us celebrate. My today is just like my yesterday. Fulfilling and rewarding. I pray that today be the same way. I am asking that He love me today just like He loved me yesterday.

Beautiful Dreamer! That is what you and I are. Feel His breath of fresh air that He is allowing you to inhale and exhale in and out of your lungs. Thank Him for allowing your heart to beat at a normal rhythm.

So, this morning, when He blew His breath of life into my lifeless body and allowed me to become a living soul all over again, I had to give "Thanks" in the humblest manner that I knew how. He is my all in all. Can't make it without Him. There is no sense in trying, you can't make it on your own. You need Divine Intervention. You need His Grace and Mercy to accompany you while you embrace the day that He has planned for you.

It is another day; His birds are singing and chirping. His birds are giving "Thanks". Have you given Him "Thanks" for this day that you have never seen before? When I open my eyes, I feel His Love penetrating my heart, mind, brain, body, soul, and spirit. I wake up to Him every morning with Him standing beside my bed ready to take my hand. He holds it so gently, smoothly, and kindly. It is sheer joy and pleasure to wake up because I know He has watched over me while I slumbered and slept.

Back to my affirmations! I began talking after I had finished up in my happy space. I sang 'Thank You Jesus" the entire time I was on my way in and on my way out. When I snuggled back underneath the covers to reclaim my spot, that is when I heard it. Say "Thank You" and I went ahead and followed the leader and done what I was instructed to do.

O Lord, Thank You for sheltering us. O, Lord. Thank You for shadowing us. Thank You O Lord for favoring us. Thank You, Lord, for covering us with Your Blood. Thank You Lord for granting us Your Grace and Mercy on a day we have never seen before, O Lord, Thank You for forgiving us of our sins because we don't always do things perfectly and correctly. O Lord Thank You for forgiving our enemies because they know not what they do, O Lord Thank You for strengthening us physically, mentally, emotionally, psychologically, morally, and spiritually. O Lord Thank You for protecting us from all plagues, pandemics, disasters, and turmoil. Thank You O Lord please prosper us physically, materialistically, financially, and spiritually, O Lord Thank You for not casting us away from Your Presence and O Lord Thank You for letting Your Holy Spirit dwell in us on this day. In Jesus' Name, I Pray this prayer - Amen.

There will be difficult days ahead, MLK said this. Suppose the jury comes back with a not guilty verdict. We must prepare ourselves because hate is trying to take over, but we are not going to allow it. We must face it head on. All nationalities of people hate black folk. They see us devils, scoundrels, misfits, savages, and barbarians. Don't you know that? If you have had your head buried under a rock for the last 400 years, then you need to come to the creek and have a glass of His Living Water.

Hate! Hate! This is what we are breathing. It is about to overtake us. It will overtake this Land that God, Jesus, My Lord, and Savior have prepared for us if we do not stand up. Stand up for justice, truth, honesty, equality, salvation, redemption, love, and righteousness. Come from under that rock. You have been hiding too long. Push the stones away from your eyes and look through the eyes that gave you. Begin to listen with the ears that God gave you.

Time out! It is not business as usual. You are blessed and highly favored, and it is about time you walk in favor and love that you are receiving from the One that sits on high. It is a new day. His light is beginning to shine. It is lit in your heart. Pull off all the covers that Satan has blinded you with all during your years here on God's sacred and solid green Earth, on His Planet, and in His Universe.

Hate will destroy us all. Man's heart must be made clean. Evil spirits, unclean spirits must be commanded to leave your mind, brain, heart, body, soul, and spirit. This is our only hope. Call hates out! Make hate leave you alone! Only God, Jesus Christ, My Lord and Savior can do this. Am I dreaming, no it is a dream of reality? Why cannot it be the way God, Jesus, My Lord, and Savior intended for it to be. Why can't we live in this Land? Why can't we rejoice in every new day we see?

Rodney King said, "can't we all just get along". No Rodney we cannot. There is an evil force trying to destroy us. It is Satan,

Lucifer, the enemy, the devil who is pushing hate among the races. Globally, it is an epidemic. Help me O Lord to overcome! Help us as a nation to survive these pandemics, plagues, disasters, and turmoil that has come upon us.

O Lord hear my cry. Hear our prayers O Lord, heal our land.

The church is about the only place you are going to hear these words. We will let us have a church, just you and me, and invite Him to come along with us.

Jesus! Will you join me as I discuss the ways of the Land. Jesus, will you tell us what to do. Jesus says, "We must love each other". The tall ones, the short ones, the fat ones, the skinny ones, the gray ones, the black ones, the white ones, the brown ones, the yellow ones, gay or straight, we must love them.

Can this be done? Dream of a dream where you can find peace, contentment, serenity, harmony, happiness, joy, salvation, honesty, truth, equality, love, and righteousness! Do this today! Set your sites on goals higher! Aim for a higher purpose so you will get a reward!

Let Him order your steps. Let Him guide your pathway. He has the plan for you and me.

Chapter 20

I am here for you - this is what He said. I will be near you at this present and the precise moment in time because you asked "O Lord please draw nearer to me and as I draw nearer to Thee. He has accepted me just as I am. He is has smiled on me, my family, my loved ones, and my friends on this "Good Friday Night". Times have changed.

Friday night used to be a raving night. Parties, friends, food, drinks, and smokes. Now my Friday night has come to a change.

I have a new beginning. I get excited about Friday because that is the day Our Savior died. I celebrate "Good Friday" as a day of remembrance and celebration. I am alive and I know how to honor the Giver of Life for forgiving me of my sins and for saving my soul. It is just Him and I. Me and Him. Just the "two of us". I am exploring all my possibilities. Some of His tv vessels are too theatrical for me. I need someone to talk to me and explain to me how I can get to the other side.

The river is wide. There are several mountains to cross but if you hold on and don't drift away from what you have been taught and what you have learned - you have got a chance to save your soul from that fire. I believe. I trust.

I have faith. I don't try to depend on my limited understanding. I seek God's, Jesus's, viewpoint. My hand is secured tightly into His and He is ordering my steps, ideas, thoughts, opinions, beliefs, traditions, and desires.

He wants the best for me, and He consistently tells me to keep the fire going.

Do not stop believing! Do not stop trusting! There is a light at the end of the road. A big light that He wants to shine on you. His rays of thought shine so bright. At least this is what it does for me. One of His tv vessels tried to tell me that I must speak in my tongue. Some of us have spiritual gifts that are different. I have not been able to speak in a tongue, an unknown language, but the tongue that I am speaking in has allowed me to shatter the ceiling of Heaven and He hears my cry.

I am spending my Friday night in His Presence. What joy, satisfaction, and jubilation, I am having. I came this far by faith, by believing. When I found myself at the point where I had to choose to live or die, I chose life. I waltzed through my mansion calling on His Holy Name, asking Him to save me. Oh, Lord! Hear my humble cry.

Honestly and sincerely, I had a one-on-one talk with Jesus. This is who you need to get in contact with. He listens and He answers prayer. He comes highly recommended. I can only tell you about what He is doing for me.

When I am quiet, reclining in His Everlasting Arms, He whispers soft words into my heart and when He does this, I know He is the wind beneath my wings. I can mount up on an Eagles' back and soar.

You and I. Me and you. We have been chosen to receive His Grace and Mercy. It is available to all His sheep in His Pasture if they enter His Presence with Praise and Thanksgiving. Psalm 100. You choose the time and place. His Holy Spirit allowed me to choose to be in His Presence at this 9 o'clock sacred hour. I am glad about it. I gave up the Friday night frolic because Jesus came into my heart and swept all the evil spirits that had set up housekeeping in my heart away. It was so easy for Him to do because I gave myself away to Thee.

I ask that He remold me, reshape me, and make me into the person He had designed me to be before I was in my mother's womb, and guess what He did? He answered my prayer. He is answering one of my prayers as I pound key after key.

He empowers me. He enables me to move my fingers across this keyboard. It is as if when I sat down, He pulled a chair up next to me and said "Wanna have church"? I could not say no because " I knew it was going to be good". A Friday night in His Presence presented with ideas to explore. I called my oldest daughter, Tamara, to tell her how much I appreciated being a guest at the Brayboy's' Mansion during the week of Easter and she informed me she has discovered another spot for us to try the next time choose to go on vacation. She, her husband, and my grandson are a joy to be around. They are living the dream. They are protected in His Everlasting Arms. He keeps them in His shadow. He continuously watches over me, you, them, him, her, she, them, and they. Is everybody covered in His Grace and Mercy from the crown of our heads to the soles of our feet? I think so!

This is what I do on Friday nights. I put on some easy listening music, open a bottle of champagne, and pull out my chair and get busy releasing the words that are meditating in my heart. Oh! He is with me. Psalm 23 tells me that He is with me. I like to say it over and over, again and again, these words "Thy art with me". It is confidence and courage that I receive after saying these words.

I know I can continue to embrace the nighttime activities that He has ordained for me.

What a beautiful Savior. He has calmed the raging fire that was burning out of control. I am at peace. I am contented and complacent with where I am sitting. He has captivated my mind, brain, heart, body, soul, and spirit and I am glad that He did. He saved me from destroying myself. I remember Him saying to me "You, you are the one, that is burdened down, heavy laden, weary, worn and tired, come unto me and rest. My yoke is easy. I will be on one side, and you will be on the other side, and I will direct your path. Isn't He wonderful? Isn't He magnificent? Want He supply all your needs? Want Him to protect you from all hurt, harm, or danger? Want He becomes your guide and steers you in the right direction so you can give Him the Praise and Worship and Honor that He deserves?

Help me praise Him. My God is the greatest. My God has the whole wide world in the Palms of His Hands and we as sheep must allow His will to be done. We want to be saved - right. We want our reward now. Not by and by - not someday - not somewhere off in the unknown. But on this day that we have never seen before, we want to be showered with His Unfailing Love, His Unconditional Love, His Unchanging Love, His Grace and Mercy, and His Divine Devotion on a Friday night! Right?

It is church time. I had no idea that this was the way I was headed. I simply sat down and started meditating on just how good He is to me. It is under His moonlight that I get a glimpse of His night sky and his shining stars. His stars are so peaceful. They are so content. They are patiently waiting for His return because they know He is returning to take good care of them. Why can't we be like the stars in His night sky? They are permanently fixated and occupying the space that was intended for them. They know their place. They know exactly what to do. They are supposed to light up the night sky so we can stroll bare feet across the sand that is located at His beach. We can sit under the moonlight and enjoy a refreshing beverage of our choice as we give thanks for all the Love and Devotion that He is showering all over us.

Early in the morning hours, when He satisfied me with His morning mercy, Psalm 90 v:14, I asked Him to please satisfy me with His morning mercy at noontime, evening time, nighttime and He is doing just that. Oh! He is mighty! Oh! He is great! There is no one like Him. He answers every prayer, but the key is to be consistent. Say your prayers over and over, each morning He allows you to open your eyes so you can embrace a new day. My first words out of my mouth are "Thank You, Jesus". The second set of words out of my mouth are "O Lord please come into my presence and O Lord please allow me into Your Presence. This is my affirmation. These words that I release from my tongue have saved my soul. These words opened a Treasure Chest of opportunities just for me.

I want Peace, Patience, Contentment, Tranquility, Harmony and Serenity, Love and Righteousness, and the only source I know to get it from is Jesus Christ. He canvases His sheep and gives them what they need to sustain them throughout their day. I can only do one day at a time. Today is the day given to me as a gift and I must rejoice, magnify, enjoy, and celebrate it. I will never see this Friday night again.

So, I am present in His Presence, and He is taking real good care of me.

When Saturday morning comes, I will find myself repeating my morning routine repeatedly. When His Holy Spirit nudges me, I will turn over, pull my head from under the covers and do what I am instructed to do. I know how to follow orders. I can obey a decree.

I am in His Presence all day, everyday, 24/7, around the clock, every hour, every minute, every second, and right at this present and the precise moment in time. Join me! There is plenty of room. His arms are as big and spacious as His big blue sky. He will not turn you away if you are sincere and honest in your desire to receive a new life, a new mind, a new opportunity, a new beginning, a new identity. If you commit, submit, and surrender your total self over to Him and allow His will to be done – you will be born again.

You will remember this encounter! You never will forget about how He saved you! You will find yourself eagerly anticipating the next time you can be covered with feathers so you can be safe and secure tucked under His wings. Psalm 91.

If I remain in Him, then He will remain in me. If I abide in Him, then He will abide in me. If I draw nearer to Him, He will draw nearer to me. He will give me the peace, love, affection, wisdom, and knowledge, and understanding that only I can dream about. What about you? Have you stopped dreaming? Because He loves me, "I will save her". Even if she just utters my Name, I will show up faster than a bolt of lightning.

Psalm 91. Jesus will come to your rescue. He has recreated me. He has reinvented me. I am a spiritual being having a human experience.

This tongue of mine has opened doors, windows, highways, avenues, and walkways for me. I am just strolling through this Friday night to share with you the Love and Affection that I am receiving from. A King. These are my true feelings. I love Him and I will say "Thank You Jesus" over and over so I can tell Him just how much I love Him. When I show honor, worship, and gratitude to Him, I am the one that is rewarded. My heart becomes so full of pride, love, and admiration.

Saturday morning - remember - you know what you must do, and you must continue doing it - nonstop. Prayer and Praise time. Shatter the ceiling in Heaven, break it wide open so He will begin to release the blessings He has in reserve just for you so you can give Him the Glory. You will walk from room to room just thanking Him for being so good to you. This is what I do. It is nonstop praise and admiration coming from my heart. I saturate His atmosphere with words of praise that I know He wants to hear.

I am going to come clean with you! Change up your words in your mouth and rewrite your destiny. Proverbs 18 v:21 says you have the power in your tongue to order up the kind of life you want to live. I did not say it, God said it. Open your mouth and let the miracles come out. There is a powerhouse of words in your mouth. Write the next chapter in your life. I am doing just that. I forecast my future. I can only do this because I made Jesus the Head of My Life. This is the best decision I could have ever made. He is the One in control of this little ship. He is the One that is allowing this little light of mine to shine. I will only shine for a certain season and now is the time for me to shine. He is keeping me alive for a reason. Is it to tell you that you can change lanes? You can cross over because He is waiting to take you by the hand

and lead you to His Promised Land. Come and go with me. Your soul must be anchored! You must stand on His Promises.

He promised to never leave me nor forsake me, and He will do the same for you. Ask Him?

Chapter 21

Do not ever grow too old to dream. Come alive! This is what Jesus wants you to do! He wants you to call on His Holy Name because you know that is where all blessings flow. They come from the Master on High. Oh! He is mighty! Oh! He is great and He knows my name. Man can build bridges over rivers to reach the countryside. Man is so smart! My questions are Why cannot man live in peace with His brothers and sisters in the North, East, South, and West. Why can't man live in harmony with himself? What is it that is keeping you from realizing your dream? There is another life that you can live under His Guidance. If you dwell in His Secret Place if you dwell in His Shelter and if you dwell in His Presence, He will take the veil off your eyes. You must ask Him? Only then you will be able to see. You will see that you need to give up the evil spirit of "hate". It is dwelling in the hearts of man and woman, boy and girl. Don't allow hate to blind you.

Ask Him to show you love through His eyes. If He has His eye on you like He, has it on me, you can't go wrong. I know who in charge is.

I intend to make sure I stay underneath His wings. I want His Love!

Don't you? I want His admiration. I want to be the one who wears a crown! I want Jesus to give me my crown every morning I open my eyes. I can't receive my crown if I have hated lodging in all four chambers of my heart. Oh! Lord. My heart is pure, it is filled with the Love you placed in it, and I have a steadfast spirit, please come into my presence, and please O Lord allow me into Your Presence. Did you hear me? I am sincere and honest when I am speaking with a King. I know what He has done for me. I know what He has told me, and I want Him to continue whispering words into my ears. My ears were made for listening to Him as He speaks to me. Are you listening to God or man?

There is a difference between the two. You can't serve God and Satan at the same time. One of them must go. Take my advice and choose to live in the Presence of a King. He is the One watching over you and wants you to enjoy your life in abundance. He is the One who wants you to have perfect peace.

I have a view out of my window of His forest. I have never seen so many vibrant colors of green. When I sat down on this computer, I had a forest across the screen. Between His trees, He has placed a river of water. He has allowed His sheep to build a bridge so high that it covers the trees and the water. What kind of architect is this? I am just a speck in His eye. He is watching over me at this 3:30 p.m. sacred time.

All time is sacred if you have a Savior watching over you. My time is sacred because I am spending it with the One that first loved me. He loved me when I was only a thought! He had big plans for me. I am finally at the place where I can take my rest.

What am I talking about! You might ask? I am talking about having faith in the One that is Faithful. I am talking about believing that the impossible can come through looking through His eyes. I am talking about trusting in the One that your mother and father trusted in. Where does your belief lie? Do you believe that He is holding His whole wide world in His Hands? If you believe that then you know that He has me and He has you engraved in the

Palms of His Hands. Didn't anyone tell you? Well, today is the day for you to know that there is a miracle in your mouth and a powerhouse of words stored in your vocabulary just waiting to be released. Don't you read? I do. I read everything I get my hands on that will open new ideas that I can use to shatter the ceiling in Heaven so He will hear me when I call His Name. He sure is taking good care of me on this magnificent, marvelous, foggy - semi-cloudy day Saturday. I love foggy days just like sunny days. On every one of His days that He gives me, He tells me He is with me. I can't imagine living my life without Him being in control of my thoughts, actions, deeds, beliefs, opinions, traditions, and desires. When a person speaks, you are to listen and think about what they said. Ponder some new thoughts on your Saturday afternoon. Is God speaking to you? It could be true. Oftentimes you have heard the expression, "that word was for me". Come and go to church with me.

Do you want to know a secret? He was standing beside my bed when I placed my two feet on His bedroom floor with His Hand stretched out to me and I grabbed it because I knew I was accepting His Unchanging Hand. It is a choice. You have free will. You have self-control. Don't let Satan, Lucifer, the devil, the enemy control your emotions, your desires, and your mind. Don't let Him control how you feel and think and what you do. This is His purpose to steal your joy and peace, kill your desire to believe in God, and destroy your beliefs. The devil is sleazy, sneaky, sly, cunning, deceitful, lying, and will move into your head and take control of your mind, brain, heart, body, soul, and spirit if you allow him to. Snatch that curtain that is covering your face. Notice I said, "allow". It is all about making choices. Do I want that extra piece of cake knowing that it will sabotage my weight plan? Will I do this or do that just because everyone else is doing it or will I separate myself away from the pack. I want to be on the Lord's side. I want Him to govern my mind, heart, brain, body, soul, and spirit. If this is what you want, then plan to accomplish your dream. Know that He is looking at you through His eyes of Love. He loves you. He loves me and I will share it with you how He does this if you are in earshot of my voice. Are you listening? Are you comfortable? You will be by the time you finish reading. I am glad that I am alive. Today is the best day of my life because I know I am loved. I feel it. I breathe it. I taste it. I yearn for His Everlasting Arms to cradle me so I can be safe and secure.

He is alive this morning in my heart. My heart is filled with love and compassion for all His sheep in His Pasture. I have had two beautiful conversations with my neighbor and one with Jerome Williams, my former aide. The three of us. We put it together this morning. We praised Him, worshipped, Him, Honored Him, and Saluted Him for being the King that He is. He is a King to me. He calls the shots. He tells me "Wake up O sleepyhead, rise from the grave and let the Lord shine on you."

After I hear His whisper, I immediately go into a sing-along with His other Angels that are calling on His Name. You are an angel too if you are calling on His Holy Name like I am. "Thank You, Jesus". Three simple but precious words. He is the author and finisher of my fate. He tells me what to do, what to think, how to act, and how to respond to any situation, circumstance, or condition I find myself in. He puts words in my mouth. He controls my actions, thoughts, ideas, and desires because I allow Him to.

I gave myself away to Him so His will could be done in my life while I am alive, breathing His fresh air and while my heart is still beating a normal rhythm. He is keeping me alive! Should I honor Him? Should I glorify Him? Should I rejoice in Him? I think.

"Yes".

Dream with me as I take you over yonder – over there at the Great Beyond. He is waiting on you and me. He is holding the door open waiting for you to come in. He wants to lavish you with gifts galore. The first gift He wants to give you is His Love and He wants you to share the love that you have received from Him to the ones around you. We must spread a message of love, hope, and peace. That is my aim and purpose this morning for confessing my soul to you. These are the words wrapped up in my heart. I must tell it. I must tell you just how good He is to me this Saturday, April 17th, 2021.

I watched the funeral of Prince Phillip. There was so much peace and ease at His funeral. No one moved a muscle other than the singers and the pallbearers. It was rigid and ceremonial. The military was in complete control. Every one of the guests appeared to be in solitude with what was occurring. They sang songs and read scriptures. Blessings were given to Prince Phillip and His family. What a beautiful day to lay one of His sheep to rest. Prince Phillip lived to be 99 years of age. The angels in Heaven welcomed him to his new home. Our Lord only gives us seventy- years, they say. Any time beyond that time is God's years. Isn't God good? Prince Phillip had to be faithful to Our Lord and Savior Jesus Christ for Him to receive the Kingdom of God. 99 years. For 99 years He showered Him with His Love and Affection and Admiration. Can we say that He was "favored" by Our Heavenly Father and Our Lord and Savior Jesus Christ?

He has favored me, and He has favored you. I am glad that I am alive. I am glad to be among the living. Everyday is a present from Our Majesty. Sit back! Smile! Know who loves you and you know who you love. Yes! I do. He loved me first and I don't know how to repay Him for all the Grace and Mercy and Genuine Devotion that He is showering over me on this magnificent, marvelous, splendid, supreme, superb, outstanding, wonderful, magical, majestic, miraculous, and wonderful day. A new day. Psalm 118 v:24. I have never seen this Saturday before so quite naturally when He woke me from the dead, I placed a smile on my face and had a heart filled with Thanksgiving because He favored me with another glorious and beautiful day, and I will celebrate it. This is what I was told to do. Love Him back for being so good to me. I do this every morning. It is my morning ritual.

Are you comfortable? If not! Make yourself comfortable because you are about to experience a day that has been set aside to honor the One who woke us up this morning. Jesus touched me with His finger of Love and allowed me to become a living soul, closed in my right mind, with a reasonable portion of my health and strength. He gets all my honor, praise, worship, and love and I invite you to join in with me as I salute Him throughout my testimony. I see His sunset casted over His deep blue seas. The sunrays are shining on His clouds, and they appear to be a sparkling yellow and a pungent red. Easy listening to music and my favorite cup of my delicious brew and some beautiful conversations have sat my mood. It just seals the deal that I know He is watching over me. I can't imagine a moment without Him. He is surrounding me just like He surrounds His globe. I am so grateful to Him for finding me. I am so grateful that He gave me a "do-over". I am so grateful that He gave me a new beginning. A new mind. A new birth. A new identity. A new day in His Springtime. He wants me to inhale and exhale His air in and out of my lungs. I opened the window to let a little of His fresh air in. I must be able to breathe, and I don't like breathing stale air. So, I open a window when the days are cool and comfortable.

Prince Phillip loved the outdoors! I love the outdoors and I am sure you do also. I hear His birds singing and chirping. I see His green trees swaying and swerving obeying His every command. His trees are here for a purpose just like you and I are here on His solid and sacred ground, we call Earth, on His Planet and in His Universe. There is a big green universe staring us in the face. It is waiting on you and me to explore.

Brown eyes! Lift My Name on High. Continue to speak to your loved ones and shine your ray of sunshine on them on a day that they have never seen before. You are the one that will get the greatest reward. I will fill your heart with joy, praise, and gratitude because you are uplifting My Name on High. This is what He is telling me to say to you. When I look into the mirror, I remain there until I see a sparkle in my eye, while telling myself over and over that I am loved, needed, appreciated, wanted, admired, adored, cherished, and idolized by a King. What are you telling yourself on this fabulous foggy morning? Are you listening to what you are saying? Stop and examine the words that are meditating in your heart? Ask yourself "are you worthy" to receive His Love?? His answer will be "yes! a thousand times over "yes". He blew His breath of life into your lifeless body and allowed you to become alive in your senses so you could think, and process thought.

Who loves you? Who protects you from all hurt, harm, and danger? Who will allow His Holy Spirit to be our comforter and counselor? What is your answer?

I am not the only one in the universe telling you to change the words that you are releasing from your mouth into miracles that will work for you. A man is known by the character and contents of his heart. Do you need to be bumped over the head with an iron pan so you can begin to think? Right now, several lightbulbs are going off in your head - right? Reexamine your beliefs and your dreams, hopes, and ambitions. Come to grips with these words; Who am I? and Whose am I?

Realize that you too, just like myself, are one of His sheep in His Pasture and we are to enter His Presence with words of Praise and Thanksgiving. When I opened my eyes, He was right there with me. I listened to my easy listening music all during the night and each time I woke up, He was squeezing me, telling me I am here, near you.

If I draw nearer to Him, then He will draw nearer to me. Keep your confession alive. Keep your morning prayer alive. He is alive and He wants you to become alive and allow Him to dwell in your heart so He will have a final resting place.

What are the toys you have in your attic? What is going around in that brain of yours? What words are you rattling off in your head? Are you controlling your thoughts and emotions? You realize by now that you can control the thoughts, ideas, and opinions you have. When you realize this, it will be as if you were made brand new all over again. You will rise from the dead. He rose from the dead, and He gave us all power through our tongues.

Black lives matter! White, brown, yellow, and red lives matter! We all come under His Authoritative Rule. Don't have wasted days and wasted nights. Know who loves you and know who you will worship, honor, cherish and obey? We all agree. It is Jesus who is in control of us and every situation that we find ourselves in. We all agree that we couldn't make it a day without Him. We all agree that He is keeping us alive for a reason and it is about time we researched and found the reason "Why".

He snatched me out of the bunch and placed my feet on solid ground and told me to read two of His Bibles so there will be no mistake in my understanding of what He meant by writing His Holy Word. I compare the verses in His Bibles. I like to hear the meaning described from a variety of sources. I see big audiences of people wavering their hands, mumbling words under their breath, falling on the floor, all being done to show praise and honor to Thee. I am amazed at the number who have never examined their hearts and swept the evil spirits away from their hearts. Surely if it is that many of us believers shouting the same prayer - then we would not have pandemics, plagues, disasters, and turmoil. Where is the Love? We gather in large groups to show our love, but do we take it back to the neighborhoods and try to minister to the ones who are not saved? No! We are afraid!

Leap of faith. That is the only way we can make it. We must step out on faith and allow His will to be done. Every morning I open my eyes I ask Him to please come into my presence and to please allow me into His Presence. I must build a fire. I must keep tending to that fire. I continue honoring, praising, and saluting Him and then I go into my morning affirmations. O Lord please shelter us, O Lord please shadow us, O Lord please favor us, O Lord please cover us with Your Blood, O Lord please grant us Your Grace and Mercy, O Lord please strengthen us physically, emotionally, psychologically, morally, and spiritually, O Lord please forgive us of our sins because we don't always do things perfectly and correctly, O Lord please forgive our enemies because they know not what they do, O Lord please prosper us physically, materialistically, financially and spiritually, O Lord please protect us from all pandemics, plagues, disasters, and turmoil, O Lord please do not cast us away from Your Presence and O Lord please allow Your Holy Spirit to dwell in us again on this day. In Jesus' Name, I Pray - Amen.

I am wise. You are wise. Our destination is to receive all the love and blessings that He has in reserve for us. We both know that we will not allow the devil to infiltrate and destroy our minds and beliefs. We know who is holding us in the Palms of His Hands. We know the One who says, "He will never forget about us", that is you and me.

Isaiah 49 v:15-16 validates my statement. Therefore, He is watching over me, you, His trees, birds, flowers, weeds, bushes, grass, bugs, insects, butterflies, and every living creature that He created.

Isn't He just downright miraculous? Isn't He just downright wonderful? Isn't He showering you with His Love and Affection and Admiration? This is what He is doing for me as I listen to His instrumental melodies blasting from the tv's music stations. I recommend Easy Listening Music. This station cascades pictures of nature across the screen and while I am writing I can glance at it and allow my thoughts to flow in succession.

Just throw me in a pile of grass, with my sun hat on, dressed in shorts and a blouse so I can feel His love from His sun that will penetrate my bones, mind, heart, brain, body, soul, and spirit. Our world needs prayer. Your prayer, my prayer, His prayer, Her prayer, Their prayer. We need everyone to pray and ask for His Grace and Mercy. I can rejoice because He sure is good to me. You too. - Right? We are separated from this wicked and corrupt world. We know who to call on foggy days as well as sunny days - right? Thank You, Lord, for sparing us. Thank You, Lord, for smiling on us and giving us another chance to get it right.

I just finished eating a bowl of cereal that came from His wheat farm. I had almond milk with my cereal that came from His Almond Tree. I had a bottle of His chilled water that He allowed to escape from His rocks, mountains, rivers, brooks, streams, and canals into a bottle just the right size for my hands to hold. Bet you will never look at your bottle of water the same as before. You will gladly sip on the beverage that He has provided for you. It is a new day. A new beginning. Old thoughts, ideas, opinions, beliefs, traditions have passed away. You are putting on new clothes this morning supplied to you by Our Lord and Savior Jesus Christ. I am a new creature in Christ. I am a spiritual being having a human experience. I don't belong here; I am just passing through and I want to leave you a reminder that I was here, and I knew how to "hallow" His Holy Name because He sure is good to me.

I am just a seed budding from the ground. I want to bear good fruit. I want to spread my wings. I want to capture your mind, heart, body, brain, soul, and spirit so you will believe and worship Him right where you are. Feel like having church right where you are. You and only you are the ones who can make this happen.

Shut it all down and spend time in His Presence. It will be just the two of you having a conversation. He is hovering over you just like a helicopter waiting to supply your every need, answer your prayer, renew your strength, and uplift your spirit.

He is so magical that He gives His love to the entire whole wide world at the same time. As I stare at His babbling brook, trees and weeds and bushes growing on the side of His mountains, I am in awe as to the amount of peace it brings. Oh! Let me run through His cornfield swiping the tree limbs away from.

Chapter 22

There is no fire burning in my soul! My soul is filled with joy and gratitude because He spared me. He could have allowed me to go under, but He stretched His Hand out to me, and in the nick of time, I grabbed it instantaneously. If you are just searching and browsing trying to find something to do, now is the time for you and me to have a meeting of the minds. Just us two, let us invite Jesus in and ask Him to have a seat? All I want is a seat at the table. This is where it was determined at the table of who I was, who I would become, and how He would bring me back to the beginning. You see a plan was made for me and a plan was made for you. I didn't determine my reign. I just knew I wanted to be in that Number of the Saints that go marching in. How about it, then spend a little time with me.

My heart, mind, soul, heart, body, soul, and spirit are filled with love. I want to share it with you because this Love was given to me by My Lord and Savior Jesus Christ. Ready to build a fire? Ready to throw on some more logs so it will keep glowing? I am. After you spend time in His Presence listening to Him speak to you, you are a forever changed person. How do I know? Because I have experienced it. Not just on one occasion but on several occasions. He is always speaking - you must be attentive and ready to listen. He chooses the time and place so you must be ready all day, everyday, 24/7, around the clock - every hour - every minute - every second to hear a word from Our Lord and Savior Jesus Christ. Me, myself, and I. You will find me at His feet listening to every word He says.

It is Sunday morning. A beautiful and glorious, sunshiny day, April 18th, 2021, here at Gene Miller Manor in Christian City, Union City, Georgia. I have never seen this Sunday before - have you? Wonder what it will behold for you and me. I am excited and welcomes the adventure that He has planned for me to embrace. I will listen to His angels sing gospel music, I will listen to some of His tv vessels, I will listen to His Easy Listening Music, instrumental melodies as He gives me my daily bread. Sometimes I get so wrapped up in what He is saying to me, I dismiss all my surroundings and recline in my happy space so I will not miss a word of what He is saying to me.

He allows me to feel His Enchanted Everlasting Arms all around me. This is a tiny slice of Heaven. His sunset glossing over His meadows, that is what I am seeing, blue skies casting a shadow over His blue waters, cottages of people living side by side in harmony and peace. The only way they found it was through Jesus Christ. That is where the peace is. It is at the hem of His Garment. I am going to that Promised Land, it is too beautiful, don't you hear people shouting about it.

Give me my land now! I can't wait until I am dead and gone to experience what He has planned for me. I am coming to the Lord through backaches because I must prove Satan wrong, I will walk up straight again. Maybe not today, or tomorrow, but One day He will - Jesus will take all the pain away and allow me just one more time to walk straight up again, I will praise you. The rocks will not cry out because I knew it is through your rocks are you able to build a foundation that will keep standing. Standing beneath His wings, aren't we? I pray. I talk. I ask that He only allow me inside His gate so I will be protected from the raging storms in my life.

Know what He did? He appeared. Dream with me. No! This is not a dream. This is reality. This is where I came from, where you could open the windows at the home and allow His fresh air, His Love to float through your house because it was "Sunday Morning." You have something to celebrate. It is "Sunday morning" and I believe more than I did last Sunday morning. He just keeps pulling me in. He tells me "Follow me" and I am not turning back. Soon it will be over, and I will not be dead in my grave waiting to die. I am asking for Eternal life.

Let me! Allow me! Let me live today. Let us relax, find our groove, take it slow, take it easy and just sit back and enjoy the time you are spending inhaling and exhaling His air in and out of your lungs. You know He is the One that breathed His life into your lifeless body and allowed you to become a living soul all over again so you could praise Him for raising you from the dead.

Ready for a second sermon? If not! I understand. If you have the time, then I have the time. You see I know a couple of things. I know if you open the window, smell His breath, He will breathe life all over you in that sin-sick soul. Satan, Lucifer, the devil, the enemy only takes over if you let Him. He can only influence. You have the final say. You know who has brought you from a mighty long way. You came from behind the fence. You just crossed over – one day – your eyes opened, and you have allowed yourself to just breathe and thank Him for every breath you take.

Don't let Him in. Put up your guards. Don't let Satan in. Use your memory. Remember your mother, your father, your sister, your brother, your auntie, your cousin, your friend told you to have faith. Have faith in yourself. You can do it. The world is wrapped up in an oyster. His soul is protected. His soul is saved just by listening to His musical instruments. He can save your soul just like He saves the life of His oyster. His oyster is sealed tight. You and I must stand on His Promises. I want to build a pearl.

Allow your heart to glow! Build a fire! Add to your fire! The more fire you have in those bones the higher your flame will glow. His written word. Words build. Words create. Words persuade. Words convince.

My mama and daddy had love for each other. Have Love for each other is what they said. Practice it. They taught it to us. They know the source of their peace and contentment. They know that if they want to continue to receive the Love from God that they must love each other. Why can't we all just get along? This is what Rodney King said. We can't just "get along" until man changes his heart and seek Divine Intervention. Jesus said, "I am the truth, the way, and the life". Follow me. Tell someone. Listen to God. Listen to Jesus. Get it straight before you spread the news. Do you know Him for yourself? Have you tried Him? If He has never failed you yet, then hold on to that string. His fabric is intricately woven. Catch the string if you can't catch His Hand. My advice to you is to try and move in so close to His chest that you can lay your head upon His chest and breathe His sweet breath forevermore. It is Sunday Morning. Come alive. Rise from the dead. Let Our God, Our Lord, Our Jesus shine on you. You deserve it.

I know how to cool down. I drink a cold chilled beverage either chilled or at the right temperature. I renew my strength and uplift my spirits. There is love, there is kindness, there is joy, there is peace, there is trust, there is faith, there is honesty, justice, and truth being passed around for those who are willing to drink from the cup of truth and righteousness.

Listen to Unchanged Melody - He is the wind beneath my wings. He has me mounted on top of an eagle. Yep! You guessed it I am one of His sheep in His Pasture just trying to make a dent in your life. Think!

Listen! You have a sixth sense. You must allow it to come to you.

You must dream both night and day that He is holding your hand and I know He is holding my hand. He is My Leader. My Commander-in-Chief, the designer and coordinator of my soul. I yield my case.

To get to God you and I must go through Jesus. Jesus is the One that is sitting on His right hand side. Jesus is our intercessor. Jesus is the One speaking to God on our behalf. I trust you, Lord. I believe you, Lord. I have faith in you O Lord. I am only one pea in the pod, and I have a story to tell. Ready for church? I will take you there. It is the sacred hour of 10 a.m. and you see where I am geared up to go. If I dwell in His Secret Place, if I dwell in His Shelter and if I dwell in His Presence, He will allow His Grace and Mercy to follow me all my days. Say that one more time. Read Psalm 23 and it says, "Thy art with me" and surely His Goodness and Mercy shall follow me all the days of my life if I dwell in His Presence. Oh! He is alive. Oh! He is dwelling within my spirit. I welcome Him all day, everyday, 24/7, around the clock, right now at this present and the precise moment in time.

Build a fire! Help me to keep my flame burning. Witness with me if you will - just how good He is to you on this Sunday morning. What a glorious and beautiful day to be alive and among the ones who chose to live their lives in the Presence of a King. We are saved! We are redeemed! We have been endowed by Our Creator with Perfect Peace. It only comes through knowing Jesus. It only comes through if you are allowing Jesus to hold your hand. You are too beautiful to be left to the fowler's snare. You are too beautiful to be left alone to fend for yourself. He wants you to come inside the gate so He can take good care of you. Psalm 23 says "The Lord is My Shepherd, and I shall not want."

Let me call you by your favorite name. Is it my cupcake, is it my brown eyes, is it my favorite, is it my shining star, is my tulip, is it my rose? Am I a butterfly? Am I a hummingbird? Am I an old oak tree? Am I a Georgia Pine? What is your favorite name to be called? Call me a child of a King, one of God's children, and one of His sheep in His Pasture. I will answer all three. He is the One that pulled up a chair right beside me when I pulled the chair out from the computer desk and began to sit down. I began early conversing with Him. It was during the wee hours of the morning when I first began to "hallow" His Holy Name for being so good to me. He allowed me to flush my kidneys and excrete my bowels. Isn't He wonderful? Isn't He glorious? I think so and I give Him all my praise, worship and honor, and love on a glorious and beautiful cool Sunday morning during the Springtime of the year. In 2021. He is mighty! He is great! Do you agree? This is my personal and private and intimate testimony.

Watch me take you to a higher dimension! I wasn't kidding when I said I was going to take you over yonder, over there to the Great Beyond. Are you ready for church? We will shatter the ceiling of Heaven with our testimony so He will release to us the blessings He has in reserve for you and me. Make yourself happy. Make yourself content. Make yourself satisfied. Accept Him as Your Lord and Savior. Bow to Him and ask Him for His Unfailing

Love, His Unconditional Love, His Unchanging Love, His Grace and Mercy, and His Divine Devotion. This is what I did. Use my recipe and see what you can accomplish and obtain. Every tongue must confess that Jesus is Lord. Ask Him to dump buckets and tons of His Love right over your shoulder. Let His Love drizzle all over you. It is only His tender Hands of Mercy that He wants you to feel. Release that stress. Breathe, take in the beauty that surrounds you.

Want peace, contentment, tranquility, harmony, and serenity this morning? Renew your strength and uplift your spirits. You must do this on your own. I opened the door. Now it is your turn to knock, seek and see what you will find. I know what I have got. I know what my tongue has enabled me to accomplish. I know how to reveal to you the contents of my heart. I want to be like Him. I want to be with Him. I don't want Him to ever leave me alone. We belong together. He belongs in my heart so He can dwell and have a final resting place. It is Sunday morning, rise from the dead and let the Lord shine on you. Let Him scour your heart clean. He will scrub it clean then massage it with His Love, His Kindness, His Softness, His self-control, His Faithfulness, and His Love all rolled up into one soft ball and it is at your doorstep. Stop walking over your blessings! Thank Him one by one. I can't stop believing. I can't stop worshipping. I can't stop honoring. I can't stop saluting Him because He is so good to me. He gave me a platform. He gave me the table to sit at. Stay close and I will shine a light on your pathway. This is what He said to me. If I remain in Him, then He will remain in me. If I abide in Him then He will abide in me, if I draw nearer to Him then He will draw nearer to me. Magic. Majestic. Miraculous. Wonderful. Spectacular. Faithful. He is my all in all. He is holding my hand and He will not let it go if I hold on to a tight grip. He will follow me from one happy space to another happy space. He has me surrounded. I am in a bubble, and He is causing me to bounce back and forth with knowledge, wisdom, and understanding. He is holding me in the Palms of His Hands. Isaiah 49 v:14-16. We are! You and me, him, her, she, he, them, and they carved in the Palm of His Hand. He has the blueprint for our lives. Allow Him to order your steps. Ask Him? He is listening to you. He is listening to me, and He is resting in my heart because I cleaned it out so He could dwell. You are getting it from the horse's mouth.

Read St. Mark. Chapter 7. Clean and unclean heart. Your choice, you choose. It is Sunday morning, a time of gratitude and jubilation that we see another Sunday morning. Let us get overjoyed because we are alive. One more day. I am getting closer into that Kingdom, and I want to hear Him tell me "Welcome servant" for a job well done.

Did I come down your street this morning? Did I light up your life? Did a couple of lightbulbs go off in your head? If yes! Then there is more to come. If no! Then reexamine your mind, heart, brain, body, soul, and spirit. You may need a heart transplant or a new set of eyes. I could cry you a river, but I am not in the same boat that I was in years ago. Jesus casted a wide net and I got caught. Love walked in and despair and disappointment flew out of the window. Love, Peace and Happiness. I received a new life, a new beginning, a new birth, a new mind, a new identity, and I was born again. That is what I want to talk about. Are you ready to listen?

It is time for a sip of my delicious brew that I am tasting right at this present and the precise moment in time. It surrounds His whole world. His water. That Divine Healing waters. That water that He dipped you in in the pool. That is deep water. I lean back. I take a deep sigh of relief because I know who is holding me in the Palm of His Hand.

It is Sunday morning. A time for worship. A time to sincerely and honestly listen to the words that you are reading. I love being in His Presence. I love being wakened to Him standing beside my bedside ready to take me by the hand and lead me on. I hear His birds singing and chirping. I hear them giving praises to Him for His sunshine and fresh air. Hear my praise this morning as He allowed me to be closed in my right mind with a reasonable portion of my health and strength so I could glorify and magnify and rejoice in Him for being so good to me. I am glad that I am alive. I may never get another day like this one so I will celebrate it as if it is my last. Just because I can. Just because He allows me to call on Him. Just because He will supply all my needs. Just because He will protect me from all hurt, harm, and danger. Just because He will allow His Holy Spirit to become my counselor and comforter. He is mighty and great. He is worthy to be praised. He is worthy to be saluted, honored, and cherished by little old me.

This is me sharing, caring, and giving you part of the Love and Divine Devotion that I am receiving. It is a "fine day" if you allow Him to be the Head of your life. It is a "fine day" if you allow Him to move into your heart and fill it with His Love and Divine Devotion. It is a "fine day" because I am alive, and I know who loves me. It is a "fine day" because I know who I am. Just like He has His eye on His sparrow, then certainly He has His eyes on me and you. Want to be in that number when the Saints are called up yonder? Want your name to be carved in the Lamb's Book of Life?

Well! Climb aboard this ship - there is plenty of room. His Everlasting Arms are as wide as His big, blue spacious skies and I am sure He can find a spot for you. You are His favorite. You are His Shining Star. You are great. You are His masterpiece. You are a fine specimen of His workmanship. He is keeping you alive for a reason. You have been given a reason to live. You have been given a reason to come alive in your senses so you can "think and process thought".

Your senses have been lying dormant for a long time. What do I mean? Something happened and you no longer think, and process thought. You stopped believing. You stopped dreaming. Satan, Lucifer, the devil, the enemy has draped a curtain over your eyes. He allows you to see, hear, listen, and taste what He has designed for you. He caught you asleep. Satan then breathes His fire into your bones. There is no raging fire in your soul if you love the Lord, Our Lord, and Savior, Jesus Christ, Our God. You are blinded by your own two eyes. You say, "I can see fine". Can you see the doors that Jesus Christ wants to open to you? Believe. Trust. Hope. Are you familiar with these three words? I bet you have heard them a couple of times -- right? You and I, the two of us, must walk by faith and not by sight. I believe. I trust. I hope. I have faith. This may be the last dance. Walk hand in hand with Our Savior. He loves you and He loves me. He wants you to acknowledge His Presence.

I believe that there is a better life for me to live. Stop leaning on your understanding and begin to see your life through the eyes of Our Heavenly Father, Our Jesus, Our Lord, and Savior. My cup is running over this morning. I have gotten started, and I do not know when to stop so go with me. His words are tender, kind, soft, and delicate to your heart and ears. Hear this rich man, poor man, tall one, short one, skinny one, fat one, little one, a big one, a brown one, a black one, a red one, white one, gay or straight - you are all sheep in His Pasture, and you must take up your cross and follow Thee. Face the facts of life. You could not do it on your own. You cannot live the life that He has intended for you to live without His help. You are wading in the water without a paddle. You are being tossed about like the waves in His seas. He has not left you alone. He wants you to call out, reach out and grab His Hand. He wants you to be pulled to safety. Only under His wings, you will find safety and security. Psalm 91 says "He will cover me with His feathers and under His wings, I will seek refuge."

Draw nearer to me and I will draw nearer to you. O, Lord! Hear my prayer. O, Lord! Answer me tenderly. Shine your spotlight on me, you, him, he, her, she, them, and they. Love us O Lord! Walk with us O Lord! O, Lord! Please cradle us in Your Everlasting Arms right at this present and the precise moment in time. I have been thinking about you, He says. You can always be my tulip. We will never be apart. I will love you always. I will always love you. I will watch over you every day of your life so you can show your warmth and beauty so you can bloom at a designated season of the year. I will never leave you alone. Jesus said, "I am the way, I am the truth, and I am the life." This is where you want to live. Lay down your burdens. Lay them at His feet. He has the plan. He knows the truth about your existence. In Him there is life. In Him you can live and not die. In Him there is hope. I see a brand new day.

As I peeled back the covers to place my feet on His floor, I began to sing a song "Thank You Jesus", repeatedly and again. I sang these three precious words as I entered my happy space and, on the way, out to return to snuggle up in His Everlasting Arms.

Last night when I laid my head upon His chest, I began talking. He began to cradle me, and I whispered a joyous, sincere, and honest prayer to Him because I was talking to My Savior. Then I drifted off into La La Land. This is what I call Wonderland! I went to sleep.

I woke to a kind and gentle voice. "Wake up O sleepyhead, rise from the dead and let the Lord shine on you". I began to call on His Holy Name. I began to saturate His atmosphere with words of praise and admiration. I returned to get all nestled in so I could reclaim my spot. I began to say my affirmation; O Lord please come into my presence and O Lord please allow me into Your Presence. I remember repeating this about three times, each time pulling the covers closer to my neck, and then He told me "We will never be apart."

My heart, my mind, my brain, my body, my soul, and my spirit were instantly filled with joy, pleasure, satisfaction, and jubilation. I began talking because I knew He was listening to me. I have that much faith. I trust His word. I trust Jeremiah 29 v:12 where it says, "I will listen". We will never be apart. He hears me and He has promised that He will respond. I pray a simple prayer "O Lord! Let Thy will be done for me and through me. I am a sheep in Your Pasture, and I will do what you tell me to do. I will say what you tell me to say. Philippians 1 v:6 says I am sure of this, that He who began a good work in you will bring it to completion at the day of Jesus Christ." Thank You, Lord, for what you have instilled in me. Thank You for Your Promises. I want to tell you. I yearn to tell it. I cannot keep this "good news" to myself. I must share with you how the Lord saved my soul. When I walked out on that limb, I had no idea that He had placed a safety net to catch me as I began to fall. I was leaning heavily on my understanding, but I learned quickly to throw in the towel and ask Him to "please save me".

He was standing at my door the entire time. When I opened it, in walked His peace, love, satisfaction, pleasure, honesty, truth, justice, salvation, redemption, and righteousness that only He could give. Ask any preacher, any minister, or any other vessel if you don't believe me.

He gives us our individual needs. He wants to love you. Honestly, He will put no one before you. You are His. We belong to Him. He calls the shots. He is the author and finisher of our fate. Believe Him. I am the True Vine. Ask John 15 - I am the vine, and you are the branches, whosoever abides in me then I will abide in Him, He is the one that will bear much fruit and He knows apart from Me He can do nothing. If anyone does not abide in me then he is thrown away like a branch and withers and the branches are gathered, thrown into the fire, and burned. If you abide in me, and my words abide in you, ask whatever you wish, and it will be done for you.

Can it be said any plainer than that? It is a sunny warm, day with only a slight breeze and small rays of His sunshine. He is blowing a cool breeze over my shoulders as I witness His landscape. A picture of His Canadian sunset. A picture of a "Tulip". Have you ever felt the soft petals on this flower? This is a must. They feel almost like silk. You know that fabric we can get from silkworms. His creation. You, me, Him, Her, She, He, Them and They. All of us are lumped into the pot. It is a big pot; it can hold you and me and all His creation in this pot.

Let me get away and breathe His air in and out of my lungs as I sit in the hammock, under the umbrella, in His swing and rock back and forth, ever so gently. Catch a breath of His fresh air. He is giving you His air to breathe. "Thank You, Jesus" for being so good to me. You gave me another chance and I will earn my title so I can receive my crown. I want to be one of His Queens. Don't you? He is taking applications for King's also.

I am making dinner. Stewed Turkey Wings, Stuffing, and String Beans. Sounds delicious right? Just some of what I have discovered in my Treasure Chest. He loves me and He is with me wherever my little feet may trot. I love Him. How deep is your love? How much do you love Him? Then do what He says, "Think and Process Thought". I am only one of His gifts.

The doors of the church are open in your heart. As time goes by you will recall or remember that the Same Grace that He gave to your mom and dad is the Same Grace that is available to you and me on this glorious, gorgeous, and beautiful day. Ask Him for your share! I am sure He has a lot to spare. He will never ever forget about you. You are engraved in the Palms of His Hands. Isaiah 49 v:15-16.

Chapter 23

Church time. What is a millisecond? One thousand of a second, that is loose, the is just how fast I allow myself to be in His Presence. Every millisecond, every nanosecond, every minute, every hour of the day, all day, 24/7, around the clock He hangs with me. It is my new Monday morning and when I first sat down and glanced at the computer it told me it was Monday, April 19th, 2021, at the sacred hour of 1 p.m. I rejoice. I am glad that I am alive.

Just waiting for a business associate to arrive. Let me tell you about the pictures that cascaded across my tv screen and my computer screen at the same time. One was a pool of bats flying in a pool, they were glowing, and their colors ranged from gold, yellow and brown and some black. Bats know how to live in harmony, why can't we. Man's head is buried in the sand. He keeps looking down and not looking up, around, outward, and beyond. Man, only sees what His imagination will unfold.

One screen showed me the picture of His sunset. The radiant yellows, reds, and orange colors were breathtaking. I can feel His gentle wind as it floats by. I have His window open, and a cool breeze is cascading my body and listening to some soft gentle music. I can think when I am listening to this kind of music. I hear the sound of each instrument playing in harmony. Oh! He is a Beautiful Savior! I enjoy being satisfied with whatever I dream. He is right here beside me. I can confer with Him anytime I want to because He is always listening.

Me, myself, and I, do not have much to say. I listen to His birds as they chirp, sing, fly and play. I was reclining earlier during the day, and I saw two blackbirds floating, sailing through His air with such grace. They prearranged it so they would fly past my window. I saw His big, blue spacious skies stretched out for all His children to come and seek refuge in His Everlasting Arms.

If you are like me, you can lay your head upon His chest whenever you feel like it and breathe His sweet breath forevermore. Let us do that! He will allow you to get that close? If I remain in Him, then He will remain in. If I abide in Him, then He will abide in me. If I draw nearer to Him, then He will draw nearer to me. He is all around. One of the managers placed a flier in the doorway and she had written His Psalm 23. The Psalm that saves my soul all day, everyday, 24/7, around clock - every hour - every minute and every second. Try it. Pace it across your heart, mind, brain, body, soul, and spirit. Let it cover every nook and cranny.

"I see you". He says.

I am watching over you". Recline, watch the birds fly through His big blue sky. Watch the clouds as they appear to float back and forth, from one end of the Earth to the other end. Gently, calmly, tenderly, they float not disturbing the other clouds. Each cloud has a job to do. Just like a man. Each man has a job to do. Oh No! Your job is not to eat, sleep, gossip, and sit under the shade tree. Man - Your job is to save somebody's soul for Christ. Who woke you up this morning? Who blew His breath of life into your lifeless body and allowed you to become a living soul all over again? In case you did not know - it was A Beautiful Savior, Our Lord of Lords, and Our King of Kings. That is the One. That is who is responsible for raising me from the dead.

Early in the wee hours of dawn, He nudged me and touched me with His finger of Love and told me to "wake up O sleepyhead" rise from the dead and let the Lord shine on you. It is Monday morning, move about - you have a whole day ahead of you, what will you do? I will enter my happy space and enjoy all the gifts that you have on display for me. This was our morning conversation after I had worshipped, adored, admired, cherished, and idolized Him for being so good to me to allow me to flush my kidneys and excrete my bowels. As I was finishing up, washing my hands, I took several seconds longer to finish up, because I began to feel how good His hot and cold water mixed felt to my hands. Have you ever noticed it? Bet you have never looked at a tree long enough for it to begin sparkling. This is what the birds see - they see sparkles on every leaf on His tree.

The tree is speaking out - hey - I am alive - don't chop me down. Man is alive but He continues to allow Satan, Lucifer, the devil, the enemy to chop him down by controlling every impulse in your mind, brain, heart, body, soul, and spirit. This is Monday morning and I have so much to say. How did you enjoy your Sunday? Was it fulfilling and rewarding? Did you notice who was watching over you while you went here and there? He is never far away. He hovers over you like a helicopter. This is what He is doing for me.

I watched CMA last night. Why can't the entertainers put on some clothes and cover their bottoms and their chests up? Who wants to see it? Hold some of your treasures to yourself! Don't let it all hang out! Go in reserve mode! I am saving this for later. Not now, it is too early to reveal all of me to you. What is going on in that head of yours? What do you have to offer? What can you bring to the table? Nudity? Is any common sense available – I want to know? Do you have common decency?

These are the questions you should be asking yourself when you meet one of His sheep in His pasture. It is Monday morning, April 19th, 2021, here at Gene Miller Manor in Christian City in Union City, Georgia. I am alive. I am not dead. I am just as alive as the leaves on His green trees. The color green. Can you imagine seeing pea green, lime green, money green all at the same time? This is what I see. I see bridges and highways built over canals. I have been visiting Italy and Guatemala on my adventure that He planned for me today. I saw structures built in the year 250.

Our world! It is remarkable. There is more for the human eyes to see than what you are looking at right now. There is a better world out there only if you are ready for me to describe the beauty that was preached to me that I can enjoy when I get over yonder, over there at the Great Beyond.

I can't wait. I want it now and I have the secret. It is in your tongue. You speak it, then you allow it. You believe it. You trust in it. You don't give up – right? You know what you have learned from listening to your elders. Those that know just a little bit more than you, like your mom and dad, sisters and brothers, cousins, and friends. What a wonderful world! They are trying to tell you that they have seen it before and there is another life that you can live if you would only come alive in your senses and begin to think, and process thought. It is a wonderful world – only if you make it so.

This is my magnificent, marvelous, splendid, superb, and wonderful Monday morning and I will not take "no" for an answer.

You know who loves you - right? You know who is watching over you - right? You know who is making a mental note of everything that you are saying - don't you? It is Jesus. He is keeping excellent records. He fills out a report on you daily. Daily I am recognized as a member of His household because every morning I open my eyes, I began to saturate His atmosphere with words of praise and admiration because He is taking good care of me all day, today, everyday, 24/7, around the clock, every hour - every minute - every second and right at this present and precise moment in time.

He made the decision that I could come alive and be closed in my mind right with a reasonable portion of my health and strength, did you know that? I recognize who the Giver of Life is? He allows me time to "think". He does not rush me. It is my decision. I wanted a new beginning. I wanted a new mind. I wanted a "do-over". I wanted a new opportunity to get it right and you know what He did - He answered my prayer. Is today -the day I begin to call on Your Precious and Holy Name?

Just let it be! Let His magic be showered all over your shoulders. He will massage your body, beginning with your head, then move His way down your upper and lower extremities. Has the nail technician ever massaged your hands, arms, legs, thighs, knees, and feet? Mine has! His Hands feel better because you know He is gliding His Grace and Mercy all over your body and will give you a bottle of lotion to go over your entire body. I call His lotion "Divine Devotion" because it was intended just for me.

I am hanging on this morning by the strings in His garment. George Floyd's death. We are reliving every breath he took. My daughter says "get ready mom! Expect a "not guilty" verdict. So, I am preparing myself. Justice, honesty, truth, salvation, redemption, love, and righteousness can only come from a King. It is His will that must be done. We must abide by rules and regulations. We can turn out heads in a different direction and look forward. If there is no "guilty" verdict, then we must continue to pray and know that He will make a way to shine His light over the entire situation. He has never failed me yet. He is holding His whole wide world in the Palms of His Hands.

I am glad it is being televised so we can hear the prosecution and defense. We can compare notes. It only takes one to suggest reasonable doubt and it will result in a hung jury and then what. We must act fast. Certainly, we have a world leader who will address the nation and ask for peace, patience, and calmness. Gather the facts first and then control your emotions. We as an African American Nation of people can't accomplish anything when we are looking at dust, confusion, rage, anger, lies, and deceit. Try and get a clear picture of what is going on.

Let the smoke clear and then let us sit down, gather our thoughts, and plan a strategy of what we can do to overcome, so we as a nation of brown, black, yellow, and white people can heal! We are in the middle of a storm. We are in a pandemic. We are in a plague. We are in a disaster. Our world is in turmoil. How can I sit here and compose any meaningful thought? One thing I do know that it is out of our hands. We are in the Hands of Almighty God and what He says is what we must live with. We shall overcome. Don't you feel it? Can you see it?

One day we will all be judged by the contents of our heart and not by the color of our skin or the texture of our hair. You and I have to move to a higher dimension. Ask Our God, Our Lord, Our Jesus to elevate our status so we will not be affected by the ways of this wicked and corrupt world. It is ruled by Satan, Lucifer, the enemy, the devil. Satan at work! Rage, anger, hate, savages, barbarians. Thieves, murderers, rapists, mass shootings, and mass murderers. Common everyday occurrence - right? Somehow, man must get in control of himself before we are all destroyed. Man must be able to control his thoughts, ideas, actions, desires, beliefs, traditions, dreams and opinions. Man must begin to believe in a higher power. Man must clean his hearts of all unclean spirits. Hate! This is the disease affecting our nation. Man must turn to Jesus, tell Him all about it, and ask Him to ask the Father to heal our hearts and our land.

You must put Jesus first. I made Jesus the Head of My Life, and this is the best decision I could have ever made. He answered all my prayers. It was all "just for me". at the wave of a hand, I can change just like that because I am under Divine Authority, so I know how to listen, learn, and obey. It is beautiful where I am. I have peace, patience, kindness, gentleness, softness, faithfulness, self - control combined with His Love. This is the kind of present Jesus rolled up to my door. I cannot step over either one of them. I must pick up each one and examine it and see how He lavishes it all over me.

Are you ready to take that chance again of believing, trusting, and worshipping the One who has all power in His Hands? I am! Travel with me. Dream with me. Come alive in your senses - your sixth sense and begin to just simply and honestly "Think". Take a gigantic sigh of relief, sit back and just allow your thoughts to flow out and embrace the leaves on His trees. They sparkle. His leaves on His trees are alive. Are you alive? Are you able to get enough courage to give Him praise? This will illuminate your brain, mind, and heart. You will become alive and realize that this felt so good that you would continue to do it - over and over again - there will no one who will be able to hear you - if you affix your mind on Him and thank Him for being so good to you on a Monday morning that you have never seen before.

It is a new day! Are you dead? Are you in your coffin? Just know He will tell you "I will be with you always - we will never depart from each other. I will be there right by your side. Trust in me. Believe in me. Worship me. Honor Me. Cherish me. Salute Me and glorify My Name. That is your job. No big requirement - right? Nothing you can't do - right? Then begin now when you place your feet on the bedroom floor. Honor Him. Say "Thank You Jesus" on the way in and on the way out of your happy space and repeat it softly as you nestle under the covers to regain your spot.

I fluffed the pillow and pulled the covers up close to my neck and I began talking. I ask O Lord please come into my presence and O Lord please allow me into Your Presence and then I got so comfortably, I continued and asked O Lord please shelter us, O Lord please shadow us, O Lord please favor us, O Lord please cover us with Your Blood, O Lord please grant us Your Grace and Mercy, O Lord please forgive us of our sins because we don't always do things perfectly and correctly, O Lord please forgive our enemies because they know not what they do, O Lord please strengthen us physically, mentally, emotionally, morally and spiritually, O Lord please protect us from all hurt, harm, and danger, O Lord please protect us from all plagues, pandemics, disasters, and turmoil, O Lord please prosper us physically, materialistically, financially and spiritually, O Lord please do not cast Your Presence away from us and O Lord please allow Your

Holy Spirit to dwell in us on this day. In Jesus' Name, I Pray - Amen.

Your dreams can be fulfilled! Take a deep sigh of relief. Get a sip of your beverage. Set the music. Let it marinate your bones, brain, mind, heart, body, soul and spirit. Let us get sincere and honest. Let us refrain from thinking ungodly thoughts. Let us train ourselves to think higher than the level we are currently on. Let us see each other as a beacon of light that God is shining through you. You are not a stranger to me because "I love you". I am following a royal command. I just love each one of my brothers and sisters in the North, East, South, and West and I must love myself before I can love anyone or anything else.

Tranquility, Harmony, Contentment, Serenity. All these words spell Peace! Where can you get it? It is at the feet of Jesus. You must take up your cross and follow Him. He has swung the door wide open, and you must come on in out of that rain. You do not want to drown in your sorrows. You want to belong in God's household. You have had a beautiful description given to you by the preachers, lecturers, teachers, and other vessels of how life is on the other side. Do not wait. Live now! This is the only chance you will get. Ask for His Grace and Mercy, now! Ask for His Divine Devotion! now!

It is as if I woke up one morning and realized that I was not dreaming. He is watching over you and me. He is listening to every word we say. He is living within my heart, and I want Him too. I don't want too ever be apart from Him. I want to stay in His Presence forever. Here I am saved from the wolves. Even the wolves are tired of flesh being eaten, they have begun to enjoy vegetation and berries. When will man stands up to Satan and tell

Him - okay - that is enough. I am not going to take it anymore! Put your foot down. Fall back on your beliefs. Fall back on the One who you know is cradling you in His Everlasting Arms.

Ask Him to let His will be done! You know who you are depending on! Trust me. You will feel so wonderful! Finally, you have gained your freedom. You are not burdened down with trials and tribulations. You can breathe. The veil of deceit, anger, rage, and violence have been ripped from your soul. There is no fire raging in your soul - right. You have casted all your cares on Him because He cares for you.

1st Peter 5 v:7. You read it right?

You are in good hands - right? You are deeply rooted in that vine - right? If you are not anchored to that vine, then you will not bear good fruit. You reap what you sow. Your mind will only release what you have put in it. I asked for my freedom. I ask O Lord please give me a free mind, a free brain, a free heart, a free body, a free soul, and a free spirit. He will answer prayer. He answers mine. I am sure He will do the same for you. I ask Him all of the time to shower me with His Unchanging Love, His Unfailing Love, His Unconditional Love, His Grace, and Mercy and His Divine Devotion all day, everyday, 24/7, around the clock - every hour - every minute - every second of the day. Like right now, He is surrounding me. This is what He has been doing throughout my morning routine. Isn't He wonderful? Isn't He great? Isn't He mighty? Want He answer your prayer? Have you had an intimate, personal, and private conversation with Him? I have!

I am listening to music that will soothe that fire within me. Sometimes I get overexcited about what the next prospect will be.

My heart starts palpitating fast. I begin to take short breaths and some of the time I just have to sit back, sip on a bottle of His chilled water and relax my mind and say, "what's next"? I just want to stay here and watch the red and black and blue beetles perched on the arm of an octopus. They are both so content. Calm that raging fire in your soul by slowing up. Move and glide along at the pace of a snail. Quiet that fire! Get comfortable in your skin. Get comfortable with who you are. Spend some alone time with yourself then easily ease into His Presence and ask Him to please take good care of you. Know that you are mere dust to Him and can be blown away in a mist anytime or at any place. He is the glue that holds you together if you know Him. He is the Author and Finisher of your fate. He calls the shots. Allow Him too. You only live once. Today is the day that you throw in the towel and tell Him, O Lord! Have your way with me - lead me on - guide my tongue - guide by footsteps. Expect Him too. Expect Him to show up faster than a bolt of lightning. He wants to save you. He wants you to cross over to the other side of this mountain. He wants you to drink some of His living water. He wants to quench your thirst. We will never be apart. Tell yourself. Paste these words across your forehead and your heart. We will always be together. Just me and Him. Him and I. Me and Him. Just us "two". Jus the "two of us" in our hide-a-way.

He will wrap you in in a ball of peace. Position and anchor you just where He wants you to be. Ask Him? Listen to Him as He tells you "I will always love you, and if you did not hear Him when He said it, He will rephrase it and tell you "I will always love you". What is dwelling in your heart? Is it Love and Compassion? Was your heart filled with Love from King Jesus? His Love will hold everything together. If you have received the Love that The Lord has to offer, then you have stood the test of time. You are on your way to being what He intended for you to be! Good News! You are a child of a King. You are one of God's children. You are one of His sheep in His Pasture. Now you are a member of God's Household while you live on His solid and sacred ground, we call Earth on His Planet and in His Universe.

Chapter 24

I loved you yesterday and I have returned to give you my morning mercy, love, graciousness, and righteousness. This is what He said to me. Just want to be around you! It is my pleasure and joy to shower you with My Everlasting Love, My Forever Love, My Unchanging Love, My Unfailing Love, My Grace and Mercy, and My Divine Devotion. This is what I have waiting for you if you just make a switch, cross over the other side of that field of cotton. Look at woe and weariness as mountains that you will overcome if you just trust, believe, and have Everlasting Faith in Him. It is "The Greatest Love of all - I have it! I will not stop believing that He is a mind and heart regulator, a healer, a Savior, a protector, a provider, a way maker, my strength, my joy, and my guiding light. Build a fire. I am building a fire and I want you to lay some logs on it so it will continue to glow. Did you know that the very thought of Him makes my heart, mind, brain, body, soul, and spirit be filled with pride, joy, pleasure, satisfaction, wisdom, knowledge, understanding, truth, honesty, justice, salvation, redemption, love, and righteousness?

I will not stop believing that it was Jesus who touched me with His finger of Love and whispered in my ear, "wake up O sleepyhead" rise from the dead and let the Lord shine on you. "I am here with you to give you your morning, love, grace, and mercy and you must allow it to remain with you throughout your entire day." This is what I heard Him say to me. It can last throughout your lifetime if you want it to. I heard Him say. Here today, right now at this present, and the precise moment in time? I knew you at birth! I knew you when you were only a thought! There was a plan devised for you before you were created that you would receive a life that is fulfilling and delightful.

I know if I remain in Him then He will remain in me. I know if I abide in Him then He will abide in me. I know if I draw nearer to Him then He will draw nearer to me. Have I told you lately that I will always love you? Yes! Master, you have. Let me tell you again "I will love you always. Do not doubt your faith. Do not doubt what He has told you. Do not doubt what you have seen and read with your own two eyes.

I will not stop believing that He is keeping me alive for a reason. I have been given a reason to live. I have a reason to shout with joy and sing "Hallelujah" because He sure is good to me on this magnificent, marvelous, splendid, superb, joyous, and wonderful Tuesday morning, April 20th, 2021, here at Gene Miller Manor in Christian City in Union City, Georgia. I have never seen this Tuesday before, have you? I am glad that I am alive and ready to embrace the adventure that He has planned for me to embrace. I have an upcoming planned event that I will attend because I know He will supply all my needs on this foggy - semi-cloudy, morning at the sacred hour of 10 a.m.

I will not stop believing that He is the author and finisher of my fate on the day He decided to raise me from the dead. I was asleep in my coffin. I had been buried alive. I had no hope. no future, no love, no compassion, no dream, no desire to open my eyes to see another day. My life as I knew it was over. How can I make it over? How can I overcome? Is this my end?

I received a gift. A "gift" of a brand new life, a brand new mind, a brand new beginning, a gift of new birth, a gift of a new identity.

I was allowed to come alive in my sixth sense so I could think, process, and perceive thought. Do I shout now or save it for later? Agree with me that He is wonderful, grand, magnificent, marvelous, splendid, supreme, superb, outstanding, wonderful, and remarkable?

I am off to enjoy a cup of coffee. I call it my delicious brew. It is because it is a potful of love that has been given to me by My Savior, the Master of the Universe. I love My Lord of Lords and My King of Kings. He sure is good to me. Let me shout it from the snowcapped mountains. Let me shout it as I am going through the wilderness. Let me tell you that Psalm 23 says "He is with me". Let me tell you what Joshua says in Chapter 1 verse 9 and that is "He will go with me everywhere I go. Let me tell you at the end of Psalm 23, the very last sentence, says "Surely goodness and mercy shall follow me as long as I dwell in His Presence, His Secret Place, His shelter. Now I ask you "What is the rush"?

Take a moment. Stretch out your arms and legs and admit these words to yourself. "We live in a wonderful world". Find me an island in the sun with plenty of red roses and tulips surrounding me with their love and beauty. He is alive. Want to know how I know? He is the One that blew His breath of life into my lifeless body, raised me from the dead, and allowed me to become a living soul all over again, ready, yes ready to "hallow" His Name and give Him praise, worship and honor Him for being so good to me. He is alive within my heart, mind, body, brain, body, soul, and spirit! Help me to praise Him. He is wonderful, magnificent, marvelous, splendid, superb, wonderful, and remarkable. Every chance I get I will allow my mouth to explode with words of love and admiration because He sure is good to me.

Listen to the songbird! Listen to my song! I will not stop believing that I am wanted, needed, accepted, appreciated, adored, admired, cherished, and idolized by a King. You cannot make me doubt my beliefs. Unshakeable faith is what you and I must have. No matter how many darts I may have to dodge, I am going to stay right where I am planted. We are side by side! He is holding my hand. We are walking hand in hand! I will never let go of His Hand. I have a solid and tight grip.

I am so glad I am alive. I am so glad that I can call on His wonderful name again and again, over, and over and tell Him how much I love Him, adore Him, admire Him, worship Him, cherish Him, and idolize Him because He is the first one that loved me. Relish this thought. "He sure is good to me". Let these words follow you around during your entire day on your brand new day that you have never seen before.

Do not stop now. More good news is about to come! Can I get more love today than I received yesterday? What have you outlined for me to embrace? Today is brand new. I get a brand new mind if I open up my senses and begin to think." He has blessing after blessing in reserve just for me. Into His Everlasting and Loving Arms is where you will find me, all day, everyday, 24/7, around the clock - every hour - every minute - every second and right at this present and the precise moment in time.

Rake the leaves away that are covering His plant and allow it to breathe. Allow the words of my mouth to mediate in your heart. Only His Love, the Love from Our Savior, will set us free of the shackles Satan has intertwined around your neck, brain, heart, body, soul, and spirit. The work of the enemy - this is what you are seeing and witnessing every day you open your eyes. Satan attacks your heart, mind, brain, body, soul, and spirit. He steals your dreams, destroys your desires, and kills your beliefs.

Do not get out of reach! Find yourself a safe place, secure place, a quiet time, and begin to have a little talk with Jesus. He is the One who wants to hear everything about you, your hopes, your dreams, and your future. He is present to help you accomplish your goals if you allow Him to. He is not coming unless He is wanted. You must seek Him, yearn for Him to come into your life, and give you the peace and patience that He gives to His flowers in His Garden of Life.

When I opened my eyes, I saw daylight. Then sunlight. I kept waiting on it and finally, it peaked from around the trees and shined its bright light into my bedroom. My happy space. This is where He and I were on this morning. I wake up to Him every morning. He is right beside my bed because He stood watch over me all during the night. He did not slumber nor sleep because He had to keep an eye on me. He is the decision-maker. He is the One that favored me with a brand new day. Psalm 118 v:24 tells you to rejoice in it, enjoy it, magnify it, glorify it, celebrate it and be thankful for everything that He is giving you on your brand new day. It is a gift!

2 Corinthians 5 v:17 says, "Therefore, if any man is in Christ, he then becomes a new creature and old things are passed away; Behold, stop what you are doing because all things have become brand new. It is a new day, and I cannot turn back now. Beautiful days are ahead. Dreams are fulfilled if you only would believe and accept the new life that He is giving to you and me on this day.

Romans 8 v:28 says, "And we know, yes we do, in all things God works for the good of those who love Him, who have been called according to His purpose." He is keeping me alive for a reason. He gave me an assignment. He continues to shine His light on me, and I will tell it. He gave me a new reason for living and I will cherish, honor, worship, obey and glorify and love Him all the days of my life, on His solid and sacred ground, we call Earth, on His Planet and in His Universe.

Off on an excursion! Off to my very own private island! Want to go?

Chapter 25

Want to follow my flow? Say Yes! Get comfortable. Shift into an attitude of curiosity? Buckle up it may be a first and second sermon combined. Love is all around us. It is surrounding us. You see it in your children, your loved ones, and your friends. It is okay to share your love with the ones closest to you. Try it. Light up someone's life by telling them simply "I love you". It is pure love and genuine devotion. This is what I am getting. This is what He has in reserve just for you and me.

When it is just the "two of us" in the whole wide world it becomes evident that I am the center of His attention. Tell the devil, Satan, Lucifer, the enemy that He can just circle you and then decide if He is going to attack your mind, brain, heart, body, soul, and spirit. Keep circling Satan. Know that You are alive in His Spirit and Jesus is in total control. Let Him. Allow Him to have His way with you. Submit. Commit. Surrender your total self over to Him and let His will be done. Satan will slither away from you. This I know. You will be able to walk all over him. Bury his head. Tell Our God, Our Lord, Our Jesus, just how good He is to you. He sure is good to me. I just want to tell someone, and you have been chosen to be the One who will climb to a higher dimension.

Jesus and I went to the grocery store this morning. I had arranged transportation, so it was "1-2-3". I completed my morning routine and dressed to go outside and do some shopping. It was early in the morning when I opened my eyes and said, "Thank You, Lord". I praised Him all night. I hardly got any sleep.

This morning when I opened my eyes to greet Him and thank Him for watching over me while I slumbered and slept, I was still celebrating a victory.

George Floyd opened the door - didn't he? He came to Earth and served His purpose. It was not intended for Him to stay here for a long time as you have noted. He was given an assignment and he completed it. Now he has been welcomed into God's Kingdom where he will live forevermore in the presence of a King. That Name - George Perry Floyd - is carved in the Lamb's Book of Life. He has received his crown and is worshipping, singing, and saluting His Holy Name.

We are not defeated. We recognize it is the devil who is trying to trip us up and make us fall. We know who to trust. We know what we believe. We believe that no weapon formed against me shall prosper and I can do all things through Christ who strengthens me. You guessed it! I am fighting the devil this morning. He wants to attack my right leg, hip, knee, foot, and toes. He will not succeed. I will not allow Him to stop me from doing what Our Lord and Savior Jesus Christ has outlined for me to do on this Wednesday morning. I have the authority to speak to this mountain and make it move. I promise you that I will battle. I have on the full armor of God. I have placed on my chest His breastplate of righteousness and I will not give up my beliefs, ideas, thoughts, opinions, traditions, dreams, and desires because I know He has a plan for me. I know God is in control. He orders my steps. He is my mind and heart regulator. He is my healer. He is my Savior. This is who saved my soul. Oh! How He loves me. He loves you. He loves us so much that He was willing to give His son up so I could be saved from a world of corruption, wickedness, and the evil spirit of "hate". It is a disease. Left unattended there will be a fire raging in your soul. I know. Yes! Jesus loves me and I will hold on to His Unchanging Hand.

I have a destination in my view. It is in the front of my mind. I know if I keep Jesus out in front of me then I can achieve and accomplish my dreams. What are you hoping for? What is in your future? Have you moved outside of yourself, looked around and dreamed new thoughts and ideas? His will is for you to have hope and a future. He is with you. Psalm 23, "Thy art with me", which means that every morning you open your eyes, He is there ready to give you your morning grace, love and mercy and He wants it to last you all throughout your day. Psalm 90 v:14. Hallelujah! This is the highest praise, and I am ready with a praise because He is so amazing. Amazing, Marvelous, Magnificent, Splendid, Superb, Outstanding, Spectacular, Fabulous, Fantastic, Magical, Majestic, Miraculous and Wonderful is how I can describe Him to you. You see I love the Lord because He is the First One that ever loved me. He deserves all my praise, honor, and worship. I cherish Him, adore Him, admire Him, worship Him, honor Him, and idolize Him. There is something about that Name. The Name of Jesus has all power.

He whispered in my ear, early in the wee hours of dawn, these words: "Wake up O sleepyhead" rise from the dead and let the Lord shine on you." He touched me with His finger of Love and blew His breath of life into my lifeless body so I could become a living soul all over again ready to "hallow" His Holy Name for being so good to me. Oh! I am building a fire this morning! I need your help. Will you place a log on this fire so it can keep burning?

There is no one like Jesus, God, My Lord, and Savior. To me! Wow! To me! What does He do for me? When I open my eyes, He is standing beside my bed ready to take my hand, hold it and guide me to the next phase of my day. Isn't He grand? Isn't He mighty? Isn't He great? I see greatness. I see Love, attentiveness, and devotion. Look what He did for me. He came to see about it and came to shower me with His Unfailing Love, His Unconditional Love, His Unchanging Love, His Grace and Mercy, and His Divine Devotion on a Wednesday morning that I have never seen before at this 9 a.m. sacred hour. It is wonderful to be in His Presence.

It is a sunshiny, chilly day here on Wednesday, April 21st, 2021, here at Gene Miller Manor in Christian City in Union City, Georgia. I am leaning on my Pillar of Faith. It is the day after the George Floyd verdict. Black, brown, and yellow and white America are relieved. Finally! Some justice. Finally! God has spoken and He spoke through the hearts of man. His jurors, His sheep were given an assignment. Find out the truth. Listen to the facts, then make a judgment call.

I can sing a song this morning. I lift my heart, brain, mind, body, soul, and spirit to Jesus this morning because I know His eye is on the sparrow, then His eye must be on me. I am the crown of His creation. I am someone special. I am important. I am great. I am a masterpiece. I am a fine specimen of His workmanship. His eyes were on George Floyd. George Floyd made his transition, and he was given a seat in His Kingdom, and George Floyd is watching and influencing God to make the wrong right.

My God! My Lord! My Jesus! He is alive in the hearts of man. We are open to receive Your Grace and Mercy. Please fill our hearts with Your Love, wisdom, knowledge, understanding, and allow us to embrace the adventure that you have planned for us on this day. I am praying for the whole world. O Lord please cover us with Your Blood. Let me grab a holt of the hem in Your Garment. So many people have grabbed it – now it is in strings. And the strings of justice, equality, honesty, equality, sincerity, salvation, redemption, love, and righteousness must prevail. This is what we are begging for. We give you the Honor and Praise because we know that you are watching over us just like you are watching over your entire creation. I am one vessel with a message of love, hope, and peace. I am asking for your love and protection and guidance while I am on a Divine Walk with My Divine God.

The George Floyd Act will set the pace. There is so much justice needed. The list of names goes on and on. America is seeing a new awakening. Black Lives Matter. We want a seat at the table so we can receive the justice and love that My God, My Lord, My Jesus wants to hand out to us. Are you glad to be alive on this day? I am! I see it. I see the change! I am witnessing a change. There is another life you can live if you cross over to the other side of that mountain. On the other side, there is peace, patience, kindness, gentleness, love, and righteousness.

Use his legacy as a foundation for truth, justice, honesty, salvation, redemption, love, and righteousness to prevail. Let coronavirus roll in and out. We the brown people, yellow people, red people, black people, and white people are rerecording history. Aren't we?

Has not injustice, equality, dishonesty, lies, hate, and deceit prevailed long enough? Hasn't that been the norm? Joe Biden said it. He said, "enough is enough". The day and time for systemic racism are over. We know who loves us. We know who has the final say. We know what we believe. We trust. We believe and we have faith that justice will begin to roll down like a mighty stream. Is MLK happy this morning? He must be grinning from ear to ear. God decided to use one of His soldiers to bring about a change. He is hollering to the top of His lungs "Let my people go". Satan loose your grip. Let them go back to their beginning and remember who it was that freed them from bondage and slavery.

If The Lord had not been on my side, I do not know what I would have done. He saved me. He lights up my life. Once upon a time, I had to jump over hurdles just to make it but today is a new day.

I am free from the chains that had me bound. I am free just like His blackbirds. They wander, glide, float, and coast through HIs air because they know who is watching over them. Just like His eye on the sparrow, He is looking out for me.

I am walking through a pathway that He has designed for me. I cannot see my way, but I know He is waiting there right by my side to grab my hand and I am going to let Him. Let us go beyond what we see. Look at His trees, weeds, bushes, flowers, birds, insects, and bugs. Everything that He created is at perfect peace. Why can't you and I achieve a level of tranquility? Because we do not trust Him! Throw in the towel and put your total trust in Thee and ask Him to guide your thoughts, ideas, actions, beliefs, opinions, traditions, dreams and desires. Talk to yourself. Build your fire. I built mine around 8 a.m. this morning when I glanced in the mirror. His question to me was "how are you". I stood there and tried to explain but so much joy and pleasure and delight filled my heart, brain, mind, body, soul, and spirit that I pulled away smiling and laughing.

I have so much to be "thankful for". I sat down to "thank Him" and I realized my list was long, so I concluded to say "Thank You Lord" stretch my limbs, drink my bottle of chilled water before I put the groceries away. He is good! You know that already – right? How does it feel for someone else to say it? Feels good – don't it? We are on the same page. We both believe. We both trust. We both have faith. Let the blessings that He has in reserve for me, and you begin to flow.

His sun will not catch me crying. His sun will catch me giving Him the love and glory for allowing me to see all His vibrant and brilliant colors. His bright reds, His bright oranges. His pungent yellows. His blue and pale pink colors cascade across the sky. I am glad that I am alive today. I got a chance to breathe some of His fresh air in and out of my lungs. I got a chance to see His sunshine. I have never seen so many different shades of green. Lime green, pea green, army green, money green. These shades of green are overshadowing a village of people living on the side of a mountain in perfect peace and harmony.

These people are happy. These people are living in peace and tranquility. They know who is watching over them and who will return to take good care of them. They know Him and what He can do because they love Him, and they have been placed on the side of the mountain to live in dwellings side by side to live in His Presence. These people know that He has them wrapped in His Everlasting Arms. They are being cradled.

Just like you and me. We have been spared. All things work together for those who know the Lord and who have been called according to His purpose. Romans 8 v:28. Want to tell someone? Talk to the One that made it possible first. Give honor and salute

Our King for being so good to you. I am glad that I am alive. I was favored with a brand new day just like you and we can get it right.

Where is your head dwelling? What are the words meditating in your heart?

What are you saying to Our Lord and Savior? Are you telling Him "Thank You"? These should be the first three precious words out of your mouth. Recognize the Giver of Life from whom all blessings flow.

Know who has your back. Know who you can depend on. You and I depended on Him yesterday and He has reappeared again on this Wednesday morning to shower you with His Unshakable, Merciful, and Wonderful Grace.

He bathed The George Floyd Family in His Grace and Mercy - didn't He? He dumped buckets of Love over Attorney Crump and The Reverend Al Sharpton. Jessie Jackson was there in spirit. All of them deserve a pat on the back for a job well done! We cannot forget about His other sheep that He has in His Pasture. We must look past their deeds and judge them on the contents of their hearts. What does this man or woman have to say for themselves? How are they defending themselves? Man and woman must prove their self-worth.

Man has to slow down and begin to "think and "ponder thought". Man will not slow down long enough to feel the hot and cold water mixed to get warm water when he washes his hands. Slow down! Take your time. That is all we have is time and we must recognize who is in control of our every action, deed, idea, thought, opinions, dreams, traditions, desires and beliefs. I guess I will have to sing it to you in a song.

He is the glue that is holding me together. I went to the grocery store. We had a safe trip there and back; I was able to get the items on my list. I was satisfied with my accomplishments. I know who made it possible. I know who was whispering in my ear. I listened. I listen well. I listen all day - everyday - 24/7, around the clock - every hour - every minute - every second, and right now at this present and the precise moment in time I am listening, and I hear waves crashing into a seawall.

Want to come with me? Oh! I am going there! I am on my way over yonder, over there, in the Great Beyond. There is plenty of room. His arms are as big as His big blue spacious skies. His eyes are as wide as the sky, so He is continuously watching over you and me.

His window is up, and a cool fresh breeze of fresh air is coming in through the opened window. I feel His warmth and I see His beauty. It was designed just for me. I am "grateful" that He decided to allow me to be closed in my right mind with a reasonable portion of my health and strength. It was early in the morning hours when I recited my affirmation. I ask O Lord please come into my presence and O Lord please allow me into Your Presence. After this exchange of words, I went to talk. I repeat these words every morning I open my eyes.

He knows my voice because He hears it so often.

After I saturate His atmosphere with words of praise and worship, I began talking asking O Lord please shelter us, O Lord please shadow us, O Lord please favor us, O Lord please cover us with Your Blood, O Lord please grant us Your Grace and Mercy, O Lord please strengthen us physically, mentally, emotionally, psychologically, morally, and spiritually, O Lord please forgive us of our sins because we don't always do things perfectly and correctly, O Lord please forgive our enemies because they know not what they do, O Lord please prosper us physically, materialistically, financially and spiritually, O Lord please protect us from all plagues, pandemics, disasters, and turmoil, O Lord please do not cast us away from Your Presence and O Lord please allow Your Holy Spirit to dwell in us again on this day. In Jesus' Name, I Pray Amen.

I know He loves me, and I know He knows that I love Him. I give Him all my honor, praise, worship, admiration, glory, and love.

Isn't He wonderful to be praised? He is "great". He is "mighty".

Stop and recognize it. Celebrate the moment. Be present in mind, heart, brain, body, soul, and spirit. Let your brain overflow with His music. Let your heart be soothed with His instrumental melodies.

I am glad that I am alive. I get another chance. I get a new birth, a new mind, a new beginning, a new identity, and I am born again. He raised me from the dead. Oh! I was buried alive. I was dead in my coffin but there was a plan made for me and His plan was not for me to die and get buried and never allowed myself to walk hand in hand. I got the chance to become brand new! I got the chance to be "born again". I pulled off the old clothes and put on new clothes. I moved from behind the railroad track and past the white fences. I am on a clear path. This road is headed up the King's Highway. There were bumps placed in my pathway but My God, My Jesus, My Lord, gave me the authority I needed to jump over them.

In His Everlasting Arms, I cast all my cares on Him because I know He cares for me. 1st Peter 5 v:7. Outside. Outdoors. It is calling me. Long sleeves and my sunglasses and I will dash the outside so I can inhale and exhale some of His fresh air in and out of my lungs. I "Thank Him" for every breath I take and each time He allows my heart to beat at a normal rhythm. You know we are all in His Hands.

You and I are engraved in the Palms of His Hand because He will never forget about us. Isaiah 49 v:15-16. He remembers us as suckling babes. Isn't He wonderful? It is Springtime. Things are made brand new. You are made brand new each morning you open your eyes to greet a new day. Wake up! Live! Open up like the bud of a new flower. Unfold and allow Him to satisfy you with His morning mercy and grace.

Chapter 26

Have yourself to some waa-saa time. That is how my oldest daughter describes it, I just say La La Time. I would be lost without You O Lord! Who would protect me? Who would provide for me? Who would answer all my prayers? If you were ever to leave me, I would be lost. You recreated me. You reinvented me. I will never leave you. I will stay by your side. I will remain in You if you allow me to. Your prayers are so important. The conversation you have with Him is just between the two of you.

Earlier during the morning before I got dressed to go to do some shopping, I ladled my cup of coffee, my delicious brew, back and forth and I recited His 23rd Psalm. The entire scripture. I said it all. I pause when I get to these words "For Thy Art with Me". Say it with me. "He is with me". When, how, and at what time? He is always around waiting, watching, and listening to the words that we are saying. He is hovering over you and me just like a helicopter. He is waiting on you.

He is listening for some sign that you know who the Giver of Life is.

Repeat these words; "If I remain in Him then He will remain in me." He will go with you everywhere you go. He guides the breath you take. He allows it to go in and go out. He is coordinating my breathing. I cannot breathe without Him permitting me. That is why I depend on Him. I depend on Him for everything. For every breath I take. He is a heart and mind regulator. He regulates my heart to beat at its normal rhythm. He controls my mind and tells me what to do, what to think and what to say. I depend on Him. I committed. I submitted. I surrendered my total self to Him so His will could be done.

Your blessings are only a breath away. You speak yourself into existence. What are you? Are you a child of a King, are you one of God's children, are you one of His sheep in His Pasture? What do you see yourself as? Are you a success or a failure? Truth, honesty, sincerity, justice, salvation, redemption, love, and righteousness is on the menu. Get you a big helping of each! Examine it. See how it fits into your character and makeup. Can it dwell in your heart?

We are calling on Kings and Queens, Men and Women, children, both boys and girls to raise a fist in solidarity with The George Perry Floyd Movement. We cannot get it unless we ask for it. We must go to the Source of where all blessings flow. For years I searched for love, acceptance, and appreciation. I solved that problem I began calling on the Name of Jesus. When He told me "I will love you always", I did not hear Him at first. I had never heard these words before. So, he said it again and rephrased it and said, "I will always love you". Can you imagine how this made me feel? I was in awe. Are you talking to me? His reply was "You, yes you" who are weary, worn and heavy laden – come and go with me and I will give you rest." I went. I found the scripture and I read it for myself. Matthew 11 v:28. I was convinced that I wanted to be a part of God's Household, so I went searching for the proper way to greet and salute Him.

I began to seek. I began to knock. I found the right words to say that would shatter the ceiling in Heaven. I began to write and practice. John Gray taught me how to praise Him. John Gray stopped in the middle of His sermon and said, "let's praise Him". I am tempted but I save it usually at the end of a sentence when I am coming down the side of that mountain. Oh! He is worthy? He has done so much for me and He still is at this sacred hour of 6 p.m. on a Wednesday. It is news time. I want to disappear into a sea of blue. I can do this each time I place my head upon His chest. I see blue water, blue waves, blue clouds, blue skies, all are varying shades of blue. I decided to go outside and stare Him in the face as He blows His breath on me. Thank You, Lord! I am alive! Thank You, Lord! I am not dead. I know how to praise you. I know He loves me. He loves you. He can cradle you and me in His Everlasting Arms anytime you want Him to. Ask Him. Yes! Jesus loves me. Yes! Jesus is the first one that ever loved me. There was a plan made. Jeremiah 29 v:11. I was created for a purpose. I asked that He reshape me, remold me and make me into the person He had designed me to be before I was in my mother's womb. He did. He has given me an assignment. I have been called to His purpose. Oh, Lord! Lead me by Your Guiding Light!

How great Thy Art! There is no one like Him. This is who you need to call on. This is the One you need to cherish, honor, salute, and obey. He is the One with the plan. How can you go wrong if you follow the Leader? His yoke is easy. He is on one side, and I am on the other one. If I abide in Him, then He will abide in me. If I draw nearer to Him, then He will draw nearer to me. What are you saying to yourself? Are you placing new logs on your fire every time you open your mouth? There is a miracle in your mouth. You possess it. It is a powerhouse of words waiting to give you the freedom that you desire. You must yearn for a change. You must desire a change. You must want a change. You will soon find out that the old clothes, attitudes, ideas, thoughts, beliefs, dreams, desires, traditions and ambitions just do not fit anymore. You will gladly rinse all the residue away. You just do not want it anymore. Do you want to try something different? You want to walk in the ways of the Godly! Do you want His Peace, Love and Devotion, Grace, and Mercy? Right!

When you cannot see your way then it is time not to rely on your understanding. Walk by faith and not by sight. I have been told about Him. You might say! Now is the time for you to try Him for yourself. Stretch out. Walkout. Declare you will put all your hope, faith, and trust in Thee. Do it. Just do it. Your world will change. You will begin to see what is in front of you and what is up above you. Your viewpoint will change. Your eyes will become open. You will begin to realize who has been loving you since the cradle. It is okay – you can reach out and touch Him, He is right there by your side. He is underneath your breath. He lives inside of you. Are you amazed that He would love someone like you?

In His Loving and Everlasting Arms, you will find that He accepts you, wants you, needs you, admires you, adores you, cherishes you, and idolizes you because you are a child of a King. You are one of God's children. You are one of His sheep in His Pasture. Is this high enough for you? You are special. You are somebody. You deserve to be honored for taking the necessary step to save your life, your children's life, your children's children life, their families, their loved ones, and their friends.

That is a whole lot of sheep in His Pasture, and He is looking out for each one of them. He will supply all their needs. He will listen and answer every prayer that is sincere and honest. Speak to Him. Let Him know what is meditating in your heart. He is waiting.

Do not let anything stop you from spending time in His Presence. This is what you must do. This is where you will find Divine revelation, wisdom, knowledge, and understanding. Read His word! Understand His word! Knowledge is power. Your tongue has power. Life or death.

Proverbs 18 v:21. You raise an umbrella of words over your head and watch them come back to rest on your shoulder.

Chapter 27

Where are we going? An escapade! An adventure! Let me take you with me as I have just finished enjoying a bowl of His delicious bran with raisins floating around in almond milk that He allowed to be squished into a carton. Did you know that I found peace in that bowl? I began chewing and tasting the bran flakes mixed in with raisins. I began looking and hunting for the raisins. As I was thankful for every spoonful, I kept saying "Thank You Lord", I got lost in a sea of whiteness. I was mesmerized by the color of white and my mind began to flow. I gently breezed into green pastures. The unknown. Where am I going? Do not ever forget about me O Lord! I am just a sheep in Your Pasture of Life.

Oh! Bright Eyes, Sparkling Eyes, Brown Eyes, Black Eyes, Hazel Eyes, Spanish Eyes, White Eyes! I will never forget about you. He has you and I cradled in His Everlasting Arms. Want to know how I know? He told me when I read the Book of Isaiah. Isaiah also told me that "He is My God". No one else. Nothing else. He will never forget about me.

I am out in the dessert waiting for it to rain! I am ready! It only took a moment's notice to realize that I am where I want to be. In His Presence. I have an aerial view of His forest of green trees, bushes, weeds, animals in a circle of Love. It is an oasis of different shades of green.

Now I see mounds and mounds of dirt phased into clay. A desert made from clay. Different sizes, different shapes, different colors. Hey! I am only a piece of dirt in His Pasture. There are so many mounds of dirt in that Pasture. I am among that group. It is a beautiful, magnificent, and marvelous occasion and I am in your presence, and I am in His Presence. Walk with me! Grab my hand. You are safe only if you believe, trust, and have faith in the unseen. You know it is there - cannot quite put your finger on it yet! Grasp the whole picture. Do not be left in the dark. I just finished looking at an abstract painting and I saw so many vivid colors. The artist was expressing himself and this artist appeared to be free in these thoughts, you can tell by the way he swerved his brush. He stroked up and down, far, and wide. He was enjoying using His brush on his canvas. A Divine Spirit was leading his hands and fingers and mind.

Oh! I enjoy writing. Can't you tell? There is so much to say! There is only a short window open for me, so I must get it all out. Words are meditating in my heart, and I just want to share it with you that when I asked for Him to let it rain, little did I know I would receive buckets, tons of His Unfailing Love, His Unconditional Love, His Unchangeable Love. It is here, now what am I going to do about it? I believe I will stroll down a dirt road, kick some rocks, smell His honeysuckle vine. Breathe. Breathe His fresh air in and out of my lungs. I will praise Him because He blew His breath of life into m lifeless body and allowed me to come alive in my senses so I could begin to think, and process thought. Isn't He able? Isn't He magnificent? Isn't He awesome? Isn't He miraculous?

He is to me! He is so good to me I want to talk to somebody. I just want to share! He touched me this morning with His finger of Love and whispered in my ear, words of wisdom and inspiration and encouragement. "Wake up O sleepyhead, rise from the dead and let the Lord shine on you. It did not take me long to respond because I knew He had returned to give me His love, grace, and mercy on a Thursday morning that I have never seen before. Psalm 90 v:14. He is alive. He came early in the wee hours of dawn nudging me to get up, rise, and do what I needed to do. I sang my song; "Thank You Jesus" the entire time I was up moving around and when I found my way back to His Everlasting Arms located in His sky. He had saved a spot for me, and I got nestled in and began opening my mouth and my heart. I began to tell Him "How Great Thy Art!" Good morning Sunshine.

Oh! Your Splendid Wonders! You and I should be praying for peace on all mankind.

There is a lot of sheep in His Pasture.

He has sheep located in the South, East, North, and West. They are all different colors, shapes, and sizes. Some are tall, some are short, some are thin, some are fat, some of big, some are little, some are white, some are black, some are brown, some are yellow, some are red, some are blue, some are green. There are so many varieties of flowers in My Garden of Life, and you are one of them. Peace for all mankind. How can we go about achieving this goal? You, me, him, her, she, he, them, and they. We all need to be on one accord. We all need to be praising Our Lord and Savior Jesus Christ. He is the One that saved my sole.

He gave me a banana, my meds, and a bottle of water. I was praising Him throughout the time I was cutting the banana into bitesize pieces. I had a mound of banana, a bottle of His chilled water that He allowed to escape from His rivers, brooks, streams, canals, mountains, and rocks into a bottle just the right size for my hands to hold. Ah! He is wonderful? You and I both know it. I do! I do! I do!

It is Thursday morning, a morning we have never seen before. I had chores to do, and I gladly embraced each one of the adventures that He wanted me to embrace on this brand new, glorious, and wonderful day. We are among the living! We are not dead! Act like it!

Come alive in your senses, breathe His fresh oxygen in and out of your lungs. Say "Hallelujah Anyhow". Talk to Him, He is listening. He wants to hear your praise. He wants you to worship Him for giving you a life to live in the Presence of a King.

Just one more time! Thank You for my do-over. Thank You for another opportunity to get it right. Thank You for allowing me to breathe Your fresh air in and out of my lungs. Thank You for allowing me to be closed in my right mind with a reasonable portion of my health and strength. Thank You for deciding to wake me and let me rise from the dead. Look around you! How many people do you see who is sleeping? Sorry! Every spirit you meet will leave a lasting impression upon you. You must greet them first in their native tongue. You must speak their language. If you listen closely that will have a tale of sorrow, weary and woe. Not you! We have been raised from the dead. We have been born again. We are no longer a part of this corrupt and wicked creation that Satan, Lucifer, the devil, the enemy has made.

Matthew 11 says "my yoke is easy". Am I willing and am I eager to embrace another day that I have never seen before at this 1 o'clock hour? You bet I am, all day, everyday, 24/7, around the clock - every hour - every minute and right at this present and the precise moment in time I am in His Presence ready to preach another sermon and tell you just how good He is to me.

Oh! He is good! The best thing I ever felt, tasted, seen, and witnessed. Softness, gentleness, kindness, tenderness, soft melodies, soft violin strings, light harp sounds, a faint drumbeat, a trombone, a sax, I hear them all. Let me hear it one more time. Let it rain down on my head. I am in the desert just waiting for His manifestations, revelations, wisdom, knowledge, and understanding to be transported down to me. I will wear a cap. I will bat when it is my turn. I know who is stepping up to the plate with me and His Name is Jesus. I allow Him to go to bat for me. I am just a bystander. He leads the way because He has the plan. I will do as I am told and that is to follow the leader.

Night and day! He is with me! He holds my hand throughout the daylight hours, and He gently tucks me away at night while He watches over me while I slumber and sleep. I ask for His grace and mercy. I ask Him to shelter me. I ask Him to shadow me. I pray for you, too. I pray for mankind. I say "us". I mean "us". Oh, Lord! All of your children. All of your sheep in Your Pasture. You are The Sheepherder.

Let it rain on me. Listen to His piano keys while you read. You should have soft melodies surrounding you. Want some peace, contentment, joy, and happiness?

Find it wherever you can. It is right at your fingertips. Turn the dial. Select a channel of music. Let it soothe those tired aching muscles in your heart, head, brain, mind, body, soul, and spirit. Let it engulf you. Let His music led you to that far-a-way land. The land over yonder - the land over there at the Great Beyond. This is where I am!

I am a spiritual being having a human experience. I am fascinated by how He recreates me. I am fascinated with how He has reinvented me. It is a joy and pleasure to be able to hit key after key, sharing with you the words that are meditating in my heart. I am curious! What is meditating in that heart of yours? Are you traveling? Are you stuck? Come alive!

There is another life that you could live. Do not enjoy leftovers by Satan. Open your world. Choose your very own personal, private, and intimate thoughts. I know someone who wants to hear every one of your thoughts, ideas, opinions, beliefs, traditions, dreams and desires in detail. It is Jesus!

He is my soul and the source of my inspiration. I call on Him. I go to Him in prayer. I ask Him humbly, softly, gently, and kindly to please come to see about me. Guess what? He does. He shows up. O Lord please come into my presence and O Lord please allow me into Your Presence. He swings the door wide open. He welcomes me in with open arms. He wants to cradle me in His Everlasting Arms so I can be safe and secure, and I let Him.

He says, "You can climb every mountain"! He says, put your trust, faith, and hope in Thee. He will make that mountain become a molehill. He is able. He will walk with you as you face that mountain. He will hold your hand. He will allow the rain to come down on your shoulders. Want Him to rain on you? He already has! Think about it! What has He done for you? What is He doing for you at this present and the precise moment in time? He is keeping me alive for a reason. He is keeping you alive for a reason. Was it by some chance that we were supposed to meet up?

I see you standing behind that white fence. I see you peeping out of the window curtain. I see you looking up and I want you to continue looking up, around, and above your head. Do you see light? Do you see life? Do you see a new beginning? Do you see a new birth? Do you see a new identity? Are you born again? Yes, you are born again. You did shed those old clothes. You have on new clothes. You see hope. You see a future. You see the love and you see it is waiting just for you.

I had to stop and enjoy a bottle of His chilled water! Join me! Take your time, all we have is the time! I am not going anywhere. I will not stop writing. God has shown me the way to worship Him, praise Him, honor Him, and salute Him. Surely His Grace and Mercy shall follow me all the days of my life if I dwell in that Secret Place, that shelter, or in His Presence. This is what He wants to do for you. He wants you to take a deep breath, relax and allow Him to calm the raging seas in your soul, mind, heart, brain, body, and spirit. Let Him remember you as a suckling babe. Rest now. You are in His Arms, and you are seeking shelter from the storm. Praise Him. Rejoice in Him.

Honor Him by letting Him know that you know who has all power in His Hands. If you cannot catch His Hand, then grab a piece of the hem in that garment. If you cannot catch the hem, then catch a holt to one of His strings. He is canvassing the area. He is casting a wide net to see what He can catch. He is circling the globe this morning looking for someone like you. Can she carry a message? Can she light up somebody's life? Can she be trusted with wisdom, knowledge, and understanding? Will she tell someone?

Cannot keep it to myself! His works are marvelous, magnificent, splendid, superb, terrific, wonderful, and spectacular. Look at the hills from which comes our help. Look up. You too can disappear into a sea of blue. Green. Orange. Red. Yellow. Brown. Black. White.

Just one more day is all I am asking for! A day just like yesterday! Yesterday! You showered me with Your loving grace and mercy, and I am asking You to remain in me because I will remain in You. Oh, Lord! If I just abide in, you then you will abide in me. Oh, Lord! If I draw nearer to you then You will draw nearer to me. That is His Promise. Hebrews 13 v:5, says "He will never leave me nor forsake me."

Looks like I am covered from the crown of my head to the soul of my feet in His Grace and Mercy. He is taking good care of me. He has His watchful eye on me and you. Let Him fill you with His pride and joy! Let Him cradle you just like you are His own. Let Him place you in His Flower Garden and let you see all the beautiful colors that He has on display for you.

It is a joy and pleasure to be alive. Do you know that you are loved, wanted, needed, appreciated, accepted, admired, adored, idolized, and cherished by a King? Try to remember! Try recording these words into your brain, mind, heart, body, soul, and spirit. He is hovering over you and me like a helicopter. Just waiting. He has time. This is the only thing you have is the time! Time to think, wonder, prepare, and plan. This is what Easy Listening Music, Jazz, allows me to do. I think, I wonder, I prepare, I plan, and my moves are carefully orchestrated by a King. Stroll with me under His light coming from His sunset as I walk through His sand between my toes trying to make it to that palm tree that is bending over for a perfect shady spot.

Today is Thursday and it is a business day for me. I had several letters to get in the mail. You can always depend on the mail. Once you complete it and get it on its way to its destination is a great accomplishment. I save Tuesday and Thursdays as business days. The rush is over, and people are settling down to embrace a new week. I go about my daily routine and activities because I know I am being glided by another power that is not my own. Where He leads me, I will follow.

My God, Jesus, My Lord, and Savior has shown me the way. He has the plan. He knows where this ship is headed. I do not - I am just at the wheel and it just keeps on turning. It takes me here, it takes me there, I never lose sight of where I am trying to get to.

The phone keeps ringing and when someone comes on the line, I tell them I am celebrating, "George Floyd" and ask them if they want to join me? Click! I am. We are on our way. Root out that evil spirit of hate! It is embedded in their bones, heart, mind, brain, body, soul, and spirit.

Savages. Barbarians. Madness. Ugliness. Rage. Anger. If left unchecked, this is what it produces. Monsters of every shape, color, and size. Moses spent 40 years in the wilderness because the people would not listen and think.

There comes a time and place for you to get serious! I cannot stress the importance of listening and reading and understanding. Somewhere out there is a different life for you to live. Your job is to look for it, seek it and you shall find it. What are you looking for? What is most important to you on this adventure that you have been charged with overseeing. You are the overseer. You make sure everything is done exactly right.

Tell your brothers and sisters in the North, East, South, and West that we must love each other. It has been ordered. It is His Divine Will.

Will man allow this knowledge to float past him? Yes! He will because man is blinded by so many passions. Man is not looking through God's eyes at His magnificent and marvelous creation. Man's head is buried in the sand! Man is too busy looking down to look up and see the beauty that He has in reserve just for you and me.

I see a redbird. This bird is so peaceful. It is so happy fumbling around trying to make a nest so He will have a dwelling place so He can rest. Guess what!

I hear His birds chirping, singing, and praising His Holy Name for creating a day for them full of sunshine, warmth, and beauty.

Let us, you and I pretend that we are "birds". Oh! I am so free!

I can glide. I can float. I can slowly, methodically land on the branch of His trees. I am light as a feather and they will hold me, I am sure of that because I have landed on this branch before.

He is the glue that is holding me together and I will honor, praise, worship, and salute Him for just keeping me alive to see another brand new day. Psalm 118 v:24, tells you what to do when you have a gift of a brand new day. Rejoice in it. Magnify it.

Enjoy it. Glorify it. Celebrate it and be "thankful" for everything in it.

Want to try it? Today is my brand new day and I will celebrate it as if it is a Sunday. Want to go to church? I am available all day, everyday, 24/7, around the clock - every hour -every minute -

every second to take you there. May Jesus bless all His tv vessels and radio vessel for all their hard work. They are trying to motivate you the best way they know how. Some I cannot get. Some vessels take me around and around, up, and down, back, and forth. I need it only plain and simple. No theatrics, please. No long white robes. Dress comfortably for me. Just put on some clothes. Attire fitted for the occasion. Clothes are not important. Your message is what is most important. You are trying to save souls for Christ.

Isn't that your aim and purpose? Then give the people what they need. Cold, hard, honest facts. We are on a collision course with death unless someone pulls up the brakes! Show me another way! The road I am on is not working! I need a new sense of direction. Can you lead me out of this wilderness? Can you point me in the right direction? Look! Take my name and steer someone in my direction. I want to tell them how Jesus saved my soul. I want to tell them what Jesus has done for me.

He fixed it. He fixed it so I would never be thirsty again! He fixed it so I would never be hungry again! He opened His book of knowledge and His Holy Spirit allowed me to thumb through the passages until I came upon a scripture that is quite fitting for today's message. Matthew 11. "Come to me, all who labor and are heavily laden, and I will give you rest. Take my yoke upon you, learn from me, I am gentle and lowly in heart and you, only you will find rest for your souls. For my yoke is easy and my burden is light. Just worship Me! Just honor Me! Just praise Me! Just salute Me! It is just that easy. Simple huh?

There is a miracle in your mouth. This is all we have is "talk". Conversations. You tell me and I tell you just how good He is to me.

We both can agree on this one thing. He sure is good to me.

His Holy Spirit and I went into one of my happy spaces. I sang a song the entire time I was going and, on the way, out. This is what I do each morning when I open my eyes. I cry out "Holy" because He is worthy to be praised. I know what He has done for me. He gave me a new reason to come alive in my senses so I could "think and process thought". I can think. He has me engraved in the Palms of His Hands.

I had to get refreshed so I could continue the pathway that has been outlined for me. I am glad that you are with me! I have a lot to say! In solitude is where I renew my strength and uplift my spirits. When I pulled out the chair to this computer, He pulled out a chair and sat right beside me and told me "I will help you". I see where you are headed, and you may need some help to get there. If you remain in Me, then I will remain in You. Spend some time with me. There is so much for you to learn, to do, to think, and to experience.

I cannot forget your smile. I cannot forget your smile. I see you each time you look in the mirror. I see the sparkle you have in your eye. I see you searching for clues. I see you searching for answers. It is only love that I am showing you when I allow you to adjust the water temperature to one that is comfortable for you so you can wash your hands. Thank You, Lord, for my hands and fingers and the mindset you have given me to wash them properly and thoroughly. Do you take the time, pray while you are washing and rinsing your hands? Nope! This is such an everyday occurrence; you pay it no attention. It is just something that you do - right? Stop! Think! This is sacred. You know who provided the water, the soap, the cloth for you to wash your hands. Oh, Lord! I am grateful that you chose me to receive your loving grace and mercy on this brand new Thursday afternoon.

Time will bring about a change. You have never stopped, examined what you were doing before - right. Well, now is the time to "thank" the One from whom all blessings flow. "Thank You, Jesus, "Thank You Jesus". You are only showing me just how much love you have for me.

He says "I love you, while you are drinking a bottle of my water at room temperature. I did it all for you and I will do it again tomorrow if you allow me to. If I put Jesus first. Just remember! I will provide all your needs if you trust me, believe me, and have faith in me that I will listen to your prayer.

This morning, after I finished up in my happy space, I nestled back under His covers and reclaimed my spot, and I began talking. O Lord please shelter us, O Lord please shadow us, O Lord please favor us, O Lord please cover us with Your Blood, O Lord please grant us Your Grace and Mercy, O Lord please strengthen us physically, mentally, emotionally, psychologically, morally and spiritually, O Lord please forgive us of our sins because we don't always do things perfectly and correctly, O Lord please forgive our enemies because they know not what they do, O Lord please protect us from all plagues, pandemics, turmoil, and disasters, O Lord please prosper us physically, financially, materialistically, and spiritually, O Lord please do not cast us away from Your Presence, and please O Lord allow Your Holy Spirit to dwell in us again on this day. In Jesus' Name, I Pray - Amen.

Am I covered from the crown of my head to the sole of my feet? I think I am. I believe I am. I trust that I am. So, I will continue with the plans that He has outlined for me on this glorious, beautiful, gorgeous, windy sunshiny day that He has given me.

My goal is to take Jesus with me everywhere I go and consult Him about everything I do. He has led me to the river now it is up to me to quench my thirst. He has opened the door and it is up to me to walk in and receive the blessings that He has in reserve just for me. I give Him all my worship, all my honor, all my praise, all my glory, and all my love. He is worthy to be praised, admired, saluted, cherished, and idolized. Do you agree?

Chapter 28

I have a duty. I have a job to do. What would you do if you had been assigned a task that you had no earthly idea of what to do? Go crazy! Stay Calm! Think! What are the possibilities here? What options do we have? My only recommendation is that you go to the Source of your beliefs, faith, trusts, ambitions, opinions, traditions, dreams and desires. Anybody tried Jesus! O Lord please help me! Tell me what I am missing here. I am thinking, nothing is coming in clear, let me interject here, who are you listening to. I am getting my knowledge from the Horse's mouth. So, who is your Source? Simply Jesus Christ. He is the Only One I know who can save a sin-sick soul, a feeble wrinkled old body, just like mine. He did it. It is Friday morning. A "good Friday", He gave His life up on Friday to save me from a world of sin, regret, delusion, illness, and shame. He is the Only One I know who was willing to give me another chance to become alive in my spirit and praise His Holy Name. He is calling me His bird, His flower, His butterfly, His tree, His mountain, His river, His High Seas, His Blue wind and His Blue ocean. I can listen to Him until the end of time. I can listen to Him honor me all day, everyday, today, 24/7, around the clock, at this present and precise moment in time.

Okay! I want the world to know what I know. Can you help me tell my story? You have an open invitation to go to my website. bettiejeangrose.com and share your wisdom, knowledge, and understanding. I want the world to know that His eyes are upon all of us. He is watching over me just like He is watching over you. How does He do that? His eyes are as wide as the sky. His big blue spacious eyes are watching over me, him, her, she, he, them, and they. Did you know that? Did you know that He has His eyes on the Ones in the North, East, South, and West and that means He is watching over me? You too! Right?

I know you know Him just like I do. He is hovering over me like a helicopter waiting for any type of response to let Him know that they know you. Just like I do. I know what you can do. I can witness that this morning when I opened my eyes, I peeped out and up and saw a foggy - semi-cloudy - gray day - I began to pray. "Thank You Jesus" and He said to me "You are the most beautiful girl in the world!" I am addicted to that smile. I recognize your voice. I can hear really good. I heard your mamma, your daddy, your sisters, your brothers, your loved ones, your family, and your friend. I will listen to you. Jeremiah 29 v:12. Bettie Jean!

What are you doing? Reading Your Word. Your Honor, Your Majesty, drinking Your water and listening to Your music that You have provided for my ears to hear.

I have developed this habit and that is waking up after hearing Him speak to my heart, mind, brain, body, soul, and spirit. He talks to me! He tells me "Wake up you, O sleepyhead, rise from the dead and let the Lord shine on you. That is joy and music to my ears. I know who woke me up and I know who is going to guide me on the adventure that He has planned for me to embrace on this gorgeous, beautiful, precious, magnificent, marvelous, fabulous, fantastic, tremendous, and terrific Friday morning.

It is Friday morning, April 23rd, 2021, here at Gene Miller Manor in Christian City in Union City, Georgia and I am glad to be in His Presence one more time. I was challenged this morning and I went to God, My Lord and Savior Jesus Christ, in prayer. I ask O

Lord please make Satan leave my back, neck, stomach, intestines, leg, knee, ankle, and toes alone. My Lord and Savior replied. Satan! Satan went to talking – telling Him it was not He – then He added – you told me not to touch your anointed. That is right. I know who will fight my battle. I know who has been leading me thus far on a day that I have never seen before. I am following Jesus! I followed Him when He opened the door for me to go into my happy space and perform normal body functions. Did you "Thank Him" as I did? Did you sing Him a song? Did you honor Him? Did you salute Him? Did you pay tribute to the One who made it all possible?

Well, if you have not, then you need to read Psalm 145 v:15-16 – the first line – the first sentence – gave me the word that I needed for today. There is a message interwoven in this sentence structure. Think and read between the lines, what is this author saying? It says to me that all the eyes of the world will be on Him waiting for His return because everyone wants to see the One who made a way for me. Don't you want to see Him, the One that blew His breath into your lifeless body and allowed you to become a living soul all over again so you can "hallow His Holy Name"? Don't you want to meet the One who made the decision that you could come alive in your senses and begin to wonder, ponder, think and process thought. It is "Good Friday", don't you expect miracles to happen – I do! It was a miracle that I am sitting here at this 1 o'clock sacred hour on a day I have never seen before telling you just how good Our Lord and Savior Jesus Christ has been to me.

Ah! This morning! The day Our Lord has given to us as a time and place so we can rejoice, magnify, glorify, honor, and salute His

Name. In our domains, in our homes, in our apartments, in our manors, in our rooms. That is where I am - in my room - it is just us "two. The "two of us" are having a fireside chat. He is talking to me, and I am listening, and I am talking to Him, and He is listening to me. It is a two-way conversation. Right here on His solid and sacred ground, we call His Earth, on His Planet and in His Universe. Want to hear more? I dealt with Satan. He kept getting in the way! I resorted to my only means of Protection and that was to keep talking to God about my aches and pains, beliefs, desires, opinions, ideas, thoughts, traditions, dreams and desires. He wants to know just how I am!

I had a lot of boulders in my pathway early this morning, but I was able to work my way around them. This morning, His Holy Spirit told me to read, open the window, get a little fresh air, and begin to sit, think, ponder, and wonder and this is what I did, and I saw pyramids made from dirt and dust. That is all we are. Dirt and dust. He has allowed us to come alive just like the Tulips that He has planted in His Flower Garden of Life. Flowers are so sacred. You know all these flowers are found in the wild - don't you. They grow in bunches. They accumulate and their seeds scatter when He blows His breath on them. They live for only a season. This tulip is only living for a specified period. This is my due season. I am supposed to be in your daily life. Everyday there is something different. Everyday there is new knowledge that I want to share with you.

He is with me "always". Tell yourself this "He is with me always". He will never leave me nor forsake me.

He will watch over every step I take, if I continue to believe, trust, and have faith in Thee. I am trusting. I can go the full distance. I don't see my way - I am just taking it one day at a time. I remembered yesterday. He was with me and today He has reappeared to pick up from where He left off yesterday. He is here!

He is present! He came early this morning in the wee hours of dawn, and I followed and obeyed His every command.

When I opened my eyes, I saturated His atmosphere with words of praise, admiration, and amazement. I saw His gray skies and I also saw His trees, weeds, bushes, flowers standing at full attention. They were waiting on Him to come to see about them. Aren't trees smart? Their leaves cry. Their leaves cringe. Their leaves dry up, fall off the branch, go away and sleep and return in another season. That is the way man does it. For a particular season, he is allowed to blossom, bloom, and grow.

It is my due season. I am eating meat. I am eating my daily bread. I am going to the Source of My Inspiration and Encouragement. Pardon me if I get a little long-winded, I have kept it all in during the morning hours and now I am ready to explode with my message of love, hope, and peace. Call me "tulip". I will call you "tulip". When I think of you, I will think of you like a rose or a tulip. Make sure you answer when He calls. He maybe calling you to give you a special message. He may want to tell you these three most precious and sacred words that are in the Universe. "I Love You". Why is that so hard to believe? I listen for my name to be called. I was in His basement, but I got my foot wedged in the door and if I keep knocking - someone will let me in. I just want to be in His Presence. When the roll is called up yonder- over there - at the Great Beyond, I will be there.

Human Spirits come and go! Some you want to leave them at the door! Some you want to avoid altogether! You will encounter so many different spirits, it is best to allow His Holy Spirit that He has placed in you to lead the way. He is your comforter and your counselor! Let Him do His job. You don't know what is best for you yet? You have not asked Him what was His plan for you before you were in your mother's womb - have you? Mistake! This is the first item for discussion after you develop your personal, private, and intimate relationship with Him. You have had a little talk with Him - right? Have you had a little talk with Jesus and posed your questions to Him? Have you asked Him why, what, where, when, and how?

What is most important. You need to know who you are! That is the only way you can succeed. I am following a long list of High Achievers and I must keep the faith that He is with me, and He is with me everywhere I go. His Holy Spirit guided me to open the windows and let some of His air in so I could breathe it in and out of my lungs after spraying the air with aerosols. It is a "Spring Breeze" that He is allowing to cascade throughout the house.

It is our mansion, our little hide-a-way. My bed of roses.

I read that this senior citizen was bedridden, and she went to sleep on a bed of red roses and when someone asked her "how did she sleep", she said the Lord came, got her body, and placed her in His Everlasting Arms and His Arms were made from red and white roses. The senior citizen replied I am fine! I am good! Do you have the courage the senior citizen had to allow the Lord to engulf your mind, brain, heart, body, soul, and spirit? The senior citizen saw the red roses as they were a gift from God through Jesus Christ, Our Lord, and Savior.

Thank You, God, for My Savior! My Savior saved my soul! I was pacing back and forth, praying in silence. Giving honor and glory to the One who watched over me while I slumbered and slept. I remember waking up and singing my song and pulling the covers tightly around my neck and I went to talk. I ask O Lord please come into my presence and O Lord please allow me into Your Presence. I drifted off into La La Land, but I woke myself up and remembered I had not said my affirmations. I started humbly and meekly talking to the One who is listening to every word I say. He wants to know immediately what is meditating in my heart and I position myself to submit my request boldly and honorably to Thee. Oh, Lord! I began with these words! O Lord they are so important to me. I am honoring. I am saluting the Giver of Life. I want to make sure He knows who I am and whose I am. So, I will speak out. No rock will need to cry out for me. O, Your Majesty! I am your humble servant – what must I do?

Read John 3 v:16, says "For God so loved the world that He gave His only begotten Son that whosoever believeth in Him shall not perish but have an Everlasting Life." Only for me. Only for the chosen few.

I am one of the ones who is receiving everlasting life every time I open my eyes. I become brand new. I come alive again. I live again. I am not dead. Today is the best day of my life. I am glad that I am alive today. Everyday, all day, 24/7, around the clock – every hour – every minute – every second and right at this present time He is with me. Psalm 23 tells me. I believe what I read. He is hovering over me like a helicopter. He has me surrounded. He has me captivated. I am under His spell. He has the plan. I am listening to the One who knew me before I was in my mother's womb. I am listening to the One who rose from the dead to save my soul.

Stop now! Renew your faith. Renew your strength. Put a couple of logs on the fire. The hotter it gets the more you want to move away from direct heat. Have you ever met spirits that made you want to just disappear? I have! These are the most awful kind. They don't love themselves and you either. They are so wrapped up in themselves that they cannot see beyond their nose. They look at you with hate and scorn in their eyes. Satan, Lucifer, the devil, the enemy has captured your eyes. He has you looking at what He wants you to see. Blind them and you can have complete control. I was blinded by idol gods and now I am not. I have money to do what I need to do. Thank You Jesus for Your abundant supply of resources. You just keep my blessings coming. Again, and again, over, and over.

Earlier during the morning hours, I was challenged physically, mentally, emotionally, morally, psychologically, and spiritually. I woke up early with stomach discomfort. I went to praying. I went to work. I did this and I did that as His Holy Spirit was directing my every footstep. It is now around lunchtime; noon and I find myself just unloading all on you. These are the words that are meditating in my heart.

This morning I ask Him, O Lord please shelter us, O Lord please shadow us, O Lord please favor us, O Lord please cover us with Your Blood, O Lord please grant us Your Grace and Mercy, O Lord please strengthen us physically, mentally, emotionally, psychologically, morally and spiritually, O Lord please forgive us of our sins because we don't always do things perfectly and correctly, O Lord please forgive our enemies because they know not what they do, O Lord please protect us from all plagues, pandemics, disasters, and turmoil, O Lord please prosper us materialistically, financially and spiritually, O Lord please do not cast us away from Your Presence and O Lord please allow Your Holy Spirit to dwell in us again on this day. In Jesus' Name, I Pray - Amen.

My heart is made from gold. It is full of putty. My love smears. My love covers you like a blanket. Once you open your heart and let Him fill it with His Love, you will never be the same anymore. This Love is not ordinary. It is Extraordinary Love just waiting for you. This Love has your name written all over it. It is free! That is what is so good about it. He has tons and tons of His Love that He wants to give you. You must ask Him. You must acknowledge Him as the author and finisher of your fate. He is my beginning and my end. He loved me yesterday and He has reappeared to do it all over again.

How is that possible? You may ask! Everyday is my birthday. Everyday I open my eyes I get a new mind, a new brain, a new heart, a new body, a new soul, and a new spirit. Take a deep sigh of relief! I had to. It is true when you accept Jesus as Your Lord and Savior, you are born again. Old clothes have been replaced with new clothes.

2nd Corinthians 5 v:17. You will not be the same. Something wonderful, magnificent, marvelous, splendid, superb, spectacular, and wonderful will drape a curtain of pure pleasure, satisfaction, kindness, gentleness, honesty, truth, justice, salvation, redemption, love, and righteousness all over you. It has been a mighty good year for me. 2020 and 2021 are the years that I spent in His Presence. He is mighty good to me. He is mighty good to you. Help me admit it. He is Our King of Kings and Our Lord of Lords. He deserves all of the praise, honor, and worship. I will serve Him the rest of my life. Surely His goodness and mercy shall follow me all of the days of my life as long as I dwell in His secret place, dwell in His shelter, dwell in His service and dwell in His Presence.

After adjusting and adapting to my morning routine I survived by only placing my hope, faith, and trust in Thee. Yes, I am ready! Ready to embrace the adventure that He had planned for me. I believe I will sing a "Love Song". Thank You, Jesus! These are the only words. Just three precious words. These words are so sacred. These words saved my life. These words opened the doorway to Heaven and allowed me to come walking in. I am never going to let Him get away from me. So many people are holding on to the hem of His garment, it has turned into strings. I am holding on to a string.

Are you holding on? If you need a word of encouragement, remember never let go of what He has given you. If he has given you hope, love and a future then stay with Him because He has a plan just for you. Hold on to His Unchanging Hand, His Unfailing Hand, His Unconditional Hand, His Grace and Mercy, and His Divine Devotion.

He is my divine companion. He is my constant companion. He goes with me everywhere I go. This is what it says at Joshua 1 v:9. "For Thy Art with Me". This is what it says in Psalm 23. He will keep His promise. If He promised it to you then He will give it to you. If I remain in Him, then He will remain in me. If I abide in Him, then He will abide in me. If I draw nearer to Him, then He will draw nearer to me. What a beautiful Savior?

Just the way you are! This is how accepting He is! No special preparations are needed. No precautions need to be taken. Step right up and step right into His Presence. Ask Him! O Lord please come into my presence and O Lord please allow me into Your Presence. He will accept you faster than a bolt of lightning. Just as you are. Weary, worn, tired, and heavy laden come unto Me and I will give you rest. My yoke is easy. I will be on one side, and you can be on the other one and allow me to guide the way. Matthew 11 v:28.

I submitted. I committed. I surrendered my total self over to Thee so His will could be done. I ask O Lord please reshape me and remold me and make me into the person You had designed me to be before I was in my mother's womb. I got a chance to prove my self-worth. I came alive in my senses so I could "think and process thought". I cry "my country tears for thee". His eyes are filled with tears because he sees that so many of His sheep have hardened their hearts. They are pulling away farther and farther from the truth. His sheep are being misled. His sheep are forgetting that Satan, Lucifer, the devil, the enemy's job is to steal, kill and destroy. Steal your desire, kill your joy, and destroy your beliefs in God, The Father of Our Lord and Savior Jesus Christ.

Just give me a reason to keep talking and I will take you into a second sermon. It is a new day. I knew the era in time. A new awakening. A new opportunity to beat Satan at his own game. You know who you trust! You know who you believe in! You know where you have placed your faith!

Ask Him to come to see about you just like He comes to see about His Flowers in His Garden of Life.

He comes every morning to give His creation their morning mercy and love. Psalm 90 v:14. He satisfied me early with His love and told me to let it last me throughout my day. So, I got busy after shaking the devil loose and began to complete my morning routine.

Prince said he saw "Purple Rain". Prince, I see "blue rain, blue skies, blue waters, blue ice, trees growing from inside of rocks, trees growing on the sides of mountains, a pyramid of dust and dirt. I am standing

at the base knowing that we will all return to what we came from. We will all return to dust. Wait! It is not too late for you to live again – before you turn into dust.

Change the words that are meditating in your heart. Proverbs 18 v:21 says "the tongue" has the power of life or death. Choose life. You want to live a life in the presence of a King. You want the shackles that have accumulated over time to be removed. Ask The King! This is what I had to do. I pushed past Satan and went directly to the Source. I went directly to the One who watched over my mamma, daddy, sisters, and brother, cousins, family, loved ones, and friends. I received my reward. I knew I had a fighting chance because I knew what He did for them. The Same Love back then is the Same Love that I have today. They believed. I believe. I trust. I hope. I have faith in the unseen. I am walking by faith and not by sight. I am hooked on Him and what He is doing for me.

He comes highly recommended. I am glad that I can tell you about a Savior who saved my life. I am glad that I have the opportunity to invade your space. It is with delight and pleasure that I am allowed to share with you just what Jesus and I talk about daily. It is joy and pleasure to be in His Presence. I am at peace this morning. I have talked with my two daughters, my son, my brother, and some random unknown callers. I am answering my phone each time it rings, and I tell the caller I am celebrating George Floyd Day, did they want to join me? Click!

This is what I expect. It was a surprise to me that the phone went silent. Since this is what I wanted to talk about. You see what was on my mind, on my heart, in my brain, my soul, my body and spirit.

It is time to celebrate a new beginning. We are moving in closer. Our feet are in the door. Justice! Truth! Honesty! Equality! Sincerity! Salvation! Redemption! Love! Righteousness! Leave the doorway open. I am coming through because He is always on my mind. I made Jesus the Head of My Life, and this was the best decision I could have ever made.

I made "Jesus First". Jesus. J E S U S. Spell it out loud. He is the One that made a difference in my life. He is the One that gave me a reason to live.

He is the One that allowed me to be closed in my right mind with a reasonable portion of my health and strength ready to praise, honor, cherish, worship, and obey Him for being so good to me on this glorious and wonderful Good Friday on this Springtime Day.

Turn down my street of dreams on this Friday morning! One day man will not be judged on the color of His skin or the texture of his hair, but by the contents of his character and the contents of his heart! Did you know that? Man must come to grips with the reality! Man must begin to realize that there is another life he can live.

Man must begin to realize that he does not have to live in a corrupt and wicked world. Man must realize that he is buried in his grave. Man must realize that he is the walking dead. Man must realize that his life is over unless he stops being eaten alive through his flesh and desires. Man must open his eyes and begin to look upward, outward, around, and beyond and see what His eyes can behold. Look at the trees! Have you ever seen so many varying shades of green! Pea-green, lime green, yellow green, money green, army green. All these colors are blended in, and they give off a magnificent color and peace. Slow up. Stop and look at His trees. His trees are a beauty for your eyes only. There are so many shapes and sizes. Just like mankind. He satisfies the desire of every living thing.

You want love, He has got it? You want peace, He has got it? Do you want companionship? He has got it. Do you want joy and happiness? He has got that too. You want honesty, truth, integrity, justice, salvation, redemption, love, and righteousness, then He has got that also? Man must be in the right posture to receive all the blessings that Our Lord has in reserve for Him.

I am alone and it is so easy for me to continue the relationship that we have daily. He was with me yesterday and He is with me again today. I ladled my coffee back and forth and I recited His 23rd Psalm.

Surely His goodness and mercy shall follow me all the days of my life if I dwell in the Presence of the Highest. If I dwell in His shelter, if I dwell in His secret place. God told the Israelites when they pass through the waters, I will be with you. Whatever you go through, remember Me. I will be with you all day, everyday, 24/7, around the clock – every hour – every minute – every second and right at this present moment in time if you allow me to. Let the truth prevail.

Me, myself, and I can't live without Him. He came early and distracted Satan. Satan slithered back in His hole because He saw that I was covered by His Blood. Jesus chose me after I began to honor Him, cherish Him, obey Him, worship Him, praise Him, love Him, and glorify His Name for being so good to me. Listen to the gentle sounds of His raindrops on a tin roof. They are so peaceful. They fall so gently and delicately. The sound transforms into peace, patience, and contentment. This is the sound of nature that He wants you to hear. Drift off into La La Land. Place your head upon His chest so you can breathe His sweet breath forevermore. This is what I do at a moment's notice.

This is all I am asking for! Just to be in His Presence. Just to be in His Household. Psalm 91 says "He will cover me with His feathers and under His wings, I will seek refuge. In His Everlasting Arms is where I am safe and secure at this 4 o'clock sacred hour. He is taking good care of me.

Why do I say sacred? Every moment I spend in His Presence is sacred to me because He made the choice that I could inhale and exhale His air in and out of my lungs. He is the One that made the decision that my heart could beat at a normal rhythm. He is the decision-maker. I honor Him.

I praise Him. I worship Him. I adore Him. I admire Him. I idolize Him.

I cherish Him because He is the first one that ever loved me.

Chapter 29

Okay, I have renewed my strength and uplifted my spirit. Listen to what He said to me! I will always love you! I will love you always! These are the words that greeted me early during the morning hours. These are the words that I have been operating off of. It is great to know that you are wanted, needed, cherished, admired, adored, appreciated, and idolized by a King. It has been a cold – chilly – day with tidbits of sunshine peeking through. I see His sun shining. I see its shadow overcasting the landscape of trees in His forest. I see big, humongous trees with moss growing out of the side and top of them. I see a stream of water finding its way through the meadows. I am looking at a floating palace in Jaipur, India. It is gold and its shadows over the water with a glare. Looks like a place in Paradise. Looks like a place in the Great Beyond.

I am only one vessel with a message of love, hope, and peace. My method of delivery might not be conventional. Nope! I am not yelling and hollering, I only want to have a chat with you and tell you that I will not stop writing until all the eyes of the world are waiting anxiously and excitedly about His return. One day He is returning to gather the souls who have stayed in the boat. He will be back to get the ones who believed in Jesus as The Messiah – A Savior – My Savior. Wherever I go and whatever I do, I place Jesus first. He is my Savior, and I will let Him be my Savior. I will follow His every command. He is the Author and Finisher of my fate, and I will let Him lead the way. Whichever way He wants this ship to sail, then this is the direction it will drift off into.

I had to fight with Satan. Guess who won? Jesus Christ, the Only One took control of the situation. My heart pounds so fast when I talk about My Lord and Savior. I must stop recline, listen to some easy listening music, and pray. I calm myself down. I place my head upon His chest so I can breathe His sweet breath forevermore, become content and satisfied, trusting that He has got me. Banjoes, violins, accordions, trumpets, sax, drums, guitars, and pianos are excellent sources to relax your heart, mind, brain, body, soul, and spirit by. They provide a need for comfort, patience, peace, and joy. I want to belong somewhere. I want to fit in. So, I will play by your rules. Now that is the way things are done around here. You have an idol --someone who you worship, praise, salute, admire and adore. My idol is Jesus Christ. He is My Lord and Savior. I don't know who you worship but I still leaning on The Pillar of Faith. That promise that He would never leave me nor forsake me. He had remembered my smile, He had remembered my name, He called my name. I heard Him. I took my seat at the front of the class. I was on the ground floor then I moved to the top of the floor. Determination to learn more than my mom and dad did. They would often tell us to "make me and pappa proud". They would immediately pray and ask O Lord please protect and guide my child to make the right decision so he can come back home alive.

Fear - Panic switch in - confusion comes into play - they have no idea of what to do next, they know they want to get away from the police real fast, little do they now the police are trained to shoot to kill as this is justice done by The God Father Movie. Shoot to kill? Stop and just talk to someone.

Look! We are taking our eyes off the prize. Jesus promised Understanding, Peace, Patience, Contentment, Tranquility, Harmony, Joy, Happiness. There are dreams made up in those clouds. Ever just sat and watched the sky at night. All kinds of colors. You see sparkles before your eyes because He lights your way. You look back and wonder how I made it. Barriers, Suitcases, Boulders, Rocks were thrown in my face, it always blocked my view until I day I crossed over to the Other Side of that Mountain. I was always looking for a brighter day. Remember!

He is with me. Thy Art with Me. These are scriptures in the Bible. Find them and read them to your loved ones, sisters and brothers, mother and father, nieces, nephews, family members, and friends. Psalm 23. Paste this scripture across your heart. Seal it in tight and never forget it. This is the Name that God wanted you to call on. It was His Only Begotten Son. In Jesus' Name. Let it be. Tense down. Do not be afraid of me, I am just riding along. Let all of us three meet up together and have a meeting of the minds. You, me, him, she, he, her, them, and they. Did I grab your attention? Yep! I am preaching! Have no concept of time. I listen to melodies that fly me to the moon and back each time my fingers move across this keyboard. Thank You, Lord, for my body, my hands, my fingers, my arms, my mind, my brain, my heart, my legs, my knees, my ankles, foot, and toes. Just because "I Love You", You are my Only Love.

Listen to me singing a song! I sing a song with my free mind, free brain, free heart, free body, free soul, and free spirit. Yep! It is all clear of the clutter? It is time for your loved ones to speak to you from the grave. They are saying to you before it is too late, get the word out that He will not be satisfied and full of contentment until all heads bow unto Thee. The One that He created as a gift to us. Our Savior! Our Majesty! Our King of Kings, Our Lord of Lords. Jesus Christ, Our Lord, and Savior.

Ready to shout yet? I am because I have a lot to shout about. No covid - no pandemic, no plague, no disaster -no turmoil will stop us. We will continue to praise His Name. Right. Shout! He spared me one more day. I opened the windows and enjoyed a little of His fresh air. Those houses are too tight. Oxygen cannot get in and that is why you must find a breath of fresh air, inhale it in and exhale it out of your lungs. Sit back, relax, and let yourself go to over there, over yonder, in Paradise, in that Promised Land.

In La La Land is where you will find me when I place my head upon His chest so I can breathe His sweet breath forevermore. Every night I come in a little closer. Each morning the sun shines, I go into overload. I wake up preaching. Just talking and singing and praising Him for being so good to me by favoring me with a brand new sacred hour of 9 p.m. on a night that I have never seen before.

Star Bright! You remember at night you use to talk to me. Why did man stop listening to God, Jesus, Our Lord, and Savior? Blindness. These animals that we are eating are giving off fumes like gas. We are slowly rotting away. We will become like the dust from where we came from. We are withering. We are like falling branches, dying on the vine.

I will not return the same way I was while I was on His sacred and secret ground, we call Earth, on His Planet and in His Universe. I am going to tell it - who will listen. I will speak if you allow me to. You have too much to say! No one wants to listen! Is there any chipper in that voice? His bird chants, chirp, and sing

Praises to His Name early in the wee hours of dawn. They start early.

When I peep from under the coverings, I begin praising Him. just like the birds are doing. They are praising Him, so I join in. Okay, Holy Birds keep chirping. I will strengthen my eardrums so I can hear You when You speak to My heart. He gave me a life to live, and I am going to live it to the max.

Honey! I will not be home for dinner. Not today – not ever – can't you see the difference between the two of us, he wants it his way and I want things my way – Let us compromise. Nope! Separation needed. He is on one side of the mountain, and I am on the other one. This is the best thing that will work for me. You see! I would be lost without His Guidance and His Love. I know my source of strength. I know who will delight my spirits. Oh! Jesus, I would be lost without You. Look how He wants to shed His tears. Rain and Thunderstorms. Use this time to pray, talk with Jesus, and ask Him to become your comforter and counselor. He will come and bring you His Holy Spirit as a gift.

Do not get bent out of shape if you don't speak in tongue. Some have this as a spiritual gift and another one of His sheep may have something different. Examine that tongue. Is it giving you life or death? What is meditating in your heart? Psalm 19 v:14 says "may the words of my mouth and the meditation of my heart be acceptable in Thy Sight, My Lord, My Redeemer, My Rock.

Won't He promptly remove you from the corner? That corner in your heart, brain, mind, body, soul, and spirit that has a raging spirit of fire in their hearts towards all of mankind? One day! One day! There will be an awakening and every one of us will be on one accord. He will be listening to see what you are saying. He will be reading your mind the whole time you are talking. He is just that close to me on my Friday night. I have been celebrating by sharing the good news from my camp.

I took my brother to church. His voice perked up; He became quiet and at ease when we are talking. His favorite expression is "Peace". I asked him one day why do you say "peace" at the end of our conversations, and he said because I am at peace, and I want you to have peace also. Okay, I am at Peace!! He is at peace because I know who is holding my hand and I had my brother agreeing that we knew the One who was holding our hand. Wavelength. Just an Arm away. Just between those ribs, you can find a heart. and it will not be made from stone. Your heart will become free! Your heart will become brand new! You agree! That we should receive a golden heart because of what we had to go through. Another Angel said "we made it" one more day. He has been watching over us the entire time, during the hours of the day, and is getting ready to shift into some night gear.

I have had so many interesting conversations today. I have not had time to relive my early morning sickness. I have been so wrapped up in rejoicing in His Name about His goodness until this morning is only a faint memory. It is a blur. I can see, I "Thank Him" for my sight. My eyes - my brown eyes - I can see with a faint amount of light. Turn some of the light down or downright off. You are not sitting in the dark, you are getting ready to put on the hat of mom and dad, sister or brother, husband and wife. Morning seemed like it was so long ago. It is now 6 p.m. on this Good Friday afternoon. News time. I caught it earlier and I don't want to hear repeats.

Politicians, Democrats call it as you see it. It is "hate". This is what about to destroy us if we do not stand up and face reality. The reality is that black folk, brown folk, yellow folk, red folk, white folk are hated because of the color of their skin and the texture of their hair. This is an underlining evil spirit that has consumed the hearts of many. It will take Jesus showing up in the hearts of man to fight this evil. Rev Al Sharpton. Ask Jesus to come into their hearts and minds and make them change their beliefs, ideas, thoughts, opinions, dreams, desires and traditions. This is your prayer. Ask Him for the words to say and He will direct your path. Time is changing. Satan knows his time is up.

What they use to do they cannot do anymore. What they use to think has been replaced with stone hard cold facts. Jesus said, "Love each other". What is so hard about this decree? Why can't we? Hate is in all four chambers of man's heart. Hate, Rage, Anger produces savages and barbarians. Can't you see them being transformed into evil beings? Don't you see steam coming from their ears and mouths? They are spewing "hate". It is up to us, brown folk, black folk, red folk, yellow folk, white folk, to put an end to Satan, Lucifer, the devil, the enemy's tactics. Far too long we have been subjected to unconstitutional and unlawful acts perpetrated by the devil. Enough is enough. We will not take it anymore! We will call it just like we see it. It is "hate".

Man hates himself. How can a man love you when he hates himself? Loaded question, right? It is true! Blacks, browns, yellows, red ones, white ones, hate themselves and each other. Scrape that hate away that is climbing the walls of your heart. Go into every nook and cranny and clean all the evil spirits that are destroying you. Make them go away, out, gone for good. Don't ever let the evil spirit of "hate" come back. Stand up to "hate" and demand it to leave your heart, brain, mind, body, soul, and spirit. Free will and self-control. You possess a heart and a soul just like all His sheep in His Pasture.

What is in that heart? Hurray! It is a new day. It is "Good Friday", and we always can expect miracles on a Good Friday. Without Him, as my constant companion, I could not make it. Without Him leading the way, I would crash, burn, and wreck. Without Him whispering in my ear words like; I will always love you and I will love you always, I would be lost. Like a ship without a sail. I would be drifting far and wide with no sense of a clear direction. Thank God that He saved my soul! "Thank You, Lord" for sending me a lifeline. "Thank You, Lord" for saving my soul. You did not let me drown in my sea of terror. You stretched out Your Righteous Right Hand and I grabbed it. Today! I am holding on to His Unchanging Hand because He is showering me with His Unconditional Love, His Grace and Mercy, and His Divine Devotion. Isn't He grand? Isn't He mighty? Isn't He great? Isn't He magnificent? I see blue water, gray water, cathedrals, villages, cottages, places, trees growing out the side of mountains. He is mighty. He is great.

Isn't He marvelous? Isn't He spectacular? Isn't He miraculous? He is to me because He performed a miracle on me when He raised me from the dead. I was sleeping in my grave. I had given up. It was the end of me, so I thought. One afternoon I came face to face with Satan. I told Satan that I had changed my address and He wasn't welcome around me anymore. I did not need Him any longer. I had been listening to Him for too long and it was time for me to make a change. This is what I did!

I became a sophisticated lady. I wanted more. More of what I didn't know. I just knew there had to be more. That this was not all there was. I went searching. I went knocking. I began believing. I began reading. I began trusting. I began not to lean on my understanding but lean on what the Bible said to me. The very first thing I learned was that there was a powerhouse of words in my mouth and my mouth had miracles in it. My words gave life to my thoughts. I began to think. I began to process thought. I began to imagine what my life could be like.

I began to seek out other avenues and other opportunities for growth and development. I was not satisfied with the old clothes that I was wearing. I wanted to become brand new, and this is what I did. I learned that I had to shed the old ideas, thoughts, opinions, beliefs, traditions, dreams and desires. They had destroyed me, and I was convinced that I would no longer allow myself to be a part of them. I no longer wanted their influence.

I got the opportunity to find out that I was great! I got the opportunity to find out that I was a masterpiece. I got the opportunity to find out that I was a fine specimen of His workmanship. I got the opportunity to find out that if He crafted my body under His moonlight, when He turned me over to look at me under His sunlight, then suddenly I was His shining star. Stay just as you are, you will be a useful tool as you go across the country to tell the world that all eyes of His sheep should be waiting on Him to return. What a great day? Until that day I will keep shouting His Name in Praise. All the days in my life, along with every breath in my body I take, I honor Thee. I thank Thee.

Bid this world goodbye so you will be ready when He returns. Don't wait until you are on your death bed to ask Him to save your soul. Do it now while the blood is still running warm in your body, and you can make a choice. You have free will. You have self-control, then control your desires and emotions. Don't you want your voice heard?

Go ahead. Tell Him what you want. Be sincere and honest in the conversation you have with Him because your aim and purpose are to establish a relationship whereby you can go to Him in secret prayer and ask for what you want, need, yearn, and desire. Want a second helping?

Okay! Who is sleeping in their grave? Boy! Am I eating meat during my season? Just send me Your Love, Grace and Mercy, and Your Divine Devotion. Don't ever leave me to be snared by the fowler. Please O Lord hear my prayer. Lead me on through this foreign land. This place is not my home. I am only passing through trying to get to the other side and with Your help I know I can make it. Ears have not heard; eyes have not seen what the Lord has waiting for those who love the Lord. I am listening to some easy listening music and allowing my thoughts to go there, here, over there, over yonder, and right where you are.

In His Presence - Yes! I am. I am proud of it. I know where my health and strength come from. I know who I trust. I know who I believe. I know who I have faith in. There is only one of us who should be on the road at the same time. That is Jesus Christ. Let's you and I invite Jesus in to have a seat. We will wait and see what the Savior has to say. It is getting to be my bedtime.

So! Has He been beneficial today? Did you see any waterfalls? Did your raindrops drop on the tin roof? I did. The raindrops are splashing up the side of the walkway. I must wade through the type of snow that I experienced when I lived in the State of Maine.

Slushy, mushy cold blue ice. The river would freeze over. I would look out and say, "I wish it was Spring". More soups, stews, pies, and cakes. Something good to the tummy tum.

To tell if a man hates you, try to look them in the eye. Lock eyes with them and let them speak to you with a message from their heart. You talk out your tongue, mouth, forehead, nose, ears, eyes. What are you spewing out of your heart? Is it Love? I thought so. Do you know who is the Source of that Love? If you do then you and I can become best friends because you will always be truthful when I give you, my love.

I see a palm tree 100 years old. It is big and lean. The shadow of the sunset has it lit up. Like a dust storm. It was white dust. The spring had carved its pathway. White sandy beaches, blue water, blue skies, one or two stationary clouds, a bed of green grass, bushes, and weeds that cover the walkway. It is like walking through the woods. There are so many good spots to grab along the beach. I am going to see my great-granddaughter, Luna Skye. She is four and I understand she is quite an "active" four-year-old. She asked my youngest daughter, Aishah, "So, do you want to take a selfie"?

Already wise. She hails from a group of high achievers. Her mom and her dad. Her grandparents. Grandmother and Grandfather were game changers. They fought the fight. They never gave up. They depended on God. They will tell you quickly "I know the Man". All right Grandmother Suzanna Tharpe. She lived to be well into her hundreds. She knew day from night. Closed in her right mind with a reasonable portion of her health and strength. She would often remark to me that "she knew the big guy".

My mama knew it took two incomes to raise a family with fifteen people in a two-bedroom house with one bathroom. Ah! He is able! Ah! He is wonderful? Look into the bathroom mirror, wash your face, do what you need to do, and let's go. You did not get a chance to see the sparkle He had placed in your eye. You were too busy to notice. The next morning you were back in the mirror, did you see the sparkle?

I "Thank Him" for giving me eyes to see. I "Thank You" for opening a peephole for me. I see your sheep who are content and have peace. I want that same kind of Love, peace, and contentment. You can have it because you are engraved in the Palm of His Hand.

Isaiah 49 v:15-16. I am Your God. I am the One you should seek first. I hold the key. You cannot get past me without acknowledging my Presence. Tell them that "I do exist" and how do you know that? Because He has brought me from over yonder, down in the valley. I was badly bruised. One day He opened my eyes and placed my feet on the solid and sacred ground we call Earth on our Planet and in Your Universe.

My life has not been the same. I dance to different music. I think. I have new ideas floating in and out daily. All day, everyday, 24/7, around the clock I remain in His Presence so He will remain in me.

Rocks coming up out of the water. Mountains formed in the oceans. Just to name a few of the pictures that are cascading across my tv and computer screens. Five minutes ago, I was full and content as I was preparing for bed. I am drinking water so that should fill me up.

I will not stop writing until all eyes are affixed to getting to know Jesus. He is a heart regulator. He is a mind regulator. He is a heart fixer. You will never know unless you tried Him for yourself. He is a way-maker. He is my pride and joy. He is My Savior, the one that bled and died so I could come alive in my senses so I can think, and process thought. You will never know what it means to have someone in your corner, cheering you on until you meet Jesus. He will be your bridge over troubled water. He calls the shots. Your ears must be tuned in to His frequency. Your ears must be listening for the slightest noise. You must want to hear Him. You must learn to listen so He will come right-a-way. He does not keep you waiting. Like a bolt of lightning, He appears. He wants you to be in His shelter, His secret place, His Presence. You must recognize where you want to be. Are you destined for greatness? I think we are! We will crush Satan at his own game.

You and I will change our focus. We must learn to be content, happy, joyous, and peaceful regardless of what state we are in. Good times, bad times, it does not matter if you remain in His Presence. He will take care of you and provide for all of your needs. One thing to believe and that is He will never steer you in the wrong direction. He wants to take good care of you. He is the Sheepherder. We are His sheep. We belong here. Take your life back from Satan through Jesus Christ and His Holy Spirit.

Just do it! Make Satan loosen the shackles he has tied around your neck, mind, brain, heart, body, soul, and spirit in Jesus' Name. Oh! We are going there. I see a bunch of blue clouds coming right at us and now I see a pooch taking a nap in the sun. I see two birds, perched out on a limb appear to have a prayer meeting. You must realize what words are capable of doing. Words can build. Words can destroy. Words will tell you to add some more logs in the fire because this is getting good. Where are going? We are going to explore Our Planet in His Universe.

The trees are crying out stop! You are killing us. If you remove the trees, you will be inhaling gas from the cars, airplanes, animals, and yourself. Trees develop into instant springs of water. Suddenly water starts gushing out of the rock showing us a "rainbow". Have you ever seen a rainbow? I have! I can angle my head away from the sun and I see sparkling blues, greens, reds, orange, yellow, and pink colors, like the stained-glass paintings at some churches. All these colors are so prominent and vibrant.

I am listening to an organ. It is music to my ears. I can dream, float, glow, glide in and out of His Presence.

I see a patch of red tulips. He is watching over me, and He is watching over you. There is so much He wants to show you. He wants you to know that "He will always love you" and if you did not hear Him the first time, He waits and turns it around and tells you "He will love me always. Old ones, young ones, tall ones, skinny ones, short ones, fat ones, black ones, brown ones, yellow ones, red ones, white ones, gay or straight - must submit themselves to Him so His will can be done.

Jesus gave us roadmaps, blueprints, and guidelines, the secret to Eternal Life. We must go through Him before we can ever have any peace, patience, joy, happiness, truth, honesty, justice, equality, integrity, love, and righteousness. I love Him. He died for me. He died for you. Shucks! Man - He gave up His life for me. Would you give up your life if you were asked to? No! This would be your reply. What are you going to do in a life and death situation? You must act fast.

My hand is in Jesus' Hand. He calls the shots. I trust in Him. I believe Him. I have faith because He has the plan. Jeremiah 29 v:11. He is the best of Planners. This is the only way you cross over to the other side where righteousness lives. Put Jesus first. Make Him the Head of Life. When I did this, I realized that this was the best decision I could have ever made. I don't go anywhere without Him. He is always on my side. We are hand in hand!

I remember yesterday. My entire day was fulfilling, rewarding, and simply delightful. I have a clean house. I used domestic help to mop, to get it spic n span. Isn't God good? He is a "great God". He is an "awesome God". Today, tonight, tomorrow, He will keep His Promise.

Chapter 30

Want to travel? Want to ride with me? Want to check out the latest in my world. You must see how the Kings lived! Floating Palaces. It is partly submerged into His pond of water that is traveling around in His oceans. The most beautiful fish. The widest turtles, man is moving a tad bit too fast. Get in the slow lane and ease with me. Travel with me as I explore the great beyond after spending all morning in His Presence while He serenades my body. He touches you ever so smooth and gently, just like I want Him to. Nice. Slow Easy. We have a lifetime together, so just slow down and listen to my flow. I am living in that Palaces at the bottom of the feet of My King. I am down on my knees begging Him to please do not forget about me. I am doing your Will O Lord I am doing what you told me to do. I accepted my responsibilities and I sat out to make You proud of me.

You bet I am happy, content, and thankful on this Saturday morning that I have never seen before. I have a clean house, clean furniture, and clean clothes. I remember growing up cleaning house from top to bottom. Everything was pulled out from the walls, and we gave the floors a good scrubbing. Time has changed. I was the best domestic help in the business. I knew I could clean and cook. Those were my two main objectives. If I saw something that needed to be done, I did it. I needed no convincing or prodding. I decided to do the job and I did it exceptionally good. I have a determination that was instilled in me by my mother, father, sisters and brothers, aunts, and uncles. Do not wait to be told - get the courage and enthusiasm to tackle whatever is before you.

I woke up to a gray - rainy - foggy wet day. Saturday, April 24th, 2021, here at Gene Miller Manor in Christian City in Union City, Georgia. Listening to some of my favorite music. I am just coasting through my morning routine. I have eaten my banana, taken my meds, and drank a bottle of His water at room temperature. I enjoyed it. I was not in a rush. I slowly, carefully planned my morning. I had listened to music throughout the night so quite naturally when I woke up, I was in perfect peace and ready to embrace the adventure that has been planned for me.

Jesus came early and satisfied me with His morning mercy, love, and grace and told me to let it last me all during my day. Psalm 90 v:14. This was after He had touched me with His finger of Love and told me to "wake up O sleepyhead, rise from the dead and let the Lord shine on you." I know My Savior! I know who did it. I know who was responsible for me waking up this morning. It was Jesus. Only a five-letter word, a word above all words, He is my Savior and I want to tell you just a little about Him. He is on time. He never fails, He is with me in illness and in good. I turned over on my side very slowly and placed my two feet on His floor and began to "hallow" His Name because He allowed me to get up and do what I needed to do. Once again, He favored me. Once again, He smiled at me. Once again, He carved a pathway for me to travel. After I had finished up in my happy space, I climbed into my happy space so I could reclaim my spot. After I did this, I pulled the covers up close to my neck and began talking. O Lord please come into my presence and O Lord please allow me into Your Presence. I snuggled in tighter to His Everlasting Arms and began to say; O Lord please shelter us, O Lord please shadow us, O Lord please favor us, O Lord please cover us with Your Blood, O Lord please strengthen us physically, mentally, emotionally, psychologically, morally and spiritually, O Lord please forgive us of our sins because we don't always do things perfectly and correctly, O Lord please forgive our enemies because they know not what they do, O Lord please protect us from all plagues, pandemics, disasters, and turmoil, O Lord please prosper us materialistically, financially and spiritually, O Lord please do not cast us away from Your Presence and O Lord please allow Your Holy Spirit to dwell in us again on this day. In Jesus' Name, I Pray - Amen.

It brings joy and pleasure to my heart knowing I can speak to the Ruler of The Universe and to the One who has all power in His Hand when He was raised from the dead. He came alive so that I may live again. He taught me to knock, seek and ye shall find. He laid the groundwork; all I must do is to keep the torch burning. Keep His Name alive. Tell him, her, she, he, them, and they, how Our Lord and Savior Jesus Christ saved my soul. I must tell you of an experience I had at one time in my life. I hated to look at my pictures. There was a smile on my face but deep down in my heart, there was sorrow and woe. The smile on my face and the contents of my heart did not correspond. My face told a different story. My heart told the truth. I had to come to grips with myself and begin to love the person I was looking at in the photo. I hated her. I did not love her.

What happened you ask? One fine morning I shed that overcoat of hate and shame and humiliation. That is what I lived with on a day-to-day basis. 2nd Corinthians 5 v:17 says, "therefore if any man is in Christ, he is a new creature; old things are passed away, behold all things have become new." I opened like the bud of a flower. I became brand new. I had a new mind.

I had a new beginning. I had a new birth. I had a new identity. I was born again. I was a new creature in Christ because He had come to see about me, and He promised He would take good care of me. I began to see myself through His eyes. He says hey "sweet pea". All I had to do was to believe, trust and have faith in The One who I have not seen, walk by faith and not by sight. This I can do. I pulled out my Bibles. I began to chart my affirmations. I began to chart what I would say each morning I opened my eyes to see another great, spectacular, and marvelous day. It is a day that Our Lord has made and gave us specific instructions at Psalm 118 v:24 to rejoice in it.

I read Psalm 23 and I tattooed it across my heart, mind, brain, body, soul, and spirit. The Psalms reads "Yea though I walk through the valley of the shadows of death, I will fear no evil, for Thy Art with Me." I read Joshua 1 v:9 and it said, "I will go with you everywhere you go". So here I am reading and digesting His word and letting it stick to me like glue. Just knowing He is near me gives me so much courage and confidence. When I pull out the computer chair and place my fingers on the keyboard I began to think and ponder the thought. I allow my thoughts to flow freely because I am saying the words that are meditating in my heart. I am a good listener.

It is a joy and a privilege to be alive in my senses so I can "think and ponder thought". Knowing that He blew His breath of life into my lifeless body and allowed me to come alive ready to praise, worship, salute and glorify Him for being so good to me. He made the decision that I could wake up, breathe His air, and allow my heart to beat at a normal rhythm. He is worthy to be praised. Isn't He wonderful? Isn't He wonderful? Answer the question. Is He wonderful to you? Look down in your heart (bow your head down to your stomach and when you raise your head with the answer look at the smile and contentment you will feel throughout your bones. It is smooth because He glides His Love all over my body, He is taking good care of me, He allows me to eat, drink, sleep, slumber, shout, hoop, jump, dance, wiggle, walk, glide, and coast right along. Put some more logs on that fire. Don't let it smolder. We are alive. We are not dead. His birds praise His Name. Let's you and I join in with birds and shout praises to His Name.

Something as tiny as a bird knows how to worship Him for being so good to it. I will not be satisfied until the eyes of all will wait upon Thee. My God, My Jesus, My Lord, and Savior knows every fiber of your being. He knows your thoughts. He knows your actions. He knows your ideas. He is watching over you, and He is watching over me waiting to see if we will saturate His atmosphere with words of praise and worship. He is listening to every word we say. Jeremiah 29 v:12. He is taking mental notes, so He knows what is always going on with you. This is what He does to me. He surrounds me. He follows me around. It is me and Him in a bubble. We are bouncing here, there, and everywhere. Isn't it amazing that Our Savior can be here, there, and everywhere at the same time? Is He magical? Is He majestic? Is He miraculous?

Oh Yes! He is. He is a beautiful Savior. Watch me as I write this song. He performed a miracle on me when He raised me from the dead. He is the reason I am living. He gave me a reason to come alive in your senses so I could begin to love myself and love Him. I had to learn that I could not love Him or anyone else until I began loving myself. After I began accepting myself as to who I was, He brought to me His Gifts of His Spirit. Galatian 5 v:22. His Fruits are kindness, gentleness, joy, happiness, faithfulness, self-control combined with His Love all wrapped up into one gigantic ball "just for me". I took each fruit and bathed in it. I felt my fingers and hands. I began "Thanking Him" for my fingers and hands, brain, mind, heart, body, soul, and spirit. I thanked Him for it all. He permitted me to "think", I ask for it. I ask Him to strengthen me physically, mentally, emotionally, psychologically, morally, and spiritually. In Jesus' Name.

God knew what I needed before I did. He knew I would need to be wrapped up in His Everlasting Arms because I was taking baby steps. I was just beginning to say my affirmations each morning I opened my eyes. Practice, practice, and more practice, now My affirmation rolls off my tongue because this is what is meditating in my heart. Several times of the night I honor the One who allowed me to flush my kidneys and excrete my bowels and expel my bowels. It is a joy and privilege to go into my happy space because I know who is holding my hand the entire time I am in there and on the way out. I look forward to talking with the One who watched over me while I slumbered and slept. I am grateful" to the One that stretched His Righteous Right Hand out to me, and I grabbed it. This is the same Hand that I am holding on to at this noonday hour. This Hand gave me a new reason for living. This Hand sustains me from sunup to sundown and in between.

I know who is watching over me on this magnificent, marvelous, foggy gray-looking day. It is Jesus Christ the One who was holding my hand when I drifted off into La La Land. It was in His chest that I laid my head so I could breathe His sweet breath forevermore. Memories, that is all we have. Yesterday, He was good to me. Yesterday, He was good to you, and He did it again. He returned to give us more of the same love that He gave us yesterday. Aren't we blessed and highly favored? I believe we are. Say it to yourself. See what it feels like to paste these words across your heart, lips, mouth, soul, and spirit. Yes, Queen Bettie, I am blessed and highly favored, and thank - you for bringing it to my attention.

My sister, Hilda Joyce Grose, always said these words, "I am blessed and highly favored". She would plain bore me. She was so bossy, messy, sometimes, never sure of herself. So, I did trust nothing she said except "I remember her saying to me, "Sis, what is the rush".

It took her thirty minutes to chew one bite. Stop, eating so fast. Dad would say, it will make you poor to tote it. Meaning, after you eat so much you can't do anything. You cannot even move a muscle and you call that a good thing. Wake up! Now, who is sleeping? We all are! Some are more awake than others and those that are awake have a job to do. Man, beast, slob! You choose. Convince them. Convince her. Convince him. Convince she. Convince he. Convince them and convince they, the Ones in the East, North, South, and West that the King is scattered His most prized possessions among the masses. Man, woman, King, Queen, boy, girl, princes, princesses. Man, woman, or child. Listen! His trumpets are sounding.

They are blowing smoke. He is raising the dead. He is canvassing the area to see who has the righteous heart and a steadfast spirit. He found one, two, three, four, five, six, seven, eight, nine, ten, I will stop counting. This is the majority, and the majority says let's follow the Leader. She sounds like she knows the way to the Kingdom. She talks about going over there, over yonder at the Great Beyond! Any ideas? No! Let's trust her. Let's listen. Give me your full attention, nothing else. Rock with me. Just listen - do you hear any silence. Do you hear any noises - there is too much noise in your ear? You cannot hear Him when He calls you. Listen! He is calling your name. That is why you must be at perfect peace. In His Presence is where you want to be.

Ah! His green foliage growing on the side of mountains, water spewing over rocks at a waterfall, the bluest skies, the whitest clouds, the blackest birds, the roaring thunder, all part of His Plan. He is replenishing His solid and sacred creation, His Earth, on His Planet and in His Universe. I know who I am, and I know whose I am.

Psalm 121. I am trying to walk straight. I walk with my back bent over. This is not how I want to walk so I will lift my eyes to the hills from whence cometh my help. My help cometh from The Lord, who made Heaven and Earth. When I stand up, I call on Him and ask to Help Me, Jesus. I will not shift my focus from Him. I am going to call on Him all the days of my life if I am walking on His sacred and solid ground we call Earth, on His Planet, and in His Universe. After I make the cross-over I will be praising Him singing "Holy - Holy - Holy" because He allowed me to lay my head upon His chest and breathe His sweet breath forevermore. I know the Lord is my keeper. He neither slumbers nor sleeps. He is always around. He is watching over me right at this present and the precise moment in time. He sees me sitting here, searching for the next clue that He wants to reveal to me.

The Lord shall preserve me from all evil; He shall preserve my soul. The Lord shall preserve my going out and thy coming in from this time forth and forevermore. The Lord is in control of my destiny. I am only a tool that He is using to tell you that in due season, you too will spring forward, like a bud out of a new flower, and tell the world that all eyes should be focused on Him, what He is doing in your life and what He has done in your life. If He saved your soul, then you know you cannot be quiet. He wants to make His children happy. That is the reason He continues to shine His Grace, Love, and Mercy upon you.

You are accepted, wanted, needed, appreciated, adored, admired, cherished, and idolized by a King. This is the truth that is being told to you. Testify as you look around at all the green foliage that is cascading before your eyes. I have never seen so many rich colors of green. Pea green, lime green, purple, green, army green, money green. It is springtime and everything is being made brand new and we should find harmony and contentment in knowing that He is feeding His creation. He is giving His creation what it needs to flourish and grow. He is giving me what I need. I owe Him a debt of gratitude. Ten thousand tongues would not be enough. Just Love me forever O Lord.

Philippians 4 - beginning at verse 11, says we should be content with whatever. Happy or sad, good, or bad, up, or down. We should be alright because God has ordered us to be not anxious for anything. He has promised that He would return to take good care of us. Just like His Tulips in His Flower Garden. God, Jesus, My Lord, and Savior has put His foot down. Are you going to believe it? Do you trust me? I will carve your pathway, just hold unto my Unchanging Hand. I know how to follow a decree! I know how to take orders!

Let us sail on the lakes that He has designed for us down here on His green Earth. If we believe and trust and have faith, He will protect us from all hurt, harm, or danger, He will provide all our needs and He will allow His Holy Spirit to be our comforter and counselor then just do it. Stand on your convictions and beliefs, opinions, traditions. The Apostle Paul was speaking, and he said "I have learned in whatever situation I am to be content. I know how to be brought low and I know how to abound. In any and every circumstance I have learned the secret of facing plenty and hunger, abundance and need. I can do things through Him who strengthens me.

This morning, are you content, happy, joyous, satisfied, at peace, and in harmony in your heart, brain, mind, body, soul, and spirit? Ponder this one before you answer. Have you learned to be content with "just whatever"? Are you resting your soul in His Hands? If you rest your soul, you will automatically become complacent and content. You know without a shadow of a doubt that He is with you, He is watching over you, and He is taking good care of you. I knew He was smiling on me when I placed my two feet on His floor, and I began to sing my song; Thank You, Jesus, all the way in my happy space and on the way out. I have completed my morning routine and find myself with peace and contentment to share with you just how my morning has been unfolding. I am dreaming of a brighter day.

I had to stop writing and take a sip of His water at room temperature. It was so refreshing and filling and satisfying. Sometimes you need to just slow it down and taste the water and allow it to renew your strength and uplift your spirits. Take a break. Relax in your happy space knowing that You have a Savior who is watching over you, me, him, her, she, he, them, and they. At the same time! How remarkable is this?

I am alive. I am not dead. I want to live again. I am grateful for everyday that I see. I will not be satisfied until your eye, my eye, his eye, her eye, their eyes are focused on waiting for Thee. Psalm 145. The eyes of all wait upon Thee and Thou give them their meat in due season. Thou open Thine Hand and satisfies the desire of every living thing. Oh, Lord! Just let me get closer to Thee. If I remain in Him, then He will remain in me. If I abide in Him, then He will abide in me. If I draw nearer to Him, then He will draw nearer to me. I desire to complete the assignment I have been given. I believe if I walk, tread lightly, focus on what I was told to do I will complete my destiny.

My mamma uses to say to us kids, "child, I am preaching my funeral everyday that I live". She lived to please the Lord, feed, and clothe and teach her children. She was a great teacher. We kids were taught to learn and recite His 23rd Psalm and we had to do this at Sunday School and home. Now I say it all day, everyday, 24/7, around the clock - every hour - every minute - every second and right at this present and the precise moment in time. He has got me. I can't fall because I am leaning on His Pillar of Faith that He is providing "just for me". It is only us "two" on this soggy, wet, rainy day. A wonderful and beautiful day to read our Bibles, religious books, meditate, write, and pray. Everything is so still. Man and woman should use this time as quiet time to be in His Presence. When will man slow down and begin to think, and process thought? Can't anything be accomplished when you are in a rush? I know. So many times, I get up and begin rushing and His Holy Spirit must slow me down and just have an old-fashioned talk with me. I listen. There was a plan made for me. Jeremiah 29 v:11. He plans to prosper me, not harm me, give me hope for my future.

We all are engraved in the Palm of His Hand. His Hand is so big. It is enormous. He can hold you, me, and his whole wide world in the Palms of His Hands. What a mighty hand? This is where I belong. This is where I want to be. I will wait my turn. I will move along at the speed I am at. I will be content in that I am adding my voice to the list of believers. Everyday I get another opportunity to witness to you just how good He is to me. Join me in my celebration. I need your input. I need to know if you know that God made you and me perfectly holy and happy and we have let our emotions, the way we feel, get in front of reality. Man has self-control and free will and He must learn how to control his emotions. God, Jesus, My Savior, wants us to stop and think and process thought. We are the crown of creation. He made us in His image and when He had finished, He said "it was good".

He has given us everything we need to prosper and grow and flourish on the Land with our beliefs, opinions, desires, hopes, desires, dreams and traditions. We owe Him a debt of gratitude for giving us a life to live in the Presence of a King. There is another life you can live other than the one that you see under your nose. For God's sake! Look up. Look around. Look over there. Look over yonder. What do you see? Houses, land, trees, shrubs, weeds, bushes, grass, pine straw, flowers, insects, and bugs. This is all His creation. You are His creation and if He takes good care of the sparrow then certainly you should realize that He will take good care of you on this rainy chilly Saturday afternoon.

Today I will read, write, meditate, pray, talk, converse, share and listen to the Savior call my name. I am coasting through my routine and now it is time for some Saturday morning brunch. I hear His birds in-between the rain clouds. Yep! They are singing their songs. They are happy birds. I will join them.

Chapter 31

Got a minute? I began preaching the moment I opened my eyes. I cried out "Holy" is Thy Name. You are worthy to be praised. It is Sunday morning. Want to go to church with me? There is good news being tossed here and there. Let's you and I go beyond tomorrow. If I can do it so, can you. Suppose everyone you meet would say when you ask them how they are, they would reply with "I am blessed and highly favored". What joy, pleasure, happiness, and satisfaction are wrapped up in these words. I can see you tomorrow. Martin Luther King said, "I have been to the mountain top". Did he look over and see a nation of people with all their eyes turned to Heaven and their hearts resting on the words from Jesus' mouth?

Did he see "man's heart" filled with love for each other? Did he see "love" for all mankind? Did he see it being spread among the masses? Young, old, tall, short, skinny, fat, big, little, gay, or straight! Did he see that this nation was paying honor to Almighty God, The Creator and His Son, Our Lord, and Savior Jesus Christ? Did he see man's heart clear of any hate and confusion? Did he see man's heart filled with "love"? Did He see all the brothers and sisters in the East, North, South, and West praying to the Same God that watched over their mom, dad, sisters, brothers, nieces, nephews, cousins, and friends?

If Jesus, did it for me then He can do it for you. Read Ephesians 4. Pay close attention to verses 22 - 24. It says "You, man, must put off concerning the former conversation of the old man, which is corrupt according to the deceitful lust. Be renewed in the spirit of your mind and put on the new man, which after God is created in righteousness and true holiness."

Divorce yourself from the old you, your old ways are corrupt and wicked, renew your mind and become a new creature in Christ that follows righteousness and true holiness. The old ways have got to go. You are putting on new clothes. A brand new you. A brand-new mind. A brand-new birth. A brand-new identity. A brand-new beginning.

This is what I received on this brand new gorgeous and glorious Sunday morning in His Presence. Ah! The sound of His musical instruments playing soft melodies in my ear. I am listening as they go up high and they go low. I dream. I think. I ponder. This is what you need to do. You need to just "let go". Enjoy some downtime. Waa-Saa time. Just take some deep breaths and feel the present. In my presence I see His trees sway and swerve as they appear to frolic and dance by bumping into each other as they "hallow" praise and thanksgiving to Him for creating them. His sun is shining. It has His trees, shrubs, flowers, weeds, bushes, insects, bugs, and all His creation in His shadow this morning. Surely, He has me and you in His shadow. Don't you agree?

Let's me and you go to Paradise. Find the Mangrove trees in Palawan, Philippines. Disappear into an island of blue water, blue sky, blue sand amid His lighted trees. Watch penguins dive into a sea of blue water under a blue sunset. They are marching one by one in succession. Peacefully, gracefully, and taking their time. They dive over with such grace and precision. These were the pictures cascading across my computer screen. Of course, I had to just sit, stare, and imagine being amid all this action. These pictures of nature renewed my strength and uplifted my spirit. I had no idea I would be writing. I reread one of my testimonials and I said to myself "where are you this morning?" I was talking to myself.

I had listened to Dr. Charles Stanly last evening. He quoted several scriptures. The only one that comes to mind is Joshua 1 v:9. It says, "Haven't I told you to "be courageous and confident, I will be with you everywhere you go". If He told Joshua these words, then He is telling you the very same words. His words have not changed. He created you and He want you to be healthy and happy so you can grow, flourish, and reproduce. Produce the young minds that you oversee. Teach them about Christ. Teach them about the love that Christ wants for all the children that occupy the land to know about. Teach them about the man who saved your soul. Teach them about the man who blew His breath of life into your lifeless body and allowed you to become a living soul all over again so you can "think and process thought". Teach them to give "thanks" the second they open their eyes. We see another day.

Have you ever seen this Sunday, April 25th, 2021, before? Psalm 118 v:24. Rejoice! Raise your voice and shout "Hallelujah" it is a new day and I get a new mind. On this day I am raised from the dead. On this day I am no longer sleeping in my grave. On this day I will shed the overcoats that have held me in bondage. The devil, Satan, Lucifer, the enemy has stopped you from being all you can be. Satan has blinded your eyes and has deafened your ears. You cannot see because there is too much before your eyes. You can hear Jesus call your name because you are allowing too much noise into your ears.

It is time for a new beginning. Help me add a log to this fire! You deserve a life to live in the Presence of a King. You need to paste three words across your chest and let them be released from your mouth and they are "Thank You, Jesus". This is the only way you can get into The Kingdom of God. Have a personal, private, and intimate conversation with Him so you can develop your relationship with Him. Nobody can do you like Jesus. You must try Him for yourself. You must give Him your heart and ask Him to return it to you filled with His love and compassion. Oh, Lord! I want to be like You. Oh, Lord! I want to be with You. Oh, Lord! I want to live the life that you intended for me to live. Oh, Lord! I want to live up to Your expectations. If you find a plank in my eye, please remove it, and give me the courage I need to run this race. I am Your chosen One. You are the One who decided for me to come alive and inhale and exhale Your air in and out of my lungs. You are the One that decided for my heart to beat at a normal rhythm. Nobody but You Lord who had mercy on me. I am grateful that you favored me with a new mind, a new beginning. Only You, Lord, only You allowed me to be closed in my right mind with a reasonable portion of my health and strength to complete my morning routine.

Live! Love! Come alive in your senses and begin to just "think". It is a new day. It is a new sacred hour. It is the ten o'clock hour and I find myself in His Presence. I am beyond tomorrow. I see the Promised Land. I am living in Paradise. My little private hide-a-way. Only us "two". Just He and I. Just Him and me. We are the perfect combination. He knows me and I know Him. He knows my name and I know His Name. I heard Him speak to me and tell me to "wake up O sleepyhead, rise from the dead and let the Lord shine on you." Put on your new clothes. Put on your new mindset of ideas and get ready to embrace the adventure that I have outlined for you in this new era in time.

Put some more logs onto that fire. It is the Springtime of the year. Feels more like fall - right? My sister, Vivian, says, "she believes we might just go from spring right into summer". She could be right. I will enjoy each day that He gives me, whether, warm, cold, snowy, rainy, and hot just as long as I know the difference. Is He alive in your spirit? He is alive in my spirit. I say this all the time. I can only tell you the words that are meditating in my heart. Nothing else. My mind stays on Jesus and just how magnificent He is to me. I can't turn loose His Hand. I can't give up receiving His Unconditional Love, His Unfailing Love, His Unchanging Love, His Grace and Mercy, and His Divine Devotion. I want more. Yes! I want Him to continue to shine His light on me. I see the light. I can see Him uplifting my spirits and renewing my strength every morning I place my two feet on His floor to go into my happy space and do what I need to do. He holds my hand. He carves the pathway for me to travel. If I remain in Him, then He will remain in me. If I abide in Him, then He will abide in me. If I draw nearer to Him, then He will draw nearer to me. James 4 v:8.

John 15 v:5. "I am the vine; you are the branches. If you remain in me and I in you, you will bear much fruit; apart from me, you can do nothing. I am overjoyed at how He blesses me. I am overjoyed in the way He loves me. I am overjoyed that He gives me what I need and when I need it. I am overjoyed that He allows me to be in control of all my faculties so I can think, and process thought. If it had not been for the Lord on my side, I don't know where I would be or what I would be doing. I would not have the peace, patience, solitude, and desire to write a testimony daily. This is my contribution. I can tell you, him, her, she, he, them, and they just how much He loves me. He loves me so much. He was willing to listen to me as I ask O Lord please come into my presence and O Lord please allow me into Your Presence. I received so much confidence and encouragement, so I continued to speak the words that were meditating in my heart.

You have heard them before. This is what I say each time I open my eyes in the wee hours of dawn. I pull the covers up close to my neck after I have nestled my head back into my spot. I go to talking. I position myself at His feet and I ask O Lord please shadow us, O Lord please shelter us, O Lord please favor us, O Lord please cover us with Your Blood, O Lord please grant us Your Grace and Mercy, O Lord please strengthen us physically, mentally, emotionally, psychologically, morally and spiritually, O Lord please forgive us of our sins because we don't always do things perfectly and correctly, O Lord please forgive our enemies because they know not what they do, O Lord please protect us from all plagues, pandemics, disasters, and turmoil, O Lord please prosper us materialistically, physically, financially and spiritually, O Lord please do not cast us away from Your Presence and O Lord please allow Your Holy Spirit to dwell in us again on this day. In Jesus' Name, I Pray - Amen.

I went directly to the Source. I opened my heart, brain, mind, body, soul, and spirit and cast all my cares on Thee. Eat the bottom of His feet. 1st Peter 5 v:7. I became as a little child talking to my Master. I know He has all power in His Hands. I knew He was listening because I humbly and meekly placed myself before Him. I was so satisfied and overjoyed that I got a chance to communicate with My Savior that I drifted back off into La La Land.

This is how much love that He had granted me. I ask for His Grace and Mercy, His Love and Divine Devotion. He is the Source of where all my blessings come from. Just keep them coming! Just keep my mind and heart regulated so I can receive the love that You have in reserve "just for me".

Put some more logs onto that fire. Where does your health and strength come from? Who woke you up this morning? Who enabled you to place one foot before the other one? Who woke you just in the nick of time to flush your kidneys and excrete your bowels? Who is the Author and Finisher of your fate? Who favored you, your family, your loved ones, and your friends on this Sunday morning? I saw a blackbird just as I was opening my eyes. He was floating, gliding, coasting so peaceably through His air. It went forward, it went backward, it went around in circles before flying off into the Great Beyond.

Can't we tell someone just how good He is to me and you? Yes! I can. He watched over me while I slumbered and slept and was right beside my bed to take me by my hand and lead me to the next phase of my morning routine. His Holy Spirit told me to check the time and to turn on some easy listening music. "He did it all for me". He told me "Now is the time for you to come alive". After He raised me from the dead, I went into singing a song; "Thank You Lord", "Thank You, Lord". These are the only words to my song. I can sing it anytime I want to and as often as I want to. Man can't take away my praise.

Think about yesterday. Was He good to you yesterday? Slow it up a bit and begin to think about all the things that He allowed you to do, and it went unnoticed to you until now. Think about it. He gave you everything you needed yesterday. He answered your prayers. He listened to you and prepared a way for you to travel so you would accomplish what you sat out to do. "Thank You, Lord" for watching over me. "Thank You, Lord" for letting me hear Your birds sing praises to Your Name. "Thank You, Lord" for Your soft rain that saturated Your solid and sacred ground we call Earth, on Your Planet and in Your Universe.

Who are you? What are you? Simple questions, right? Take your time before answering. Find solace in getting to know yourself. Find solace in knowing that you are a child of a King. Find solace in knowing that you are one of God's children. Find solace in knowing that you are one of His sheep in His Pasture and you will come into His Presence with words of praise and Thanksgiving. Psalm 100. It is Sunday morning. Church day. O Lord on this day, please give me my daily bread. Feed me until I can't eat anymore. Make my heart, mind, soul, brain, body, and spirit content in knowing that You will take good care of me. Psalm 23 says "The Lord is My Shepherd, and I shall not want". Dig down deep into these words. Do you know who is keeping an eye on you? Do you know who will supply your every need? Do you know who will protect you from all hurt, harm, or danger? Do you know who will allow His Holy Spirit to be your counselor and comforter? It is Jesus! J E S U S. I spelled it. It is "Jesus" who is keeping a watchful eye on you, and it is "Jesus" who is waiting for you to saturate His atmosphere with words of praise and admiration.

Slow up from reading and just take "five". Think about what you read. Get you a bottle of His water whether chilled or at room temperature and just throw your head back, investigate your heart and find you some joy, glee, and satisfaction in knowing that He gave you a bottle of water that He allowed to escape from His mountains, rivers, brooks, streams, and canals into a bottle just the right size for your hands to hold. All I know is that He loves me. He showered me with His love all during the nighttime hours. He showered me with His Love when He touched me with His finger of Love.

Look! I am awake. Look! I am alive. Look! I can think. Look! I can move my limbs. Look! I can move my fingers. Look! I can share with you what is meditating in my heart. All I know is that "He loves me, and He loves you". Do you believe that? Do you believe Him? Look around you, look in front of you, what do you have? Do you have all that you need and some surplus? Do you have the most important thing of all and that is His Love and Admiration?

Know that you are wanted, needed, appreciated, adored, admired, cherished, and idolized by a King. Don't you feel special? Don't you feel important? Look at what He has done for you this Sunday morning. Look at the clock and be in His Presence. Utter these words under your breath "Thank You, Lord". No one must know just how much faith you have in your heart. It can between the "two of you". You know and He knows. Then sashay off into the next phase of your morning knowing that He is providing coffee, a banana, your morning meds and vitamins, and a bottle of His water so you can complete your morning routine.

Join me! Salute Him! Glorify Him! Magnify Him! He created you, me the Heavens, and the Earth just for me and you. There is so much to see. We have a lifetime. We don't know when the end will be! You and I must live everyday that we see as our last day. Celebrate your birthday. You received a new birth when you opened your eyes. You received a new mind now go and think with it. Just for today. Find peace and satisfaction in everything you do.

I will find peace when I slice my banana into bitesize pieces. I will find peace when I peel my boiled egg and when I pour myself a glass of juice that He allowed to be squeezed from His fruit trees. I will find peace when I ladle my coffee back and forth to get it at its desired temperature. I will find peace when I recite His 23rd Psalm. Surely His goodness and His mercy shall follow me all the days of my life if I dwell in that Secret Place, in that Shelter, and His Presence. I will do this all day, everyday, 24/7, around the clock - every hour - every minute - every second and right at this present moment in time.

Chapter 32

Without Your Love, where would I be? P.S. I Love You! Come away with me. Climb into my hammock. I see white sand, blue water, a blue sky, and I am swinging back and forth with His fresh breeze of air cascading my body. Are you a dreamer? Are you a believer? Do you wish upon a star? I do! I talk to the trees, birds, animals, His creation. I will talk to you too if you allow me to. Allow me to speak to your heart, brain, mind, body, soul, and spirit! It is all "good". Nothing to hurt you. Nothing to get upset about. My heart will go on and on into the land after tomorrow. Want to hitch a ride on this old buggy? Only if you want to. No one is forcing you to do anything you don't want to. You have free will. You have self-control. Do this or that because you want to. Let whatever you do bring you peace, joy, happiness, contentment, tranquility, harmony, and serenity.

The only Source I know to tell you about is "you will find this type of Grace and Mercy in His Everlasting Arms that are in His big, blue spacious skies that you see up over your head. His Arms are just that wide. He has room for you, the whole wide world in the Palms of His Hands. Isn't He marvelous? Isn't He magnificent? Let's you and I look at a Canadian Sunset and see the vibrant colors that He has on display for me and you. His signs and wonders. They are surrounding you. Find His Mangrove Trees located in Palawan, Philippines. Peace. Magical. Majestic.

His Holy Spirit urged me to get ready to go outside. I did and took a detour before getting to my destination. I was scolded for not following through with the plan that was outlined for me. He called me His "Tulip" and I immediately "regrouped" to continue to complete my mission. I aimed to go outside, breathe His fresh air in and out of my lungs, and feel His sunshine. This is what I eventually did. I marched to the swing, sat down, removed my mask, and began to rock back and forth, view the landscape, watch the trees sway and swerve, and listen to His birds sing their songs.

One bird told me to "give" give", just give and one bird told me to "speed it up". Give your time and devote it to finding the pieces to the puzzle. Speed it up, tell them, him, she, he, her and they, that He is getting ready to close the door and it is time for them to come on the inside before it is too late.

I will preach until I am blue in the face. I want to tell someone, somebody, just how good He is to me. It is Sunday morning, and I am alive. I am not dead, and I wish you would come alive so you can witness that there is another life for you to live. It is evident all around you.

Where are you looking for answers? What side of the road are you on? Do you have the faith of a grain of mustard seed? That is all you need! You must trust, believe, and have faith that He is getting ready to turn His world upside down. He is going to allow you to shake the devil loose. The devil has been holding on to you too long. Reach out. Reach up. Reach beyond what you see and depend on faith and not by sight.

Watch Him send in the clowns. Satan will! Satan will have you second-guessing your thoughts and ideas. Don't let Him control your thoughts, mind, ideas, emotions, body, heart, soul, and spirit. Get rid of this demon once and for all. Tell Satan to take His hands off God's anointed ones. Tell Satan, you have changed your address. Tell Satan you heard about Jesus from Galilee, and you want to give Him a try. Satan has been holding you by your coattail long enough. Take your life back through the Presence of Our God the Father of Our Lord and Savior Jesus Christ and His Holy Spirit.

Like now! This is your day, a day of complete relaxation and pleasure. You want to spend all your available time in His Presence because you know He will take good care of you. Chances are you have never read a testimonial quite like mine. Right? I only want to tell you what I know. Each day I get more love than the day before. Everyday is a new beginning and I get new thoughts, ideas, beliefs, opinions, traditions, dreams and desires. I began to come alive as I add logs to the fire. There is no fire raging in my soul, my heart, my brain, my mind, my body, and my spirit. Every part of me is at perfect peace, in harmony enjoying The Fruits of His Spirit.

There is so much more for me to tell you! I may not get the chance again so let me share with you the words that are meditating in my heart. You have never received this kind of Love and Admiration before. No greater Love I know. No greater Love can we receive on this Sunday afternoon. It is a glorious and gorgeous day to be alive and in His Presence. He is breathing down on us. He has His eye on me and He has His eye on you. Aren't you glad that you are alive? I am.

I am glad to be able to see His flowers that grow wild in the dessert come from the dirt and display their beautiful colors. When I come back, O Lord, let me come back as a flower, a tree, a bird, a butterfly, and let me "hallow" Your Name. These are my ancestors. They lived long ago, and they continue to flourish and grow.

How did I survive all my previous years? By always attending church. By always looking for a brighter day. I looked around and I saw that He was blessing His sheep that got up every morning to go into His Pasture then certainly and surely, He would get a glimpse of me and hear my cry. When I rose this morning, I had no clue that the weather would just invite me to come outside and enjoy the outdoors.

I had no idea that He would speak to me while I was swinging back and forth and tell me "Peace on Earth and Goodwill toward all Men. Can it get any clearer? He is looking for the men to stand up and fight for the cause they believe in. Women take your role in history and give them the encouragement they need to succeed in what their endeavor is. Stand by your man. Listen to him. Help shape his ideas and thoughts. You know you can always depend on mamma; she will never lead you astray. Mamma is always going to put you on the right road. The mommas must be the papas too. You must listen. Come! Gather around! There is a news flash, and you should not miss it.

Today, Sunday afternoon is brand new to me. I have never seen this Sunday afternoon before. What a joyous occasion it is. His sun is shiny, His sheep are going back and forth. The little children are crying because they want some attention. Everyone wants your attention. Who do you turn to? Don't ask "what am I going to do", simply turn it around and say, "O Lord "what do you want me to do." What are the ways that you want to handle this? I come under His Authoritative Rule so I will let His will be done.

Whichever way you want this ship to sail - I will go. Whichever way you want my light to shine - I will let it shine. Whatever you tell me to say - I will say it. Whichever way you tell me to go then - I will go.

Let's you and I share this world. It was made for you and me. Let's take it back. Give me my land and give me my freedom. You have stolen the gifts given to me at birth. The right to peace, health, and happiness. My head is no longer buried in the sand. I have shaken the dirt that was covering my eyes, my ears, my nose, and my mouth. It is a new me.

New ideas, new thoughts, new ambitions, new dreams, and new beliefs.

Let's you and I dream in that far-a-way land without leaving the comfort of your happy space. Put some more logs on the fire. Allow me to rock back and forth in the hammock while enjoying His sunshine therapy. I have on sunscreen so I should be perfectly safe for about an hour or two. He says "He will be with me today, tomorrow, and forever.

What kind of confidence is this? What kind of courage is this? One thing I know and that is "we are happy - together". Happiness, sheer joy and bliss, perfect peace, and harmony. We are on one accord. I allow Him too. I gave up the reigns I had over my life to Him so His will could be done. I gave myself away to Thee. Use me to glorify Your Kingdom. Use me to fertilize the land. Use my voice, use my tongue, use my heart, use my brain, use my mind, use my body, use my soul and spirit for Your Glory.

I love you and I want to share with you just how much love you can receive on this beautiful, gorgeous, magnificent, marvelous, splendid, superb, spectacular, and wonderful day. All I must do is dream. Stick my head up in His clouds. Let me dream that I am a bird, floating along, gliding, coasting through His Heavens going here, going there, sometimes around in circles, just let me be me. Let me be free. Let me roam about in His atmosphere and if somehow, we meet then let you and I celebrate our new beginning.

Let's you and I agree that we are spiritual beings having a human experience. It is nice to be alive and free. It is nice not to be saddled with ugly memories from your past. Yesterday was here, now it has come and gone. You will never see another bright sunshiny day such as this one. Open your eyes, feel His sunshine, breathe His fresh air and just "Thank Him" that you are living and not sleeping in your grave. Come alive and live. You have moved so far away from that coffin. The world is yours. Find your place and take a stand. I will not give up my beliefs, opinions, ideas, thoughts, traditions, dreams and desires. I love Him and He loves me. This I know and you can't take God, My Jesus, My Lord, and Savior away from me. I am His. He orders my steps. He is keeping me alive for a reason and I am to tell you again that Jesus saved my soul. Yes! I was lost but now I am found and destined for greatness. This is what He told me. I can't argue with an Expert. He has a plan for me. He knows the plan. I must simply believe, trust, and have faith. He will let me continue to sing my song of peace, hope, and love. This is what He has waiting on those of us who love Him.

I had to take a break before I began my second sermon. I dined on an oven-baked Italian sandwich, buffalo wings, and a garden salad. I organized my medicine into a container that will last me for two weeks. He was watching over me with His eyes of Love while I ate my dinner and prepared my medicine dispensers.

It is news time. 6 p.m. I will listen to the latest and draw my conclusions. I can't take too much of the news. I watch just enough to be in the know. I want to know what is going on with the sheep that He has in His pasture on this wonderful and glorious Sunday afternoon.

I have been listening to some of His tv vessels talk about the relationship that they have developed with Him. This comes through listening. Your ears must be tuned to the right station so He can come in loud and clear.

Escape into the Great Beyond. The door is wide open. There is room for you and me, him, her, she, he, them, and they. Don't believe me?

Try it and see where you fit in. The most comfortable spot you will ever find. Being cradled in His Everlasting Arms. It is safe and secure up here. Join me. I will lay my head upon His chest and breathe His sweet breath forevermore. This is such a "grand occasion". He is "mighty"!

He is "great"! He is worthy to be praised.

Chapter 33

Let me warn you before we get started. I am speaking the words that are meditating in my heart. He pulled out a chair when I sat down and yeah! Once again, He said "let's go", just me and you. A one-on-one conversation, don't you like it? I am glad that I have someone to talk to and someone who will listen to me releases into His atmosphere my words of wisdom, knowledge, and understanding that have been relayed to me during my 74 years of tenure. He is keeping me alive for a reason and on this day, I hear His birds. I see His birds. I know the life of a bird because I watch them so often. Let me tell you what a bird does. A bird wonders, a bird glides, a bird coasts, a bird floats through His atmosphere. They know they are well protected. Are you? Did you ask Him? I did. I will explain it later when you read my affirmations. I talk to Him. He talks to me. I listen. He listens. We share. I belong to Thee, and He directs my path.

It was early in the wee hours of dawn, about the crack of dawn and He said "Hey there! It is time, so I rejoiced, opened my eyes, and saw a gray sky, I went back into La La Land. Nope! That was not the plan, so I rose early to get my day started. He had prepared everything I would need to cleanse and clothe my body and I said "Ohh Wee! Something good is going to happen to me today! That is what He said. I will be happy and content in whatever He brings. I know it will be good. I have faith. I trust and I believe. I know who is the Author and Finisher of My fate and He has never failed me yet. This time He will allow it to rain on me. If I remain in Him, then He will remain in me, if I abide in Him then He will abide in me, If I draw nearer to Him then He will draw nearer to me. So, it will be beautiful - whatever He wants to delight me with. It is all left up to Him. I will wait my turn. I will keep hope alive "Jesse Jackson," said this. I am confident that He will give me His best, that is what He has been doing throughout my golden years. A new awareness, a kind of love that you have never experienced before comes alive in you. I should have been told about this sooner. Oh! I wish upon a star.

I am listening to music for dreaming! Easy Listening Music, Lawrence Welk, his kind of music is filling my ears, what joy, comfort, peace, and pleasure it brings to my mind, heart, brain, body, soul, and spirit. It is a great morning to be alive. He did it again. He decided to allow His little light to shine on my little heart. I heard Him when He whispered in my ear early in the wee hours, wake up O sleepyhead, rise from the dead, and let the Lord shine on you. How would I know that He would be standing by my side, ready to catch my hand and lead me into my happy space to do what I needed to do now that I had opened my eyes. Thank You, Lord, once again You came to see about me. It is with sincere joy and pleasure that You allow me to call on Your Holy Name. May I? Sure! you know my name and I know your name and I will allow my Grace and Mercy to follow you all the days of your life if you dwell in His Presence. That Secret Place - you go to - in the front of your mind - that place when you relax and say O Lord! Have thy way! "Thank You, Lord" for watching over me. After I say this renews my strength and uplifts my spirits.

Today something good is about to happen to me. This is what I was told when I opened my eyes. Something good is going to happen to you today. Joy, happiness, peace, tranquility, contentment. I was overjoyed to know that He is watching over me and listening to every word I say. It was early in the morning when He touched me on my shoulder with His finger of Love, telling me to rise and shine and get ready to embrace the adventure that He has planned for me on this day.

Okay! I am glad that I am alive. You guessed it! Yes, I am, I get one more day among the living to spread the word that there is someone who loves you, admires you, adores you, idolizes you, and cherishes you. His Name is Jesus. That is who it is. Did you know that you are great, a masterpiece, a fine specimen of His workmanship? He raised me from the dead. I am a new creature in Christ, and I know I must tread lightly when I say these words. You can't say this unless you are sure, and I am sure I am walking under a Divine Light. He opened my casket and allowed me to become alive. I became brand new. He stretched His Righteous Right Hand out to me, and I grabbed it.

He said "You, you, who are weary, worn and heavy laden, you, come and go with me and I will give you rest. I will give you a new reason to come alive in your senses so you can think and be ready to praise my holy name for being so good to you. I went. He was so convincing! I began to surrender, submit, and commit my total self to Thee so His will could be done.

Are you with me? Do you see me? I am traveling, once it was on Blueberry Hill, now I am in Hollywood, sitting in a swing, near the Gazebo here at Gene Miller Manor in Christian City in Union City, Georgia, South of Hartsfield-Jackson Airport. The largest in the United States. Congratulations Maynard Jackson! You earned your crown. He received several awards and accolades for his achievements.

I see another day and He has decided that it was my turn to be first in line to receive a gift of a brand new day. Why was I chosen? Because I know how to rejoice, magnify, glorify, and celebrate the arrival of my new day. It is a time to reflect on the many memories that I must behold. I talked with my oldest daughter, Tamara, she is always a ray of sunshine. I prayed for this little girl. I used to dress her up as a Princess and gave her everything she needed and wanted. She was my gift from the Lord because I asked for a little girl since I had two boys and they were hardheaded. At an early age, they did not want to listen. I had to keep telling them, over and over about this and that until they finally caught on. Oh! You want me to do it this way, they would ask, and the answer would be a happy "yes", you got it.

I don't struggle with being glad that I am alive on this Monday, a sacred and great day, April 26th, 2021. I am glad that I am alive because He came to see about me. How do I do it? Day after day, write about the conversations that I am having with the Lord right in my office. It is true, it is as if, when I pull out the chair, He pulls a chair out right beside me and tells me "Ok - let's go".

His Holy Spirit had me looking at Lake Matheson in New Zealand. It is known as the Mirror Lake because of its reflective surface. It is a reflecting pond of water. I see clouds, mountains, trees, grass, snow-covered mountain peaks in the water. It is under His moonlight, so it is simply beautiful and oh so peaceful. You can see it was designed for His sheep to come and rest their souls knowing that it was given to us by Our Creator, of Heaven and Earth. No greater Love can be seen or shown to mankind. His love was written upon every blue cloud, every blue mountain, all the green grass, shrubs, weeds, bushes, and trees.

Man, woman, boy or child, woman, man, and child! Newsflash! Let go and let God have His way on this magnificent, marvelous, serene, sunshiny, breezy day during the Springtime of the year here in April of 2021. Without His Love on this morning, which I have never seen before, I could not make it. I would be lost like a ship without a Captain. I am following Jesus this morning and I am grateful to Him because He came to see about me. Now, this is "true love". No matter what I am doing or where I am at, He is never too busy to give me His undivided attention. I remain in His Presence. I have His 23rd Psalm tattooed across my chest, and I reach for it and use it. I am walking in the light.

He is keeping an eye on me, you, your loved ones, my loved ones, your family, my family, your friends, and my friends. Isn't He mighty? He can love on me, you, him, her, she, he, them, and they at the same time. He can do this because He has you, me, the Earth, and everything He created in the Palms of His Hands. He has promised that He would never forget about me because He has me engraved in the Palm of His Hand. Isaiah 49 v:15-16 validates my claim. Just how big is His heart? His heart is as big as His big, blue spacious sky. He has so much love to give. He wants to fill your heart with His Unfailing Love, His Unconditional Love, His Unchanging Love, His Grace and Mercy, and His Divine Devotion if you have the time to accept it and if you want it.

Okay! Deep breath! Breathe! Know that He is close by your side. He never left. He watched over you while you slumbered and slept. Did you "thank" Him for being so kind and gracious to favor you with a new beginning. He has made you brand new. I can live again. I am free. I know who woke me up this morning. I know who reached for my hand and allowed me to flush my kidneys and excrete my bowels. He is miraculous. He performed a miracle on me when He allowed me to become a living soul all over again after He breathed His breath of life into my lifeless body.

I am alive! I must tell someone about the joy, pleasure, happiness, faithfulness, truth, honesty, justice, salvation, redemption, love, and righteousness that I am being overwhelmed with. He loves me and I am not afraid or ashamed to tell you, the ones in the North, East, South, and West how He saved my soul. Jesus came to my rescue. He re-invented me. He re-created me. I asked. I asked O Lord please reshape me, remold me and make me into the person You had designed me to be before I was in my mother's womb. Guess what! He started scattering my message of love, hope, and peace to all four corners of the globe. Today is a great day! It comes with all sorts of surprises.

I received a flyer in the door and on it were Bible verses recorded in scripture. One of my favorite verses is Isaiah 41. v:10. I have referenced this verse quite often in my first book "You Can Be My Tulip" by Bettie Jean Grose. Amazon or Barnes & Noble. This verse is relevant today and I am quoting it for you. Read it. It says. "So do not fear, for I am with you; do not be dismayed, for I am Your God. I will strengthen you and help you; I will uphold you with My Righteous Right Hand.

I stake my claim. I know without a shadow of a doubt that He watches over me. Sometimes I feel like I am His only true Love. There is so much love, tender devotion being given to me on this magnificent, marvelous, splendid, and superb Monday morning, that I have never seen before. He says "I am with you" not tomorrow, not only on Sunday but today and forevermore if you allow me to be. Don't fret! Don't panic! I am there. I will be here for you all day, everyday, 24/7, around the clock, every hour - every minute - every second only if you let me. Somehow, someway, you must allow Him to enter your heart and remove the evil spirit of hate that has given you lies, deceit, and confusion. He wants to give to you His peace, His Love, His Admiration. This is what He wants to replace in your heart once you clean it out of all unclean spirits. Hate! Rage! Anger! must be removed before He can dwell in your heart. He needs a place to rest. Will you open your heart and let Him in? He wants to rest in your heart. After all, it was a "golden heart" that He gave to you at the time of your birth.

Before you and I were in the womb, there was a discussion held about me and you. What should she become? The question was raised. Let's make her a public speaker! Let's allow her to speak truth to injustices, favoring her with a long span of life, entrusted to become a mother, father, wife, sister, daughter, niece, auntie, cousin, and friend. Let her go. Let her loose in the field of dreams. She will be back!

Today! I salute Him. Today! I glorify Him. Today! I am breathing His fresh air in and out of my lungs. I am inhaling and exhaling His air in and out of my lungs. He is regulating my heart to beat at its normal rhythm. Isn't He grand? Isn't He marvelous? Isn't He fantastic? Isn't He supreme? Isn't He magnificent and wonderful? I am an angel in His eyes. He follows me around. He surrounds me. He has me and Him in an inflated bubble and we are bouncing, here, there, and everywhere. I am along for the ride. I am going with the flow. Wherever He wants to take me, whichever way He wants to go, is fine with me. I know how to follow the Leader. I know who in charge is. I know who calls the shots. I am a true believer that He can. I can do all things through Christ who strengthens me.

Time for the second sermon? You can turn me off. I will be waiting to tell you these words when you return. He says, "I am your God". You can depend on me to be right by your side at your every twist and turn. He will be with me if I go into the bathroom, bedroom, kitchen, computer space, or living room. Each time I sit down to begin writing He is right by my side, urging me to say this or say that. He is present in my life today so that I may come alive in my senses, begin to live, and think and process thought.

2nd Timothy 1 v:7 says "The Spirit God gave us does not make us timid, weak or shy, it gives us power, love, and self-discipline. I choose to be in His Presence. I am glad that I am a member of His Household. I am glad to know that He is watching over me just like He is watching over His trees, weeds, bushes, flowers, shrubs, insects, bugs, and all His creation. I choose to. I choose to believe in not what I see but I choose to believe in the unseen. I can dream, can't I? This is your God-given right! Do it. You have the power. Give yourself the authority to get a dose of reality!

I have faith. I am not blinded by what I see. I look beyond what I see. Sure, I see trees, sure I see birds, sure I see bushes and weeds, but do you know these trees, weeds, bushes and flowers, birds, insects, and bugs have a story to tell. They are alive. They know how to pay honor and tribute to the One that created them. They continue to flourish and grow after He allows His rain and sunshine to supply them with the needed nutrients they need to survive.

Let me compare man to His creation. In walked man into this great big picture. Where does man and woman, boy or girl fit into His puzzle pieces? I am all about rejoicing in that He has given me a new beginning, a new mind, a new birth, a new identity on this glorious and gorgeous day. Join me in my celebration. He did it and I am grateful. Again, I rose from the dead on this Monday morning. A repeat of yesterday! I can take all that He wishes to deposit at my doorstep. We need to slow up, come to a complete stop and recognize who it is that favored us with a brand-new day. Did the Lord do that? He allowed me and you to be closed in our right minds, with a reasonable portion of our health and strength? Say it again! I checked and I was all there. I had the sense of mind to begin and complete my morning routine. I had the presence of mind to read verses in scripture and relate to you just what I learned after reading them. Our Lord has given us self-control and free will. It is up to us to be in control of our emotions, thoughts, ideas, opinions, beliefs, traditions, dreams and desires.

I ask every morning I open my eyes; O Lord please come into my presence and O Lord please allow me into Your Presence. After I humbly and meekly make my request known I am so confident that He heard me because He rules in my heart and when I am talking, I am conveying to Him the words that are meditating in my heart. He says, "I am with you" and I am listening to every word you say. Jeremiah 29 v:12. I have the confidence I need to keep talking. He wraps me up in His Everlasting Arms and I begin my morning affirmations. O Lord please shadow us, O Lord please shelter us, O Lord please favor us, O Lord please cover us with Your Blood, O Lord please grant us Your Grace and Mercy, O Lord please strengthen us physically, mentally, emotionally, psychologically, morally and spiritually, O Lord please forgive me of my sins because we don't always do things perfectly and correctly, O Lord please forgive our enemies because they know not what they do, O Lord please protect us from all plagues, pandemics, disasters, and turmoil, O Lord please prosper us materialistically, financially and spiritually, O Lord please do not cast us away from Your Presence and O Lord please allow Your Holy Spirit to dwell in us again on this day. In Jesus' Name, I Pray - Amen.

After placing my head upon His chest, I drift back off into La La Land. This is where I rest comfortably throughout the night. I climb into bed, find my spot, and began just "chatting". I tell Him "Just how good He is to me" and I praise, worship, salute and glorify His Name for being so good to me. He allowed me to write my testimony yesterday and He has started me on my way again. You can't make me doubt Him, He will come through. He will answer prayer, lean on that Pillar of Faith, My Rock, and My Redeemer.

On my computer, I saw a house built out of rocks scattered on about two acres of land and it had a rock fence. A pond filled with colorful rocks. Rocks of all shapes, colors, and sizes lined its foundation. This home looked so peaceful. You could tell it was surrounded in love and was well protected from the snare of the fowler. It gave a vibe of "don't you want to be here"? It was so inviting. I can use this image when I lay myself down to sleep. As I get nestled into His big blue spacious and Everlasting Arms, I will have this as a memory.

This is all too real; I feel like I am in the cottage, and He is welcoming me again into His Presence. I see two red birds perched on a limb and they appear to be talking, both of their heads are only a breath away. They are just that close. They appear to say "hello again" just like the Father does when He allows His Son, to reach out His Righteous Right Hand to you.

He did it again! He woke me up on due time. The time and hour that He had appointed me to rise from the dead. I tried to watch the Oscars last evening. It became boring when they began to thank him, her, them, and they. I wanted to hear about their achievements and how grateful they were to become honored for their great work. It resulted in a lot of name-callings. Only they knew them, the audience didn't have a clue of who these people were. Very disappointing. I tuned them out and began listening to some Easy Listening Music and floated off into The Great Beyond.

Here I am again, at this 3 o'clock hour, telling you about a Savior, who I can call my very own. His eyes are only made to shine on me. Want to know how I gained so much privilege? I began "thanking Him" for everything. This is what I was told to do. I was told to be "thankful" for everything that concerned my day. I read Psalm 118 v:24 and it says "rejoice" be "thankful" for everything and I did just that. What a privilege and honor to know that I am loved, appreciated, needed, adored, admired, cherished, and honored by a King. King Jesus is His Name just in case you did not know who I was referring to. I am worshiping the King of Kings and the Lord of Lords. Jesus Christ, My Lord, and Savior.

I can call on Him anytime I want to. He is always available. I got His Name engraved in the four chambers of my heart. Jesus!

Jesus! The greatest Name I know. Oh! He is great and mighty. He is alive in my spirit. I am a spiritual being having a human experience. Nope! I don't belong here. I have moved on to a higher dimension. I am on the ground floor, just knocking, searching, and seeking to see what I can find.

I found a gold mind. I found a treasure chest. I am sounding my horn. Don't you hear the "choo choo"? The birds are talking. They are telling us to speed it up. Come on inside the gate before He closes the door. His gate is open wide. There is plenty of space available. Claim your seat early while you still have the time. While blood is running warm in your body, kneel as His feet and tell Him all about it. Lay your cares, concerns, wants, needs, interests, beliefs, dreams, desires and opinions at His feet. Try to catch one of the strings that are hanging from His garment if you can't get to the hem. It is truth, honesty, justice, love, happiness, faithfulness, self-control, salvation, redemption, and righteousness that He wants to shower all over you.

Do you see over the rainbow? This is what He has waiting on you and me. I am getting the portion of blessings that He has in reserve just for me. He gives it away freely to the Ones that love Him and know Him, His peace, patience, love, joy, happiness, contentment, tranquility, harmony, and serenity. It is not hard to crossover. His yoke is easy. He is on one side, and you are on the other one. I gave up the reigns I had over my life to allow His will to be done. This is the best decision I could have ever made. I made Jesus the Head of My Life. I placed Jesus first.

Because I was able to do this is the reason, He decided to grant me His Unconditional Love, His Unfailing Love, His Grace and Mercy, and His Divine Devotion. I started calling on His Name. The Name that can save your soul. The Name that can keep you from having a raging inferno in your mind, brain, heart, body, soul, and spirit. Jesus! OH Jesus! What a joy for me to bring all my cares, wants, and dreams to you and let you decide what is best for me. I trust you, Jesus. I believe in You, Jesus. I have faith in You, Jesus. You are the author and finisher of my fate and I love You for being so good to me one more day.

If today was my last day, I can be content and complacent in knowing that You are near me. You O Lord, are the One who is directing my tongue, mind, brain, ideas, thoughts, hopes, and dreams. Knowing You are near me empowers me to continue to write sentence after sentence. I am a living witness that I have got the Lord on my side. I brag nor boast. It is a fact. He is here near me. He is holding my hand. We are hand in hand! Want to join me.? You can. You can hold His Hand, I can Hold His Hand so can she, him, her, him, he, them, and they.

I have a constant craving and desire to be in His Presence. I don't want Him to ever get away from me. He is with me morning, noon, and at night. In between times also. Did I tell you that He came early during the morning hours and satisfied me with His morning mercy and love and told me to let it last me throughout my day? I complied. Therefore, I am so blessed and highly favored. I listened. I obeyed. I heard.

I was listening with the ears He gave me. I am selective about what I let go off in my ears. I choose the right sound at the right time of the day. It is news time and I have no desire to peek at the headlines. I will get them later during the afternoon.

Somehow, we must educate ourselves, our kids, and the entire population that the police are trained and taught to kill you if they see any kind of threat. Some police officers act before they have time to react. They roll up not asking any questions, scope out the layout, and perceive you and me, the public as a threat to their safety. The police need to be retrained. The police have hate in their hearts for mankind. You black brothers and sisters, you brown ones, you yellow ones, you red ones, you white ones, get ready, there is an outright assault on your life. Do you see who is being shot and killed? Racial injustice. Must we tolerate the behavior of the police, or do we make them come under an "Authoritative Rule" and ask them to "think and process thought" before they fire these weapons intent on destruction.

Who is sleeping in their grave? Police Reform! You bet! Raise a fist so we can keep "hope" alive. Raise a "fist" if you want freedom, truth, justice, honesty, and equality to prevail! The police must be held accountable for their actions. They have a responsibility to uphold the law and to keep everybody safe. Not insight vigilante law. The first thing they do is "draw their gun". The gun should be the last resort.

Police need to show restraint, compassion, and love. What did you say?

Police are looking for ways to detain you. Police do not believe that you have every right to a peaceful and rewarding life. Police see us as hoodlums, scoundrels, misfits, the worse of the kind. Police do not see us a "human beings". Their take on us is distorted. That is why we cannot give them any reason to shoot. My advice to anyone stopped or detained by the police is to follow their orders. Do what they tell you to do if you want to come home alive. Follow their orders. Don't try to run or escape. This triggers their minds to fight. Don't give them the opportunity. You control your emotions so you can control the situation. Ask the Savior to take charge. Know that some things are out of your control, and you need Divine Intervention. This is the time to ask Our Savior, Lord what do you want me to do. Charles Stanley says, don't say O Lord what am I going to do, change it around and ask O Lord what you are going to do with me at this appointed time on Your Earth, on Your Planet and in Your Universe.

He wants to know that you rest your soul and spirit in Him. Show Him where your faith lies. I know if I trust in You O Lord, that You will make everything all right. It will turn out in your favor because you conceded the rights you had over your life to Him and allowed His will to be done. It is okay to know that O Lord I am in Your Hand.

Remember the outcome must be successful if you have placed all your faith, hope, and trust in Thee. Has He ever failed you yet? Hasn't He always answered your prayers? Well, today is a great day because He will answer your prayers today just like He answered them yesterday if you ask. I repeat myself often. Have you noticed? Each day, each morning I open my eyes I recite my affirmations because I don't want Him to ever forget about me.

O Lord it is me O Lord, who is calling on Your Holy Name, asking that You come to see about me.

Chapter 34

God is great! God is great to be praised. This is what the song says. This is what His angels are singing. Oh!

He is great! Here it is Springtime and last season during the fall of the year, I was in His Presence. What began in one season has transferred over into another season. I am still singing. I am still humming. He was by my side during last season. Yesterday! He was faithful! He stayed right beside me. I was anchored to Him at the hip. He is My Rock. He is My Redeemer. Psalm 19 v:14 says, O Lord "Let the words of my mouth and the meditation in my heart be acceptable in Thy sight". He is with me. That is what it says when I read His 23 Psalm. Yea though I walk through the shadows of death, fear no evil, for Thy art with me. That means He is right by my side. Again, He pulled up a chair.

I know who I can depend On. I know who I am leaning on. Yes! He is great. He is mighty. He is magical. He is majestic. He is miraculous because here it is again in the afternoon, and the Same Grace and Mercy He gave me in the wee hours of dawn are now moving their way into my afternoon hours. Hallelujah! He knows my name. I know His Name. I call Him by His Name! I call Him Jesus! That is not a hard name to remember! Have you ever heard it before if not get used to me saying "Jesus" this and "Jesus" that? I must talk about the King. I must talk about the One who made it possible for me to be able to rise from the dead.

I believe Him. I trust Him. I have faith! Hallelujah! March at the sound of your drumbeat. What are you telling yourself? What are you telling those who are at your knee? Are you telling them that they should put all their faith, hope, and trust in the One they cannot see with the naked eye? Are you telling them to trust in the One that woke them up this morning? It was Jesus! He did it. He blew His breath of life into my lifeless body and allowed me, yes me, to come alive in my senses so I could "think and "process thought". Sing Hallelujah anyhow, just because, you can. He has given you a voice to speak. Use it. Don't let the rocks cry out, let Him hear your voice. Let Him hear you say three precious words and they are "Thank You, Jesus". These words saved my life. These words woke me up. I was dead. I was in my coffin. It was about to be a nailed shut then I heard a voice.

That voice, said, "You, yes you who are weary, worn, torn, sad and heavy laden, come unto me and rest." I opened my eyes and I saw a Hand. It was stretched out to me, and I grabbed it, and this is the Hand, that I am holding today.

Isaiah 41 v:10 said He would. I believed. I trusted. I had faith that I was making the right decision. I had been searching for this type of freedom for a long period.

I found Him. He found me. I am glad that He gave me another opportunity to come alive and worship Him, salute Him, adore Him, admire Him, cherish Him, idolize Him while the blood is still running warm in my body. He is Lord of Lords. He is King of Kings. Want to go to church? You know that is where we are headed.

I will not be quiet until all His sheep's head is looking in one direction. That is up. We need to focus our attention on what is up there. Use your imagination and begin to dream without any shackles or chains around your brain, your mind, your heart, your body, your soul, and your spirit. Ah! Shucks! I have all my ducks in a row. Somebody, please put another log on that fire. It is burning out of control. You see I don't know when it is time to quit. I just go on and on. Nonstop. Right. It is an impulse that I can't control. This computer draws me. The telephone draws me. His Holy Manuals draws me. His handwritten notes draw me. I am so glad that I get a chance to witness Him for His greatness. He is the greatest. He is strong and mighty. He is great and powerful, and no one can do the things you do. You take over and allows me to follow the leader. I let Him have His way. I follow the leader. Let Him have His way in your life. Listen to Him tell you that you don't need all that food – not everyday. Give your body a rest. You asked it to digest an Italian Sandwich, Tossed Garden Style Salad, Buffalo Chicken wings, and soda. Today – go it light. Eat something soothing and easy to digest. You can treat yourself later – at another time. This is what He said to me. Isn't He great? Isn't He remarkable? It is so easy to listen to what He has to say. His voice is always gentle, soft, persuasive, and clear. He makes sure you hear every word He has to say.

That reminds me of a story that I can share with you. The boat came near my shore. Jesus was the Captain and He told me to "get in". When I stepped in with one foot, He told me, "I will always love you", I didn't hear Him at first and then He said it again "I will love you always". I had never heard these words before. I was amazed at what these words did for me. They saved my soul. They made me set up and take note of who was talking. It was Jesus! These are the words that came from His mouth. My life changed. My ideas, my thoughts, my opinions, my beliefs, my traditions, my dreams and my desires went out of the window only to return with pure satisfaction. This is where I have been searching to go. This is where I belong. I belong with the One who has the greatest power. He comes highly recommended. My mamma, daddy, sisters, and brother, all said: "try Him". I am only doing what they told me to do. They told me to listen so I could hear His voice. They told me to keep still until He told me what to do. I waited. Then He revealed Himself and told me what to do. This is what He did!

He raised me from the dead. He gave me a new beginning. A new birth. A new identity. A new mind. A new brain. A new heart. A new body. A new soul. A new Spirit. Praise His Name. He did it. Worship Him for His goodness. Honor Him for being so good to me. I will.

During the day I float, glide, coast throughout my day until I get close to this computer. Then I take off my hat because I know I am going to be here for a while because this position is where I am most comfortable. I try to watch tv from time to time, but it doesn't hold my interest. I come to life once I realize "you can write". So, I get the courage and I get started. I maybe in the middle of a sentence and His Holy Spirit will tell me to "hold up", make this call. I stop what I am doing and begin to follow the order that I have been given.

You see I only have time. That is all any of us have is time. Take some time and just feel His Presence. Take some time to invite Him into your Presence. Take some time and ask Him to please allow you into His Presence. Take a deep breath, get a bottle of His water, relax, sit back, let Him enter your consciousness. Ask Him if He is there and He will tell you "I am here, there and everywhere" and today I am here to take real good care of you.

Psalm 23. The Lord is My Shepherd, I shall not want. We are sheep in His Pasture. Psalm 100. Okay, sheep - enter His Presence with Praise and words of Thanksgiving. O Holy One! I worship You. I honor You. I praise You. I glorify You. I Love You. Please hear my cry. Please hear my plea at this sacred hour of 7 p.m. He is listening. Thank You for favoring me with a new afternoon on this brand-new Monday that has never seen before. Thank You, Lord, for allowing me to center my thoughts on you. Thank You, Lord, for listening to me as I release into Your atmosphere words of praise and admiration. I give You all my honor, praise, and worship. He is worthy to be praised. Agreed?

I can't dream of ever being without you. What would I do if you left me alone to fight the wolves, please keep them from devouring me? I see them coming but I am going to stay close by You so I will be safe and secure. Psalm 91 says "I will cover you with My feathers and under His wings, I can seek refuge." I am believing what I am reading. I am going to trust in His written word. I am going to believe in the unseen. I am leaning on the pillars that are outlined in His Manual. In His Holy Bible. This is where I placed my trust. Are you with me? Are you onboard? Are we traveling in the same direction? Do you believe it? Do you trust? You got faith to go with to the end - right. You are going to stay with me to see what direction I may go off into next - aren't you?

I coming to the end of today's adventure. He has made my day alright. I followed His instructions. I am winding down. I will be reclining as I lay my head upon His chest to breathe His sweet breath forevermore. I am putting on some nice easy flowing music, going to light up a candle, and open a bottle of His chilled water that He allowed to escape from His rivers, mountain, rocks, brooks, and streams into a bottle just the right size for my hands to hold. Isn't He great? Isn't He mighty? Isn't He powerful? Does He love me? Yes! He does. I see it. I taste it. I hear it. I feel it. I think it. Jesus loves me, for the Bible tells me so.

Tell yourself the same thing every day for thirty days and you will develop it as a habit. Tell yourself the same thing every day for sixty days then it will become a part of your total makeup. You will begin to believe what you say. Dream with me. We can go to the Philippines, New Zealand, South Africa, Japan, China and see the Reflective Pools at a moment's notice. Peace. Oblivion. Contentment. Happiness. Joy. You will be overwhelmed once you immerse yourself in His signs and wonders. This is our world - let us take it back. Let's begin to love ourselves first, then we can begin to love each other. Remove the evil spirit of hate away from your heart. Refuse to hate. Hate destroys. Hate tears down God's anointed. Hate begins in the heart, travels to the mind, brain, throughout the body, in the soul, and destroys your spirit. The devil's, the enemy's, Satan's, Lucifer aims to steal, kill, and destroy. He steals your joy and happiness, kills your desire to believe in yourself, and destroys your faith in God.

Do you see how sly, sneaky, and diabolical Satan can be? Public enemy number one. Evade Him at all costs. You know who has a fence of protection wrapped all around you - don't you? The Lord is your help! He never slumbers nor sleeps. He is always with you. Joshua 1 v:9. Haven't you been told to be courageous and never doubt yourself because I will always be near you. Our God, Our Jesus, Our Lord has shown me the way. He has been shadowing me just like I asked. He is watching over my shoulder to make sure I get it right.

You see when I placed my two feet on the boat, I knew I had made the right decision. I went into my happy space and made myself some dinner. After I finished eating and cleaning up the kitchen I migrated back over to my computer and pulled out a chair. God is working in my life. I know it. I am aware of what I have been able to obtain and achieve. He continues to allow me to see the sparkle in my eye each time I investigate the mirror. I do this quite often because I am in my happy space several times throughout the day and I look up into the mirror when I am washing my hands under His hot and cold water, caught at the right temperature, to lather up my hands and rinse them. I greet myself. I listen. He is forever searching to find out if I am okay. I look up and say I am ok and place a smile on my face because I am confident that He is watching over me. So, I recompose myself and continue working on the mission I was on.

Everything is possible when you believe, trust, and have faith. What do you want? What is your heart's desire? He is listening. You can lead the horse to the pond, but it is up to him to drink. Drink some of this water and you will never be thirsty again. I am writing my eulogy every day of my life. The honor goes to Bertha Bond of Dry Branch, Georgia. She is the one that called my attention that I was recording history every day of my life.

He is holding my hand. I am holding His Hand. We are hand in hand! He is guiding me. I am skipping and hopping all the way. My feet are as light as a feather. My feet are as light as a bird. A bird has so much precision that it can land on a thin line in the air. The birds know that if they can land on a tree limb that they will be safe landing on the power lines. A bird knows when it is time for a time out. Does man know when he needs a time out? Man and woman slow down to eat, then collapse at the nearest couch or bed. Wake up sleepyhead - you are killing yourself - dying a slow death imposed by you. When you were younger your body could digest heavy foods and meals. Now that you are getting into your golden years, your body does not need much food. It needs to rest. You have overworked it for a long period. Now it is time to take a rest break.

You will live longer and be free of aches and pains if you eat less and drink more water and juices. This has worked for me. I can only clue you in on what I know has worked for me. I don't have body aches. I take two Tylenol with arthritis pain pills each morning and nothing else is needed throughout the daytime and the nighttime.

Just keep living. Per James Bond, Mt Gilgal Prominent Member. These are his famous words. Just keep living and keep believing and keep trusting and continue to have faith. I will not stop believing that He is keeping me alive for a reason. I will not stop believing that He is watching over me. I know He is near me.

Chapter 35

It is evident that once I began spitting our words, they become nonstop. Speak the word - my Sis. Speak the word. Call me pastor, preacher, teacher, leader, lecturer, a smooth talker, a motivational speaker, one that convinces you so easily. I am at the mountain top. I am looking over a cliff and I see what is going on? His sheep are astray, it is not their fault. They were tricked by what they saw and were controlled by the words they heard, Jesus. Jesus. Jesus. Get adjusted to hearing me say the word - Jesus. I will use it a lot. Want to go to church. There is a second sermon attached. It is okay - just digest part of it now and then another part later. I must go in the direction that I am guided in. In other words, I go with the flow. I never tire. I can go on and on, over and over, again and again. I have a "favorite subject". Yes! You know - right? If after reading for a while, you need a change, then take it. I will be here. I can't shut up. There is so much to say during my season. One day I will float away and be a faint memory, just like a mist of vapor. Just that fast, I will vanish into a world of the unknown. Heaven. Paradise.

My name is carved in the Lambs' Book of Life. Somewhere - over yonder - somewhere over there - at the Great Beyond.

When I had no vision or sight, you taught me how to love my brothers and sisters in the North, East, South, and West. You turned my life upside down. You gave me new ideas, new thoughts, new opinions, new beliefs, new traditions, new dreams and new desires when You used Your Resurrection Power from the grave to raise me from the dead. It is a fight every morning you open your eyes. You can choose to center your thoughts on the One that blew the breath of life into your lifeless body and allowed you to become a living soul ready to praise, admire, worship, and honor the Giver of Life. I am closed in my right mind with a reasonable portion of my health and strength and I have already won the victory because I can "think" and "process thought" in a nanosecond.

Satan, Lucifer, the devil, the enemy, has you blinded. You are looking at yourself and your surroundings through the eyes of the devil and you have blinders on. Your sense of sight has gone dark. You only see what the devil wants you to see. Has anyone ever told you these words "just look around and see what you see"? Has anyone ever told you to be "present", to engage in the present moment in time? Wait! Just one second. Reread what you just read and adjust yourself. Spend a comfortable day in California on one of its beaches and watch His blue waves come in and go out. So where are you located, in the den, in the living room, in the bed, at your computer desk? Wherever you are - make sure it is your favorite spot because this is where you and I will have our "one on one time."

Do you know who is wonderful? Do you know who is all-powerful? Do you know who woke you up this morning? Did you have a little talk with Him this morning? I did! He touched me. He touched me with His finger. His finger was filled with love, and it brought joy, pleasure, and Thanksgiving to my day. I am glad that I am alive.

Today was my day to go to the grocery store. I made transportation plans yesterday. So, I had given my Uber driver the heads up. We both agreed on a time. Lunchtime is good for me, and it was good for him. This worked out just perfectly. Looks like Someone was watching over our shoulder and had already worked out a plan because He knew what I had to do. He worked it out! Say it again! He worked it out. I went to the store, gathered groceries, checked out, returned home, and went and retrieved the grocery cart from the first-floor stairway. I had to push the buggy. This was not easy; the buggy's legs were wobbly. Thank You, Jesus! I made it. He had a light shining down on me because I completed what He allowed me to embrace on a day that I have never seen before.

It is Tuesday, April 27th, 2021, and I need His Grace and Mercy. The second day of the week. On the second day, He was in the process of creating Heaven and Earth, and He said, "it is good". I had to take a break. I had to break away from the moment and attend to some personal needs. He was holding me - you see I made it back - I didn't miss a beat. He was with me the entire time showering down on me His Grace and Mercy because I prayed and I asked O Lord please grant me Your Grace and Mercy, Cradle me in Your Everlasting Arms. Hold me close dear Lord. Don't ever let me go! I will never let go of the Hand that I am holding. I am holding on for dear life. I owe Him a debt. He gave up His life so I could be saved.

Me, myself, and I say it is time to take your life back from Satan through believing, trusting, and having faith in Our Lord and Savior Jesus Christ and His Holy Spirit. Oh! He is on time. He is right here with me at this present and the precise moment in time. The man should not be judged by the color of his skin or the texture of his hair. A man should be judged on the contents of his heart. Hate! Hate! Man hates each other. I will say it again, man, despises himself and you. Man sees no self-worth in himself and surely, he cannot find any self-worth in you because you don't value what God, Jesus, My Lord, and Savior has created.

It is a brand-new morning. Tuesday morning, April 27, 2021, here at Gene Miller Manor in Christian City in Union City, Georgia and I have got a message for you to hear. It is a brand-new day. A brand-new morning. A time set aside for you to come alive in your senses and begin to think. I know a man who lost His life on Calvary and rose to victory. His Name is Jesus. Jesus. Jesus. Say it slowly! Say it gently! It is the "Sweetest Name" I know and how I love it. Do you know what He has done for me on this brand new glorious and sunshiny day?

Let me fill you in on the latest.

He came early in the wee hours of dawn and satisfied me with His morning mercy and love. He had Grace and Mercy on my right, Grace, and Mercy on my left, Grace, and mercy in front of me, Grace, and Mercy in the back of me, Grace, and Mercy on top of me, Grace, and Mercy underneath me. He has me covered from the crown of my head to the sole of my feet. Ain't He grand? Ain't He marvelous? Ain't He magnificent? Right at this present and the precise moment in time! Yes! He is. Glorify Him with me. Rejoice in what He is doing for you at this nanosecond. Each millisecond - He is with me. We are just that close. It is Him and me. He and I. Me and Him. Us two. The "two of us". We are together. He is leading me around from trough to trough telling me what kind of water I should be drinking. I should be drinking His Holy water, His water that He allowed to escape from His mountains, rocks, brooks, rivers, and streams into a bottle just the right size for my hands to hold.

Drink the verses in His scriptures. It is written. Do you have peace like the river? Perhaps you have never sat, starred at a forest of trees, just sat, and studied His rivers, lakes, brooks, and streams. Perhaps you have never seen a pond of water. There is the various color of rocks lining the bottom of the water.

Peace, contentment, harmony, and tranquility – all from one source. His sacred and solid ground we call Earth, on His Planet and in His Universe.

I will sing the song "Thank You, Jesus". Sing it with me. Take a deep breath. Sigh and relax in knowing that He has done it again. He has reappeared and showered me with His Unchanging Love, His Unfailing Love, His Grace and Mercy, and His Divine Devotion. Do you know how I know this? I felt Him. He has been following me since I placed my two feet on His floor and went into my happy space to do what I needed to do. Ah! He is wonderful! Ah! He is mighty! Ah! He is great!

You do know we are covered by His blood. Because He shed His blood, so that I could be saved, I am going to tell it. I am going to spill the beans. I am going to shout, hoop, speak, talk, and write and tell the ones in the North, East, South, and West just how good He is to me. He watched over me while I slumbered and slept and when He released my head into His atmosphere, I felt the Presence of My Lord and Savior. He was there at my bedside with His Hands stretched out to me and I began talking. Oh, Lord! You are great. Oh, Lord! You are the greatest because You favored me with another day to be alive on your solid and sacred ground we call Earth, on Your Planet, and in Your Universe.

I know the Ruler of the Universe! I owe Him a deep amount of respect, love, and honor. He is the King and I salute Him for being so good to me. He found me. I was a tulip. I found my way to the top of the surface and now I am blooming. I am opening to you and giving you the knowledge, wisdom, understanding that I have been able to receive during my sacred time here on Earth. I have a lot of stories to tell. I will celebrate God's Grace. Previously in my earlier life, there were a lot of boulders on the road. I hopped over them. I got out of the way, they didn't destroy me, why not, because God was working in my life.

God is at work this morning. I heard Him when He whispered these words into my ear, "wake up O sleepyhead" rise from the dead and let the Lord shine on you." I turned over and decided to allow Him to lead me on the adventure that He had planned for me to embrace.

It was about the break of day when I first opened my eyes. I was on a mission, and I got the job done. After I finished, I hurried back to reclaim my spot. My head was nestled in His Everlasting Arms. Once I got comfortable, I began talking. I ask "O Lord please come into my presence and O Lord please allow me into Your Presence. I snuggled down under the covers and went to talking. O Lord please shelter us, O Lord please shadow us, O Lord please favor us, O Lord please cover us with Your Blood, O Lord please grant us Your Grace and Mercy, O Lord please forgive us our sins because we don't always do things perfectly or correctly, O Lord please forgive our enemies because they know not what they do, O Lord please strengthen us physically, mentally, emotionally, psychologically, morally, and spiritually, O Lord please protect us from all plagues, pandemics, disasters, and turmoil, O Lord please prosper us materialistically, financially and spiritually, O Lord please do not cast us away from Your Presence and O Lord please allow Your Holy Spirit to dwell in us again on this day. In Jesus' Name, I Pray.

Worship Our Lord, Praise Our Lord, Honor Our Lord. Let Him know that today we worship You for being so good to us. O, Lord! Thank You for listening to the words that were meditating in my heart. O, Lord! Please continue to answer our prayer. This is my affirmation. What is yours? I know you have a morning meditation, morning prayer, morning confession, morning mantra. You must have. You want to walk under His crown. You want to be able to go here, there, everywhere knowing that He has His eyes on you. Have you called on Him and asked Him for His Grace and Mercy? If not, you must get busy, time is wasting, you are losing precious moments. It is the sacred hour of 10 a.m. on Tuesday, April 27th, 2021, and you can tell "Me, myself and I, is in the Presence of a King.

I was in His Presence all day yesterday and today He has shown up again to give me the same kind of love that He gave me yesterday. A repeat performance. I will not balk. I am happy. I am content. I have joy and pleasure radiating from my heart. My heart is filled with love and compassion. I am compassionate, considerate, and tolerant. This is what I was told to do, and I knew I had work to do, and God showed me how to love. "Love yourself first." Be compassionate to yourself! Be kind to yourself! Tenderly touch yourself, pinch yourself, see what pain feels like. Nothing to it. That is what Our Savior said when they crucified Him on the cross.

Somehow, young man, young woman, young boy, young girl, young child, You must listen. You must clear your head of all the noise and just simply plainly listen for your name to be called? His voice is a low, gentle whisper.

My living arrangements changed. I am on the second floor of the building. Moving on up. I have the most beautiful and serene view. It is a forest of trees. All different sizes and shades and colors. I see a big spacious blue sky. I see clouds moving about - traveling with the wind.

I talk with the Lord each millisecond of my life, that is just how fast my heart is beating. I am glad I am not in control of my heartbeat. I would probably collapse under stress. I am glad I know who controls my heartbeat. It is Jesus! He is the One that is regulating my heart to beat. Surprise Info? He is the One that is allowing your heart to beat.

Give Him some Praise! Ah! He is worthy! I am not ashamed to say His Name. His Name is Jesus, The Ruler of The Universe. He knows my Name and I know His Name.

Here is a story. Satan blinded me with so much light, division, and confusion. Satan was moving so fast. He sat up roadblocks. I hopped and skipped over them too. Uh! Huh! Satan. Not anymore, I listened to you for too long, and look where I am. I had blinders on. I could not see the light that Jesus was shining in my direction. I was a disaster until I heard a slow, soft, kind, and gentle voice. He said to me "You, yes you, you are weary, you are worn, you are scared, you are torn, you are heavily laden, you are confused, come and go with me and I will give you rest. Matthew 11 v:28. Keep reading. "Come on, my yoke is easy, I will be on one side, and you can be on the other one." I went. I was so tired. He saved me. Jesus saved my soul. Jesus! Jesus! He is the One that did it. He cast His net real wide, and I got caught. I made Him the

Head of My life. I made Jesus first. Oh, Master! Wherever you lead me, I will go. Oh, Master! Whatever you tell me to say, I will say it. I owe you, my life.

I was warned about the changes He could bring about. The rest is history. I became brand new. I got a brand new mind, a brand new beginning, a new birth, a new identity when He raised me from the dead. This morning is a day of "gratitude". Thank You, Lord, for every breath I take. Thank You, Lord, for allowing my heart to beat at its normal rhythm. You have given me a new life to live in the Presence of a King. He chose me. He pushed the weeds, bushes, garbage that was covering His tulip and it began to grow.

If I am lifted, I will draw all men unto me. This is what He said. Let's you and I began to lift His Name on High. O, Lord! You are mighty. O, Lord! You are great. There is no one like you Lord. You are one of a Kind. There is no one else like you. I submit. I commit. I surrender my total self over to Thee so Thy will be done.

It is blessing after blessing that I receive daily. I am getting my daily bread each morning I open my eyes. I must write. It is an uncontrollable impulse. I have so much to "Thank Him" for. I have so much to say. There is never a quiet moment because it is time to recognize who woke you up this morning. Did you saturate His atmosphere with words of appreciation and gratitude for making the decision that you could come alive today and be raised from the dead?

Yesterday, the day before that one, I was glued to this computer and today is more of the same. I am so glad to be alive. I am alive. I am not dead, and this is what I will portray to the world, I am alive, and I want to live my life pleasing A King who sits high and looks low. He was looking around and He found me. I was willing to take up my cross and follow Thee. He said I was the right one for the job. He had confidence in me that I could complete the assignment that I was given, and I will not prove Him to be wrong. I will write. I will talk. I want to hear Him say "Servant! Well done".

He allowed me to come back to Thee and start my life over. I got a new start. I was made brand new. I was born again. I pulled off those old clothes and tried on the new garments that He had designed just for me.

I can do all things through Christ who strengthens me. I had no sight nor vision. I could not see but today is a great day to be alive under the guidance and leadership of the One that made me. I am here. I am present in your life to tell you that there is another life you can live in the presence of a King. You must come under His authority. You will never be lost again. He has a plan. He knows the plan and He wants you to allow Him to work His plan.

Prayer will change things. When you pray know that you are talking to the One who has the plan. My prayer is so simple. I say "O Lord please come into my presence and O Lord please allow me into Your Presence. Once I say these words, I know He is listening and recording everything I say. He hears me. I am confident that He heard me and will answer my prayer, so I drift back off into La La Land.

This prayer has worked for me, and I believe it will work for you. You are the one that will need to contour your lips to let these words roll off your tongue. Now I know what direction I am going in because He is with me all day, everyday, 24/7, around the clock and at this sacred hour, sacred minute, sacred second, and right at this present and the precise moment in time. How do I know this? I can feel Him. I can taste Him. I can smell Him. I can hear Him. I can "think". I know who to praise. I am praising the One who is holding my hand and guiding my footsteps. I listen very well. I follow orders. I understand His Decrees. They are meant for my eyes only. I hear the messages that He is allowing to resonate in my heart, mind, brain, body, soul, and spirit. I will be with you always. My love will last forever. This is what He is saying to me. I know if I remain in Him then He will remain in me. If I abide in Him, then He will abide in me. If I draw nearer to Him, then He will draw nearer to me. It is written. Believe, trust, and have faith in the unknown and the unseen.

He makes me lie down in "green pastures", the unknown but I have courage and I am confident that He is with me. Psalm 23. Dream! Who took your privilege away? Yank it back! Begin to stand on your own two feet and just "think" and "process thought". Why is this one way, when it should be another one? Why do you hate me so? Do you hate yourself? Strong terminology -right? It is true. You must find out why and what you hate about yourself.

Me, myself, and I. I love me. Yes! I love myself some Bettie Jean because He first loved me. Jesus! That is who. He loved me before I knew myself. He loved me when I was a thought. Jeremiah 1. He loves my face, nose, eyes, mouth, ears, hair, and scalp. He loves my body, my mind, my brain, my heart, my soul, and my spirit. He keeps supplying my every need. He will do the same for you once you establish a relationship with Him. You must make yourself known to Him.

He knows my voice because He hears it so often. He knows my thought before it is a thought. We are just that close. There is so much to say. He orders my steps. He orchestrates my thoughts and aids me in forming my ideas, thoughts and beliefs, traditions, dreams and desires. These are the words meditating from my heart that need to be released into His atmosphere.

We are living in fear. What will they think if I go forward with the plan, I must tell the world that Jesus can save your soul? Come unto me - you can rest now. No more hassle, no more trials, and temptations, once and for all no disappointments because you trust, you believe, and you have faith that He will never leave you nor forsake you.

This is His promise to you and me. Hebrews 13 v:5. Whichever direction you choose to go in - I will be there right by your side. I will never forget about you. You are one in a million. You don't need any credentials - I will be your passport. Oh! He is able! Oh! He is remarkable! Oh! He is outstanding. Oh! He is spectacular. Oh! He is wonderful and miraculous. Did you know all of that? If yes! then make some noise. I can count on you to say "Amen". I know.

When I sat down on this computer, Jesus had a surprise waiting for me. He said "since I love to look at His trees, He was going to provide me with a picture of trees, row after row of green forest, all shades of green, all varying colors, carefully manicured lawns that can be found somewhere in Italy. This is the land of our brothers and sisters. I have deep respect for them because it certainly appears that He has had His eye on them and gave them the peace to develop His forests into wonderlands. I can breathe His fresh air right now. I feel the breeze coming in through the window. He is allowing me to inhale and exhale His air in and out of my lungs. Isn't He wonderful? Isn't He kind? Isn't He gentle? It automatically comes in and goes out. What a blessing to be able to breathe! What a blessing it is to be alive and in His Presence? Just to know Him. Just learning what He is all about.

We owe Him our life. He is the reason I am alive. He is the reason you are alive. It was Jesus' decision as to who would wake up this morning and who would not. I just simply say "Thank You". Humbly, meekly, I open my heart to Thee to say, "Thank You". I am glad to be alive. I will worship, honor, and praise you on this day because I may not get another day to "hallow" and praise Your Holy Name. Today could be my last day. I am glad to know that He is sheltering me. You, too, right? I am glad to know the He has you and me in His shadow. He is keeping an eye on me and you. I am glad about it - aren't you? He is searching for a clean heart and a steadfast spirit. To know that He is showering His Unfailing Love, His Unconditional Love, His Grace and Mercy and His Divine Devotion all over me is a joy and a privilege. He didn't forget about me when He came early to satisfy me with His morning mercy and love and told me to let it last me throughout my day.

I followed His command. I did as I was told. His plan was well coordinated. He executed His plan, and I was satisfied with my accomplishments and achievements. He guided me back and forth. He shines His little light on me. He had me under His protective covering. I am His. I belong. Join me. This is the best decision you could make. Make Jesus the Head of Your Life. Put Jesus first. Let me take the lead. His yoke is easy. You can depend on Him to lead the way because He has the roadmap in His Hand.

All He wants you to do is reach out and up and grab His Hand. To You! Oh, Lord! I give you, my life. Take control of my mind, brain, heart, body, soul, and spirit, and allow me to come under Your Authority.

Who do you believe? Who do you trust? Who do you have faith in?

Do you know He will make a way out of no way? Do you know He will answer your prayer? Your answer maybe; yes, no, not yet. Whatever answer He gives should find you content, complacent, and full of praise. I know who will make the best decision for me. I gave up the reigns I had over my life to Him so His will could be done.

I am sitting at the computer, and it is saying "you need a break". Join me, get you a bottle of His water, chilled or at room temperature, get some of His hard candy, moisturize your mouth. The water and candy will curb your appetite. You will not feel the urge to eat. You will find relief and contentment by sipping on your water and hard candy. This is what I am doing. I know when to stop and take a break. My daughter calls it "Wuu-saw Time". When I stop, I pay honor and tribute to A King for making everything possible.

He loved me when I did not love myself. He allowed His will to be done. He knew one day I would return to my roots from whom all my blessings flow. I am anchored to that vine. I am holding on for dear life. Like a sparrow on His tree, I am confident that He will take good care of me. He prepared my dinner for me while I was in the grocery store. I am going to dine on some Lemon and Herb Rotisserie chicken, bread, and watermelon bites in the Presence of a King.

I am "still the one" that He loves. He prepared for me, and I didn't even know it. He is magical. He is majestic. He is so surprising. It is so fulfilling to know that you are loved, wanted, accepted, needed, admired, adored, cherished, and idolized by a King. Okay! Take a deep breath, investigate your heart, and bring about that smile on that face. You know He loves you. You know He wants the best for you. He knows you adore the baby that was in a manger and had nowhere to lay his head.

Wouldn't it be great if a man were to begin to love each other? This dream can be a reality if enough of the believers began to speak against the evil spirit of hate. Hate kills, Hate destroys, Hate steals your strength. Hate steals your joy. Hate left to fester creates rage, answers, lies, and deceit. Hate blinds you. Man and woman must begin today at this present moment in time to speak out against hate and not allow it to continue to grow in the hearts of man and woman around the globe.

Think about it! Think about "hate". Why do men and women hate themselves so much? They have never been told three simple words and they are "I Love You". Not until now. They get to hear these words from the mouth of a King who has loved them since birth. Beginning at the cradle, He granted us His Grace and Mercy, Love and Tender Devotion. Isn't He wonderful? Put your log on the fire. Make your contribution. We are praising, honoring, and saluting a King. Join in. He is listening. The more voices He hears we might shatter the ceiling in Heaven.

Chapter 36

"For God so loved the world that He gave His only begotten Son that whosoever believeth in Him shall not perish but have everlasting life." John 3 v:16. Jesus - The Prince of Peace. Jesus says that He will pour out His Spirit on all in the land. Let's you and I lift His Name on High. Bow your head, open your heart, meekly and humbly call on His Holy Name, and ask Him to come into Your Presence and ask Him to allow you into His Presence. Man and woman, boy, girl, and child need to posture themselves before a King and ask Him to shower you with His Unfailing Love, His Unconditional Love, His Grace and Mercy, and His Divine Devotion.

Put another log on the fire. Reach, reach, knock, seek and you shall find. What are you looking for? Are you looking for His Love and Tender Devotion? It is so close to you. It is right under your breath. He is there waiting to hear you salute, worship, and honor Him just for being so good to you on a day that you have never seen before. It is Wednesday morning, at the sacred hour of 9 o'clock and I am in His Presence. He touched me with His finger of Love early in the wee hours of dawn and told me "Wake up O sleepyhead, rise from the dead and let the Lord shine on you." I received His undivided attention as He allowed me to go into my happy space and do what I needed to do. For this I am grateful, and I sang my song the entire time I was going in and coming out. "Thank You Jesus" are the only words to my song. I was skipping, hopping, and running all at the same time while "hallowing" His Name for being so good to me.

I was so sleepy! He held my hand on the way in and on the way out. I finished and I hurried back to reclaim my spot. My head was nestled in His chest, lying in His Everlasting Arms, and breathing His sweet breath forevermore. After doing this I went to talking. I ask O Lord please come into my presence and O Lord please allow me into Your Presence. I was so happy and thrilled that once again I get to honor, worship, and salute A King, who has watched over me while I slumbered and slept. Preaching, teaching, talking, singing is nothing new to me. I can do it all day, every day, 24/7, around the clock - every hour - every minute - every second and right at this present and precise moment in time. This millisecond. This nanosecond. He is watching over me.

I see Him. I see Him casting His sunlight over His entire creation. He has everything He made in His shadow. Therefore, He has me and you. Praise Him. Once again, He decided that I could come alive in my senses so I could praise His Holy Name for being so good to me. He allows me to "think". He allows me to "process thought". Ask Him! This is the One who supplies all your needs. This is the One you talk to too early in the wee hours of dawn. He will come early let me warn you. If you hear a knock, it is just Jesus. He wants to come in - now let Him.

Earlier during the morning hours, after I had said the most important affirmation, asking Him to come to see about me and asking Him to please take good care of me, I went into the remainder of my morning prayer. O Lord please shelter us, O Lord please shadow us, O Lord please favor us, O Lord please cover us with Your Blood, O Lord please grant us Your Grace and Mercy, O Lord please forgive us of our sins because we don't always do things correctly and perfectly, O Lord please forgive our enemies because they know what they do, O Lord please strengthen us physically, mentally, emotionally, psychologically, morally and spiritually, O Lord please protect us from all plagues, pandemics, disasters, and turmoil, O Lord please prosper us materialistically, financially and spiritually, O Lord please do not cast us away from Your Presence and O Lord please allow Your Holy Spirit to dwell in us again on this day. In Jesus' Name, I Pray - Amen. He will answer prayer. I tried Him for myself. I don't have to listen to anyone else give Him Praise, I can do it myself, I can praise, worship, and honor the One who gave me my life to live in the Presence of a King. Yes! This is a lot to say. It rolls off my tongue so easily because these are the words meditating in my heart. I am in His Presence. Every day, every morning I open my eyes I know who to honor, salute, cherish, praise, and obey. As I peeked from under the covering, I could see His sunlight. His daylight. I immediately went into praise mode. Oh, Lord! You are great! Oh, Lord! You are mighty! Oh, Lord! Thank You for coming to see about me. Oh, Lord! Thank You for not forgetting about me. Oh, Lord! You are wonderful. Oh, Lord! Thank You for Your Love and Admiration. This morning when I opened my eyes, He was standing beside my bed, ready to catch my hand. It was such an encouraging and tender touch. I wake up to His Love each morning I open my eyes because I had no idea when I closed my eyes, trusting in His Holy Word, that I would wake up on this morning. He just keeps on blessing me each day.

Jesus is the One that made the decision that I could come alive, begin to "think, and "process thought". He is the One that favored me with another day. He is the One that made the decision to blow His breath of life into my lifeless body and allowed me to become a living soul ready to praise, worship, honor, and cherish Him for being so good to me. Once again. A Wednesday morning, April 28th, 2021, here at Gene Miller Manor in Christian City in Union City, Georgia, He is alive, canvasing to check on His sheep who is determined to hold on to their beliefs, thoughts, ideas, opinions, traditions, dreams and desires.

I know who woke me up this morning! I know who touched me, my family, my loved ones, and my friends. Tamara, my oldest daughter knows who woke her up, her husband, and her son. There is no greater Love. There is no one like Jesus. I love Jesus and Jesus loves me. He loves you just like He loves me. Remarkably, He can love on me, you, my sisters and brothers in the North, East, South, and West, and His whole wide world at the same time. Isn't He miraculous? Isn't He magnificent? Isn't He marvelous? He satisfied me early with His morning mercy and love and told me to let it last me all during my day.

I began being happy when I opened my eyes. When I opened the door up to my happy space, I had been given everything I would need to cleanse and clothe my body. Say that again! Yes! I was showered with gifts. Yes! I had a washcloth, a towel, soap, hot and cold water, clean clothes, clean shoes, and socks to adorn my body. Is He great? Is He wonderful? I just stopped looked around and took a mental note of all the things He had provided for me, and I said "Hallelujah". Praise His Name because He is showing me that He loves me and the ground I walk on. He is keeping me in His shadow.

I marched into my happy space under the direction of His Holy Spirit and made myself a pot of coffee. Let me tell you what He did for me. He gave me the coffee, the filter, and the coffee pot. All I had to do was to measure the exact amount of water and coffee to make two cups. This I did under supervision. After it finished brewing, I poured it into the cup, along with the creamer and sweetener. I had my napkin and spoon in my hand. I moved to the table, ladled it back and forth, and recited His Twenty-Third Psalm. Oh! What peace and contentment these words gave me? I put another log on the fire. I renewed my faith; my strength and these words uplifted my spirit because I knew He was listening to me. My coffee tasted so good. I call it my "delicious brew". Help me praise Him! Don't wait for someone else to do it. Join in and share in the fun. Salvation is free. Open your mind, heart, brain, body, soul, and spirit and "hallow" His Name. He is just that "good" to me. He is saving souls. Let Earth receive its Savior. There is healing power in Jesus' Name. I call on Him often. He knows my voice. He knows my thoughts. He knows my dreams.

He did it again. He returned to grant me His Grace and Mercy. He took my feet out of the miry clay. He placed my feet on solid ground. He saved my soul. It felt good to be saved. I had joy in my heart. I have love in my heart. There is compassion, softness, gentleness dwelling in my soft meadow. He said, "she'll be back". How did I know I would be testifying about what He has done for me so early in the morning. This is what I have this morning, His Grace and Mercy, His Unconditional Love, His Unfailing Love, and His Divine Devotion. This is "goodness" that only can come from Our Lord and Savior Jesus Christ. Don't you agree? I can't give up. I can't stop now. I am moving right along up the King's Highway. I am on my way to receive my crown. I shatter the ceiling in Heaven every morning when I open my eyes because I saturate His atmosphere with words of praise and admiration. This is what I did this morning. I know who gave me a life to live in the Presence of a King. Jesus came to allow me to live my life to the fullest. Jesus rescued me. Jesus recreated me. Jesus re-invented to me. I am a new creature in Christ. I am a spiritual being having a human experience. I don't belong here in this corrupt and wicked world. So, I will call on His Holy Name and let Him Save me.

Each day that I move about, I know that "He is with me". His 23rd Psalm says this. "Thy art with me". He is keeping me alive for a reason. Pull out your Bibles, find Psalm 23, and read it. It begins with "The Lord is My Shepherd and I shall not want". I know who has His eye on me. I know who is guiding my footsteps. I know who is guiding my thoughts and ideas. I know who will protect me from all hurt, harm, or danger, I know who will provide all my needs and I know who will allow His Holy Spirit to become my counselor and my comforter.

I stand on His word! I stand on His Promises. I stand on My Rock. I stand on My Redeemer. I place Jesus First. When I made Jesus the Head of My Life, this was the best decision I could have ever made. My mind was on Jesus when I went into La Land and my mind was on Jesus when I opened my eyes to embrace a magnificent, marvelous, splendid, supreme, fabulous, fantastic, spectacular, and wonderful day that I have never seen before. God is Love. 1st John 4 v:8. He shows us His love through every flower that He allows to bud out. He shows us His Love through His birds. His birds praise Him. I will join in with the birds and tell Him "He is the greatest".

John 14 v:27 says "Peace I leave with you, my peace I give to you. Not as the world gives do I give to you. Let not your hearts be troubled, neither of them is afraid." Jesus is the Prince of Peace. I found peace in the hem of His garment. I found peace in the string that I grabbed a holt of. I started believing it a long time ago. I held on to my beliefs. I went to church. I listened to the vessels. I heard a word. I heard the preacher say, your life is the way you made it because this is what you chose to do. You decide what kind of life you want to live. Preacher – I am looking for a brighter day.

I was responsible for my fate. I was responsible for what happens to me. Of course, these words did not digest well. I started asking questions. I started to try to find out the answers to this question. Did I do it to myself? The answer came back, yes! You did. You made your bed now you must lie in it. I began to shake the devil loose. I did not want to be in the company of the devil anymore. I had been on this road too long and I have been asleep the entire time. Walking with blindfolds on. My eyes opened and I began to walk up to His castle, knock, seek and see what I could find.

I woke up! The Lord only helps those who help themselves. I knew I wanted a change. I knew I wanted a new direction. I knew that the ball was in my court and could bounce it in any direction I chose. I started with changing the words that I release from my mouth into His atmosphere. Proverbs 18 v:21. It says the tongue is your determining factor. You forecast your future. You write your eulogy. Whatever words you speak over yourself will return to rest on your shoulders. I had never formed a morning affirmation before, so it was all new to me, but I got busy and crafted the words that I wanted to say and then I put them into practice. So off I went determined to change my life. Since I had been given a choice, I chose to change my life. I wanted His Peace, Love, and Admiration. So, the search began.

I started calling. I started reading. I started writing. I started believing. I started trusting. I started to develop faith in His Bible and His Word. He said, "I am the sheepherder, and I will take good care of you". I plastered these words across my chest. I continued to read, and it said, "Thy art with me". I began to believe that He was with me all day, every day, 24/7, around the clock, every hour – every minute – every nanosecond, and right at this present and the precise moment in time. I cry out "Holy" because He is with me at this computer orchestrating my ideas, telling me to say this, and telling me to say that. I am under an Authoritative Source. I am listening to the One that woke me up this morning. I hear His voice. I hear Him talking to me. He is telling me that "I am the only one" that He loves, admires, adores, cherishes, and idolizes me. I have been sat apart from the rest. I am to receive His specialized care because there is no one else like me.

It is a time for a cross-over. It is time for you to change lanes. Don't you have everything you need? Hasn't He answered your prayers. He has been good to me, and I will tell it "He is mighty good to me. Peace. Patience. Tranquility. Serenity. Justice. Truth. Honesty. Salvation. Redemption. Love and Righteousness. Come on in the boat. There is plenty of room. This is the directive that I have been given and I want to share it with you. Get in the boat because He told you to. Praise, worship, and Honor Him for being so good to you. Listen! I hear the cry of a babe, telling you that He is just about ready to close the gate. It is time for you to put your foot in the doorway to Heaven.

Now that you are in the boat, you are safe and secure. Psalm 91 says "He will cover me with His feathers and under His wings, I will seek refuge from the snare of the fowler. I am protected from the enemy. I have a protective barrier covering me. I am in a bubble. It is just me and Him. The "two of us" bouncing here and bouncing there. Jesus is leading me to the trough so I can get a drink of water. Where is your faith? Do you think He would lead you this far and then leave you? Nope! He will not snatch the rug from under your feet because you are standing on solid and sacred ground, we call Earth on His Planet and in His Universe. You are standing on His Promises. Hebrews 13 v:5, says "I will never leave you nor forsake you". In Jesus' Name. I Pray.

Don't give up on His Love. Who are you trying to please? Who are you trying to satisfy? Who gave you a life to live on this Wednesday morning? It was You! Jesus! It was You who came to see about me. It was You who told me to turn on some music and listen to Your angels sing songs of praise and worship. When I turned it on, I heard moaning, hollering, and hooping. I could not take this kind of music so early in the morning. My spirits were high. I wanted to celebrate so I chose another station. My favorite, instrumental music. Joy to my ears and pleasure to my heart. My soul was satisfied because I know who loves me. There was fire shut up in my bones and I wanted to tell someone, so I migrated to this computer, pulled out a chair, placed my fingers on the keyboard, and went to release the words that are meditating in my heart.

His love came out of nowhere. Suddenly, like a bolt of lightning, He appeared. And how do I feel? I have His peace, patience, contentment, tranquility, harmony, and serenity. He promised me I could have it if I trust, believe, and have faith in the unseen. Don't you know He is there? I do! He is near me. I can touch Him if I want to. He allows me to hold His Hand.

Can't no one take God away from me? Now that I found Him, I will never let Him go. I am alive. He is allowing me to inhale and exhale His air in and out of my lungs. He is keeping my heart regulated to beat at its normal rhythm. Isn't He wonderful? I have life in my bones. I will not be satisfied until all the eyes of man will be turned toward Heaven waiting for our King to return. Until that day I am going to live - His Presence! I will be happy! I will live every day as if it is my birthday. It could be my last, so when my time comes for me to leave this world, I pray for a short span of sickness and a swift rise in death so I can lay my head upon His chest and breathe His sweet breath forevermore. Are you ready to go? It could be a car accident, a bomb, a mass shooter, a stray bullet. From out of nowhere there comes death. Aren't you scared? This is how Satan, Lucifer, the enemy, the devil wants you to feel. This is how He wants you to think.

Let Jesus come into your heart and fill it with His Love, compassion, joy, happiness, gentleness, faithfulness, and righteousness. Oh, Lord! Please come into my heart. I want to praise You. I want You to love me just like Your other sheep in Your Pasture. Anoint me with Your Love, Presence and Grace and Mercy, your strength, and the courage to believe in that I have not seen. I have not seen Him, but I know He is there. I was crafted in His image so each time I look in the mirror I see what He made was great! What He made was a masterpiece! I am a fine specimen of His workmanship, and I can tell you from experience that He is a Beautiful Savior. There is no one like Him. Ask Bryan Popin and Tasha Page Lockhart. There is no one like you. No one makes me know I can think, believe, and trust in every word that He says. Do I have to shake you? Nope! I will listen.

There is no one like You. I walk with Him. He walks with me. We are hand in hand. It is a new day. It is a new era in time. We are only passing through and some of His sheep are moving faster than a speeding bullet. Slow down! Stop for a minute. Stop for a second. Take a deep breath. Sigh and release it and realize that we serve a mighty God. He came to see about me and when He came, I asked O Lord please take good care of me and He heard my prayer. He heard my plea. He heard my cry. He smiled at me. I can honestly say I am blessed and highly favored just like you - right? We agree - right?

This morning. This morning. A morning that I have never witnessed before. He did it again. He came back to repeat His performance. He strengthened me physically, mentally, emotionally, psychologically, morally, and spiritually because I asked for it. He took me and made something wonderful and now that He has, I will tell the world just how Jesus saved my soul.

On this Wednesday morning, when I woke to His Presence, He gave me a new mind, a new beginning, a new birth, and a new identity. I was grateful that He did not forget about me. I knew I was in His Presence all day yesterday and I knew I kept His Name alive, so I rolled over with the sweet Name of Jesus on my lips. I will keep singing and keep praising Him for being so good to me.

A mist! A vapor! That is all you are. You are here one moment and then the next moment you have faded away. What do you want to say now that you have been allowed to speak for yourself? Do you know Him? Do you know who I am talking about when I say, "He and Him"? Make no mistake about it – I am talking about a man named Jesus. The man from Calvary and Galilee. He died on Calvary so that I could have Everlasting Life. I am ending now so I can enjoy some of His Grace and Mercy and Divine Devotion.

Chapter 37

I am trying to get into Heaven while I am living here on His solid and sacred ground. So many things stepped in the way. But I tapped into an energy that rules the World. It can happen if you ready to dream. I just finished looking at some of His ducks. They were all in succession bringing grass, leaves, and straw to build a nest. Wow! This duck has a brain. They can think. They know how to prepare. They know what they need to do to survive another Spring, they are getting ready to lay some eggs and their hatchery must have a place for them to lay their eggs. They are getting ready to mate and lay some eggs. His ducks are so graceful, cautious, tolerant of each other and consider that they too must have their space so we can get this job done. Could these ducks be making preparation for whatever storm that comes their way. Man, woman, boy, and girl, you have been given one directive all your life and that is "think". Think! Ponder some thoughts. Listen to another person's song. Listen to my lyrics. Church time. Are you ready?

It is another evening in the Presence of the One who sits High. The Most High! The One over all things. Oh, how I love my Beautiful Savior. Ask Bryan Popin. This is my second time hearing his song. These words on His album will penetrate your mind, brain, heart, body, soul, and spirit. Allow Him to take control of the reigns you have over your life and turn them over to Him so He can be in control of you, me, him, her, she, he, them, and they.

We are sheep. We have a sheepherder. Psalm 100 and Psalm 23. Let Him take control. Let Him be the Ruler of your fate. Allow your destiny and purpose in life to become fully open so your bright eyes can see the hidden messages. You have been passing by these two scriptures all your life but today is a day that you should stop. Read it for yourself and let each word in the verse define itself within that brain, mind, heart, body, soul, and spirit of yours. Examine each one. You have the time. One verse a day, that is all. Read Psalm 23 and it says, "Yea though you may walk through the shadows of death, fear no evil, for Thy Art with me". He is my way maker. God sees the way. He has proved Himself to me and this is who I will trust. He knows the way. He planned for me before I was a thought. He watched over me when He formed me like an egg. He talked to me the entire time I was being formed. He took good care of this egg. I had to be born again. I had to return to the womb. I had to get started all over again and begin to live the life that I was intended to live before I got snatched up in that grave. Man is in his coffin. I am slowing up long enough for you to come out of that trance that Satan has laid for you.

I am hungry. I want more. I want more of His Love, His Unchanging Love, His Unconditional Love, His Grace, and Mercy and His Genuine and Divine Devotion. It is genuine. There is no other love like it. Its envelopes you into a cocoon. The more I say these words, the clearer my connection is. If I remain in Him, then He will remain in me. Get there, any way you can, come by bus, come by train, come into that Secret Place, come into that Shelter where you can dwell in His Presence. Let me continue with my salute and words of honor that reveal my gratitude. I am trying to get there and if I abide in Him then He will abide in me, if I stay in His Presence, if I keep a song in my heart and praise on my tongue. "Thank You, Jesus, for my eyes so I can see. Thank You, Lord, for sight. Thank You, Lord, for my brain, my mind, my heart, my body, my soul, and my spirit. You gave it to me, and I am mighty "grateful". Yes! He is a way-maker. He made a way for me. I ask Him to strengthen me and prosper me each time I open my eyes.

I see the handwriting on the wall. Time is winding up and now it is the time to hear a word from the Lord. If I draw nearer to Him, then He will draw nearer to me. He has healing power. He will heal you physically and spiritually. Man is dead spiritually. Your beliefs, trusts, hope, and faith have drifted slowly away. You don't even have the desire to seek, knock, so you shall find. The urge to read His Holy Word, His Bible, or any religious book, newsletter, or email has vanished. All I want to do is be in His Presence. The window is open, and a light breeze is coming in through His window at the 6 o'clock hour. Sorry, I broke away - I just had to "thank Him" for the way He is showering me with His Love and Affection on this Wednesday afternoon. He is so "amazing". Jesus is. I use His Name often so if you see me referring to Him - then you know who I am talking about. I Love You, Lord. I Love You Jesus because You are the first one that ever loved me. It is written. Yes! Jesus loves me for the Bible tells me so.

Let's you and I call on Him. Jesus! Jesus! Oh, Lord! Oh, Lord! Please come into our presence and O Lord please allow us into Your Presence. God says I am what I am. I am a child of a King - I am a child of God and I am one of His sheep in His Pasture. Am I covered or what? I should be covered from the crown of my head to the sole of my feet in His Grace and Mercy. I went to a waterfall! I got in the shower and just let the water come down on me in a mist. I was drenched from head to toe. I just stood there, under His water, and just allowed it to massage my neck, back, legs, arms, face, head, neck, mind, brain, all over my body, my soul, and my spirit were immersed under this waterfall. Yes, I "Thanked Him". Yes, I showed my gratitude to Him for allowing me to stand up and wash every nook and cranny two times over. I scrubbed and scrubbed, rinsed, and rinsed until I was satisfied that I was clean. I was bathing up in His Grace and Mercy and when He gave me a lotion to put on my skin, I gave it a name. I call it my Divine Devotion. I placed lotion all over me, every toe received its share.

I am reading a newspaper named "The Union Review", The National Baptist Union Review. The March issue has photographs of some prominent, famous, knowledgeable, and influential women. The newspaper was celebrating "Women's History Month". Let me name a few; Kamala Harris, Michele Obama, Shirly Chisolm, Rosa Parks, Cicely Tyson, Hilary Clinton, Harriet Tubman, Oprah Winfrey, Elizabeth Warren. The captain read "Women in Leadership" Setting new standards for Diversity and Equality. It was an interesting read. There is a powerhouse of knowledge located in all the pictures shown. Each one of these women was a high achiever because they had a miracle in their mouth. They placed their sights on the unseen. They believed in themselves and what they can do. They had a dream. They see the future. They see what we are leaving to the children. These women want to see change. These women want to see men, women, boys, and girls not judged by the color of their skin or the texture of their hair but judged by the contents of their hearts.

Let me recommend your subscribing to it. It is a voice that we have. We can speak through written words. That is how the world, you, and I were created. Through words. It is in your Bible. Genesis. He created everything by using a word. He spoke to me, you, and His world into existence by using His tongue. If a man can speak it then He can believe it and become it. You cannot "wait". Time is getting away from you. Words create. Words suggest. Words propose. Words persuade. You write the next paragraph. You write the next sentence. You write your eulogy. There is a miracle in your mouth. Proverbs 18 v:21.

We are traveling fast. Now we are lifting mask mandates. Not me! I am wearing mine. I am not ready. I am going to continue to take precautions. This I must do because I pray and ask Jesus to protect us from all pandemics, disasters, plagues, and turmoil. I am tucked safely in His Everlasting Arms.

I do not have Covid and am not seeking to find Covid. I am grateful for on this day that it is passing by my house. I am so glad to be alive, breathing His fresh air, looking at His green forests, trying to find a pea-green tree, a lime green tree, a money-colored green tree as I smell His Tulips. His Tulips are opening. I have three outside my bedroom window. I love my view. I see His blue spacious skies and sometimes I drift off into a sea of blue, blue skies, blue water, blue snow, blue rain, blue waves on this Wednesday afternoon.

Make sure to set aside some time to hear President Biden speak to Congress. History will be made. Two women. The VP and the speaker. What are women doing? They are slowly changing history with one mind at a time. I know if I lift His Name on High, He will draw all men unto Him. I have a contribution to make. I will tell them that it is the evil spirit of "hate" that is trying to rule in the hearts of man. The first thing we need to do is to call out hate each time it rears His sneaky, sly, cunning, diabolical, ugly head.

We women can't sit still and allow our children, husbands, fathers, princes, princesses, boys, and girls to be consumed by that fire. The fire that is raging in the mind, brain, heart, body, soul, and spirit. Restlessness. We are moving too fast. Our world is turning around the globe faster than the speed of light. Time is winding up. Time is all that you have, and you resent time. When you get a chance, just flop, relax, and realize we are under the ceiling in Heaven, and we have a Savior listening to every word we say. This takes self-discipline. This takes self-control. This takes free will. You possess all three. You choose where you want to spend Eternity. You decide what side of the road you want to be on. You decide what shelter you will dwell in. You decide to go to Paradise or live in Hell. Decision time. Ready to commit. Do it with me, promise Him you will serve Him the rest of your life if you are a human being having a spiritual experience. Plan to move up a little higher because I say I am a spiritual being first having a human experience. I am a new creature in Christ.

We are flesh and it is hard to contain flesh, lusts, deceit, lies, and hate. These evil spirits creep up in your mind, brain, heart, body, soul, and spirit. These evil spirits linger. It is hard to get rid of them because they can justify themselves for being present. Pretty soon – you are agreeing with the devil. Well, everybody else is doing it I might as well do it too. Hasn't your mom ever told you not to follow the crowd? Hasn't your dad told you to remember that you are a man, and you should think before you act? Where are the mamas and papas, we need them? We need them to begin teaching these children when they gather around their knees. If you can kneel then you can hear. If you can kneel then you can listen. If you kneel then you can begin to think. Some of us need to go back and kneel at His feet and let Him teach you like He taught Mary and Martha. It is never too late to pick up your Bible. This is the manual that you have been given. This is the only guide and resource you need to achieve an Everlasting and Eternal Life. John 3 v:16. Jesus Christ, My Lord, and Savior, I adore You, I admire You, I cherish You, I worship You, I honor You, I love You, I idolize You. You are My King of Kings and My Lord of Lords. Look and listen at the Declaration I just made. Declare these words in your heart. You are trying to save your soul and it begins with your mouth. Your tongue is a powerful weapon. Use it against the enemy. Mow Satan down to size. Put Him under your feet. Stomp His head. Stand on your beliefs and principles. Remember what the 23 Psalm said, Thy Art with me. He is good to me. I have to tell it.

I believe we can come together and begin to love each other. I believe that we can come together just like His ducks and plan our strategy. We have an enemy to fight. I believe Jesus will be the conqueror. I believe Jesus will win this fight. Jesus wants to replace those evil spirits that man has in his heart with His Fruits of His Spirit. Galatians 5 v:22. His Fruits are kindness, gentleness, softness, faithfulness, self-control combined with His Love. Move to the front of the line so you can receive a clean heart with a steadfast spirit. David asked for this type of heart. Let's do what David did. Let's ask Jesus to come in, sweep each chamber of our hearts clean. If He finds anything that does not belong here, ask Him to remove it, now, at this present and the precise moment in time. This millisecond. This nanosecond. Please stroke the walls of my heart with your finger of love so you can dwell so You will have a final resting place. I got the strength. You got the stamina. I can plant a seed. You know you reap what you sow. I can see Him. I can hear Him. I can taste Him. I can do all things through

Christ who strengthens me. He is with me, telling me to get something to quench my thirst but I got to keep moving these fingers because revelation and manifestation are coming all through my toes and feet, in my hands and fingers, and my ears. What are you listening to? Do you want to add any more logs to this fire? Everything is possible in Jesus' Name. I should know because I ask my prayer to be answered in Jesus' Name.

Making Jesus the Head of My Life was the best decision I ever made. Putting Jesus first in everything I do and say has become a daily, hourly ritual. His Name is so sweet. Sweeter than a honeycomb. How sweet is that? I only have good thoughts when I say Jesus' Name. I become intrigued and delighted and elated. I know He is answering my prayer at this 7 o'clock hour. I know He will continue to answer my prayer as I go forward to embrace the rest of my adventure today. Oh! Yes. He will make everything alright if you have developed a relationship with Him. Your move! Have you consulted Him at all today? Have you acknowledged His Presence at all today? He is only listening to hear three precious words "Thank You, Jesus".

Acknowledge that He is good to you and know that He will continue to be your guide, protector, comforter, way maker, strength, and joy because you are asking Him too. You are allowing Him to be in control of your circumstances and situation. You are in control of your emotions, and you can choose to be in His Presence. This is what you must do. You must make a choice. Know that you have defeated the devil when you said O Lord, I put all my hope, faith, and trust in Thee.

Chapter 38

Beat that beast into submission. Calm the raging fire that is burning in your soul. You need to catch this Hand. You need to grab a holt. This Hand has dropped the charges. I am free because Jesus had a special Love just for me. He freed me. I got a free heart, a free mind, a free brain, a free body, a free soul, and my sweet, sweet spirit. There is a joy about me, and I just want to share it with you. He saved me. He woke me up. I was asleep. Not now, there is too much to share. You don't have time to give it, your mind, your heart, your brain, your body, your soul, and your spirit rest. Stop! Time out! You say, no, this is not what I want to do. Your reply is No. I will only catch a brief nap. You see where I am you want to be. I am at His knees, biding my case and I am shouting joy, praises to His Holy Name for being so good to me. In case you have figured it out, we are going to church, and I want to take you with me. Up the King's Highway, that is the route that I will be taking, because Jesus, I Love You because You are the first one that ever loved me.

You, Jesus, stayed by my side while I paid the price for not obeying your every command. You only told me to listen and now that I am listening, tell me more. Tell them like it is, tell them it is not a fairytale, there is another life you can live. You are welcomed into His heart. He has time for you but don't wait too long! Time is getting close, Satan is about to reveal Himself if we, me, you, don't put a stop to it once and for all.

Begin to love yourself. Begin to accept yourself, get some peace and while you are doing that, get you some concentration and will it to be your way. Will your life to change. I will not stop believing that it was My God, My Jesus, My Lord and Savior who touched me with His finger of Love and allowed me to become a living soul all over again ready, yes ready to praise, honor, worship, cherish and salute Him for being so good to me. I will not stop believing that He loves me, and He wants to see me prosper in everything that I attempt to do. He is a deliverer this morning. He delivered me from the snare of the fowler because I exalt His Name on high. Do not give Satan, Lucifer, the devil, the enemy time to creep in your mind, heart, body, soul, and spirit and make you detour your thinking. Jesus is the greatest! He is mighty! He is wonderful! So, push these thoughts through your mind, body, soul, and spirit. Depend on the One that is holding your hand. He is holding my hand. We are hand in hand! And how is that? Because I believe. I trust. I hope. He is cradling me in His Everlasting Arms ever so gently and kindly. There is nothing like this kind of Love.

I was created to be a winner on this magnificent and marvelous, fabulous, and fantastic Thursday morning at this 10 o'clock hour. I am going to praise Him. I will begin on a small scale and then work my way up to His ladder that He has laid out for me to climb. Thank You Lord for my bed, pillow, and the ability to slumber and sleep in Your Presence. Thank You, Lord, for watching over me. Thank You, Lord, for extending Your Righteous Right Hand out to me. Once I opened my eyes, I realized I was surrounded by Your Unchanging, Your Unconditional, Your Unfailing Love, Your Grace and Mercy, and Your Divine Devotion. Am I glad? Am I elated? Am I thrilled? Am I satisfied? Yes! I am. I know who loves me. I know who is considerate, compassionate, and tolerant of me and my behavior. Ask me has He been good to me? Yes! He has. He has been good, mighty good to me.

When I opened my eyes to go into my happy space to do what I needed to do, I sang my song. "Thank You, Jesus" in and on the way out. He is so good to me. He held my hand the entire time. He aided me and guided me back to reclaim my spot. My head was buried in His chest, being cradled in His Everlasting Arms on a morning that I have never seen before. He did it again. He raised me from the dead. He allowed me to come alive in my senses and begin to "think". Who made all this possible? Who is leading me? I am following Jesus. I will listen. I will say what you tell me to say. I will do what you tell me because I trust, believe, and have faith in the unseen. I know He is able. He has proven Himself to me over and over, again and again and I am grateful that He chose me to be the recipient of His peace, patience, contentment, harmony, tranquility, and serenity. Where am I? on such a marvelous occasion as a new day.

When I opened my eyes, I immediately went to my Source of Strength, my joy, my way maker, the author and finisher of my fate, and sought to find His Love and His courage He wants to extend to me. After I finished up in my happy space, I pulled the covers up close to my neck and began talking. O Lord please come into my presence and O Lord please allow me into Your Presence. I pulled the covers tighter because I was so content and comfortable. I knew He had heard my prayer, so I continued talking. I ask O Lord please shelter us, O Lord please shadow us, O Lord please favor us, O Lord please grant us Your Grace and Mercy, O Lord please strengthen us physically, mentally, emotionally, psychologically, morally and spiritually, O Lord please forgive us of our sins because we don't always do things perfectly and correctly, O Lord please forgive our enemies because they know not what they do, O Lord please protect us from all plagues, pandemics, disasters, and turmoil, O Lord please prosper us physically, materialistically, financially and spiritually, O Lord please do not cast us away from Your Presence and O Lord please allow Your Holy Spirit to dwell in us again on this day. In Jesus' Name, I Pray - Amen. I know I am in His Presence.

This prayer, this confession, this affirmation, this mantra has saved my life. I have come this close to communicating with Heaven and I am not going to stop now. These words are my source of strength. He is keeping me alive for a reason. My destiny and purpose are about to meet. You can be victorious with the words that you allow to meditate in your heart. The words meditating in your heart will save your life. These words will add new meaning to your life. These words will renew your strength and uplift your spirits because you and I are communicating with Our Savior.

Once again, we are alive. Once again, He has raised me and you from the dead. You and I are going to see the world through the eyes of God. When I look at myself in the mirror, sure I see flesh and bone, but I also see a child of a King, one of God's children, and one of His sheep in His pasture. He promised in Psalm 23, that He is my shepherd, and He will take good care of me. Want to know how I know? I tried Him. I change the words meditating in my heart. I will defeat the devil at His own game. I will exalt the Name of Jesus. I will exalt His Name of High. I give Him all my honor, my praise, my glory, and my love because He is worthy to be praised. He saved my life. He gave me a new life to live in the Presence of a King.

I have a new mind, a new heart, a new brain, a new body, a new soul, and a new spirit because I asked that He return day after day to satisfy me with His morning mercy. Psalm 90 v:14. I am to let His morning mercy and love last me throughout my entire day. I see His sun shining. I see His trees standing still, at ease, waiting for the next time they get a chance to "hallow" His Name. There is a lesson here for mankind. Wait! Wait on Him. He is there. Here is here and everywhere. He is just a breath away from you, you can call on Him whenever you want to and wherever you want to. He is always close to you. He is to me. Want to know how I know? I just sit back, relax, and say I am glad to be in His Presence one more time. This feeling of comfort, joy, peace, and pleasure overwhelms me. Let's praise Him. He is worthy to be praised. Thank You, Lord, for breathing Your breath of life into my lifeless body and giving me one more chance to praise you, honor you, salute you, worship you, and cherish you just for being so good to me. I am inhaling and exhaling your air in and out of my lungs. My heart is beating at its normal rhythm. You! O, Lord! Made it all possible. I will trust you all the days of my life because when I recited Your 23rd Psalm, you made me remember that "Thy Art With Me". You let me know that you were watching over me while I sipped on my cup of delicious brew that I prepared with my own hands. You are the One who gave me the wisdom and knowledge and understanding that I needed to complete my morning routine.

It was early in the morning when He picked me up and placed my feet on solid ground. It was early in the morning when He whispered these words into my ear, "wake up O sleepyhead" rise from the dead and let the Lord shine on you. I wanted to. Yes! It was a delight and pleasure for me to rise again knowing that He is looking out for me. Knowing that He was there to take good care of me. I had no qualms about turning over, placing my two feet on His floor, and do what He allowed me to do. I was blessed early in the wee hours of dawn. You were too! I can make you recall just how blessed you are! You were permitted to flush your kidneys and excrete your bowels. He was waiting for you to show Him your gratitude for allowing your body to function properly. Say "Hallelujah". Glorify, magnify, and salute Him for being so good to you. Man, woman, boy, and girl, stop and just "think".

Do not allow Satan to continue to keep blinders on your eyes. Do not allow Satan to control your thoughts. You have free will, you have self-control. You have self-discipline. Tell Satan, tell the devil, tell the enemy, tell Lucifer that you are not going to take it anymore. Tell Him that you have changed your address. Tell Him that He cannot live in your heart anymore. It is a new day. It is a new beginning. Now is the time for you to sift through fiction and facts. Do you know who woke you up this morning? Are you praising Him? Are you talking to Him? Are you telling Him how grateful you are to be alive? Do not give the devil time to come into your thoughts and ideas. Shut the door. Keep Him out. Exalt the Name of Jesus on High. Know where your help and strength come from. I know who allowed me to be closed in my right mind with a reasonable portion of my health and strength. Nobody but Jesus. Nobody but Jesus. Jesus came to my rescue. He reinvented me. He recreated me.

He is proud of my accomplishments and wants me to continue spreading my message of love, hope, and peace. I only want to go higher. It is Jesus who empowers me with words of encouragement and inspiration. There is never a dull moment when you are being guided through the power of the Almighty. It is just me and Him. It is just He and I. It is just us "two". His yoke is easy. I am on one side, and He is on the other side. Oh, Lord! Guide my tongue, my heart, my brain, my mind, my body, my soul, and my spirit. You are the Ruler of my universe! I believe in Your miracles. You came, saw, and sought the ones who you knew would make a difference. Women! Are you ready for some justice, some equality, some honesty, some truth, some guidance on this morning?

Thank You for coming into my world. Thank You for coming into the world of the Land of the Living. There is another world out there waiting on you. You can embrace what He has in His plans for you. It will never be a journey, a chore, or just something to do, it will be an adventure because you are trusting in the Almighty because He has a plan for your life. You are told to come alive, pull off those old clothes, and put on some new clothes. Let us embrace each other's opinions of where they see themselves on this brand new day. I will tell you what is meditating in my heart. Got time to listen?

I will never burn out of words to say. I know I am holding on to the Hem of His garment and He is leading the way. I place all my trust, belief, hope, and faith in Thee. Each morning I open my eyes, I become "grateful" that I have another chance to get it right. I am going to stay on the battlefield. My prayers and my affirmations have resulted in my being a success. He hears my prayer. He comes to see about me and when He does come, He takes real good care of me. Psalm 23. The Lord is My Shepherd, I shall not want. I open my heart to you and ask you to fill it with Your Love and Admiration.

This same Love and Affection that He gives to me I want to share with you, my brothers and sisters in the North, East, South, and West. I have a love for you, me, him, her, she, he, them, and they. Have I included everyone? This is what He wants, He wants us to come together as a nation and begin to focus our attention on the One that created Heaven and Earth. I will write. I will teach. I will preach. I will lecture. I will tell it from my point of view. My opinion matters. Your opinion matters. You are important! You are special! You are His Shining Star in His Eyesight! He has His Eyes on you and me at the same time.

Aren't we special and important to the One that created us? I am. He listens to me. I talk with Him. He hears me. He answers me. I am sticking close to His chest because He has brought me a long way. A mighty long way. Today, right at this moment in time, He is still in the Blessing Business. He can bless you and me at the same time.

Isn't He wonderful? Yep! He is Awesome. Tell Bryan Popin those words. They will only inspire Him to go deeper into His Secret Place, His Shelter, into His Presence. As I praise Him, I build my fire. Do you want me to add another log to the fire?

Psalm 145 says, "The eyes of all wait upon Thee". O, Lord! I pray to Thee from whom all blessings flow that you would open the eyes and hearts of man to be able to see the self-worth that you have placed in them. Man needs to know that He has a Savior who accepts him, needs him, appreciates him, admires him, adores him, cherishes him, and idolizes him. Like a bolt of lightning, He wants man to know that He is loved and protected from all hurt, harm, and danger. Man needs to know that He has a Savior who will provide all His needs. Man needs to know that Jesus Christ will enter the hearts of man and allow His Holy Spirit to become his counselor and comforter.

Do you believe these words? Do you firmly affirm that this is the truth then put on the full armor of God? Put on His breastplate of righteousness, turn from their wicked and corrupt ways and seek to find God's favors. I am blessed and highly favored and so are you on this glorious and gorgeous day that Our Lord has created for us. Psalm 118 v:24, tells you what to do when you have received a gift of a new day. He orders us to enjoy it, rejoice it, magnify it, glorify it, celebrate it and be thankful for everything in it. This is an order given to us by our King. Can you follow orders? Read this passage of scripture for yourself and let the words fly off the page and enter your consciousness. Wake up and do what Our Lord has instructed you to do. He said Live! Come alive in your senses and begin to "think".

Know the One who shelters you in the time of a storm. Know the One that set you free! Know the One that permitted you to live again. It was Jesus! He is the Light of The World. Try calling on that Name! Try it! Make it tender and sweet. Find comfort in that word. Find joy, pleasure, and jubilation as you begin to follow His instructions. "Love each other" as I Love You". Tell each other, show each other. Be patient with each other. Wait! Let them catch up to you. He is leading. I am just a follower. I do as I am told. I listen to make sure I hear it right.

Our Lord will open His hand and satisfy the desire of every living thing. Psalm 145 v:15-16. When I say my affirmations, Our Lord and Savior open His Hand and distribute to me my daily bread. I know who I confided in early in the morning hours when I saturated His atmosphere with words of praise and worship. "Thank You, Jesus" for one more opportunity to come alive in my senses so I can "think and process thought". The ability to "think and process thought" has been stripped away from you. Satan tells you what to think, what to say and how to think and act. Remove those chains. Remove those shackles. There is a new way of thinking.

I want the best and I will do what is necessary to have an abundant and Everlasting Life. Your old way of doing things has not brought you wealth, fame, and success. Toss those habits away. Toss them out of the window and put on some new clothes.

Ephesians 4 v:22-24 reads, put off the former ideas of the old man, his mind is corrupt and wicked and deceitful, be renewed in your mind, put on the new man with his new ideas, beliefs, opinions, traditions, dreams and desires that will seek God and His righteousness and true holiness.

Do you love the Lord on this morning? Tell Him! He is waiting to hear the words that are meditating in your heart. You want to talk to your Creator, the One that formed you before you were in your mother's womb and thank Him for giving you a Savior. Yes! I want everlasting life. Yes! I want eternal life. I want to live every day as if it is my last because I don't know. If I draw nearer to Him, then He will draw nearer to me. I want to keep my hand in His Hand. I want Him to hold my hand and lead me on the adventures that He has planned for my life.

Let me shout from the mountain top that Jesus loves me, and Jesus loves you. We need to join forces with our brothers and sisters in the North, East, South, and West and tell them "I want to love you just like Jesus loves you. Talk about turning some heads. Talking about shifting the words in the atmosphere. Let's you and I talk about how good He is to me and you. Jesus is my help. Jesus is the One waiting to douse me with buckets of His Love and Devotion at my every twist and turn. When I opened the door to my happy space, I had everything I would need to cleanse and clothe my body. Let me start small in honoring Him. Let me praise Him for being my constant companion, my overseer, my healer, my provider, my protector. Without Him, I can do nothing. Nothing. I trust Him. I believe Him. I have faith that He will order my steps, orchestrate my thoughts and opinions into complete sentences that I can use for thought. Do you understand my translation? I am getting my thoughts from the Source. I went there. I kneeled at His feet again this morning. I cast all my cares on Him because He favored me with a brand new beginning on this mild summer-like day.

There is nobody like Jesus. Again, I say it, "there is nobody like Jesus". He woke me up this morning and said to me. "I will love you always" and then He repeated himself and said, "I will always love you". How much freedom do I have? I have the freedom to discover all the love that He has for me. He loved me so - that he provided me with a bed and pillow to lay my head when I laid down to sleep. I have to say it again "He watched over me while I slumbered and slept and when I opened my eyes, He was thereby my side allowing me to wake up in His Presence.

Isn't He wonderful? Isn't He magnificent? Isn't He marvelous? Isn't He spectacular? Yes! He is wonderful to me. I can't live my life without Him. Making Jesus the Head of My Life was the best decision I ever could have made. Putting Jesus first has opened doorways, avenues, freeways, and byways for me to travel. I can never know what He will do next. I am just confident that He has a plan, and He knows the plan.

This is the knowledge, wisdom, and understanding that He has allotted for me. You must plug in and get your very own personal, private, and intimate relationship so you can hear Him when He speaks to you. You are not a finished work because you have a job to do. You have a purpose and a reason for being alive. Knock, seek and you shall find. Ask Him! I can only tell you about me and what He has allowed me to accomplish. I have found what works well for me. If I remain in Him, then He will remain in Him. He is the first one that I think about! He is the first One that I honor when He allows me to complete any task that I begin. Hurry, you have work to do. God, Jesus, My Lord, and Savior has shown me the way and I have work to do. Every day I will write. Every day I will forecast my future. Every day I will write my own eulogy. He is not finished with me yet. There is so much to say. There is so much to do. I pray that I am given the time I need to make Him proud of me.

Save a soul for Christ! This is my job. I take it very seriously. I have been chosen and I am proud to be a member of God's Household. He takes good care of His own. He will never see the righteous forsaken. Oh! How He loves me. Oh! How He loves me on a Thursday morning, April 29th, 2021, here at Gene Miller Manor in Christian City in Union City, Georgia. His love and protection come with joy and pleasure. I am His. I belong to Him. I will wait upon Him. He knows the direction that this ship should set sail in. He tells me what to say and how to say it.

There is no one like Our Beautiful Savior. There is no one like Our God. He is directing my path and is giving me my daily bread if I "hallow" His Name. It is just that simple. Replace all those negative and destructive thoughts with His peace that He wants to give you. It is time to "shut up" and stop talking. It is time to allow His gentle and kind voice to penetrate your heart and fill it with peace and contentment now that you know who the Giver of Life is. Oh, Lord! I give You all my praise, worship, glory, and love for being so good to me. You have provided for me everything I would need on a day-to-day basis. Hour by hour you give me your love and devotion. Yes! I am grateful.

Let me witness for you. He will shower you with His Unfailing Love, His Unconditional Love, His Grace and Mercy, and His Divine Devotion all day, every day, 24/7, around the clock - every hour - every minute - every second and right at this present and the precise moment in time. Yes! He is leading the way. I am in His Presence and there is no one like Our Lord. He saw me. He found me. He asked if I wanted another chance. I bowed my head and said "yes" Lord. Then He said, "you, you who are worn, weary, tired, torn, and heavy laden, come and go with me and I will give you rest." I went. Yes! I got in the boat and took my seat. I am just so glad that I was raised from the dead. I was saved before I got to my grave. He gave me a new life to live in the Presence of a King.

I want more glorious days. I want more days so I can glorify Him for being so good to me. He pushed back all the dirt and debris that was keeping me from living my life the way He had intended for me. He allowed me to come alive, breathe and look around at His wonderful creation for my eyes only. I see a piece of rock sitting in the middle of a lake, on this rock, there are trees, bushes. The water is clear blue and if I were sitting on this rock, I would be forever content and filled with joy and jubilation because I see the beauty that He has for me. His Peace! This is what He wants to give to you! His Peace! His Love! His Devotion! His Grace and Mercy! It is His signs and wonders.

I stare at this picture each time I sit at the welcome table to enjoy my coffee, water, banana, and meds. This picture blankets me with peace and contentment and patience. Knowing that I can escape to His island makes my coffee taste so good.

When I sat down to the Welcome Table in the Presence of a King, I thanked Him. I said my "grace". I know all of this is made possible by My Lord and Savior Jesus Christ and I honor Him. "Thank You, Jesus". Honor, worship, praise, obey the One who made it all possible.

He is waiting! He wants to know what the words are meditating in your heart. Are you grateful? Are you thankful? Tell Him! Worship Him. Salute Him. Glorify Him. Lift His Name on High. Sing with His Angels. They are saluting their King. Join me as I salute My King. Jesus is looking at me through God's eyes. He sees what God has created! He created something great, superb, and magnificent when He created you and me. We have been sat apart from the rest and given specific instructions and what to do, how to act, and what to think. There was a plan devised for you and me. Jeremiah 29 v:11. A plan to prosper us and not harm us, a plan to give us hope for our future.

You have only one obligation and that is to "love" yourself first. Before you can love anyone else you must first love yourself and realize there is more for you to achieve, accomplish and obtain.

Once you begin to love yourself, He will give you the peace that you are seeking. This is what He has for each one of His human beings. Peace as they graze. Peace as they glide. Peace as they float. Peace as they coast from one world to another one. Oh! It can be done. Know that somewhere out there, over yonder at the Great Beyond is Peace. Come unto Me and I will give you rest. You can rest now you are safe in His Everlasting Arms, the Arms that were holding you at the time of your birth. That Unconditional Love – That Grace and Mercy – That Divine Devotion that He gave to your mom and dad is the Same Love He wants to give you today.

If it was good enough for mamma and daddy, then it is good enough for me. I trust. I believe. I have faith. I will be lounging and reclining on the coast of Georgia this weekend. Like a little family reunion. Everybody is coming! All our loved ones and friends will get a chance to mix, mingle and elbow hug. Pray for us. Remember us in your prayers. I am not selfish; I pray for all of us. You, me, him, her, she, he, them, and they. We are all sheep. He is watching over you just like He is watching over me. I Love Him for being able to love each one of us at the same time.

You do know you are loved – right? You must know that you are cherished, admired, and adored by Our Lord and Savior Jesus Christ. He just wants some recognition for giving you everything your little heart ever desired. That was a total joy, happiness, and satisfaction because He is showing me just how much He loves me.

I need to know how He loves me! His spring-like breeze is flowing through the air. I have a chilled bottle of His water that He allowed to escape from His rivers, mountains, rocks, creeks, brooks, and streams into a bottle just the right size for my hand to hold. Isn't He wonderful? Isn't He magnificent? It is remarkable how He has thought of everything. He reassures me that He loves me because we are attached at the hip. His heart is made from gold, and He wants you to have the same kind of heart He has.

His heart is filled with love, kindness, softness, justice, honesty, truth, salvation, redemption, equality, and righteousness. He has declared these words "Peace on Earth, Goodwill Toward All Men". He only wants you to have His Peace. He wants you to experience it within the four chambers of your heart. He wants to cradle you and me in His Everlasting Arms so we can be safe and secure only if we believe, trust, and have faith in the unseen.

Can't you see His Kingdom being unfolded? Can't you see the handwriting on the wall? The time is near. You, me, she, him, her, he, them, and they must get ready for that "Great Day". A day where we will be free to worship Him all day, every day, 24/7, around the clock - every hour - every minute - every second and right at this present moment in time. I am waiting on the Lord because I have my eyes glued to Heaven. I am looking up, outward, and around so I can get a glimpse of My Savior.

This can happen if you and I spread the word. Jesus saves. Jesus is magnificent and marvelous because He woke me up this morning! I am going to praise His Name. I will do more than praise Him, I will worship Him, honor Him, salute Him, and cherish Him for being so good to me. It is a joy and pleasure to be alive - don't you agree?

Chapter 39

Ready for church? I am! I must share with you that Jesus is my everything. Jesus is my closest friend. Jesus is my constant companion. Jesus and I are "together" so count us as one. It is Monday morning, tornado watch, lots of rain and wind, we must be obedient and realize the Lord is doing His work. He is busy at work making you aware of His Presence. We honor, respect, adore and admire Him for keeping us safe through all pandemics, plagues, disasters, and turmoil. Don't we? Yes! We do. I will answer you because I know what He has done for me. He gave me a life to live in the Presence of a King. Caution! Enter His Presence with praise and Thanksgiving. Get ready for a second sermon. After three days of not writing, there is a lot for me to say. I am back home again, alone and in His Presence.

He wants to have His way with me, and I have no objections because where He leads me, I will follow, and what He tells me to say, then I will tell it. After all, I know it will showcase His Love, Grace, and Mercy. We will glorify Him together. I will open the doorway. A little bit of your time. You have so much time on your hand, then follow me as I am back home again. I am in the room where Jesus and I live. This is an everyday occurrence. I never go anywhere without my constant companion. Joshua 1 v:9, says, "I will go with you wherever you go, be filled with gratitude and courage. I adore Him. The baby that lay in a manger that had nowhere to lay His Head. I will honor You and worship You as the Giver of Life. He is My Sustainer.

Oh Jesus! Oh Jesus! You are so good to me. You gave me Your Peace, Happiness, and Love throughout my vacation days at Jekyll Island and St. Simon Island located on the coast of Georgia. A lot of family love was shared by all. We were caring, giving, and sharing each time we were together. We were a family. It was a group of 17, and we celebrated some of our family members' accomplishments and achievements through the Year 2020. The Year 2020 and 2021 has been good for us. Aishah Hayes, my daughter had the idea for us to share by asking us "what are we looking forward to". We shared some of the upcoming events in our lives that we were looking forward to. Everybody participated. We stop and pay honor and tribute for His sheep who has now embraced being over there, over yonder at the Great Beyond.

He is showering me and you with His Unconditional Love, His Unconditional Love and His Faithful Love, His Grace and Mercy, and His Divine Devotion all over our shoulders at this present and the precise moment in time. This is what He did for all 17 of us. We loved every minute of the most beautiful memories one can behold. Love was shared by all of us. We showed each other that we do mean it. "I Love You" was my famous echo. I was telling them the words that were residing in my heart.

We began our adventure on Friday morning. His Holy Spirit awakens me at the right time. I began to say "Thank You Jesus" when I opened my eyes. I trotted off to my happy space and finished up so I could reclaim my spot so I could continue to give Him praise and honor. This is what I did. I began to pray. After I finished asking Him to please come into my presence and O Lord please allow me into Your Presence, I was told, "Bright eyes" go and have a nice time. After I heard these words, I had confidence that everything would be alright". Love, Peace, and Happiness were waiting on me. I received a lot of hugs, kisses, well wishes, gratitude, and honor. I am getting some of my flowers while I am living. Memories!

I remember going to the beach. I had to walk almost a mile to get to the destination. Guess what! I did it. I took rest breaks on the way, but I had a destination in mind and Jesus was holding my Hand as He allowed His Holy Spirit to be my guide. I had His Love. He had His eyes on me. I had His Peace because this was what I had decided to do. I had His happiness because I was grateful for everything that He had allowed me to do. Isn't He magnificent? Isn't He marvelous? Isn't He magnificent? I believe so. I believe He is because He sure is good to me.

When I turned on the computer, I had several emails that needed my attention. After I had read, deleted, and spammed what I did not need to see anymore, the screen moved to a mountain of rocks. His rocks were covered in green - all different colors of green. There are so many. I will be green for wisdom, knowledge, endurance, understanding, and dedication. This is what I have this morning. I will be a brown rock surrounded by weeds, bushes, moss, and grass, all living things. There are so many ways you can come back. You can come back as a flower, insect, bug, animal, tree, shrub, bush, or weed. Our ancestors are here. They are covered in mountains of rocks, dirt, and sand. They are living things.

I am a tree planted by a river and the Bible says that He satisfies the desire of every living thing. Psalm 145. It was apparent in the picture on the screen. There were people on an island living in peace and harmony, somewhere in the Land. These people are getting what they need and want. They want His Love, peace, and happiness and it appears that they have it all on an island surrounded by water. These people are happy and are spreading God's Love and Tender Devotion. These people have been established to have everything they need because they know they are under His watchful eye.

Do you know who has His eyes on you? He showed me row after row of a green forest. So, I took a deep breath and took the entire view into my memory bank and in my heart. You can rest assured that there are sheep in His Pasture, and He is taking good care of them. This is what He wants to do for you and me. He wants you to be happy, content, joyous, full of happiness, love, and cheer. This is what He gave me on my four-day adventure. I am still celebrating. I am all alone now and I can show Him and tell Him how grateful I am for watching over all of us. He placed love in our hearts for each other. Love! Love! You can never get enough. My God! My Jesus! showered us with buckets and buckets of love to share. This is what we decided to do, and I find myself in His Presence on this rainy, cloudy, gray day. It is a day that Our Lord has given us, and we are to rejoice in it.

Psalm 118 v:24 tells you what to do when you open your eyes on a morning that you have never seen before. Rejoice! Enjoy! Glorify! Celebrate it all day, every day, 24/7, around the clock, every hour, every minute, every second, and right at this present moment in time I am happy, content, satisfied, and overwhelmed with joy because He favored me with a brand new day. Jesus made the decision that I could come alive and be closed in my right mind with a reasonable portion of my health and strength on this magnificent, marvelous, splendid, and supreme Monday morning.

I am glad that I am alive to witness to you just how good He is to me.

Jesus gave me the desires of my heart. We all said our prayers before we entered the vehicles. Once we were seated comfortably, we went into prayer. We recited prayers each time at the dinner setting. My second oldest son, Nate, led us into prayer. We all agreed that Our Lord and Savior head heard our prayers and we said "Amen" with a hand clap for Praise.

It is Monday morning and I greet you with a Smile because Our Lord and Savior has smiled on me this morning when He touched me with His finger of love and told me "Wake up O sleepyhead" rise from the dead and let the Lord shine on you. I had to readjust to my surroundings. I was at home safely and securely in the Presence of a King. So, my morning got started. I said my affirmations, just like I do every morning I open my eyes. I said, O Lord please come into my presence and O Lord please allow me into Your Presence. I saturated His atmosphere with words of praise, tribute, and song.

When I was nestled in my spot, I had a smile in my heart because He was there. He was present in my mind, brain, heart, body, soul, and spirit so I continued speaking. I said, O Lord please shadow us, O Lord please shelter us, O Lord please favor us, O Lord please cover us with Your Blood, O Lord please grant us Your Grace and Mercy, O Lord please strengthen us physically, mentally, emotionally, psychologically, morally, and spiritually, O Lord please forgive us of our sins because we don't always do things perfectly and correctly Lord please forgive our enemies because they know not what they do, O Lord please prosper us physically, materialistically, financially, and spiritually, O Lord please protect us from all plagues, pandemics, disasters, and turmoil, O Lord please do not cast us away from Your Presence and O Lord please allow Your Holy Spirit to dwell in us again on this day. In Jesus' Name, I Pray - Amen.

I gain so much peace and comfort after I have saluted the One who is in charge of me. Oh! He is able. He can bring us together as a family and allow us to love each other. He followed each of us around because we were in His shadow. He has His eyes on me as I went to the office to deliver my rent check and to check the mail. I was prepared, I took a bag with me so I could carry it all and not be dropping it from my hands. Love, Peace, and Happiness are what He will give you if you believe, trust, and have faith that He is watching over you.

Courage! Confidence! Faithfulness! Salvation! Redemption! Truth! Honesty! Justice! Peace! Love! Righteousness! This is what Jesus is giving to me and He wants to give you the same but first He wants to hear you declare Him as Your King. He wants to hear words of glorification coming from your heart and lips. He wants to know if you are eternally grateful for His Love, Affection, and Admiration. O, Lord! You are the greatest. There is no one like You, Jesus. No one will love me, accept me, adore me, admire me, cherish me, and idolize me but You, Jesus. He will love you in the same manner. I am grateful for Your Unfailing Love, Your Unchanging Love, Your Unconditional Love, Your Grace and Mercy, and Your Divine Devotion. Aren't you?

It is me this morning invading your space. Thank you for allowing me a small amount of time to preach, teach and lecture on my relationship with "Jesus Christ." Jesus Christ is my Lord and Savior and I owe Him all the honor, praise, worship, love, and glory. He is the One who is allowing my heart to meditate on His goodness for me and my seventeen seeds that has my blood running through their veins. Each of us felt the love that was being circulated. Each of us had a "good time" this past Friday, Saturday, and Sunday.

I praised Him, I honored Him for allowing me to complete my morning routine and embrace the adventure that He had planned for me after the storms had passed. During the storm, I was reclining in my happy space, and I was praying. I was talking to my Savior, asking Him to please keep me safe and to have mercy on all His sheep in His Pasture. I am so glad that He came to see about me. He touched me early and satisfied me with His Morning Mercy and Love and told me to allow it to last me all during the day. Psalm 90 v:14. I did just this and attached His 23rd Psalm to my heart, mind, lips, and brain. Off I went with His assurance that He would take good care of me on this Monday morning just like He did over the weekend. It was nice.

I was reclining at the beach in a lawn chair. Our family members were grouped enjoying the sun, water, the children playing games, the dogs running around in the sand. They did not like the sand, so they sat on the end of the lawn chairs. We enjoyed running in the water, then coming out, back and forth they went. I enjoyed His sunshine shining on my brown skin. I pointed out to the other grandmother, Alberta Daniels, that I saw waves in the water, and it was glistening like diamonds under the sunlight, and she said, "I do". We were both mesmerized as to His goodness. As we lay and play on the beach, He had His eyes on all of us. How do I know this? Because I said my prayers, my affirmations each morning I opened my eyes and I asked the question, "have you sent up a praise for a brand new day" I had, and I found a way to get them to praise the Lord.

When I arrived home, I got settled in and I turned on some music and got a chilled beverage from the fridge and just meditated, prayed, and showed Him how grateful to Him that I had gone on vacation and returned home safely. Indeed! He deserved some on my time. So, I sat quietly in His Everlasting Arms as I had memories galore. My most intense memory is that He took good care of us. He told me to "go and have a nice time". This is what I did. This is what I am doing on my marvelous, magnificent, splendid, and superb Monday morning in His Presence. I am having a happy day. He is present and is watching over me while I tell you what is meditating in my heart.

It feels wonderful to be in the presence of the Lord! It feels comforting to know that He is with me. Psalm 23 says this "Thy art with me". He was with me this past weekend, and He is with me on this glorious, rainy, gorgeous semi-cloudy day.

My 15-year-old grandson, Bryce Elijah Williams Young, drove the car for about four hours on Interstate 16, 95, and 75. He is a good driver. While I was riding, I filled the car with lively conversations, and I read one of my daughter's books. I had confidence and courage that Jesus was watching over Bryce, the driver, my daughter, Aishah, and myself. The Lord gave me peace and patience to know that He had everything under control. He is a "Good God". He is a "Faithful God". He will keep His Promises. His Psalm 23 tells me that "Surely His goodness and mercy shall follow me all of the days of my life if I dwell in His shadow, His secret place and in His Presence.

It is with peace, love, and happiness that I want to give to you. He is empowering me with only a portion of His wisdom, knowledge, and understanding. That is how He does things. If you speak it, then you can achieve it. I want to keep adding logs to this fire that He is stirring up on the inside of me. I have 74 years of thought pinned into my soul and it is hard to stop once I get started. You see! He made it all possible. He is the One that gave me a new beginning, a new start, a new identity, a new birth, and a new mind.

He is the One that told me to pull off my old clothes and put on my new clothes. He buried my old clothes and gave me hope for my future. He said He would never leave me nor forsake me. Hebrews 13 v:5. I believe in His Promises. We love each other. He knows my name and I know His Name. I know what He has done for me. I know what He is doing for me at this present and the precise moment in time. I am looking at a Canadian Sunset. His yellows and reds are so bright. He knows how to light up His sky and He knows what He wants His sheep to explain to the world.

He is keeping me alive for a reason. There is no one like Our Lord. The song says He is stronger than strong and greater than great. He is an "Awesome God". He is "mighty". He is "great". He is "just plain old wonderful". He is the way maker. He is my strength and joy. He is the One that gives me His Perfect Peace so I can sit here and honestly share my thoughts with you. Oh! To me, He is great. Today! I am overwhelmed with His Goodness and Mercy. If I remain in Him, then He will remain in me. I recited His Psalm 23 around the clock, 24/7. This was my way of keeping a Divine connection open. I was talking to the One who made it all possible.

My Lord and Savior, Jesus Christ. If it had not been for Him, where would I be, what would I be thinking and what would I be doing? I have no idea but I am closed in my right mind with a reasonable portion of my health and strength and I know how to bow in submission to the One that blew His breath of life into my lifeless body and allowed me to become a living soul all over again so I can "think and "process thought". Isn't He magnificent? Isn't He magical? Isn't He majestic? Isn't He miraculous?

Yes, He is! He is miraculous to me! He has given me 74 years of His love, His Peace, and His Happiness and I want to continue to preach about His love, hope, and peace. Oh! It is available for you and me. He wants to love you just like He loves me, her, she, him, he, them, and they. He can do this because He has so much love to share with all His sheep in His Pasture if they would only allow Him to.

We have developed this beautiful relationship. It is me and Him. It is He and I. It is just us "two". He is my constant companion, and I cannot count the many blessings that He has given me. I have a reserve. He is releasing His blessings to me as He sees fit. I can wait. I do not want to rush Him. I can patiently wait for Him to love on me today and tomorrow. I will enjoy the love and devotion that He is giving me on this day. I will continue to praise Him, honor Him, worship Him, cherish Him, adore Him, admire Him, and idolize Him because He taught me to be still and receive what He wants to give me.

He is giving me His Love and I cannot ask for anything else because He dumps buckets of His Love over me at my every twist and turn. It is a limited amount of wisdom and knowledge. Take it slow and take it all in. It is a new day that you have never seen before. You are alive! You are not in your grave! It is time for you to glorify Him for being so good to you. He woke you early in the morning hours and you should rejoice in the fact that you have been given another opportunity to get it right.

One more time I get a chance to honor, worship, and praise His Name. If I abide in Him, then He will abide in me. Jesus is my solid Rock and on Him, I am leaning. In the time of rain, sun, tornadoes, cyclones, hurricanes in my life I know who I can depend on. I know who to call on. I know how to go to the Source of all my hope, peace, love, inspiration, and encouragement. If I draw nearer to Him, then He will draw nearer to me. He wants to satisfy the heart and the desire of every living thing. Psalm 145 v:15 - 16.

Quiet down! Quiet your thoughts! You can do this. You have willpower. You have self-discipline. You have self-control. You have free will. Soft lightening and instrumental music, candle, wine, and champagne. Set the tone. Set the stage because you are about to enter the most important relationship in your life. You are about to enter His Presence. Alone time is what you need. Quiet your surroundings. This is an important time for you. It will be just the "two of you". You and Him. You and Him. Enter His Presence with Praise and Thanksgiving. Establish a connection. Saturate His atmosphere with words of praise and admiration. You want Him to enter Your Presence and you want Him to allow you into His Presence. Remember "I can do all things through Christ who strengthens me." Now begin your conversation. Know that He will pull up a seat right beside you. Let Him tickle you by bowing your head, look into your heart and pull out pride, joy, happiness, and love and realize that you know who gave it to you.

His smile, His Love will drape itself all over your shoulders because He loves you with all His heart.

Don't you know that He loves you? He loves me at this 3 o'clock sacred hour. Any time you spend in His Presence is sacred time. You are needed, accepted, wanted, appreciated, admired, adored, cherished, and idolize by a King. Remember that you are somebody. Remember that you are important. Remember that we are all sheep in His Pasture, and He wants to take good care of each one of us. He can do this if you allow Him to. Become consciously aware of who you are and who you are. I am a child of a King. I am one of God's children. I am one of His sheep in His Pasture. I belong where He has placed me. I am in a soft meadow, and He is shining His bright light on me. He is the author and finisher of my fate. He determines what I say, what I do, and how I behave. I am totally under His control. I released the reigns I had over my life a long time ago so His will could be done.

Yes! I am satisfied with what He has allowed me to achieve and accomplish. My mission is to save somebody's soul for Christ. I am to tell you who saved my soul. I am to show you that there is another life you can live. I am to convince you that you can live your life in the Presence of a King if you will just listen, honor, and obey.

Open your Bibles and read Matthew 11 v:28 and it says, "You, yes you, you are the one who is weary, worn, torn, scared and confused, come and go with me and I will give you rest." He has assured me that I can "Rest Now" because His yoke is easy. He is on one side, and I am on the other side. We are hand in hand. He is leading the way and I trust Him because He has a plan. A plan to prosper me and not harm me, a plan to give me hope for my future. Jeremiah 29 v:11.

So, until the end of time, I will trust Him. Today could be my last day and I don't want to miss a day of honoring and worshiping the One who is so good to me. I will celebrate today as a birthday, Sunday, and holiday. I can only tell you partially about what has been taking place all morning long. I have been glued to this computer because there is so much to say and only a short window to reveal it.

Look for a star. Look for something good about yourself and your day. You may find yourself as being the star for the day. You are alive just like me and I want you to join me in praising the One that woke us up this morning. Join me as I praise the One who loved me first when I was only a thought. Say Hallelujah. He knew you when you were a thought, an egg that had not been planted in the womb. He had plans for you. He engrained His desire in your heart for you to love Him. You got sidetracked but you found your way back to His Throne of Grace and like me, you cast all your cares at His feet because the Bible says, He cares for me and you. 1st Peter 5 v:7.

He knew what highway He wanted me to travel on this Monday morning. He had His ideas of how He wanted my adventure to be. I know He will make it alright because I know who is holding my hand and orchestrating, my thoughts, ideas, opinions, beliefs, traditions, and desires. He is gentle with His encouragement and that is why I love Him so. He calmly attaches me to Him and sometimes He will not let me go. I want to say this, and I want to say that. He is my everything. He has His arms wide open. He is cradling me in His Everlasting Arms. In His Arms, I can talk to

Jesus. Anytime, anywhere, all day, 24/7, around the clock, every hour, every minute, every second of the day.

Early during the morning hours, I had my head nestled in His chest and I said "Thank You" for being so good to me, my family, my loved ones, and my friends. We know we are loved by a Savior. His music was playing in the background, and it was so soothing and comfortable. I went to sleep "praising Him" and when I woke up this morning, I was listening to music as I woke up "praising Him".

It is in Jesus' Name that I am alive. He is keeping me alive for a reason. Let me tell you that this Name is your saving grace. Want to be saved?

Want to be redeemed? Want to be filled with His Holy Spirit? Then do it in Jesus' Name. Jesus is forever the Same if you place Him first. Above everything else, salute His Name. If I remain in Him, then He will remain in me. Try saying this verse over and over until the words become alive in your spirit. Know that if you keep a song in your heart and praise on your tongue, He will forever grant you His Grace and Mercy

Chapter 40

Let's go. Let's me and you go to church. I begin with words that you can identify with. Jesus is good to you - right? I know Jesus is good to me. Yes! He is! That is why I can glorify His Name. He did it again. Again, He touched me with His finger of love and allowed me to become a living soul all over again ready to praise, worship, and honor Him for being so good to me. It is Love. It is understanding. It is wisdom and knowledge that He wants to share with me. It is early in the morning, and He wants to share His Love, His Peace, and His happiness with me. He is ready to give you some of the same. He is shining His light on you, and He wants you to turn on the Love, Peace, and happiness that He has in reserve "just for you". I feel good this morning. It is Tuesday, May 4th, 2021, here at Gene Miller Manor in Union City, Georgia, and I am alive in my senses so I can "think and process thought". Isn't He wonderful? Isn't He mighty? Isn't He great? Yes! He is and I am grateful that I am alive, able to breathe His fresh air in and out of my lungs. I am grateful that He allows my heart to beat at a normal rhythm. He is keeping me alive for a reason, all I need to do is to keep praising, worshipping, and honoring Him for being so good to me.

Surely His Goodness and Mercy shall follow me all the days of my life if I continue to dwell in His secret place, in His shelter, and His Presence.

It is Tuesday morning; a semi-cloudy gray-looking day and He promises to take good care of me just like He does on His sunny days. He has not left my presence, and this is all I need to remember. If I remain in Him, then He will remain in Him. Yes! I will continually praise Him. He is worthy to be praised and He deserves all my honor, worship, praise, love, and glory. How many ways can I say it? You see! God is at work in me, and He wants me to release the words that are meditating in my heart to let you know that He is alive in my Spirit because I chose to put Him first and make Jesus the Head of My Life on a Tuesday morning that I have never seen before.

He is at work giving me what I need to enjoy a magnificent, marvelous, splendid, superb, fabulous, fantastic, outstanding, wonderful, and spectacular day. It has started great. I opened my eyes, and He was there – ready to take me by my hand and lead me into my happy space so I could do what I needed to do.

I was so grateful that I began singing my song "Thank You Jesus" on the way in and on the way out. Hurriedly, I finished up so I could reclaim my spot. It was so warm and comfortable. I was being cradled in His Everlasting Arms and I began to confess the words that were meditating in my heart. O Lord please come into my presence and O Lord please allow me into Your Presence. This is the Same God that watched over my mom and dad and answered their prayers, and it is the same God who watched over me while I slumbered and slept.

How many of you know that prayer changes things? How many of you know that you must establish your own private, personal, and intimate conversation with Our Lord and Savior Jesus Christ? I do not know how long I will feel this way – I am connected to Him. He is my constant companion, and He is attached to me. Jesus guided me into my happy space, and I was allowed to clean and clothe my body. Earlier I had been given the assurance that He was listening to every word I said.

After I nestled under the covers I went into soft meditation. I began to speak humbly and sincerely. I know what He can do, and I asked Him to please come to see about me and when He does to take real good care of me. Keep me safe from the snare of the fowler, the enemy, the devil, Lucifer, Satan. O Lord please shelter us, O Lord please shadow us, O Lord please favor us, O Lord please cover us with Your Blood, O Lord please grant us Your Grace and Mercy, O Lord please forgive us of our sins because we don't always do things perfectly and correctly, O Lord please forgive our enemies because they know not what they do, O Lord please prosper us physically, materialistically, financially and spiritually, O Lord please protect us from all plagues, pandemics, disasters, and turmoil, O Lord please do not cast us away from Your Presence and O Lord please allow Your Holy Spirit to dwell in us again on this day. In Jesus' Name, I Pray - Amen.

It is a privilege and an honor to be able to communicate with My Savior. He is my personal Savior, and I am forever indebted to Him. I committed, I submitted, I surrendered myself to Thee so His will could be done. There are millions more just like me and I want you to be able to share with me my accomplishments. I know I was on a road to death and destruction, but Jesus allowed me to change lanes. Jesus rescued me. Jesus reinvented me. Jesus recreated me. Jesus threw me a lifeline and I became anchored to His word. I am one of His branches on His trees and He is my lifeline and that is who I am putting my trust, hope, belief, and faith in. I did not know my life would change so dramatically. Jesus did it. He gave me a new beginning, a new birth, a new identity, a new start, and a new mind. He said, "pull off those old clothes and put on your new clothes" that I am providing for you.

This is what He told me. "You, yes you" who are weary, worn, torn, sad, confused, and heavy laden, come unto me and I will give you rest." Matthew 11 v:28. Jesus gave me a new mind with new ideas, new thoughts, new ambitions, new beliefs, new opinions, new traditions, and new desires. He began whispering in my ear telling me what I could have. I could have His peace, patience, love, kindness, gentleness, faithfulness, self-control if I walked in His direction. If I listened and if I believed, had trusted, and had faith in what He was saying then I could change my life. I wanted a change. I yearned for a change. It began when I changed the words that were being released from my mouth. The words that were meditating in my heart were destroying me. These words brought to me death and destruction.

I read Proverbs 18 v:21 and it says, the tongue is a powerful weapon. It brings life or death. I had a choice to make. I could change my life simply by changing the words that were residing in my heart. I sat out with a specific goal in mind and the first scripture that I remember is His 23rd Psalm. It says, "Thy art with me", so I gathered pen and paper and begin to craft the words that I would release from my mouth. Jesus saw me setting out to make a change and He helped me. He allowed me to focus on the words that I was putting into my spirit.

I learned my life is the way it is because of the choices that I made. I was responsible for my fate. I was responsible for what I am and what I can become. I was told to speak life over my life. If I speak it, believe it, then I can achieve it.

The first words out of my mouth when I open my eyes set the stage of how my day will unfold and what my life will be like in the future. I began to worship Him and give praises and honor to Him for being so good to me by allowing me to see a brand new day. Psalm 118 v:24 told me what to do when I receive such a gift. It said, rejoice, enjoy, glorify, magnify, and celebrate it because I was favored to see another day. He made the decision that I could come alive in my senses and be able to "think and process thought". He is Holy and worthy to be served. On a day that I have never seen before, He deserves all my honor, worship, praise, love, and admiration for being so good to me.

He whispered words of inspiration and encouragement in my ears as I turned over and lifted my head from under the cover. He said "Sleepyhead" rise from the dead and let the Lord shine on you. He was talking to me. He touched me with His finger of love and allowed me to be closed in my right frame of mind with a reasonable portion of my health and strength. Once again, He smiled at me. Once again, I glorified His Holy Name. Once again, He allowed me to put another log on the fire.

Long ago, I decided, this is not the direction I want to go in, so I sat out to change the course that I was on. Nope! I did not love my old self. I disliked her very much. I hated her. But Jesus turned on a lightbulb in my heart, brain, mind, soul, body, and spirit when He told me "I will love you always". When I first heard these words, they did not register and He saw me still in a distraught condition, He rephrased it and told me "I will always love you". This changed everything. This changed my demeanor and outlook on life. Suddenly, I had a new reason to live. Suddenly, I had been allowed to believe in myself. Suddenly, I was allowed to love myself. He began to shine a light in my direction. So here I am telling you that Jesus saved my soul. Jesus allowed me to change my life. Once I began loving myself, He allowed His Holy Spirit to become my counselor and comforter. His Holy Spirit led me to read the right scriptures. His Holy Spirit led me to read the right book and to listen to the right tv vessel. Jesus changed my life.

I remember on one occasion, I was having an altercation with one of His sheep in His Pasture and I called on His Holy Name, I said Jesus" there is Satan" and Jesus grabbed me by the hand and told me lets you and I go outside and enjoy the sunshine and look at the beautiful flowers that are in bloom. Simply put, He said, "let's you and I go outside". This is how He showed me that He was in control and that He was watching over me. Jesus! Jesus! He is the One that is showering me and you with His Unfailing Love, His Unconditional Love, His Grace and Mercy, and His Divine Devotion on a day that we have never seen before. He is miraculous! He is magical! He is majestic! He is wonderful and magnificent to me. He is all I need on this glorious and gorgeous day because I am in His Presence, and He is taking real good care of me.

If you lift His Name on High, then He will drape a curtain of Love and Affection over your shoulders, and you will find yourself saying "I never knew I could feel this way". You will feel His Love as He encourages you to continue with saturating His atmosphere with words of praise and admiration. All-day, every day, 24/7, around the clock, every hour – every minute – every second and right at this present and the precise moment in time – He is all you need. Thy art with me. He has me surrounded. I am in His cocoon. We are in a bubble, and we are bouncing here and there.

Everywhere I go He is there. He is listening to every word that I say. Jeremiah 29 v:12.

He is with me, and I will tell it. I am not ashamed to tell you that I know if it were not for The Lord on my side, I do not know where I would be nor what I would be doing. He saved me before I got to my grave. I was walking around dead. I was in my coffin and just before they were about to nail it shut, Jesus showed up and said, "take my hand". He stretched out His Righteous Right Hand and I grabbed it. This is the same Hand that my mother and father, my sisters and my brother, my loved ones, my cousins, and my friends were holding, and it saved them. I made up in my mind that I am never turning loose His Hand. I have a tight grip because this is the Hand that saved my soul.

When I went into my happy space, I had been given everything I would need to clothe and cleanse my body. For this I am grateful. After I finished His Holy Spirit glided me out to my happy space and I made myself a pot of coffee. As I ladled my coffee back and forth, I began communicating with my Savior by repeating His 23rd Psalm. The Lord is my Shepherd, I shall not want. I was talking and He was listening. He told me to recite it. So, I began stirring and praying and confirming that He was right there over my shoulder listening. Thy art with me. If I remain in Him, then He will remain in me. If I abide in Him, then He will abide in me. If I draw nearer to Him, then He will draw nearer to Him.

I believe. I trust. I have faith in the unseen. I know who loves me. I know who is watching over me. I know who is protecting me from all hurt, harm, and danger and I know who my guide is. Here we go, ready to face another day. He is alive in my spirit and His blessings keep coming again and again. He did it again. He gave me a reason to come alive. He is keeping me alive for a reason. Is it to tell you about the relationship that I have developed with Our Lord and Savior Jesus Christ?

My world has changed. I am not living on the edge because Jesus has got me. He picked me out of the bunch and placed my feet on the solid and sacred ground on His Earth, on His Planet, and in His Universe. What kind of God is this? He is so kind, compassionate, tolerant, and considerate of me. He calls me names. When I wake up, I never know what label He will be pinning on me. It could be "shining star", "bright eyes", "tulip", "rose", "my delicate flower". When He labels me, I am walking on air? When I look into the mirror, I greet myself. He greets me back when He sees the sparkle in my eyes. Have you ever looked in the mirror long enough for Him to call your name? Look long enough so you will see the sparkle in your eye and remember who put it there? Who made the decision that you could be raised from the dead and allowed to look into a mirror and see yourself?

Are you ready to receive His Love and Divine Devotion? Are you ready? The time has come for you to shift your ideas and opinions, beliefs, and thoughts. You want His peace, His patience, His kindness, His gentleness, His understanding, His guidance, His faithfulness, His self-control combined with His Love - Right? It is available to you at this present millisecond. All you must do is ask. Talk to Him, He is listening. Tell Him what is meditating in your heart. Let Him carry that heavy load. 1st Peter 5 v:7 says, "Cast all of your cares on me because I care for you." Want to know what I did? I cast all my cares at His feet because I knew He would take care of them. I could waltz and glide about my day because I had pasted His 23 Psalm across my heart because I had given up the evil spirit of "hate".

There is a miracle in your mouth! The power of life and death is coming out of your tongue. There is a powerhouse of words engraved in your heart! Ears have not heard, eyes have not seen, what the Lord has waited on those who love Him. Get ready for your miracles. Expect a miracle every day you open your eyes by being "thankful" for everything that He provides for you. The song says, "He will make it alright". If you recognize who it was who woke you up this morning? If you recognize who is in control of your life. If you know who is directing your footsteps and if you know is orchestrating your thoughts and ideas, then you will know He will make your pathway brighter and your eyes clearer. Are you reading the handwriting on the wall? He is the One who can renew your strength and uplift your spirits by the words that are meditating in your heart. He is a miracle worker. He performed a miracle on me when He raised me from the dead and gave me a brand-new reason to live.

What do you want this morning? Is it hard to pinpoint? My desires can be identified in one sentence. I want more of His Love, His wisdom, His knowledge, His understanding, and His direction for my life. I shattered the ceiling in Heaven when I began praising His Holy Name. I want the blessings that He has in reserve for me to be released because I have a lot to share. There is so much to say. I feel like I am just getting started. Yes! I will tell it. I will tell just how good He is to me. Yesterday was Sunday and He was good to me throughout my day. On today, just like yesterday, He satisfied me early with His morning mercy and grace and told me to let it last me all during my day. I know how to obey a decree. I can follow orders. I know if I continue to love Him, honor Him, and obey Him, then He will continue to allow me to glorify Him for being so good to me. His Grace and Mercy.

I was raised from the dead. So many of His sheep are asleep. They are merely existing. Their lifeblood has been sucked out of them. Embrace, rejoice in your new gift of a brand new day. You can do this once you find out what is your purpose. Know that there was a plan devised just for you. Jeremiah 29 v:11. Get ready! Prepare yourself! A change is about to come because you will readily recognize that you are a child of a King, one of God's children, and one of His sheep in His Pasture. Are these words hard to digest? They shouldn't be. You are alive. You are not dead. Do you know who is the first one that ever loved you? It is My God, My Jesus, the Giver of Life. He is the decision-maker. He blew His breath of life into your lifeless body and allowed you to become a living soul ready to give Him praise for being so good to you.

Oh! He is a beautiful Savior. He sat me free. I asked for a free mind, a free brain, a free heart, a free body, a free soul, a free spirit. I asked Him to make Satan remove the shackles He had placed around my neck, my mind, my brain, my heart, my body, my soul, and my spirit. He made Satan remove the chains that were holding me captive. I was lost. But guess what He did? He began to love me. He began to cradle me in His Everlasting Arms. This is where I want to be. I learned that there was another life for me to live in the Presence of a King. I sat out to find this Love and this life. I met Jesus. He was knocking on my door the entire time of my 74 years. I opened the door wide and allowed Him to come in and He changed my entire belief system. There is nobody like

Jesus. There is no one like my Beautiful Savior. Hallelujah! Praises to His Name!

I lay my head upon His chest. This is where I can seek refuge. There is safety and security in His Everlasting Arms. I hear His bird singing. They are praising His Holy Name and I will join in with them and sing praises to His Name. I am in His Presence, and He is taking real good care of me. He is giving me His peace, patience, understanding, justice, honesty, truth, salvation, redemption, love, and righteousness. I have the victory. I have love in my heart for my brothers and sisters in the North, East, South, and West. This is what I was told to do. I know how to follow orders. Jesus said, "We must love each other". If we bow our heads in His Presence, then He will fill out hearts with love and compassion for each other.

Hate produces rage and anger in some of His sheep in His pasture. This causes His sheep to become savages, barbarians, hoodlums, and scoundrels. If hate is allowed to flourish, hate will destroy you physically, mentally, emotionally, psychologically, and spiritually. Hate is embedded in their bones. Hate spews from their ears and mouth. This is what is separating us. Man, and women must stop hating themselves first before they can love anyone else. Do you love yourself? Stop and examine these words. They are not words just for you to merely gloss over. They are meant for your ears and your eyes only. You can't love mankind until you love yourself. Rake yourself over with a fine-tooth comb and if you find any hate ask Jesus to come into your heart and replace that hate with His Love and Affection. Place yourself in His Hands, knowing that He will answer all your prayers. Prayer changes things. Are you talking to your Savior this morning? I am! He and I are chatting away, can't you tell? I am listening. I am writing. I have His peace, patience, love, and encouragement to continue to post sentence after sentence.

Prophesize to yourself. Keep telling yourself the truth. Keep telling yourself that you know who is watching over you. Keep telling yourself that it is He alone that we praise. We worship Jesus because He sure is good to me, and He sure is good to you. He is wonderful! He is great! He is mighty! Prophesize while you are sitting there reading - stop reading and feel that you are alive, and you have no aches and pains. Isn't that joy? Stop and realize that you have a sound mind, and you are in control of how you feel and how you think. You control your emotions and beliefs. You have self-control, self-discipline, and free will. This is what He has given to you and me. Your choice! Life or death? Aren't you glad that you are alive and not dead? It is a great day to be alive. Tell Jesus just how glad you are. He is listening. He is just underneath your breath trying to reside in your heart. He wants to come into your heart so He can dwell and have a final resting place.

Are you as excited as I am? I am taking a break and drinking a bottle of His water at room temperature, taking a big sigh, and ready to continue. I have good news! I am glad to be alive. I am not dead. Jesus gave me a new life to live, and I am glad about it. Therefore, I write. There was a plan designed just for me. Now that I have located my purpose and my destiny, it is so fulfilling and rewarding. Peace. Love. Devotion. Salvation. Redemption. Righteousness. It is all available for those of us who choose to believe that there is another life for us to live. I am in this world, but I am not a part of this world. There are no chains on my mind, my brain, my heart therefore I can "think and "process thought". I am free to love. I am free to care. I am free so I can be kind, gentle, considerate, and tolerant. I know who loved me first. I know who loved me before I was a thought. I am following Jesus. He has the plan, and He knows the plan that was developed for me. I will keep soldiering on. I am moving forward. I am not going to stay stagnant. I must move to a higher dimension. I must seek higher ground. I don't want to stay just where I am. I want to branch out and see what else He has in reserve for me.

It is an opportunity for growth and development each day that I open my eyes to. I am confident that each day He will love me. No one has ever spoken to me the way my Beautiful Savior does. He speaks in a kind, gentle and delicate manner. When He begins to talk to me, I listen intently because I don't want to miss a word. So, while I am writing, there is soft music and soft lighting that encourages me to listen harder. It is nonstop. I know how to wait and do what He tells me to do. I know what my needs are, and I know what my expectations are. I know if I remain in Him then He will remain in me. If I abide in Him, then He will abide in me. If I draw nearer to Him, then He will draw nearer to me. Wait for Him patiently and eagerly turn your eyes to Heaven and wait expectedly for Him to return. Has anyone told you that He is on His way back? You don't hear these words nowadays.

Satan has manufactured hate in the hearts of mankind. God's sheep have gone astray. They don't know what direction to go in. They are being guided in so many different directions. You need to identify yourself. Who am I and whose am I? Position yourself in your happy space and ask yourself "what do I believe"? Do you know who you are and whose you are? Who is it that I am trying to please? Who is the first one that ever loved me? Who wants me to be happy and content? Who is the one that wants me to succeed? Who is the one that wants me to be fruitful and multiply? Who is the one that wants me to produce good fruit? Who is the One that has me anchored to that vine? Who is the one that woke me up this morning? If you say it is "Jesus" then you know that He loves you and He will be with you everywhere you go. He is a way maker. He knows the way that He wants you to go in. I am putting another log on the fire.

Your life can change. You must identify what you want and what you will accept. Satan will try to defeat you every chance he gets. He is sly, slick, cunning, sleazy, and will attack your brain, mind, heart, body, soul, and spirit. He is evil like that. Satan does not want you to have peace. He will steal your joy and strength.

He will convince you that you do not need God - that you can do everything on your own. Lies. Deceit. This will leave you on a path of self-destruction. You are in control of your future. You forecast your future when you open your mouth. You write your eulogy.

Whatever words you send up will come back to rest on your shoulders.

Just change your vocabulary and find out the words that He wants to hear. O, Lord! You are mighty! O, Lord! You are great! O, Lord!

You are wonderful! So, I embrace You O Lord with words of gratitude.

Thank You Jesus for shining Your light on me. Thank You Jesus for allowing me to be one of Your sheep in Your Pasture who is willing to tell the world, "Jesus loves me". He wants to love you. You must allow Him too. He wants to shower you with His Unconditional Love, His Unfailing Love, His Grace, and Mercy and His Divine Devotion all day, every day, 24/7, around the clock - every hour - every minute – every second and right at this present and precise millisecond.

Allow Him to love you! This is what He wants to do. Allow Him to shower Grace and Mercy all over you. His Grace and Mercy is on my left, His Grace and Mercy is on my right, His Grace and Mercy is in front of me, His Grace and Mercy is the back of me, His Grace and Mercy is on top of me, His Grace and Mercy is underneath me. Looks like I am covered from the crown of my head to the soul of my feet in His Grace and Mercy. Ain't it grand? Worship Him with all your heart, mind, and soul. He has His "gift" of Love just waiting for you.

We are sheep in His Pasture and there is a job to do. Can you tell anyone just how good He is to you? Can you share in His glory with anyone? This is our job. This is what we must do. We must tell how Jesus has saved your soul. We must tell anyone who will listen that He is holding your hand. You cannot share your knowledge and wisdom with just anyone. His sheep will reject you at every angle. His Holy Spirit will guide you to the right person to talk to. Ask Him to direct your path.

Ask in Jesus' Name and He will say "yes, no, or not yet". Once you grab a holt of His Hand, He will direct your footsteps and guide that tongue, heart, mind, brain, body, soul, and spirit. This I know! This is what He is doing for me. I am never alone in my thoughts. I can move to the couch, bedroom, kitchen, bathroom, and He is right there. He never leaves me alone. He is constantly assuring me that He is watching over me, my family, my loved ones, and my friends. Isn't He fantastic? Isn't He fabulous? Isn't He splendid and superb? I am talking about Jesus, Our Beautiful and Wonderful Savior, who gave us a life to live in the Presence of a King.

Since He gave me a second chance, I promised that I would serve Him all the days of my life while I have a chance. While I am alive, I will accept His invitation to become alive in my spirits. I am a spiritual being having a human experience. I escaped the wicked and corrupt world that Satan has created. I can shout Hallelujah and glorify His Name in the middle of a pandemic, crisis, plague, disaster, and turmoil. So can you! He was good to you and me throughout 2020 and now He has allowed His and Mercy and Grace to roll over into 2021. I know who I owe a debt of gratitude for watching over me, you, him, she, he, them, and they. O, Lord! Please save us.

Chapter 41

I am having church early in the morning hours. I can't help it. This is something I must do. I am loved. I am admired. I am adored. I am alive. Every day is Sunday. Every day is celebration time. Come alive in your spirit and life. Join me! Want truth, justice, honesty, salvation, redemption, love, and righteousness? Jesus is an "Awesome God". He is stronger than strong. He is greater than great. Want to hear my testimony? Watch me glorify Him. Watch me lift His Name to the Highest. Watch me rejoice in peace and happiness and hope. This is what He has given me on my brand-new day. Peace, joy, hope and happiness.

Gloom, disappointment, and discouragement comes and drapes themselves on your shoulders but you have been given Grace and Mercy so you can shake these feelings off your back. Sometimes we are overwhelmed with disbelief. We have no sense of direction. This can change when you realize it is a new day. What am I to do and what am I to think? That is when you must reach deep down inside of you and pull on His hope and promises of love and peace that He has for you. Begin to softly meditate on His word. Know that "He is with me". Know that "He will go with me everywhere I go". Know that He has His ear tuned to hear the words meditating in your heart.

I see His sun shining and that is enough for me to realize that once again He is shining His light in our direction. Lift His Name in praise and worship Him because He sure is good to you and me. Know how I know? I was touched with His finger of love early in the wee hours of dawn and told to "wake up" O sleepyhead, rise from the dead, and let the Lord shine on you. Immediately I began to chant these words; "Thank You Jesus" and trotted off to my happy space so I could do what I needed to do. He was watching over me as I slumbered and slept. He had watched over me all night long. When I went to La La Land, I had my head buried in His chest and I began praising Him. While the music was playing soft and low, I drifted off into a night of sleep gently honoring Him for being so good to me.

His "amazing grace and mercy", may it follow me all the days of my life if I dwell in His shelter, in His secret place, and His Presence. Glory Hallelujah to His Name. Psalm 23. God is Love.

2nd John 4 v:8. Do you see His love when you look at how it is written on His green forest of foliage? Do you see His love when you look at every rose on the rose bush? Do you see His Love when you feel the petals on His tulips? I see His Love when I hear His birds chirp and sing. I believe the birds are giving Him, honor, and praise. I see His various colors of green trees appear to dance and frolic when a breeze comes through. The branches on the tree move backward, forwards, and sideways. They appear to bump into each other, they are so happy.

Mankind needs to stop, slow down, look up and outward and see what is surrounding him. God wants His sheep in His Pasture to be content and happy. God wants us to worship Him through His son, Jesus Christ. He gave us a Savior and that is who I am leaning on, on this brand new Wednesday, May 5th, 2021, at Gene Miller Manor in Christian City, in Union City, Georgia.

This is where I belong. I am devoted to my writing because there is so much to say. His spotlight is on you. He wants to hear your praise. He wants to hear you testify as to His Grace and Mercy. What was your conversation like when you opened your eyes to see another day? I can describe mine to you. O, Lord! You did it again. You made me come alive in my senses so I could think, and process thought. Thank You, Lord, for not forgetting about me. Thank You, Lord, for favoring me to be closed in my right mind with a reasonable portion of my health and strength.

Thank You Jesus for allowing me to flush my kidneys and excrete my bowels. Thank You, Lord, for smiling on me. After I had finished up in my happy space, I was guided back to my happy space by His Holy Spirit so I could reclaim my spot about the break of day. As I got nestled in, I began talking. O Lord please come into my presence and O Lord please allow me into Your Presence. It was pride and joy because once again He showed me that He loved me and was pleased with the words I used to glorify Him for being so good to me. I began talking. Softly, humbly, meekly, I said O Lord please shelter us, O Lord please shadow us, O Lord please favor us, O Lord please cover us with Your Blood, O Lord please grant us Your Grace and Mercy, O Lord please strengthen us physically, mentally, emotionally, psychologically, morally and spiritually, O Lord please forgive us of our sins because we don't always do things perfectly and correctly, O Lord please forgive our enemies because they know what they do, O Lord please prosper us materialistically, financially and spiritually, O Lord please protect us from all plagues, pandemics, disasters, and turmoil, O Lord please do not cast us away from Your Presence, O Lord please allow Your Holy Spirit to dwell in us again on this day. In Jesus' Name, I Pray - Amen.

The reason I say my affirmations is because I want to talk to the One who raised me from the dead and had mercy on me by blowing His breath of life into my lifeless body allowing me to become a living soul all over again. I am eternally grateful that He is smiling at me. I am ready to praise, honor and worship Him for being so good to me.

Years ago, He permitted me to become a member of God's Household and I have my foot wedged in the door. I am trying to get all the wisdom, knowledge, and understanding I can get. I am overwhelmed with all that I am learning and experiencing.

Am I reaching anyone with my message of love, peace, and hope? Jesus! Jesus! Our Savior of the world. We must put all our hope, trust, belief, and faith in Him. He knows the way. I don't know my way. When I tried to lead me, I failed. I gave up the reigns I had over my life a long, long time ago so His will could be done. I committed, I submitted, I surrendered my total self over to Him. He knows the way He wants me to travel. He knows what He wants me to say. I can only reveal the words that are meditating in my heart. It is by His Grace and Mercy that I can compose any thought or idea. I give Him all the praise, honor, and worship for making it possible. He is keeping me alive for a purpose. I am fulfilling my destiny.

I know what I was told. I have an assignment to complete. My testimonials are written with the intent of saving somebody's soul for Christ. My job is to give, share and care. Let me give you thoughts to ponder. Let me share with you the Love that I am receiving all day, every day, 24/7, around the clock – every hour – every minute – every second and right at this present and the precise moment in time. I care about the direction His sheep is heading and I want them to know that there is another life they could live. Making Jesus the Head of My Life is the best decision I ever made. This is who I honor, worship, cherish and obey. He told me "Love each other". Love me, you, him, her, she, he, them, and they. Try digesting this decree. Try following His order. Your heart must be clean, and you must have a steadfast spirit.

Mark, Chapter 7, says "it is what comes out of man's heart is what makes him unclean." Evil spirits occupy the hearts of man. The evil spirit of "hate" controls you, resulting in your becoming savages and barbarians whose primary aim is death and destruction. Satan, Lucifer, the devil, the enemy's job is to steal, kill and destroy. Steal your joy, peace, and compassion, kill your desire to love God, and destroy your beliefs that there is a better life for you to live.

You and I, both know, that each one of His sheep in His Pasture needs to put Jesus first in their lives. We want Jesus to know that we honor Him as being the sustainer of our faith and beliefs. We worship Him as our Savior because He recreated me and reinvented me. I became a new creature in Christ. I had to pull off the old clothes and put on my new clothes. My old ideas, thoughts, opinions, beliefs, traditions, and desires had to disappear because they were not contributing to my growth and development. They were destroying me. When I put on my new clothes - I learned who to lean on. Psalm 19 v:14 says, "O Lord, let the words of my mouth and the meditation of my heart be acceptable in Your sight, My Rock and My Redeemer.

Help me put another log on the fire! Lift the Savior! Praise His Holy Name! He touched me with His finger of love, and I opened my eyes to greet Him. He was extending His Righteous

Right Hand out to me and I grabbed it. It was such a soft and delicate touch to let me know how much He loved me. Aren't we special? Aren't we important? It is His Unconditional Love, His Unfailing Love, His Grace and Mercy, and His Divine Devotion that He wants to shower all over us. Draw near to Him, then He will draw near to you. Expect a miracle. Don't you know what you have? You have the Love and Devotion from a King. You are wanted, needed, accepted, appreciated, admired, adored, cherished, and idolized by a King. That is worth shouting about. If you cannot shout, then surely you can pull a smile from that heart because you know who loves you. Skip, hop, waltz, dance, and prance because you, yes you are loved. Now that we both know who loves us, we can turn to our brothers and sisters in the North, East, South, and West and share our love with them.

We have been raised above the evil spirit of hate. This evil spirit is no longer part of our makeup. We have been set aside because there was a plan designed for us. Jeremiah 29 v:11. We are no longer a part of this wicked and corrupt world. We have found the gift of peace, patience, contentment, tranquility, harmony, and serenity. How does it feel to know that we are saved? How does it feel to be cradled in His Everlasting Arms? We seek refuge in His Everlasting Arms anytime we want to because we both know that Salvation is free. So, you, lean back, realize that you are resting your head in faith, hope, and promise. We have got peace this morning. His tulips, His roses, His shrubs, His trees, His weeds, bushes, insects, and animals are waiting on Him to give them their morning grace and mercy. They will be content in waiting because they know He is coming to see about them. He will give them what they need to sustain them throughout their season. His rain, His sunshine, and His Love are what He has waiting for them. What is man, woman, boy, girl, infant and child waiting on? He is coming to give you His Grace and Mercy if you allow Him too. You must want it. You must yearn for it. You must ask Him? You must recognize Him as being the Commander-in-Chief in your life. He is the One in-charge. Allow Him full reigns over your life so His will can be done. I give myself totally away to Him. He is the Ruler of my Universe.

Psalm 145 v:15-16 says, "the eyes of all wait upon Thee, and Thou gives them their meat in due season, thou openness Thy hand and satisfies the desire of every living thing." We are engraved in the Palm of His Hand. So, he knows our needs before we do. He knows what is meditating in our hearts. He positions me in front of this computer and when I first begin, I have no idea of what road I will be traveling. I know He is feeding me. It is my season to tell the children of the world that Jesus Saves. Calling all adults, men and women, boys, and girls, gather around, you need to hear three simple words and they are "Jesus Loves Me" and "Jesus Loves You". His sheep in His Pasture does not know this and perhaps no one has ever told them "I Love You". Every one of us needs to hear these words. These words will change your life. These words opened a new beginning for me.

It was through trust, belief, and faith that I was able to move the boulder that was covering my heart, my mind, my brain, my body, my soul, and my spirit. Satan placed it there. But when I heard these words; "I Love You" coming from the mouth of a King, it changed my life. I received a new beginning, a new birth, a new identity, a new opportunity to begin my life in the Presence of a King. This changed me. I never knew I could be loved like this. I found considerate, compassionate, and tolerant Love from a King.

I became free. I received my freedom. The first thing I did was to go boldly before His Throne of Grace and said "Thank You Lord" for saving me. Thank You, Lord, for waking me up before I got to my grave. Thank You, Lord, now I see brighter days ahead. I have a reason to come alive each morning I open my eyes. I must witness that Jesus Christ is so good to me. He woke me up this morning and when He did, I had a smile on my face.

I was "amazed" that I was alive to see another day. I knew immediately what to do. I had read Psalm 118 v:24 and it told me to "rejoice, enjoy, glorify and celebrate it". This could be my last day. So, I will rejoice to know that once again He has reappeared to shower me with Grace and Mercy on this magnificent, marvelous, splendid, superb, spectacular, and wonderful day. I am alive. I am not dead. I have expectations. Today will be grand because He woke me up this morning showering me with blessing after blessing. I know how to say, "Thank You", I know how to honor the Giver of Life because He made the decision that I could be raised from the dead.

HAVE THE TIME OF YOUR LIFE

REJOICE

Bones are talking. The spirits that came before us left their mark on the world. All I have to say is "Thank You Jesus". Each time I say "Thank You Jesus" His smile gets bigger, wider and deeper. He says, "there she goes", dreaming, believing, hoping and aspiring for one more day. He says "of course you can have a brighter day". This is what you have been asked to receive, remember. How was I to know that I am forecasting my future all day, everyday, today, 24/7 around the clock, every minute, every second, every nanosecond and every millisecond in time. There is power in Your Name. I am talking to My Savior. I call Him Jesus. He is My God. I have sat Him on High. I raised a praise. My mouth, my brain, my heart, my mind, my body, my soul and my spirit have been captivated by His Presence.

Who has the final say? I must follow His lead. I must climb this mountain, I want to get to the other side. I am proofreading my second book. I am reading and I have discovered there is life, hope, joy, peace, satisfaction, happiness, contentment, tranquility, harmony in my voice. God is amazing, magical, majestic, miraculous. His Name is Jesus. Jesus is My Savior. He pulled me away from the fire by breathing new life into my tired, lifeless body. I became alive again because I discovered He was amazing, wonderful, divine, outstanding, magnificent, marvelous, fabulous, fantastic, splendid, superb, superior and spectacular. This is what I am thankful for this Thanksgiving, November 25th, 2021. I have a Savior.

He calls me a snail. He says "you move so slowly". You allow me to embalm you with my kindness, gentleness, tenderness, softness, graciousness, love, hope, peace and righteousness. Sing you a song. Just relax - you are in His Presence and you deserve to move as slow as a snail. Allow His spirit to overtake your spirit. Put Jesus out front. Let Him lead the way. He has the plan so says Jeremiah 29 v:11. He has the plan for my future. He has the layout. He has the outline. He has the blueprint. He is the only who knows how this is going to end. He is investing time and energy into me to see what I can become. I am always looking for a brighter day. I am always singing a song. I am always praising Him for being so good to me. Once again Jesus works miracles. I told you about the miracle He performed on me on this brand new Tuesday morning, November 23rd 2021. It is my sister's Vivian Ann's birthday. She is 67 years of age. I wished her 67 more and she showered me with "Thank You" and said "she is grateful that she was able to witness her 67th birthday.

Jesus is a miracle worker. I have made a statement and I stand by what I said. I know what He did for me. He is working tiny miracles in my life. He is giving me hope for my tomorrow. I am so thrilled with how my morning routine is going. It is the sacred hour of 3 p.m. A golden moment of reflection, I am in His Presence and He wants me to tell you that I have a new life in the middle of a pandemic, plague, disaster and turmoil. Can you really praise Him for what He is doing for you. He gave me life. He yanked me up from that grave. I was dead and buried. Jesus can raise the dead. Here I am, a live 74 years old, praising, honoring, worshipping, saluting and obeying a King. I try too. I give it my best shot. I know what He told me. I know what He showed me with my very own two eyes. He is watching over me. I see Him with His eyes fixated on me. He knows me by the shadow of my smile. He sees me as a "Shining Star", a Tulip, a Rock, a Diamond and fine Gemstone. He knows me by the sparkle in my eyes.

Somewhere out there is another dimension. We have to have our feet planted solid on the ground. We must open up our minds, brains, hearts, bodies, souls and spirits to dram a new reality. Send the words out from your mouth, let them encircle around you. As if you were in a cocoon. He gave me such a surprise. He pained me a picture. He blanketed me with His Presence. I am proofreading my second book and He pulled up a chair beside me. He is here with me, there with you and everywhere at the same time. Are you a dreamer believer?

I admire You. I admire You. I idolize You. I honor You. I love You. You slowed down long enough for me to blow the breath of life into your lifeless soul. Before I opened my eyes I went to preaching and singing. O Lord!

You are great, mighty, powerful and strong. O Lord! Help me as I embrace the adventure that You have ordained for me on today.

I spent all of my morning hours proofreading my next book. I AM A DREAMER - BELIEVER. You must be ready to dream yourself to greater heights. We are, you, me, him, her, she, he, them and they are moving to a higher dimension. Let me take you there. Let me take you over there, over yonder, at the Great Beyond,

in Paradise, in the Holy Land, at the United Kingdom in the Promised Land. There is love, hope, peace, gratitude, satisfaction, joy, truth, honesty, justice, salvation, faithfulness, redemption and righteousness in that Land. That Land over there. Let's go there. There are birds that will give you your very own magic show. That is why I say He is magical. There are trees that glisten like diamonds. This is what the birds are attracted too. They are attracted to light just like we are attracted to the light that He is shining down on you, me, her, she, he, them and they. Don't you see His sunshine? He is shining a light in your direction. He wants you to become alive in your own thoughts, begin to think, process, perceive and ponder thought. You must have an imagination. In that Land where there is only you "two". Him and I. Me and Him. Just the "two" of us. Just us "two".

I have come up out of that valley. I see Him. He is at the corner of the rainbow. He is the beginning of my sunset and my sunrise. He is My Bright and Morning Star. I see His light. He has me in His spotlight. He is shining His light on me. He is satisfied and amazed as to how I am able to devote so much time and energy to a cause greater than myself. He is keeping me alive for a reason. Today is my new birth. I will celebrate as if it is my birthday. I honor Thee. I worship Thee. I love Thee. I obey Thee. I idolize Thee. I treasure Thee. I cherish Thee. Is He good? Let these words marinate in your spirit. Don't rush through them. Say them one at a time and let Him engulf you with His spirit. He is worthy to be praised.

He has reached a conclusion about me! I am determined to go the last mile of the way. I am on a path to holiness and righteousness. I want my name carved in the Lamb's Book of Life. Dream with me. The last time I checked I had a Savior watching over me. The last time I checked I had a Savior who is willing to listen to the words meditating in my heart. I ask Him O Lord please orchestrate my thoughts, ideas, beliefs, opinions, attitudes, behaviors, traditions, dreams, hopes and desires for my future. I project. I plan. I forecast my future. I use a mountain of words and descriptions. I prayed. I earned the right to be a member of God's household based on the words meditating in my heart. I talked my way into His Presence. I simply asked for a favor. O Lord please allow me into Your Presence and O Lord please allow me to enter into Your Presence.

I am talking to My Savior. He is listening to me. Jeremiah 29 v:12. Steal away, just you and me so we can have a talk. Come in, close the door, get comfortable, there is something we need to discuss. He says. He is always ready and waiting on you to seek out a quiet space for just the two of you. Can you obey an order? Can you follow a command? Can you honor a Decree? Listen! Just listen! Just listen to yourself think, perceive, process and ponder thought. This is a guaranteed right. You have the power and authority to make your own decisions.

I can only influence you based on my opinion. Do you want a new life to live in the Presence of a King?

Glorify Him. Magnify Him. Celebrate Him. Enter into His Presence with praise, hope, admiration and Thanksgiving. Have Thanksgiving everyday. Do you know who you are and whose you are? You are a child of a King, you are needed, wanted, appreciated, accepted, admired, adored, idolized, worshipped, treasured, honored and cherished by a King. He is so proud of you. He wants to keep an eye on you. He is proud of His accomplishment. Come with me and share with me. Thanksgiving means to give, share and care. We have so much to be thankful for. He has provided everything we would need to spread a feast on the table. What about those babies who are starving. Only if they could just get the crumbs. When you look at your Thanksgiving Table, know that you are eating from the backs and spines of your ancestors, descendants and fore parents. They sacrificed their souls so you could have food on the table. A moment of golden reflection. Is He good to you? Has He smiled on you? He is showing you just how much He loves you by making a plentiful table for you, he, him, she, her, them and they to enjoy.

Join with me at this sacred hour of 4 p.m. Rejoice that you are satisfied and elated that you have received a gift of a new day. Psalm 118 v:24.

Jesus came through early in the morning hours satisfying me with His Grace and Mercy and told me to let it last me all day long.

Psalm 90 v:14. Lamentations 3 v:22-23. I do as I am told to do. I am told to love me, you, him, her, she, he, them and they. I am told that I must have love in my heart for my brothers and sisters in the North, East, South and West. We have brothers and sisters we have never ever seen before. We know them through voice only. Let me share my love with you.

His Blood is running warm throughout my veins and your veins. He is keeping me alive for a reason. Is it too reach out and touch you with His Finger of Love. Listen! Hear me out. O Lord! I call on His Holy Name and then I complete my sentence. O Lord! Thank You for blowing Your breath of life into my lifeless soul and allowing me to become a living breathing human being all over again ready to praise, honor, worship, obey and salute you for allowing me to come alive in my sense of hearing, seeing, tasting, smelling, feeling, touching, dreaming and believing. I can think. I can process, perceive and ponder thought. I can dream for myself a new reality.

Come away with me. He says. Come away from the evilness, wickedness, corruption, hate, lies, deceit, deception and diabolical thoughts and desires. Set aside quiet time for Me and you so we can develop a personal, private and intimate relationship with each other.

Let me put my name on the roll. I want to be the first One to tell Him that I love Him. He is the First One that ever loved me and I want to show my respect, love and gratitude for raising me from the dead. He made a Dreamer Believer out of me. He gave me a new mind, new hopes, new dreams, new desires, new ambitions. He has plans for my future. I will allow the blessings that He has in reserve for me to be unfolded in my presence as I face today and tomorrow. O Lord! I will allow Thy will to be done.

Am I afraid? No! I have confidence in Thee. I know He will take good care of me. I must depend on Thee to see me safely across the river. I know He will make a way. He keeps doing it over and over, again and again, raising me from the dead, giving me a new life to live in the Presence of a King. Jesus breathes new life into my spirit. I become alive again. He gives me a new start, a new beginning, a new birth,

a new identity and a new reason to live again. I have been given a new opportunity to think. I can choose what kind of life I want to live. I can choose who I want to be in-charge and in-control of my life. I give myself totally away to Him so His will can be done.

We are under Divine Intervention. We are seeking guidance from a Supreme Being. I am gravitating to the Great BeYond, in Paradise, in the Holy Land, in the Promised Land. Golden Dreams. Golden Thoughts. Golden Ideas.

                                          Queen Bettie Jean Grose

                                                      In His Presence

                                        In The Name of Jesus - Amen

Printed by Libri Plureos GmbH in Hamburg, Germany